T0393001

The Ambiguous Legacy of Socialist Modernist Architecture in Central and Eastern Europe

This book examines the unique socialist-modernist architecture built in the twentieth century in Central and Eastern Europe as a source of heritage and of existing and potential value for the present and future generations. Due to the historical context in which it was created, such architecture remains ambiguous. On the one hand, the wider public associates it with the legacy of the unpleasant period of the real socialist economic regime. Yet, on the other hand, it is also a manifestation of social modernization and the promotion of a significant proportion of the population. This book focuses particularly on concrete heritage, a legacy of modernist architecture in Central and Eastern Europe, and it was this material that enabled their rebuilding after World War II and modernization during the following decades. The authors search for the value of modernist architecture and using case studies from Poland, Bulgaria, Northern Macedonia, Lithuania and Slovenia verify to what extent this heritage is embedded in the local socio-economic milieu and becomes a basis for creating new values. They argue that the challenge is to change the ways we think about heritage, from looking at it from the point of view of a single monument to thinking in terms of a place with its own character and identity that builds its relation to history and its embeddedness in the local space. Furthermore, they propose that the preservation of existing concrete structures and adapting them to modern needs is of great importance for sustainability. With increasing awareness of the issue of preserving post-war architectural heritage and the strategies of dissonant heritage management, this multidisciplinary study will be of interest to architecture historians, conservators, heritage economists, urban planners and architects.

Mariusz E. Sokołowicz is a scholar and urban activist, a Professor at the Faculty of Economics and Sociology, University of Lodz (Poland), and is the Chair of the Department of Regional Economics and Environment. He specializes in urban and regional studies, institutional economics, place marketing and economics of proximity. For several years, he worked as a real estate manager and advisor, as well as a local government official responsible for the town centre revitalization project.

Aleksandra Nowakowska is a Professor at the University of Lodz (Poland) in the Department of Regional Economics and Environmental Protection and Head of the Institute of Urban and Regional Studies and Planning. Her main areas of scientific interest are development and local policy, innovative methods and tools for managing the development of cities, smart city and development strategies of cities and regions.

Błażej Ciarkowski is an Associate Professor at the Institute of Art History, University of Lodz (Poland). He is the leader of the research team in the international project "InnovaConcrete – Innovative Materials and Techniques for the Conservation of 20th Century Concrete-based Heritage." His research interests focus on modernist architecture, mutual relations between architecture and politics and preservation and conservation of modernist architecture.

Routledge Research in Architecture

The *Routledge Research in Architecture* series provides the reader with the latest scholarship in the field of architecture. The series publishes research from across the globe and covers areas as diverse as architectural history and theory, technology, digital architecture, structures, materials, details, design, monographs of architects, interior design and much more. By making these studies available to the worldwide academic community, the series aims to promote quality architectural research.

Architecture and Affect: Precarious Spaces
Lilian Chee

Modernism in Late-Mao China: Architecture for Foreign Affairs in Beijing, Guangzhou and Overseas, 1969-1976
Ke Song

The Spatialities of Radio Astronomy
Guy Trangoš

The Ambiguous Legacy of Socialist Modernist Architecture in Central and Eastern Europe
Mariusz E. Sokołowicz, Aleksandra Nowakowska, Błażej Ciarkowski

Architecture, Ritual and Cosmology in China
The Buildings of the Order of the Dong
Xuemei Li

Art and Architecture of Migration and Discrimination
Turkey, Pakistan, and their European Diasporas
Edited by Esra Akcan and Iftikhar Dadi

For more information about this series, please visit: https://www.routledge.com/Routledge-Research-in-Architecture/book-series/RRARCH

The Ambiguous Legacy of Socialist Modernist Architecture in Central and Eastern Europe

Mariusz E. Sokołowicz, Aleksandra Nowakowska and Błażej Ciarkowski

LONDON AND NEW YORK

Designed cover image: nikolay100/Getty Images

First published 2023
by Routledge
4 Park Square, Milton Park, Abingdon, Oxon OX14 4RN

and by Routledge
605 Third Avenue, New York, NY 10158

Routledge is an imprint of the Taylor & Francis Group, an informa business

British Library Cataloguing-in-Publication Data
A catalogue record for this book is available from the British Library

Library of Congress Cataloging-in-Publication Data
Names: Sokołowicz, Mariusz, author. | Nowakowska, Aleksandra, author. | Ciarkowski, Błażej, author.
Title: The ambiguous legacy of socialist modernist architecture in Central and Eastern Europe / Mariusz E. Sokołowicz, Aleksandra Nowakowska and Błażej Ciarkowski.
Description: Abingdon, Oxon : Routledge, 2023. | Series: Routledge research in architecture | Includes bibliographical references and index. |
Identifiers: LCCN 2022054356 (print) | LCCN 2022054357 (ebook) | ISBN 9781032289274 (hardback) | ISBN 9781032289298 (paperback) | ISBN 9781003299172 (ebook)
Subjects: LCSH: Architecture and society--Europe, Central. | Architecture and society--Europe, Eastern. | Historic preservation--Social aspects--Europe, Central. | Historic preservation--Social aspects--Europe, Eastern. | Socialist modernism (Architecture)--Public opinion.
Classification: LCC NA2543.S6 S635 2023 (print) | LCC NA2543.S6 (ebook) | DDC 724/.6--dc23/eng/20230126
LC record available at https://lccn.loc.gov/2022054356
LC ebook record available at https://lccn.loc.gov/2022054357

ISBN: 9781032289274 (hbk)
ISBN: 9781032289298 (pbk)
ISBN: 9781003299172 (ebk)

DOI: 10.4324/9781003299172

Typeset in Sabon LT Std
by KnowledgeWorks Global Ltd.

Printed in the United Kingdom
by Henry Ling Limited

Contents

Introduction

The question of the value of architecture is almost as old as architecture itself. Philosophers – joined in time by other scientists – have been pondering this issue for just as long. Despite this, the concept of value, due to the diversity of people and societies, is still ambiguous. When we talk about the value of friendship, love or family life, we mean something completely different than when we talk about the value of a business, property or labour. Misunderstandings around the issue of value have led not only to semantic disputes but also to ideological or political ones. In turn, the values into which we are born and raised significantly condition our perception of other people and the environment in which we function. In other words, how we define value and what we consider valuable determines, on the one hand, our perception of our places and, on the other, it influences how these places shape our aesthetics.

The above is not uncommon in architecture and urban planning. It is even very significant in this domain, as it is strongly connected to what we consider to be heritage – both tangible and intangible. Historical buildings and complexes, being heritage on a global, national or regional scale, determine the identity of communities and build up a legacy, acting as a link between successive generations. In this view, heritage is a value in the broadest sense of the word. In the global dimension, it translates into the essence of civilization, while in the regional and local dimension, it determines the uniqueness of individual villages, towns, cities and regions and allows identities to be built that are territorially embedded and hence spatially differentiated.

However, the value of heritage can also be understood in a more tangible way. A monument is not only a *sacrum* but also a *commodum* – subject to market power (Purchla, 2015). Historic urban districts and architectural monuments become sources of revenue – directly, by providing a base for activities such as museums, entertainment, culture and tourism, and indirectly, by building a positive image of the place, increasing the value of neighbouring properties and contributing to the improvement of the quality of life of the inhabitants. Identifying these mechanisms at the level of specific urban centres is becoming an important and inspiring subject

DOI: 10.4324/9781003299172-1

of research for architects, planners, economists, sociologists, anthropologists, psychologists or cultural scientists. These researchers realize that the spatial heterogeneity of the impact of heritage on the value of places can explain differences in the attractiveness of towns and cities for economic activity (including tourism), differences in their image and variations in the inhabitants' perception of their life quality.

An important subject of research nowadays is the contradiction between what is assumed to be the intrinsic value of heritage or the value of a legacy (which is immaterial, intangible and therefore difficult to measure) and the use-value, which is strongly associated with profits obtained "here and now," sometimes regrettably at the expense of current and future generations. The challenge of resolving such dilemmas confronts heritage professionals, architects, cultural scientists and urban and regional economists. It is the challenge of "measuring the immeasurable," that is, the search for diverse methods of heritage valorization. In support of these attempts, a variety of direct and indirect valuation methods are available to architects, planners and heritage practitioners. The valuation of heritage – in view of the diversity of its perception and its complexity – is obviously a major research and methodological challenge and requires an interdisciplinary approach.

This is why we have attempted to analyze heritage and its value from this perspective – drawing on the work of not only architects and cultural scientists but also philosophers and economists. We attempt to combine these approaches and show the benefits of interdisciplinarity for grasping the value of heritage in everyday practice. The key spatial level of analysis for us has become the city in its most local dimension. This is because we recognize that heritage is something that has always been created not only at a particular time but also in a particular place. And it is the place and the space (Tuan, 1977) which determine both how this heritage emerged but also how its value is perceived by current generations and what decisions are or will be made in relation to it in the future. Heritage is therefore dependent on the context of place. It is territorially embedded – in the physical environment and in the social history of the place, as well as in today's needs and collective visions for the future use of heritage.

This view of heritage also advocates a territorial paradigm of development in which cultural heritage becomes one of the elements of so-called territorial capital (Camagni et al., 2020). In this approach, it is not only the material dimension of heritage that is taken into account; above all, intangible resources are exposed, building the territorial identity and uniqueness. It is the heritage that makes the abstract space a place with social ties, local values, institutions and capacities for development. In the territorial approach, cultural heritage is the basis for a new perception of development processes, in which a shift is made from a static to an active approach to its analysis. A shift from a geographical concentration of tangible resources to a space offering unique – often intangible – resources and conditions for socio-economic activities. Embedded resources such as cultural heritage are, from an economic point of view, capital – a strategically valuable resource that determines the competitive position of a given territory (Capello, 2019; Cerisola, 2019). In this territorial perspective, the value of heritage is co-created by actors anchored in a specific place. Heritage is then a factor of development, creating opportunities for the creation of direct interactions between users of specific places, for social engagement and the growing interdependence between local actors and the territory, thus building uniqueness and an urban *milieu*.

In this approach, we focus on particular – concrete – heritage, which is a legacy of modernism in architecture. We creatively refer to unwanted or problematic (dissonant) heritage. We do so, however, with the awareness that we treat it more broadly than our predecessors, who associated this type of architecture primarily as a "product" of wars and totalitarianism. We believe it is a challenge to valuate objects and complexes that are unquestionable as heritage for purely economic purposes. Nevertheless, it is not as great as the challenge of evaluating heritage regarded by many as unwanted or dissonant. The experience of many towns and cities shows that such difficult heritage, although it stirs emotions, creates an opportunity for animated social discussions about the history, culture and identity of a place. In this way, it becomes an impulse and a kind of social glue, building relationships and bonds, territorial embeddedness and place identity. This controversial heritage, while creating an opportunity to revise ways of thinking about the place's past, also allows for the creation of its future.

Regarding monuments which are several hundred years old, such as old towns, castles, palaces or urban complexes visited by hundreds of thousands of tourists, hardly anyone questions their value. The problem is, at most, what this value is. But the situation is different when it comes to objects created only several decades ago, often in controversial circumstances and times (e.g. in the era of fascism or socialism). Then, the fundamental question of whether the object is heritage at all comes to the fore. An excellent example of such a controversy is concrete soc-modernist architecture – both because of the time in which it was created and the material that was used to create it. We refer here to Forty (2012), focusing on concrete's effects on culture rather than its technical properties. He examines the ways concrete has changed our understanding of nature, of time, and even of material. He concentrates on architects' responses to concrete and considers the role concrete has played in politics, literature, cinema, labour relations and arguments about sustainability. In the twentieth century, concrete dominated basically every continent and became responsible for modernist uniformity and the debates engendered by it. Therefore:

> concrete is often regarded as a dumb or stupid material, more associated with death than life. Figures of speech in many languages take advantage of this. In German, "*Beton-Fraktion*" is used to mean an intransigently stubborn political group; "*Beton-Kopf*", literally

> "concrete head", a reactionary political opponent. In Sweden, Hjalmar Mehr, the powerful Social Democrat leader of Stockholm's city government responsible for the drastic redevelopment of the inner city in the 1950s and '60s, was referred to as "*betonsosse*", a "concrete socialist". In French, the street slang "*laisse béton*", an inversion of "*laisse tomber*", means "drop dead". In Kate Grenville's novel *The Idea of Perfection*, the boringness of the main character is communicated through his being a concrete engineer: "Concrete!", people would exclaim at parties, "and their eyes would start to flicker past his shoulder, looking for someone better to talk to."
>
> (Forty, 2012, p. 9)

Similarly, in Poland, the functionaries of the communist party (mediocre, passive, but faithful to the system and the central authority), resistant to any progress and change, were called "the party's concrete" ("*beton partyjny*").

Actually, treating concrete as an industrial (and as such, ludic and ordinary) material with literally NO intrinsic value was its greatest... value (cf. Forty, 2012, p. 218). Concrete's immunity valuation and, at the same time, its high "technical" functionality made it an excellent material for the construction not only of buildings but also of the entire modernist society. Today, however, the heritage of twentieth-century concrete architecture is inextricably linked to the notion of dissonant heritage. This concept relates primarily to the ambiguity of the architecture of the time. However, John Tunbridge and Gregory Ashworth, who defined what dissonant heritage is, argue that all heritage is discontent in its own way – it provokes discussion, evokes diverse opinions, and is a source of disagreement about cultural, economic, political or social aspects of heritage (Tunbridge & Ashworth, 1996). In the case of concrete construction under socialism, which is the subject of the considerations in this book, this relationship is particularly clear. Following Tunbridge and Ashworth, it is necessary to ask about the essence of heritage, which can be understood as both "thing" and as "meaning." These two perspectives are interrelated and therefore the destruction of matter means "the superstructure of a new layer of heritage" (Tunbridge, 2018, pp. 284–285). And its "demolition is an act of violence," say French architects Anne Lacaton and Jean-Philippe Vassal (Khan & Devanshi, 2021), who have gained worldwide recognition for modernizing concrete apartment blocks and pointing out the cultural and economic validity of treating mass housing as heritage.

So, does the contemporary perception of concrete allow its design to be considered worthy of being regarded as heritage? And if so, is it already the case, or will it happen in the future? And if in the future, when will that future come? Is it not already too late from the point of view of preserving these structures for future generations? Consequently, we take as the main objective of this book the question of whether socialist modernism – based on concrete as a universal building material – is wanted or unwanted as a legacy? Furthermore, we take up the challenge of indicating possible ways of valuing this kind of architecture – based on our review of previous approaches to the question.

The challenge here is to change the way of thinking about heritage, from looking at it from the point of view of a single monument to thinking in terms of a place with its own character and identity that builds its relation to history and its embeddedness in the local space. This implies the need for an integrated approach to heritage management in the urban planning processes. Therefore, its valorization requires the cooperation of many actors and an interdisciplinary approach. The skilful exposure of heritage in the physical and mental urban landscape, and its integration into the urban environment, contributes to a better understanding of not only the value of the monument itself but also the place where it is located. This, in turn, influences the sense of permanence, embeddedness and social involvement in urban activities (Brown et al., 2003; Vorkinn & Riese, 2001).

We thus attempt to combine a new way of thinking about dissonant heritage and the challenges of urban planning. We suggest that attention should be focused not so much on actions aimed at eliminating the shortcoming of the single monument itself, but on projects that aim to create the capital of the place. We also assume that the problem of preserving the concrete heritage of both architecture and engineering structures built in the twentieth century is also related to the most serious challenge of present times – the need to ensure sustainable development. While only a few decades ago concrete was a synonym of modernity, today, it is defined as "the most destructive material on Earth" (Watts, 2019). The preservation of existing concrete structures and adapting them to modern needs is also of colossal importance for the planet's climate. We cannot afford to destroy concrete.

This book consists of four chapters. The first one introduces the context of the issues addressed. It is a brief description of the genesis of modernism as a movement in twentieth-century architecture and an attempt to show its peculiarities in the Central and Eastern European countries. It is worth bearing in mind that during the period of the growing popularity of modernism in the world, in CEE, the structures of socialist countries were under construction, which in the 1940s and 1950s strongly distanced themselves from this "invention of rotten capitalism." Only the political thaw in these countries after the death of Josef Stalin allowed architects and urban planners (educated before World War II, when modernism was still in its infancy) to spread their wings and undertake exceptional and spectacular projects. Moreover, architects form the Eastern Bloc were dedicated to the dogmas of modern movement even when their Western colleagues started to question, criticize, and, in the end, reject them (Basista, 2001, p. 178). This ambiguous and lush socialist modernism history has led to uncertainty in its reception – both at the beginning and (even more strongly) after the collapse of socialism in CEE countries. Therefore, the discussion around these processes is an issue of heritage, which is, at least to some extent, dissonant.

The second chapter aims to prepare the ground for thinking about the dissonance mentioned above of concrete modernist architecture in socialist countries. It addresses the question of value from a philosophical and axiological perspective and in economic thought. Indeed, reflections on this topic are rich and have a long history. We supplement this perspective with an overview of approaches to value in the theory of monuments to further emphasize the interdisciplinary nature of valuation approaches. In doing so, we highlight the complementary nature of the presented approaches, showing that evaluating space and place from the human and societal perspective by mixing different approaches is necessary for a better understanding of ambiguous heritage. In the following sections of our book, we approach the problematics from a local perspective, recognizing that urban studies have much to offer to the theory of monuments or valuation in philosophy and economics. Ultimately, the examples of ambiguous architectural heritage discussed in this book are framed not only in a particular time but also in space. Hence, the urban context is significant. We conclude the second chapter considering architectural heritage as an urban common good and as a so-called territorial capital.

The third chapter brings us closer to the elaboration and our considerations by presenting the body of work on heritage valuation methodology, particularly the ambiguous one. We intend to show that despite the numerous studies on the topic, scholars and heritage policy practitioners still present a variety of methodological approaches. So when it comes to measuring the difficult-to-measure (i.e. dissonant or ambiguous heritage), they encounter more questions than answers. Therefore, to structure the discussion on this topic, we organize and present the classification of public space valuation methods. We also remind the good old cost-benefit analysis, used widely by policymaker communities. We believe that this well-known method of assessing public projects' cost-effectiveness and actions copes well with ambiguous heritage's complexity. To support this thesis, at the end of the chapter, we present an example of the application of this method in practice, reviewing state-of-the-art research and presenting the results of our study of Warsaw Ochota Railway Station, Poland.

The book concludes with a chapter focusing on case studies from other Central and Eastern European countries. In this part, we have attempted to consider not only the peculiarities of CEE countries as en bloc but also to search for local distinctions and uniqueness in this regard. In each of the cases studied, we used source materials, photographic documentation and the results of interviews conducted with specialists in the architecture of soc-modernism in their countries. It brought us closer to local realities in diverse geographical contexts. Considering the materials and contacts we had available and the consistency with the aim of this book, we decided to present five cases from Poland, Bulgaria, Latvia and the two countries that emerged after Yugoslavia's break-up – Slovenia and Northern Macedonia. We hope that a tour through selected examples of socialist modernism will help answer the question of to what extent this legacy is wanted or unwanted and what the future holds for it.

References

Basista, A. (2001). *Betonowe dziedzictwo: Architektura w Polsce czasów komunizmu [Concrete legacy: Architecture in communist Poland]*. PWN.

Brown, B., Perkins, D. D., & Brown, G. (2003). Place attachment in a revitalizing neighborhood: Individual and block levels of analysis. *Journal of Environmental Psychology*, *23*(3), 259–271. https://doi.org/10.1016/S0272-4944(02)00117-2

Camagni, R., Capello, R., Cerisola, S., & Panzera, E. (2020). The cultural heritage – Territorial capital nexus: Theory and empirics. *Capitale Culturale*, *11*, 33–59. https://doi.org/10.13138/2039-2362/2547

Capello, R. (2019). Interpreting and understanding territorial identity. *Regional Science Policy & Practice*, *11*(1), 141–158. https://doi.org/10.1111/rsp3.12166

Cerisola, S. (2019). A new perspective on the cultural heritage–development nexus: The role of creativity. *Journal of Cultural Economics*, *43*(1), 21–56. https://doi.org/10.1007/s10824-018-9328-2

Forty, A. (2012). *Concrete and culture: A material history*. Reaktion Books.

Khan, Z., & Devanshi, S. (2021). Anne Lacaton & Jean-Philippe Vassal, the 2021 Pritzker laureates for whom demolition is an act of violence. *Stirworld.Com*. https://www.stirworld.com/see-news-anne-lacaton-jean-philippe-vassal-the-2021-pritzker-laureates-for-whom-demolition-is-an-act-of-violence

Purchla, J. (2015). *Dziedzictwo a transformacja*. Międzynarodowe Centrum Kultury w Krakowie.

Tuan, Y.-F. (1977). *Space and place. The perspective of experience*. University of Minnesota Press.

Tunbridge, J. E. (2018). *Zmiana warty. Dziedzictwo na przełomie XX i XXI wieku [The changing of the guard: Heritage at the turn of the 21st century]*. Międzynarodowe Centrum Kultury w Krakowie.

Tunbridge, J. E., & Ashworth, G. J. (1996). *Dissonant heritage. The management of the past as a resource in conflict*. John Wiley & Sons.

Vorkinn, M., & Riese, H. (2001). Environmental concern in a local context: The significance of place attachment. *Environment and Behavior*, *33*(2), 249–263. https://doi.org/10.1177/00139160121972972

Watts, J. (2019). Concrete: The most destructive material on Earth. *The Guardian*. https://www.theguardian.com/cities/2019/feb/25/concrete-the-most-destructive-material-on-earth

1 Modernism, socialism and concrete in CEE countries

A controversial heritage

Modernism in architecture – Universal genesis vs CEE uniqueness

When searching for the roots of modernist architecture, one should start with Adolf Loos' essays. The author of "Ornament and Crime" was one of the very first architects to recognize the unlimited potential of mass production (Loos, 2013). Although he is known mostly for his views on aesthetics, it was his fascination with Taylorism-Fordism and strong belief in the idea of new architecture for a new society that made him truly "modern." He and Peter Behrens, whose AEG turbine factory was a magnificent example of protomodernist *gesamtkunstwerk*, laid down the foundations for Ludwig Mies van der Rohe, Walter Gropius and, last but not least, Charles-Édouard Jeanneret, Le Corbusier.

The ideas of revolution in architectural and urban design spread through Europe. Young designers, fed up with the academic approach towards architecture, followed the concepts of architecture as "the masterful, correct and magnificent play of volumes brought together in light" (Le Corbusier, 1923). They rejected the traditional urban structure of the city and human settlement. Fascinated with new building materials (or, at least, materials which were rediscovered), modernist architects of the 1920s considered them an appropriate means by which to embody their social ideas. Reinforced concrete and steel, and glazed curtain walls became carriers of moral values (Sepioł, 2011), as modernist architects (like Le Corbusier or Loos) believed that the new style was "morally superior" to the tendencies of the past. The architect was no longer supposed to create "an envelope" for the structure of the building. On the contrary, exposing the structure and its principles was perceived as revealing "the truth" about the architecture.

One of the most important ideas related to modernist architecture was its international characteristic. Rational design based on Le Corbusier's "Five Points of New Architecture" (Le Corbusier, 1923) would lead to similar results – functional and cost-efficient, ignoring the specifics of the local landscape, climate and culture. The best example of the idea of modernity

DOI: 10.4324/9781003299172-2

without borders is Maison Citrohan, designed by Le Corbusier in 1920. Its name refers to Citroen, the popular car brand, and indicates that this type of building can be mass-produced. The architect's sketches present the house in different circumstances; however, no matter if it is the Mediterranean coast near Nice or the Argentinian pampa, the white rectangular shape supported by pilotis looks exactly the same.

Nevertheless, the modernist unification never happened. Despite the flow of ideas and concepts, and despite the same origins, several countries can be recognized as independent centres of modern art and architectural development. We can name, for example, Soviet constructivism, with its expression and revolutionary ambience, the rationality of Bauhaus or the metaphysic philosophy of De Stijl. From a broader perspective, the list can be enriched with Frank Lloyd Wright's organic architecture or the curved shapes of concrete-based structures erected in Brazil.

In 1932 Henry-Russell Hitchcock and Philip Johnson invented the term "international style," which referred to the style of architecture developed in the 1920s and 1930s that emerged in the Netherlands, France and Germany (Khan, 2009). As Andrzej Basista (2001) wrote, the essence of "international style" meant that its basic principles spread around the world, although each region found its own interpretation. Of course, it is almost impossible to find examples of pure "national modernism," as different ideas permeated and interfered with others. For example, the modernist architecture in the Netherlands was closely related to De Stijl art, and buildings such as Cafe d'Unie in Rotterdam (Jacobus Johannes Pieter Oud) or Schroeder's House in Utrecht (Gerrit Rietveld) are almost a large-scale neoplasticism sculpture.

The situation changed in the late 1920s as a result of contact with Soviet constructivism. When Johannes van den Broek and Leendert van der Vlugt designed the Van Nelle factory in Rotterdam, they were influenced by the machine-alike aesthetics of El Lissitzky's works, which resulted in a white concrete-based structure with glazed curtain walls, "conveyor belt" bridges between buildings and large letters on the roofs. At the same time, Walter Gropius implemented new technologies and new aesthetics in his project of the Bauhaus school in Dessau. However, he found inspiration in real industrial plants rather than the revolutionary spirit of constructivism. Using simple forms, he created a building manifesto, a factory that was supposed to produce future generations of architects and artists, although its organization was closer to an artisan workshop than Henry Ford's assembly line.

On the other hand, Mies van der Rohe perfected what later became his trademark – minimalism villas. They had a simple structural system, large open spaces and interiors filled with exclusive natural materials (e.g. Villa Tugenhadt in Brno). Le Corbusier was simultaneously searching for a new concept of urban settlement (the concept of the *Ville radieuse*), creating a series of villas based on formal simplicity and sophisticated spatial composition (e.g. Villa Roche). Across the Atlantic Ocean, Wright found his own way to modernity, rejecting to some extent the European fascination with machines and mass production and creating the foundations for organic architecture. In the late 1930s, another star was born. A young Brazilian architect, Oscar Niemeyer, astonished the world with Palácio Gustavo Capanema, a building which represented the features that became synonymous with Latin modernism: a concrete-based light structure integrated into the natural landscape.

The list of proponents of "international style" is much longer, but those few well-known names represent its richness and diversity. Although a description of the history of architecture through "big names" is not the right way to describe the complexity of its development, in this case, it perfectly highlights one of the main attributes of international modernism – diversity in unity. Architecture developed in different countries and regions in various directions at its own pace. Yet, it had a common base, such as the supremacy of volume over mass, the use of repetitive modular forms and flat surfaces alternating with glass and the reduction of ornament and colour (Trzeciak, 1974). Thus, the modern movement before World War II was neither a homogenous phenomenon, and nor was it after 1945.

The tragedy of World War II, which reduced hundreds of cities to rubble, was, at the same time, an opportunity to create a better world from the ashes of the old one. Large-scale concepts of the interwar period, like Le Corbusier's *Ville radieuse* or mass prefabrication praised by Gropius, were no longer a fantasy. They had become a real solution for real problems. The main task that architects, urban planners and engineers had to face was reconstructing the continent demolished by the brutal force of war. Europe became a laboratory, and designers experimented on a living organism. The numerous buildings and complexes can be considered prototypes that manifested new paradigms. Among them, Le Corbusier's Unité d'Habitation in Marseille (1945–1952) and the city centre of Le Havre, designed by Auguste Perret (1945–1964), should be distinguished. The first building was not only the implementation of a new type of multifamily housing created as a self-sufficient organism but also a eulogy to concrete. The construction of Unité d'Habitation was made with reinforced concrete cast in situ, which also determined its form. Le Corbusier compared the rough surfaces of concrete walls and pillars, with visible traces of the wooden formwork, to the hard lines of an old man's face, whose beauty is in their truth (Jencks, 1982).

Beton brut (raw concrete) soon became an inspiration for architects and one of the characteristic signs of the new current – brutalism. Rayner Banham was fully convinced that Unité d'Habitation had had a great impact not only on brutalism but also on post-war architecture in general (Banham, 1966, p. 148). The fundamental decision made by Le Corbusier and his followers was to reject the machine-like form of concrete used by pre-war modernists, who saw this material as plain, white and flawless (Niebrzydowski, 2018, p. 37). The second example mentioned above, Perret's Le Havre, was "the biggest experimental construction site [in France] using prefabrication for construction" (Chauvin, 2015). Every part of the city structure – from the urban plan, through single buildings, to architectural details – was based on the systematic utilization of a modular grid. Perret created a homogenous ensemble whose form was defined by a visible modular structure. Its uniformity was not only the side effect of the innovative exploitation of the potential of reinforced concrete, but it also reflected ideas of social justice and equality in a post-war welfare state.

Considering concrete a "material of the twentieth century," whose use somehow reflected people's main hopes and fears, one should not limit the analysis to the above-mentioned examples, that is, *beton brut* and prefabricated structures. Numerous post-war monuments dedicated to fallen soldiers and civilian victims of World War II were erected in the 1950s and 1960s in sheer concrete technology. They were not only simple outdoor sculptures, but they also represented modernism's close relationship with brutalism, both in terms of spatial concepts and philosophy. Abstract sculptures and enormous blocks of grey concrete were erected in the natural landscape, creating a strong contrast between culture and nature. The material, wrote Adrian Forty, was appropriate due to its indestructibility, anonymity and dumbness, making it perfectly suited for reflection and mental projection (Forty, 2009, pp. 284–285). With its rough surface and "ordinariness," concrete was apparently more appropriate to express the enormous scale of tragedy and the togetherness of experiencing the tragedy than noble marble or bronze. Massive blocks of grey concrete were used to commemorate Jews murdered in Majdanek (architect Wiktor Tołkin, 1968–1969) and Chełmno (designers Jerzy Buszkiewicz, Józef Stasiński, 1964) (see Picture 1.1), people executed in Kaunas Fort IX (sculptor Alfonsas Vincentas Ambraziūnas, 1984) and the Monument to the Šar Mountains Partisan Unit in Brezovica, Kosovo (designer Svetomir Arsić Basara, 1964).

Concrete was not only the material of past tragedies but also mostly the material of the bright future. The modernist faith in rapid and continuous progress applied to all sorts of human activity, including architecture and engineering. Is there anything better to illustrate their unlimited potential than a six-centimetre thin layer of reinforced concrete hovering above the ground and supported only by a few slender pillars? The continuation of pre-war research on reinforced concrete thin-shell structures conducted by individuals like Eduardo Torroja resulted in this technology flourishing in the 1950s and 1960s. Due to their dynamic, expressive image, they were often used in buildings and infrastructure related to movement and transport, thus becoming a symbol of modernity in their time. It partially explains the popularity of thin-shell structures in developing countries that were proud of their achievements. It is why Torroja's hippodrome in Madrid (1935–1941) became one of the modernist icons of pre-war Spain, with architects in Latin America eagerly creating organic forms out of concrete shells. After 1956, the countries of Central and Eastern Europe (CEE)

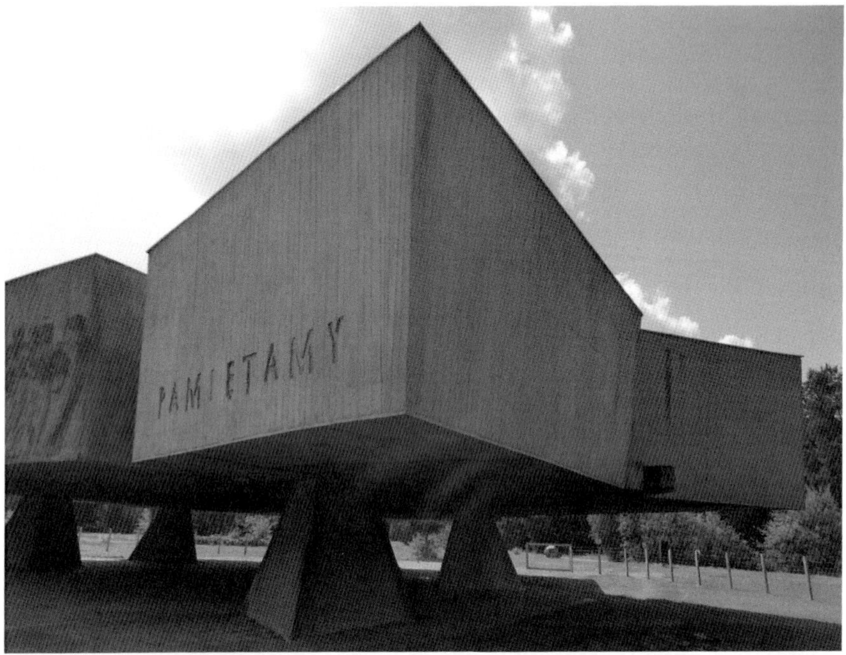

Picture 1.1 The "ordinariness" of concrete made is a proper material for commemoration of tragedies affecting the masses. The monument dedicated to victims of German Death Camp Kulmhof am Nehr in Chełmno nad Nerem (Poland), designed by J. Buszkiewicz and J. Stasiński, 1964. ©Błażej Ciarkowski.

also began to implement thin-shell structures, building upon the achievements of the Western world (Nowicki, 1960).

The twentieth century's "iron curtain," which divided Europe into two political blocks, was not really opaque and sealed. In fact, after 1956, it resembled more a "nylon curtain" – an obstacle that you could see and pass through (Crowley, 2015). At least, architects could. They were among the social groups who were able to visit Western Europe relatively often (e.g. during study visits or symposiums) (Basista, 2001), and they were able to observe the latest trends in architecture. Moreover, as architectural associations frequently imported foreign journals and books, the architects in socialist countries were aware of the latest trends and implemented them in their homelands.

However, the development of modernist architecture in socialist countries did not proceed simultaneously with the rest of the world. The doctrine of socialist realism, imposed in 1934 in the Soviet Union and in 1949 in Eastern Bloc countries, rejected the formal achievements of the modern movement and forced architects to combine neo-classicist/eclectic forms with propaganda decorations. Robust reinforced-concrete constructions were rather hidden behind facades filled with columns, cornices and sculptures. Only after the death of Josef Stalin and Nikita Khrushchev's "Secret Speech" in 1956 did the communist party in the Soviet Union declare a return to modernity in the arts and architecture. Authorities in other socialist countries followed the example of "big brother." "Let the new period be characterised by the freedom of creation. Let nobody be afraid of innovativeness," said Polish Prime Minister Józef Cyrankiewicz to encourage designers to return to the avant-garde idea (Skolimowska, 2012, p. 88). Despite its short duration, socialist realism had a huge impact on architecture in socialist CEE countries. First, it delayed its development. Second, it resulted in the indiscriminate acceptance of modernist ideas, even though they were not really suited to the local context (Basista, 2001). It took subsequent generations of designers to search for their own interpretations of modernist dogmas that would be specific to the different countries and regions.

Socialist modernism in architecture as part of the modernization policy in CEE countries

In totalitarian states, architecture, just like any other human activity, was a matter of state policy controlled by authorities. Legal acts defined the rules of practising the profession of an architect, technical standards and everything necessary in any country to prevent its architecture from falling into chaos. At the same time, numerous doctrines and suggestions made by the communist authorities played an enormous role in creating its final form. In addition to the situations related to implementing and rejecting socialist realism mentioned above, sometimes the single opinion of a politician could determine the fate of particular buildings or monuments. For example, the first secretary of the Polish United Workers' Party (PZPR – Polska Zjednoczona Partia Robotnicza), Władysław Gomułka, was suspicious about the form of the Grunwald Monument (architect Witold Cęckiewicz, sculptor Jerzy Bandura, 1960) and only thanks to the author's brilliant description of its ideological meaning was the structure completed (Ciarkowski, 2017c).

Soviet architect, Felix Novikov wrote that "the client [government, trade union etc.] occasionally acted as if he was building from his own fancies, while an architect occasionally had to accept his orders as if that really was the case" (Novikov, 2016, p. 95). He described the competition for a Moscow theatre that took place in 1947. The final verdict was given by the mayor of the capital, who was also a local Communist Party leader. He decided that the new building could not have more columns than the Bolshoi theatre and selected the appropriate project (Novikov, 2016, p. 95).These are only a few examples, but they give an overview of the situation, that is, that the aesthetic and functional values of architecture depended on the moods and whims of high-ranking politicians.

There is also another perspective, related to indirectly spreading totalitarian state propaganda. Despite its totalitarian facet, communism in CEE countries is also considered a modernization project (even during the darkest days of the Stalinist period) (Leszczyński, 2013). After World War II, material conditions gradually improved, mass poverty was gradually eradicated, and the elimination of spatial and social inequalities accelerated significantly. It happened in part due to new top-down, centralized institutions, most of which excluded active social participation and promoted loyalty in exchange for state care (Matera & Sokołowicz, n.d.).

Here, one can indicate the supportive role of architecture. Ambitious programs that were to lead to social and economic change needed a developed infrastructure. Enormous industrial complexes required new residential estates – like the ones in Magnitogorsk designed by Ernst May (1930–1933), Nowa Huta (Tadeusz Ptaszycki, 1949–1960) or Nowe Tychy (Hanna Adamczewska-Wejchert, Kazimierz Wejchert, since 1951). Due to the post-war baby boom, the number of required apartments increased; thus, housing construction was a priority sector of state policy. Simultaneously, the new housing complexes had to be filled with additional assets to serve people's living needs, for example, schools, hospitals and shopping malls.

According to the Soviet constitution proclaimed in 1936 (and similar acts in other socialist countries), hard-working people had the right to rest. Thus, the State administration authorities, big enterprises and trade unions representing specific branches built health resorts, holiday resorts and sports facilities. No matter the functional program of a single building or complex, they all represented the so-called "socialist modernist" style. The name, although it can be considered somewhat unfortunate (has anyone heard about "capitalist modernism"?), commonly identifies architecture created in the Soviet Union and socialist CEE countries after 1956.

The term was first used by Adam Miłobędzki in the early 1990s to describe the architecture of socialist Poland between the 1950s and 1980s (Miłobędzki, 1994). Even though he was later sceptical about its accuracy, "socialist modernism" became a popular and commonly understood phrase. This scepticism grew from the emotional characteristic of both words – "socialism" and "modernism." Some scholars have suggested the more neutral term "cold war modern," which refers to countries on both sides of the iron curtain (whereas "socialist modernism" describes only one side of the conflict) (Galusek, 2015). More than three decades after the collapse of the communist system, any attempts to eradicate the phrase from common and scientific language seem impossible. In fact, it is widely used and refers, for example, to post-war Serbian music, described by Jelena Janković-Beguš (2017) as a compilation of modernist form and socialist ideas. Dumitru Rusu, a Romanian architect engaged in preserving modernist architecture built in the Eastern Bloc between 1955 and 1991, defined it in a similar way, emphasizing the dissonance between the socialist ideology of creating identical blueprints and adapting them locally. At the same time, he marginalized the political background, focusing on purely architectural and social aspects. "Socialist modernism is a desire to go back to pre-World War II modernism, with architecture attempting to fulfil simultaneously cultural requirements as well as utilitarian and economic ones – the latter having priority," wrote Rusu (2017).

The post-Stalinist architecture of late modernism and brutalism was not totally free of communist ideology, even if, compared to prior socialist realistic buildings, has cut back more from it. Piotr Piotrowski, a Polish art historian, noted that after the death of Stalin, the communists did not need socialist realistic propaganda but modern art that would not affect the status quo (Piotrowski, 2011, p. 177). Idealess modernism then became a tool which was supposed to help preserve the existing political and social order. "There was no more time nor mood for ideology," wrote Krzysztof Nawratek, emphasizing that in the era of the "mature socialist society," the direct meaning of a work of art was no longer its most important feature (Nawratek, 2005, p. 92).

The communist authorities also became more open to letting socialist architects compare their achievements with the Western world. They were able to participate in international competitions, go abroad for study visits, and import foreign books and journals. Of course, the situation was different in each of the socialist countries. Designers attempted to compare their works with the latest tendencies in architectural design, searched for inspiration and tried to find their own version of "modernity." It resulted in different local versions of socialist modernism.

Although the countries of the Eastern Block shared some common aspects, for example, a political system determined by the leading role of a communist party, their dependence on the Soviet Union, and a centralized, nationalized economy, it did not translate into a unified architecture. What is more, the differences in local incarnations of modernism appeared despite the shared similarities in the creative conditions (national, multiple-branch design offices), the workmanship (national construction companies) and the technology (i.e. the prefabrication systems) of those states. This mirrored the global process that was occurring in the 1960s – the revision of modernist doctrines, which led to the creation of the phrase "national concrete," which meant architecture searching for individual characteristics rather than common traits (Forty, 2012, p. 103).

In Czechoslovakia, after 1956, Western architecture was seen as individualistic and eccentric, while its Eastern counterpart was "humanised functionalism/modernism" (Hanackova, 2014, p. 79). This opinion was mirrored by the Polish architectural press, which dubbed Western architecture "philistine modernism" (Nowicki, 1960). Although the architecture in Poland and Czechoslovakia was closer to Bauhaus productivism rather than the poetics of constructivism, "individualism, rather than uniformity, was encouraged in Yugoslavian mass-housing projects" (McGuirk, 2018).

Picture 1.2 Panelak – a large panel system housing in socialist Czechoslovakia. Multifamily housing in Petržalka estate in Bratislava (Slovakia). ©Kelovy (public domain).

The apartment buildings of Yugoslavia or Romania very often have expressive forms and sculptural details. At the same time, other countries invested in "house factories" in an effort to increase the amount of housing built by simplifying particular buildings. The forms of the Polish "blok" (e.g. the Retkinia estate in Łódź, composed of repetitive large panel system (LPS) housing) or the Czechoslovakian "panelak" (the Košík estate in Prague) derive from function and the construction system used (see Picture 1.2). Their designers saw value in the spatial qualities of the entire urban context, not in the details of a singular building (Krygier & Sumień, 1973). There were exceptions, like the Grunwaldzki Square housing complex in Wrocław (architect Jadwiga Grabowska-Hawrylak 1968–1972) (see Picture 1.3), whose organic forms were closer to Yugoslavian expressive architecture than to typical "blocks." The main differences between "national socmodernisms" were more than just a result of the architect's personal aesthetic choices. Sometimes the economy and politics were involved. In the 1960s in Poland, the authorities tried to blame the insufficient number of new houses on architects who, in their opinion, preferred to design monuments to their ego than simple and economic blocks (Ciarkowski, 2017).

Picture 1.3 Prefabrication technologies had many different faces. Housing at the Grunwaldzki Square in Wrocław became iconic due to their curved reinforced concrete facades. The housing complex at Grunwaldzki Square in Wrocław (Poland), designed by J. Grabowska-Hawrylak, 1968–1972. ©Błażej Ciarkowski.

Despite the irrelevance of this remark, the 1960s were a "golden age" of spectacular socialist modernist structures. In every socialist country, new public-use buildings were constructed – sometimes to upgrade the town's status and sometimes to emphasize its dominant role. They also played the role of social condensers. In Vilnius (Lithuania), which is a relatively small city, from 1945 onwards, new public buildings were erected "to give it the functions of a republican capital" (Hatherley, 2016a, p. 154). Among them, one can distinguish the monumental Sports Palace (architect Eduardas Chlomauskas 1965–1971) or the much more intimate Palace of Weddings. The sculpture-like building, designed by Gediminas Baravykas in 1974, sits between the greenery of the park and the street. Its form was supposed to be a reference to both, as the concrete curves of the facades are soft and organic (see Picture 1.4). In Hungary the architect, János Dianóczky, tried to find another way to connect the natural environment with modernist architecture. The ferry station in Szántód, by Hungarian Lake Balaton (1963), was based on the simple concept of the soft surface of the concrete roof hanging above glazed curtain walls so that the people inside the building could have permanent contact with its exterior.

Picture 1.4 Palace of Weddings in Vilnius (Lithuania), designed by Gedyminas Baravykas, 1974. ©Błażej Ciarkowski.

Besides the small-scale projects, a large number of impressive, monumental landmarks were built, changing the panoramas – and identities – of socialist cities. Their role was not only to impress but also to serve socialist society as a place of leisure or education. In Bacau (Romania), a new Sports Hall was built between 1969 and 1975 (architect Gheorghe Chira). It has a roof that hangs on huge, prestressed concrete arches, and it was a symbol of new technologies and a mastery of engineering. Some years later, in the Moldavian capital Chisinau, at that time being part of the USSR, Alla Kirichenko and Simion Shoykhet designed a circus (1978–1981) whose expression was achieved not only by using abstract forms in the sophisticated reinforced concrete structure, but also by creating symbolic references to local culture. The rhythm of the oblique pillars on the façade was a synthesis of the traditional Moldavian dance – the "hora" (see Picture 1.5).

In the 1970s and early 1980s, iconic architecture became popular in socialist countries. Even though architects from Western Europe and the United States had already rejected some of modernism's dogmas, many of their Eastern counterparts designed brutalist, sculpture-like concrete behemoths, monumental and overwhelming. One of the recognized architects from the German Democratic Republic (GDR), Herman Henselmann, a representative of "iconic architecture" (Bildzeichenarchitektur), designed a high-rise university building in Leipzig, whose shape was supposed to allude to an open book (Angermann, 2017, p. 196). The landmark concept was also developed by Miklós Hófer and György Vörös, who were responsible for the project of the TV Tower in Miskolc, Hungary – a 72-meter-high reinforced

Picture 1.5 The formal aspects of soc-modernist architecture not only derived from its function. The composition of the façade of the Circus in Chisinau was inspired by the rhythm of Moldavian dance. The Circus, in Chisinau (Moldavia) designed by A. Kirichenko & S. Shoykhet, 1978–1981. ©Gikü (public domain).

concrete mast with a suspended hexagonal cafeteria and viewing platform (Szendröi et al., 1978, p. 165) (see Picture 1.6) or Ivan Antic, the author of the 25 May Sportcenter in Belgrade, Serbia (1973–1975). The latter, due to the gently curved forms hanging in the massive core, evoked comparisons with Japanese Metabolist architecture and great architects such as Kenzo Tange. The resemblance of particular socialist modernist edifices to works of famous western architects was not unusual. One can easily find similarities between the Arena sports hall in Poznań (Poland) by Jerzy Turzeniecki (1972–1974) and Palazetto dello Sport in Rome (Pier Luigi Nervi, 1956–1957) (see Pictures 1.7 and 1.8). Traces of inspiration from works of the Italian master of reinforced concrete were also visible in the Maksimir Stadium in Yugoslavian Zagreb (1946–1964). Its author, Vladimir Turina, searched for beauty in the concrete structure exposed to open ambient, which “gave it a feeling of airiness and space” (Maroević, 1996, p. 112).

One cannot look at the architecture of CEE as a simple reflection of the trends that emerged in the West. Architects in every country attempted to find their own way to a “national modernism,” but, apparently, only a

Picture 1.6 The Brutalist Miskolc Tower became a landmark of the city. TV Tower in Miskolc (Hungary), designed by M. Hófer & G. Vörös, 1966. ©Mészáros Zoltán CC BY-SA 3.0.

Picture 1.7 Palazetto dello Sport in Rome, designed by Pierluigi Nervi, 1956–1957... ©Błażej Ciarkowski.

few succeeded. One of them was Slovenian Edvard Ravnikar, whose style Vladimir Kulić once called "liquid modernism." Searching for an identity, he shifted references – from the eclectic style of his mentor, Josef Plecnik, to brutalism. The result of Ravnikar's perpetual mediations was a "locally adjusted modernism" (Kulić, 2013, p. 2).

Picture 1.8 ... and its Eastern European sibling. The Arena sports hall in Poznań, designed by Jerzy Turzeniecki, 1972–1974. ©Mateusz Woźniak CC BY-SA 3.0.

Martino Stierli called Yugoslavia a "laboratory of globalisation in the cold war," highlighting a different development dynamic of the modernist architecture, distinctive from other socialist countries. This was due to the lack of a dominant position of socialist realism and the continuity of relations with Western practice and theory. According to Stierli (2018), the Yugoslavian authorities used modernist architecture and urbanism for their political goals. In this, they were not alone. Despite the end of socialist realism, architecture in the Eastern Bloc always remained a part of the state's politics. David Crowley called it "banal socialism," which served the ideology, although the buildings themselves made very few straightforward political statements (Crowley, 2015).

Socialism in CEE countries in the 1960s and 1970s was not as much an ideological struggle as an effort made by the authorities to keep the political situation stable. It could be achieved by satisfying social needs or, at least, giving that impression. Latvians sitting in the cafeteria of the health resorts in Jurmala and looking at the shore of the Baltic Sea could feel almost as if they were in Brighton. Polish tourists spent their holidays in Bulgaria, in the Pomorie Hotel, which was supposed to become a substitute for Saint-Tropez. The Arena sports hall in Poznań was a copy of Pier Luigi Nervi's Palazetto dello Sport in Rome, and the Memorial Nadia Comaneci Montreal Onexi Boxing Hall in Onesti (architect Mircea Mihailescu, 1966) did not yield to the concrete thin-shell structures of Felix Candela. Hence, on the one hand, the architecture of socialist modernism supported modernization and, therefore, improved the conditions of people's everyday lives; on the other hand, it created an imitation of Western reality – Potemkin villages made of concrete.

Concrete in post-war architecture: New possibilities for a new society

In post-war reality, concrete was the material that made it possible to reconstruct both the destroyed cities and people's identities, and it was clearly visible in CEE countries. The situation resembled that after World War I, when countries like Czechoslovakia, Poland and Slovenia regained their independence and created their identity through architecture, among other things. The impact of the villas in Prague, the Czech Cubism estates inspired by manor houses from eighteenth-century Warsaw, and Josef Plecnik's representative public spaces in Ljubljana had an enormous impact on creating, respectively, the image of a modern country and a connection with the glorious past. Yet, they did not affect the urban landscape or ordinary people's lives to such a high degree as the concrete-based, prefabricated, mass-produced buildings from the 1960s and 1970s. The scale and the range of post-war transformation were incomparable to anything in the twentieth century.

Analysing the urban space of the USRR and its "satellites" (countries dependent on Moscow), Stephan Kotkin described the unification of construction within the entire Eastern Bloc. "The Soviet phenomenon created a deeply unified material culture. I am thinking not just of the cheap tracksuits worn by seemingly every male in Uzbekistan or Bulgaria, Ukraine or Mongolia. Consider the children's playgrounds in those places, erected over the same cracked concrete panel surfaces and with the same twisted metal piping – all made at the same factories, to uniform codes. This was also true of apartment buildings (outside and inside), schools, indeed entire cities, and even villages. Despite some folk ornamentation here and there (Islamic flourishes on prefab concrete panels for a few apartment complexes in Kazan or Baku), a traveller encounters identical designs and materials," he wrote (Kotkin, 2007).

Kotkin was correct, although he focused more on general impressions than an in-depth analysis of specific technical and material solutions. Starting from the 1960s, the housing factories changed the landscape of cities and towns of almost the entire Eastern Bloc. The only exception was Hungary, where in the 1970s, prefabricated constructions comprised only 30% of all the buildings constructed (between 1970 and 1975, it was even lower – 29%). In comparison, in the same period, the numbers for other socialist states were as follows: the Soviet Union – 75%, Czechoslovakia and GDR – 60%, and Poland and Bulgaria – 40% (Molnár, 2005, p. 4). The prefabricated apartment buildings, despite having local names (*khrushchovka* in the USSR, panelak in Czechoslovakia, bloki in Poland and panelház in Hungary) and differences in their construction technology, were all different manifestations of a singular phenomenon that was the post-war modernization of socialist countries.

In 1958, the USSR bought the license and the factories for the Camus French heavy prefabrication system. It was then introduced to Czechoslovakia (Zarecor, 2011) and Poland. Also introduced were technologies created in Denmark (Larsen-Nielsen in Czechoslovakia) and Germany (Kesting in Poland) (see Picture 1.9). However, an exception to the rule was not the import of technology but entire buildings. It happened in 1973 in Poland, where reinforced concrete construction elements of so-called "Leningrad blocks" *(leningrady)* were brought from the USSR to Szczecin by ship (Wojtkun, 2008).

At the same time, domestic prefabrication systems were also being developed. New Belgrade in Yugoslavia was erected using the IMS and Jugomont systems, the Bielany quarter in Warsaw, Poland, was built using the W-70 system, and the P1.11 system was utilized for the Barrandov estate in Prague, Czechoslovakia. The construction industry in all Eastern Bloc countries could boast about having several systems implemented simultaneously. Their increasing popularity allowed the authorities to face their biggest challenge – meeting the fundamental needs of the people and providing them with housing. LPS housing estates, with simple but rather comfortable blocks of flats, allowed millions of people to raise their standard of living.

Picture 1.9 The iron curtain did not prevent from the transfer of technologies and "know-how" between East and West. LPS building in Larsen-Nielsen system, Budapest-Újpest, Hungary. ©Rovibroni (Barna Rovács), CC BY-SA 4.0.

Despite the wave of criticism (often unjustified), one should remember that those who settled in the grey concrete blocks had usually been living in substandard conditions before (Królikowski, 2017). The impact of mass housing was much greater than simply improving living comfort, however. It helped thousands of people to move from the countryside to the city and, as a result, support the development of urbanization and industrialization of every country. People started to inhabit the new housing estates before the completion of the whole investment, which resulted in problems with transport, quality of public spaces and the network of basic services, provoking strong criticism (Basista, 2001). Years later, when infrastructure was completed and the space around the blocks was arranged with lush greenery, they were evaluated very differently, with more positive conclusions.

The unified forms of housing and the limited types of apartments supported the idea of an egalitarian socialist state. It was not an isolated incident to find a worker of a local enterprise and an executive manager living in the same LPS building and sharing the same (at least, to some extent) problems of everyday life. Of course, in the communist system, all citizens were equal, but some were "more equal than others" (Orwell, 1945), although the repeatable forms of concrete blocks supported this illusion.

Prefabrication in the USSR and Eastern Bloc countries not only had a strong ideological dimension but also, most importantly, an economic one. Architects followed the instructions outlined by Nikita Khrushchev to limit the use of steel – "everything that could be made out of concrete should be made out of concrete" (Forty, 2012, p. 151). Architects in socialist countries praised the advantages of prefabrication, emphasizing its advantages over construction in situ (Cooke & Reid, 2007, p. 157; Syrkus & Syrkus, 1948). Finally, "construction sites became assembly sites" (Riabuszyn & Szyszkina, 1987). According to Adrien Forty, a paradox arose whereby the communist East adhered to the economic reasoning of prefabrication, whereas in the West, the incentives of the authorities to use precast concrete systems were purely based on ideology (Forty, 2012, p. 164).

The fascination with concrete went far beyond its advantages as a material. "In the twentieth century, the belief that concrete is the 'stone of contemporaneity' and can be rough, unpolished or have a texture of the natural print of its formwork became a matter of ethics and not just aesthetics," wrote Marcin Charciarek (2020, pp. 140–141). In fact, the "angry young man," as some critics called the generation of British architects who started their professional careers just after World War II, wanted architecture to be "closer" to reality, the problems of real life, and the truth about it. They designed buildings far from elegant forms of pre-war modernism, introducing "British austerity" to architecture (Vidler, 2011, p. 106). However, the rough surfaces of concrete walls were precisely designed and required close collaboration between the architect and the constructor at the construction site. The cast in situ concrete was, according to Erwin Heinle and Max Bacher (1971, p. 64), the highest form of craftsmanship and handicraft.

Looking back at the socialist architecture of the late 1950s and 1960s, one cannot omit the surprising popularity of thin-shell structures. Although their construction was technically demanding, reinforced concrete shells were used for assets of minor importance: urban canopies (the WKD Warsaw Railway Station, architects Arseniusz Romanowicz and Piotr Szymaniak, 1957–1963) (see Picture 1.10), sports arenas or even bus stop shelters. Apparently, the economy-oriented way of thinking about prefabricated housing in socialist countries did not refer to much more effective structures.

The reinforced concrete thin shell structure was not only a display of post-war engineering's technical abilities, but it was also optimal for certain functional programs where a homogenous open interior space was crucial. Warsaw train stations were completed in the early 1960s and can be considered an example of that functionalist approach. The Polish architect, Arseniusz Romanowicz, who designed them used to emphasize that the form of the pavilions, covered with reinforced concrete thin-shell roofs, was the rational response to specific design issues such as eliminating internal supporting structures (Romanowicz, 1964).

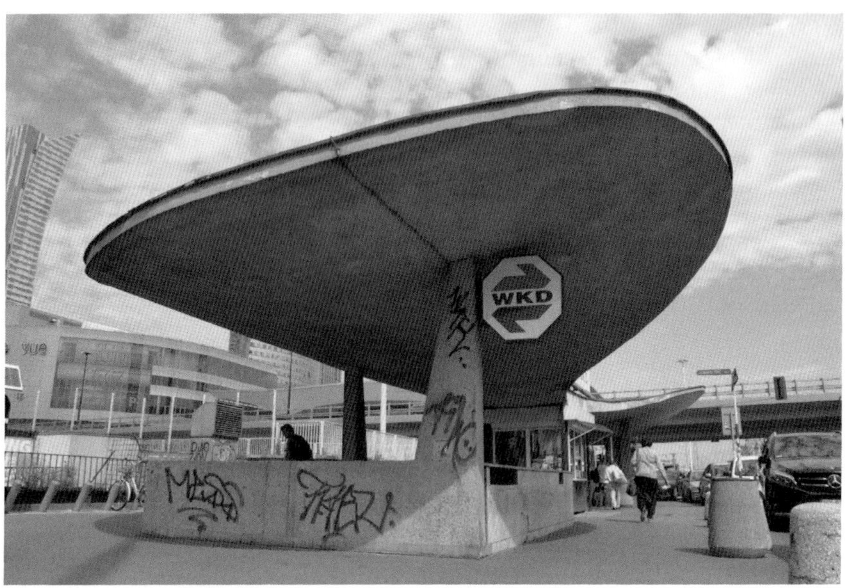

Picture 1.10 The reinforced concrete thin shell canopy above the entrance to the WKD Warsaw Śródmieście station was one of few individually designed cross-city line stations; structure in the capital of Poland. WKD Station in Warsaw (Poland), designed by A. Romanowicz, P. Szymaniak, 1957–1963. ©Błażej Ciarkowski.

However, the symbolic aspects of expressive reinforced concrete structures should also be mentioned. According to Maciej Czarnecki, they were a metaphor for the phenomena they derived from – dynamics, weight, movement and weightlessness (Czarnecki, 2017). Their forms were defined by rational principles of statics, but at the same time, they seemed to oppose them and "reveal the power of contemporary man to free himself from the impact of gravity without any effort" (Arnheim, 2016). Thus, shell structures were often implemented in structures related to transport and movement, for example, railway stations, ferry terminals and gas stations. Thin layers of concrete covering steel mesh were formed in many different styles – from hyperbolic paraboloids and other quadric surfaces to free-hand forms, whose shapes were limited almost only by the designers' imagination.

Their popularity reached its pinnacle in the 1960s when they were used in public use buildings – especially those that were supposed to create a certain spatial effect. One can easily find shell canopies in front of main entrances to administration or university buildings (e.g. Kielce and Poznań in Poland) (see Picture 1.11), thin-shell roofs of cafeterias (Restaurant Sēnīte near Murjāņi, Latvia) and exhibition pavilions, sports halls (Onesti, Romania) and even churches (Kalisz, Poland) (see Picture 1.12). Soft, folded surfaces resembled fabric more than hard, rigid concrete structures and can be interpreted as representing the dreams and ambitions of the generation who sent a man into space. They were in stark contrast to the cuboids of housing blocks made with prefabricates, which represented the everydayness regulated by the norms and laws of a socialist country.

Modernist constructions became, in their own way, abstract symbols of the new reality. Andrei V. Ikonnikov described the steel trusses of the roof structure of Vilnius's Central Post Office (architects Algimantas Nasvytis, Vytautas

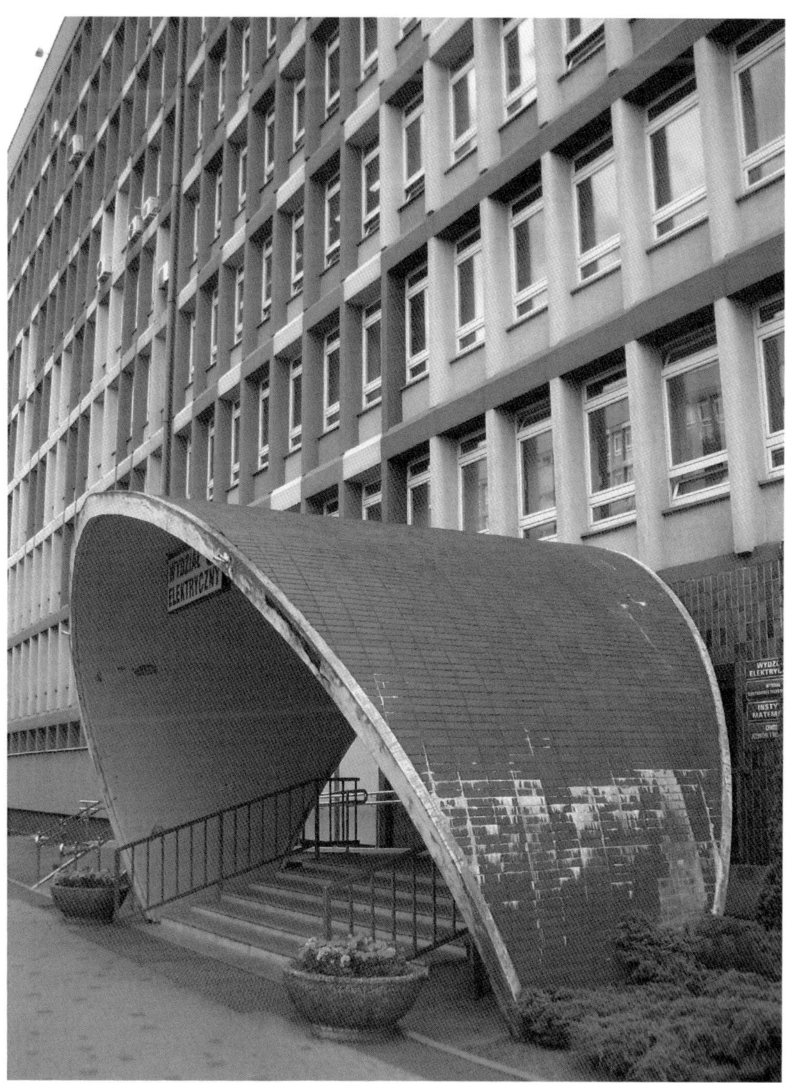

Picture 1.11 The reinforced concrete thin shell canopy in front of prefabricated building at the Technical University Campus in Poznań (Poland), designed by L. Sternal, 1965 ©Błażej Ciarkowski.

Picture 1.12 Reinforced concrete thin shell structures became popular in the late 1950s and were implemented in multiple types of buildings of different functions – even religious ones. Jerzy Kuźmienko and Andrzej Fajans designed the church of the Divine Mercy in Kalisz (Poland) in 1957, but its construction has not started before 1977. ©Stiopa, CC BY-SA 4.0.

Nasvytis, 1961–1969), which were visible in the main lobby, as "sophisticated and lightweight 'symbols of the modern technology'" (Ikonnikow et al., 1975, p. 9). Many assets were interpreted similarly. The above-mentioned Restaurant Sēnīte in Inčukalns parish, near the Vidzeme highway, designed by architect Linards Skuja and engineer Andris Bite, was opened to the public in 1967 and became an attraction due to the roof above the main hall, which was the first concrete shell construction in Latvia (Aizpurva, 2019, p. 101).

The socialist system implemented in CEE countries after World War II (except for the Soviet Union) was often regarded by society with suspicion or even hostility. To convince people that the new authority represented their common interest, the communists used different means. Among them, an important place was occupied by education, which included the creation of a new Pantheon of socialist heroes and heroines. They were mostly socialist activists or victims of World War II, as the victory over fascism was one of the foundation myths of the Eastern Bloc (in Russia, it is still the case).

The post-war period in CEE was a time when several large-scale monuments were erected. Enormous structures were built in every country to commemorate fallen comrades. Abstract concrete sculptures, designed to overwhelm visitors of the site, expressed the scale of the tragedy or the heroism (e.g. Majdanek – a monument at a former Nazi Death Camp, author Wiktor Tołkin, 1968–1969, Lublin, Poland) (see Picture 1.13). Most were made of concrete, which was justified not only for economic reasons but also for ideological and aesthetic reasons. Raw concrete, with its rough, greyish surface, resembled the artistic explorations of post-war abstractionists or representatives of *arte povera*. Architects and sculptors, working as a team, created not only single, free-standing monuments, but also whole landscapes or, in some cases, monument-buildings (Slovakia, Poland). They took advantage of certain qualities of the material – its formability and responsiveness to atmospheric conditions. Bogdan Bogdanović, a Yugoslav architect and author of numerous unique memorial sites, always developed them out of the topography and landscape as places of thinking, recalling and contemplation. His best-known work, Stone Flower, built in 1966 and located in the Jasenovac memorial park at the site of a former Nazi concentration camp, has the form of a giant lotus flower made of concrete, "a metaphor of life and imperishability" (Uskokovic, 2013, p. 87).

As a building material, concrete can be a metaphor for society in communist countries. A combination of different elements (water, cement, aggregate) makes a liquid mass, which can be shaped according to the mason's will. When ready, it becomes a monolith, hard and durable. The communist authorities and ideologists wanted to achieve the same result thanks to social engineering – several groups of people (peasants, industry workers, intellectuals), put in the frames of ideology, were supposed to turn into a homogenous socialist society.

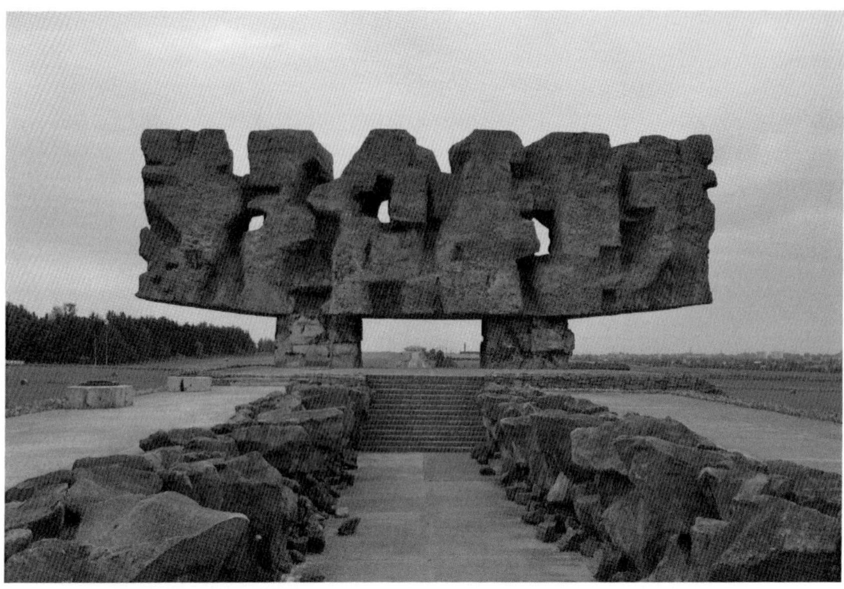

Picture 1.13 "The Gate" – a part of the monument dedicated to the victims of the German Death Camp Majdanek in Lublin (Poland), designed by W. Tołki, 1968–1969. ©Błażej Ciarkowski.

Soc-modernism architecture after socialism: The problem of dissonant heritage

The social perception of concrete architecture observed in all CEE countries can be identified and classified in the following phases. The direction of changes and development was determined by the USSR, and after 1945, the tendencies applied there were transferred to the countries of the Eastern Bloc. In the case of the People's Republic of Poland (and other communist states), the key dates were 1949 (in Hungary, it was 1951), when the ruling party introduced socialist realism as the prevailing style of architecture, and 1956 as the year of the return to modernism (Macel, 2002, pp. 110–111). From that moment, the authorities, architects and society unanimously perceived socialist modernist concrete-based architecture as one of the symbols of modernity. The situation changed in the 1980s, when society and the architects turned to post-modernism as the style to represent the social protest against the communist system (Nawratek, 2005).

After the fall of communism, grey, concrete buildings became symbols of an unwanted past. It is for those reasons that Andrzej Basista entitled the first scientific analysis of communist architecture in Poland "Concrete Heritage" (Basista, 2001). In the new, neoliberal and capitalist reality, the monuments and buildings, which had been a pride of socialist society, became a dissonant heritage.

The term is usually used to define the material evidence of colonialism or totalitarian regimes. Gregory Ashworth and John Tunbridge emphasized the connection between the feeling of dissonance provoked by certain assets and that is caused by the overlapping of different narratives and interpretative threads. Architecture may have different significance for different social groups, each assigning it different meanings. The heritage or the sheer process of its creation implies disinheritance. According to Tunbridge and Ashworth (1996), "this disinheritance may be unintentional, temporary, of trivial importance, limited in its effects and concealed; or it may be long-term, widespread, intentional, important and obvious."

Among the extensive group of objects considered to be "dissonant heritage," we can distinguish those that are "undesirable heritage." They include physical remnants of past eras that represent values that most of contemporary society does not wish to be identified with, despite understanding that they form an integral part of its history (MacDonald, 2006, p. 11). According to the above-mentioned theories and definitions, the architecture of socialist modernism can be described as the dissonant heritage of totalitarianism or authoritarianism. We will return to this topic in Chapter 3.1.

Is it justified, however, to state that the negative reception of the architectural legacy of the communist period results directly from its political connotations? The answer is not so unambiguous. Paradoxically, the social reception of socialist realism is often much more positive than the examples of late modernism or brutalism. The columns, arcades and lavish details (although filled with political content) of MDM (Marszałkowska Dzielnica Mieszkaniowa – Marszalkowska Housing Estate) (see Picture 1.14) in Warsaw trigger much more positive reactions than the simple, late modernist forms of Central Station in the same city. The aesthetics here are in stark contrast with the historical and political content, as MDM was constructed in times of Stalinist oppression, while the station was one of the flagship executions of the 1970s and prosperity. Thus, is it perhaps more than just the historical and political context that makes socialist architecture hard for many people to accept?

After the collapse of the communist system, the countries of the Eastern Bloc turned towards democracy and capitalism. The neo-liberal economy dogma became the only vision of the reality accepted by politicians, economists and intellectuals. "What is an individual? No earthly good," wrote Vladimir Mayakovsky (1972), emphasizing the power of the collective effort. Neo-liberals turned it into the opposite. "What is an individual? Earthly good," they could have said, denying "public" and promoting "private."

Many state proprieties were placed in the hands of private stakeholders or big companies. The new owners often did not pay attention to the artistic and architectural values of the existing structures, but treated them as an obstacle on their way to multiple profits from the plot of land. The number of icons of socialist modernist architecture, honoured with awards and highly praised in their time, were torn down just to prepare a space for new investments: the Supersam supermarket in Warsaw (architects: Ewa

Picture 1.14 MDM (Marszałkowska Dzielnica Miedzkaniowa) – one of the highest achievements of socialist realism in Polish architecture which was supposed to be a combination of "realistic form and socialist content." MDM in Warsaw (Poland), designed by S. Jankowski, J. Knothe, J. Sigalin, Z. Stępiński, 1950–1952. ©Błażej Ciarkowski.

Krasińska, Maciej Krasiński and Jerzy Hryniewiecki, built in 1962 – demolished in 2007) (see Picture 1.15), Hotel Praha in Prague (architects: Jaroslav Paroubek, Arnošt Navrátil, Radek Černý, Jan Sedláček and Věkoslav Pardyl, 1981–2014), the railway station in Katowice (architects: Wacław Kłyszewski, Eugieniusz Wierzbicki and Jerzy Mokrzyński, 1972–2009), Transgas in Prague (architects Jindřich Malátek, Jiří Eisenreich, Ivo Loos and Václav Aulický, 1972–2019) or the Istropolis House of Trade Unions in Bratislava (architects: Ferdinand Konček, Il'ja Skoček and Ľubomír Titl, 1956–2022). They represent different functional programs – from commercial, through public use (transport), to a building originally designed to host Communist Party congresses. The primary function of the particular building was not important, as its demolition created an opportunity for business development. For example, in Katowice, the old brutalist railway station was replaced with a new one, accompanied by a huge shopping mall (in fact, one can say that its primary function is commercial, not transport).

At the same time, those processes can be considered a battle for memory. Shabby, grey, concrete socialist juggernauts were replaced with new, shiny temples of capitalism. Probably one of the most striking examples is the history of the Moscow cinema in Warsaw (architects Kazimierz Marczewski and Stefan Putowski, 1950–1996). Demolished in the mid-90s, it was replaced by an office building with a multiplex cinema named Europlex. This was not only a replacement of one structure with another, but a bottom-up, anti-communist iconoclasm with strong symbolic meaning.

Picture 1.15 The modernist supermarket Supersam in Warsaw was recognized due to its innovative structure. Its architectural quality did not prevent it from demolition after the collapse of communist system. Supersam in Warsaw (Poland), designed by J. Hryniewiecki, M. Krasiński, M. Gintowt, 1962. ©PAP/Stanisław Czarnogórski.

From the names (Moscow replaced with Europe), through aesthetics ("Western" post-modernism instead of "Eastern" socialist modernism), to the date when the demolition began (1 May, Labour Day), everything was a sign of the victory over communism (Wiśniewski, 2012).

In recent years, the problem of preserving post-war modernist architecture in former socialist countries has ceased to be a question raised only by a group of enthusiasts and scientific circles. The gradual removal of the odium of the "carriers of bad memory" is ongoing. At the same time, the uniqueness of many architectural ideas of the second half of the twentieth century, and their links to both interwar avant-garde tradition and post-war global architectural trends, is being noticed. The discussion over the "dissonant heritage" has surpassed narrow academic scope, thanks to which an increase in the general awareness of their enormous cultural-forming potential and significance for the local society can be observed.

A number of post-war concrete-based assets have already been protected as a part of national heritage. The more than three decades that have passed since the collapse of the communist system seem to be a sufficient amount of time to analyse their architectural and artistic quality rather than considering them as monuments of the past regime. Structures of special importance (e.g. the works of Edvard Ravnikar in Slovenia or Arseniusz Romanowicz's railway stations in Poland) are seen as an important input to the history of world architecture. Yet, there are still many problems to be solved concerning the protection of post-socialist concrete heritage, including both tangible and intangible aspects.

"In general, older buildings tend to be renovated with original materials (or using as close as possible modern solutions), but with buildings of the sixties it is different. In parallel to steel, concrete and glass, the architects of the Modern Movement also worked with other new materials, such as lead, lead paint and asbestos, which are today judged to be hazardous to health and the environment. As a result, due to their toxicity, low energy efficiency and material wear, materials used during Modern Movement in restoration activities should often be replaced," wrote Luīze Marta Aizpurva (2019, p. 105). The restorers of socialist-modernist heritage often have to face the results of material and structural experiments. The latter is as important as any other. New methods of construction and new types of structures, for example, ferro-cement or tensegrity systems, were tested in laboratories, but the real test came at the construction site. In combination with the issues caused by the low quality of materials and construction works, there is a litany of possible problems.

On the other hand, those who intend to preserve the dissonant heritage of socialist modernism must consider its social reception. "Socialist monuments occupy a peculiar position in between the two opposites," wrote Aneta Vasileva and Emilia Kaleva, who analysed the situation of socialist monuments in Bulgaria. "On [the] one hand, they are considered cool art objects, indifferent to political turmoil, with [a] transcendental aesthetic value of their own. On the other hand, they inspire different practices of denial – such as destruction, oblivion, mutilation, repositioning, and intentional demolition – which are politically charged to a great extent. Other representations of emotional denial derive from the aesthetical misunderstanding of modern art, the nationalistic revival of presocialist heroes and art forms, or plain indifference" (Vasileva & Kaleva, 2017, p. 172).

The Buzludzha Monument (architect Georgi Stoilov, 1971–1984) was built initially as the Communist Party of Bulgaria's Memorial House, but it fell into disrepair following the system's collapse in 1989. Abandoned and decayed, it still should be considered "fortunate" compared to the late modernist monument "1300 years of Bulgaria" (architects Alexander

Barov, Atanas Agura, Vladimir Romenski, and Alexander Brainov, and sculptor Valentin Starchev). It was completed in 1981, and abandoned for many years, although a relatively large group of people wanted it to be preserved. Although the official reason was the poor technical condition of the structure, it should be considered a "war for memory" or the process of "rewriting the history of the twentieth century." It includes different strategies of authorities who aim to present the heritage of socialism as a carrier of bad memory.

In Poland, monuments dedicated to soldiers of the communist Polish army and the Soviet army who fell during World War II are razed to the ground with the permission of the government. In Skopje, brutalist buildings are clad with eclectic decorations – pilasters, cornices and mouldings – in order to overcome the negative impact that communist architecture had on the urban tissue (Hatherley, 2016b).

Despite the negative approach of the authorities, bottom-up activism proves that the social reception of socialist modernism is rather positive. The fascination with the architecture and monuments of socialism is not the domain of the generations who lived in the socialist systems. Young people find them interesting as landmarks and an integral part of the local identity. It is difficult to even imagine the skyline of Jena without the skyscraper designed by Hermann Henselmann (1969–1972), who wanted to shape it like an enormous telescope (Angermann, 2017, p. 197). For the same reason, the citizens of Tirana are not willing to demolish The Pyramid, a former museum that Enver Hoxha, long-time communist authoritarian leader, built between 1985 and 1988. Although the politicians distance themselves from the dissonant monument, "for the Tiranas, the Pyramid is only one of the most prominent landmarks, amongst many reference points, that help to orientate them through the haphazard web of streets and alleys produced by recent development" (Iacono & Këlliçi, 2016, p. 60). Its visibility, which was supposed to be one of the building's most important features from the very beginning, is one of the few which have lasted the test of time, in contrast to its ideological meaning as a museum celebrating the dead leader and founder of the People's Republic of Albania (see Picture 1.16).

The modernist concrete architecture of the twentieth century, especially those objects that are listed monuments, has more and more proponents and epigones. Architecture of this kind is an important element of urban identity and image in many CEE countries. It is a living screenshot of a few generations of urban dwellers, architects and developers. However, other members of society still do not treat them as a valuable part of cultural and social heritage, especially when many of them are destroyed or underinvested. Because of their age, they are neither young enough to be in perfect condition nor old enough to be fully protected as "pure monuments" (Świdrak, 2017). This sometimes provokes a negative social perception and a lack of common acceptance for post-war concrete-based

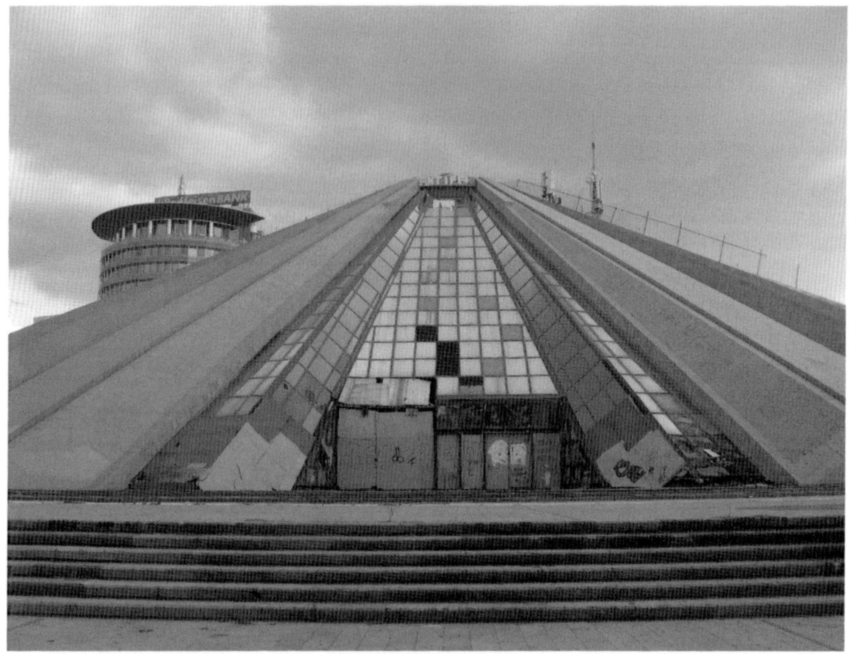

Picture 1.16 The landmark or dissonant heritage of the communist past? The Pyramid in Tirana (Albania), designed by P. Hoxha, K. Kolaneci, P. Vaso, V. Bregu, 1988 ©Inga Tomane CC BY-SA 4.0.

cultural heritage. Its specificity requires a new concept of heritage, as traditional methods and well-known theories do not respond to the needs of LPS housing estates or experimental reinforced concrete structures (Snopek, 2014).

Maybe Vaidas Petrulis was right when he wrote about the Lazdynai microrayon (architects Vytautas Čekanauskas, Vytautas Brėdikis, Vytautas Kazimieras Balčiūnas, Gediminas Valiuškis, 1974) in Vilnius, that it should be protected as one of the "most important achievements of Soviet Lithuanian architecture" (Petrulis, 2015, p. 93). "It represents the uniqueness of the socialist world. Embodying the hopes of millions of people," he wrote. He also suggested that the UNESCO World Heritage Committee consider its nomination for the UNESCO World Heritage List as representative of concrete-based prefabricated mass housing in the twentieth century – just like Le Havre, but from the other side of the iron curtain.

References

Aizpurva, L. M. (2019). The 60s of the 20th century: Modern movement public catering buildings in Latvia. *Architecture and Urban Planning*, *15*(1), 101–105. https://doi.org/10.2478/aup-2019-0014

Angermann, K. (2017). Architektura modernistyczna w Niemczech Wschodnich: Historia ochrona. In M. J. Sołtysik & R. Hirsch (Eds.), *Architektura XX wieku i jej waloryzacja w Gdyni i w Europie [20th century architecture and its valorisation in Gdynia and Europe]* (pp. 195–200). Urząd Miasta Gdyni. https://www.gdynia.pl/zabytki/cykl-modernizm-w-europie-modernizm-w-gdyni,7219/architektura-xx-wieku-i-jej-waloryzacja-w-gdyni-i-w-europie-wersja-elektorniczna,545726

Arnheim, R. (2016). *Dynamika formy architektonicznej* [Dynamics of architectural form]. Officyna.

Banham, R. (1966). *The new brutalism: Ethic or aesthetic?* Reinhold Publishing Corporation.

Basista, A. (2001). *Betonowe dziedzictwo: Architektura w Polsce czasów komunizmu* [Concrete legacy: Architecture in communist Poland]. PWN.

Charciarek, M. (2020). *Relation between the idea an matter in concrete architecture*. Wydawnictwo PK.

Chauvin, E. (2015). The city of Le Havre – The story of a modernist Utopia. In M. J. Sołtysik & R. Hirsch (Eds.), *20th century architecture until the 1960s and its preservation* (pp. 131–134). Urząd Miasta Gdyni. https://www.gdynia.pl/zabytki/cykl-modernizm-w-europie-modernizm-w-gdyni,7219/nr-2-3-en-20th-century-architecture-until-the-1960s-and-its-preservation,555278

Ciarkowski, B. (2017). *Odcienie szarości. Architekci i polityka w PRL-u* [Shades of grey. Architects and politics in the Polish People's Republic]. Wydawnictwo Uniwersytetu Łódzkiego.

Cooke, C., & Reid, S. E. (2007). Modernity and realism, architectural relations in the cold war. In R. P. Blakesley & S. E. Reid (Eds.), *Russian art and the west. A century of dialogue in painting, architecture, and the decorative arts* (pp. 172–194). Northern Illinois University Press.

Crowley, D. (2015). Nakierowani na przyszłość [Oriented to the future]. *Autoportret*, *3*(50), 77. https://autoportret.pl/

Czarnecki, M. (2017). Formy ekspresyjne jako przykład twórczych dążeń w architekturze powojennego modernizmu w polsce. In M. J. Sołtysik & R. Hirsch (Eds.), *Architektura XX wieku i jej waloryzacja w Gdyni i w Europie* [20th century Architecture and its valorisation in Gdynia and Europe] (pp. 209–214). Urząd Miasta Gdyni. https://www.gdynia.pl/zabytki/cykl-modernizm-w-europie-modernizm-w-gdyni,7219/architektura-xx-wieku-i-jej-waloryzacja-w-gdyni-i-w-europie-wersja-elektorniczna,545726

Forty, A. (2009). Beton i pamięć [Concrete and memory]. *Konteksty*, *1–2*, 284–285. http://www.konteksty.pl/numery/16,284-285

Forty, A. (2012). *Concrete and culture: A material history*. Reaktion Books.

Galusek, Ł. (2015). *Chciałbym, żeby socmodernizm był neutralnym terminem* [I wish socmodernism was a neutral term]. dzieje.pl Portal Historyczny. https://dzieje.pl/kultura-i-sztuka/lukasz-galusek-chcialbym-zeby-socmodernizm-byl-neutralnym-terminem

Hanackova, M. (2014). Team 10 and Czechoslovakia. Secondary networks. In Ł. Stanek (Ed.), *Team 10 East: Revisionist architecture in real existing modernism* (pp. 73–100). Museum of Modern Art.

Hatherley, O. (2016a). *Landscapes of communism. A history through buildings*. Penguin.

Hatherley, O. (2016b). Renowacja czy rekonstrukcja [Renovation or reconstruction]. *Autoportret*, 2(53). https://autoportret.pl/artykuly/renowacja-czy-rekonstrukcja/
Heinle, E., & Bacher, M. (1971). *Building in visual concrete*. Technical Press.
Iacono, F., & Këlliçi, K. L. (2016). Exploring the public perception of communist heritage in post-communist Albania. *EX NOVO Journal of Archaeology*, *1*(1), 55–69. https://doi.org/10.32028/exnovo.v1i0.398
Ikonnikow, A. V., Fabrycki, B. B., & Szmielow, I. P. (1975). *Współczesna architektura radziecka* [Contemporary soviet architecture]. Aurora.
Janković-Beguš, J. (2017). 'Between East and West': Socialist modernism as the official paradigm of Serbian art music in the Socialist Federal Republic of Yugoslavia. *International Journal of Music Studies*, *1*(1), 141–163. https://doi.org/10.33906/MUSICOLOGIST.373187
Jencks, C. (1982). *Le Corbusier. Tragizm współczesnej architektury* [Le Corbusier. The tragism of modern architecture]. Wydawnictwa Artystyczne i Filmowe.
Khan, H.-U. (2009). *International style: Modernist architecture from 1925 to 1965*. Taschen.
Kotkin, S. (2007). Mongol commonwealth? Exchange and governance across the post-Mongol space. *Kritika: Explorations in Russian and Eurasian History*, *8*(3), 487–531. https://doi.org/10.1353/kri.2007.0040
Królikowski, K. (2017). *Bloki*. Media Dizajn.
Krygier, K., & Sumień, T. (1973). Dzielnica mieszkaniowa Retkinia [Retkinia residential district]. *Architektura*, *5*(6), 208–211.
Kulić, V. (2013). Edvard Ravnikar's liquid modernism: Architectural identity in a network of shifting references. In I. Berman & E. Mitchell (Eds.), *ACSA 101: New constellations, new ecologies* (pp. 802–809). Association of Collegiate Schools of Architecture.
Le Corbusier. (1923). *Vers une architecture*. L'Esprit nouveau.
Leszczyński, A. (2013). *Skok w nowoczesność: Polityka wzrostu w krajach peryferyjnych 1943–1980* [Leap into modernity – Political economy of growth on the periphery, 1943–1980]. Wydawnictwo Krytyki Politycznej.
Loos, A. (2013). *Ornament i zbrodnia: Eseje wybrane* [Ornament and crime: Selected essays]. Fundacja Centrum Architektury.
MacDonald, S. (2006). Undesirable heritage: Fascist material culture and historical consciousness in Nuremberg. *International Journal of Heritage Studies*, *12*(1), 9–28. https://doi.org/10.1080/13527250500384464
Macel, O. (2002). Post-war modern architecture in the former eastern bloc. In H.-J. Henke & H. Heynen (Eds.), *Back from Utopia. The challenge of the modern movement*. 010 Publishers.
Maroević, I. (1996). Croatian architecture between socialism and new tradition. *ICOMOS – Issues of the German National Committee*, *20*, 110–114. https://doi.org/10.11588/ih.1996.0.22243
Matera, R., & Sokołowicz, M. E. (n.d.). In Pascariu, Gabriela Carmen Kourtit, Karima Nijkamp, Peter Tiganasu, Ramona (Eds.), Does history affect regional resilience in the long term? Path-dependence lessons from Poland. In *Resilience and regional development. New roadmaps*. Edward Elgar.
Mayakovsky, V. (1972). *Poems*. https://monoskop.org/images/e/ec/Mayakovsky_Vladimir_Poems_1972.pdf
McGuirk, J. (2018). The unrepeatable architectural moment of Yugoslavia's Concrete Utopia. *The New Yorker*. https://www.newyorker.com/culture/culture-desk/the-unrepeatable-architectural-moment-of-yugoslavias-concrete-utopia

Miłobędzki, A. (1994). *Architektura ziem Polski* [Architecture of Polish territories]. Międzynarodowe Centrum Kultury w Krakowie.

Molnár, V. (2005). Cultural politics and modernist architecture: The Tulip debate in postwar Hungary. *American Sociological Review*, *70*(1), 111–135. http://www.jstor.org/stable/4145352

Nawratek, K. (2005). *Ideologie w przestrzeni – Próby demistyfikacji* [Ideologies in space – Attempts at demystification]. Universitas.

Niebrzydowski, W. (2018). *Architektura Brutalistyczna a idee Nowego Brutalizmu* [Brutalist architecture and the ideas of the new brutalism]. Oficyna Wydawnicza Politechniki Białostockiej.

Novikov, F. (2016). *Behind the iron curtain: Confession of a Soviet architect*. DOM Publishers.

Nowicki, J. J. (1960). O kierunkach w architekturze współczesnej [On trends in contemporary architecture]. *Architektura*, *5*, 169–170.

Orwell, G. (1945). *Animal farm: A fairy story*. Secker and Warburg.

Petrulis, V. (2015). "Socialist realism": Timeline in Lithuania. In ICOMOS (Ed.), *Socialist realism and socialist modernism world heritage proposals from Central and Eastern Europe* (pp. 90–94). ICOMOS. https://doi.org/10.11588/ih.2013.4.20091

Piotrowski, P. K. (2011). *Znaczenia modernizmu. W stronę historii sztuki polskiej po 1945 roku* [Meanings of modernism. Towards a history of Polish art after 1945]. Dom Wydwawniczy Rebis.

Riabuszyn, A., & Szyszkina, I. (1987). *Architektura radziecka* [Soviet architecture]. Arkady.

Romanowicz, A. (1964). Przystanki ruchu podmiejskiego w Warszawie: "Ochota", "Śródmieście", "Powiśle" [Suburban traffic stops in Warsaw: "Ochota", "Śródmieście", "Powiśle"]. *Architektura*, *1*, 9–11.

Rusu, D. (2017). *Socialist modernism map. Protecting and interpreting cultural heritage in the age of digital empowerment*. ICOMOS. https://openarchive.icomos.org/id/eprint/2034/1/24._ICOA_1441_Rusu_SM.pdf

Sepioł, J. (2011). Architektura i moralność [Architecture and morality]. In B. Krasnowolski (Ed.), *Doktryny i realizacje konserwatorskie w świetle doświadczeń krakowskich ostatnich 30 lat* (pp. 117–124). Wydawnictwo WAM.

Skolimowska, A. (2012). Modulor Polski. Historia osiedla Za Żelazną Bramą [Polish modulor. History of behind the iron gate housing estate]. In Ł Gorczyca & M. Czapelski (Eds.), *Mister Warszawy. Architektura mieszkaniowa lat 60. XX wieku* [Mister of Warsaw. Residential architecture of the 1960s] (pp. 79–102). Raster.

Snopek, K. (2014). *Bielajewo: Zabytek przyszłości* [Bielajewo: Monument of the future]. Bęc Zmiana.

Stierli, M. (2018). Networks and crossroads: The architecture of socialist Yugoslavia as a laboratory of globalization in the Cold War. In M. Stierli & V. Kulić (Eds.), *Toward a concrete utopia: Architecture in Yugoslavia, 1948–1980* (pp. 10–25). Museum of Modern Art.

Świdrak, M. (2017). Jak młody może być zabytek? Przesłanki normatywne do stwierdzenia "dawności" zabytków nieruchomych [How young can a monument be? The normative premises of stating the "validity" of immovable monuments]. *Protection of Cultural Heritage*, *3*, 87–94. https://doi.org/10.24358/ODK_2017_03_06

Syrkus, H., & Syrkus, S. (1948). Architekt i uprzemysłowione budownictwo [Architect and industrialized construction]. *Architektura, 8–9*, 34–35.

Szendröi, J., Arnoth, L., Finta, J., Merényi, F., & Nagy, E. (1978). *Neue Architektur in Ungarn* [New architecture in Hungary]. Callwey Verlag.

Trzeciak, P. (1974). *Przygody architektury XX wieku* [The adventures of 20th century architecture]. Nasza Księgarnia.

Tunbridge, J. E., & Ashworth, G. J. (1996). *Dissonant heritage. The management of the past as a resource in conflict*. John Wiley & Sons.

Uskokovic, S. (2013). The "uncomfortable" significance of socialist heritage in postwar Croatia: The ambivalence of socialist aestheticism. In *Socialist realism and socialist modernism. World heritage proposals from Central and Eastern Europe* (pp. 85–89). ICOMOS. https://doi.org/10.11588/ih.2013.4.20090

Vasileva, A., & Kaleva, E. (2017). Recharging socialism: Bulgarian socialist monuments in the 21st century. *Studia Ethnologica Croatica, 29*(1), 171–192. https://doi.org/10.17234/SEC.29.5

Vidler, A. (2011). Another brick in the wall. *October, 136*, 105–132. http://www.jstor.org/stable/23014873

Wiśniewski, M. (2012). Spóźnione ułaskawienie. Kilka uwag o nostalgii za niechcianym dziedzictwem PRL [A belated Pardon. Some remarks on the Nostalgia for the unwanted heritage of communist Poland]. *Herito, 7*(2), 80–96. https://herito.pl/artykul/spoznione-ulaskawienie-kilka-uwag-o-nostalgii-za-niechcianym-dziedzictwem-prl/

Wojtkun, G. (2008). Wielorodzinne budownictwo mieszkaniowe w Polsce. W cieniu wielkiej płyty [Multifamily housing construction in Poland – In the shadow of the large panel]. *Przestrzeń i Forma, 10*, 175–194. http://yadda.icm.edu.pl/baztech/element/bwmeta1.element.baztech-article-BPS1-0033-0087

Zarecor, K. E. (2011). *Manufacturing a socialist modernity: Housing in Czechoslovakia, 1945–1960*. University of Pittsburgh Press.

2 The interdisciplinary character of heritage value

The concept of value in philosophy and economic thought

The notion of value is one of the most equivocal concepts. How value is understood depends on many factors, simultaneously objective and subjective. The objective prerequisites of values are connected with macroeconomic and macrosocial premises, and they depend on, inter alia, the level of economic development and citizens' wealth, and various elements of economic policy. Subjective premises lie in human value systems, that is, both individual and collective beliefs about what is and is not valuable in life. Therefore, it is not without reason that when two people say that something is of the highest value to us, they can talk about radically different issues. It is also reflected in everyday speech, for example, when we say "at all costs," "you will pay for that," "we paid dearly for..." "freedom at any price," "to spend time" or "to pay respect" (see S. H. Fine, 1992, p. 332).

Although the concept of value has made the greatest contribution to the field of economic sciences, it is not possible to start thinking about this term without referring to philosophy. On this basis, it is axiology that deals with values directly. In the literature that addresses axiological issues, there are several unresolved arguments about the concept of value (Białynicka-Birula, 2003, p. 63):

- The source of value – whether things themselves have value or whether value is given to them (objective vs subjective understanding of value)
- Value dependence – whether things have a fixed value or depend on circumstances (absolutist vs relativist understanding of value)
- The historical variability of value – does value change with time and historical conditions, or is it durable over time?
- The certainty of values – can a value be expressed in judgments with absolute certainty of their accuracy, or should judgments of value be more thoughtful?

Axiology – often called the science of value (from the Greek *axios*, "worthy" and *logos*, "science") – defines value in a "dictionary" way. It analyses

DOI: 10.4324/9781003299172-3

philosophically what good is, thus perceiving value in its broadest sense. A broadly understood value means, therefore, a set of features that allows something to be perceived as good, but it also simply means that it has some advantages, understood as both intangible and material benefits. But to be able to consider something valuable on the basis of such criteria, we must also define values through the lens of the principles and beliefs that underpin the ethical standards adopted in a given community.

Philosophical reflections on the concept of value developed relatively late in the nineteenth century (although the broadest reflections on value in the modern sense were introduced to philosophy in the previous century by Adam Smith, giving rise to classical economics).

The key contribution of philosophy to the theory of values was provided by Rudolf Hermann Lotze, Albrecht Ritschl, Friedrich Nietzsche (author of the theory of the transvaluation of all values), Alexius Meinong, Christian von Ehrenfels and Eduard von Hartmann. The magnum opus of the axiological discussion on value was provided by Ralph Barton (Perry, 1926) in his *General Theory of Value*, which exploited eight "realms" of value: morality, religion, art, science, economics, politics, law and custom (The Editors of Encyclopaedia Britannica, 2015).

A very important contribution to the value theory was proposed by Dewey (1922, 1939), with his division into instrumental and intrinsic value. The former tries to answer the question of what is good as a means, while the latter tells us what good is as an end. This classification – although modified and developed by successive thinkers – is a reference point for basically every subsequent classification of values, including those presented in our book. This division has now become established and corresponds to later value taxonomies, including Rokeach (1973) proposal to differentiate between terminal and instrumental values. While the first group refers to personal objectives and things a person wants to achieve through his or her behaviour (e.g. a comfortable life, an exciting life, a sense of accomplishment, a world at peace, a world of beauty, equality, family security, freedom, happiness, inner harmony, mature love, national security, pleasure, salvation, self-respect, social recognition, true friendship and wisdom), the latter indicates the personality traits a person should adopt to achieve them (e.g. ambitious, broadminded, capable, cheerful, clean, courageous, forgiving, helpful, honest, imaginative, independent, intellectual, logical, loving, obedient, polite, responsible and self-controlled) (Rokeach, 1973, p. 5).

A brief look at value from the perspective of philosophy allows us to see that axiology links this concept with the idea of good. However, different philosophical streams offer diverse answers to the question, "what is intrinsically good?" Hedonists say it is pleasure; pragmatists: satisfaction, growth or adjustment; Kantians: good will; humanists: harmonious self-realization; Christians: the love of God. Meanwhile, pluralists argue that there is any number of intrinsically good things (The Editors of Encyclopaedia Britannica, 2015).

Given that value is strongly linked to the notion of good, the taxonomy of value from the perspective of the individual remains dependent on what he sees as good or whom he sees as a good person, both in the instrumental and intrinsic dimensions. Such a philosophical taxonomy of value is proposed by Rabinowicz and Rønnow-Rasmussen (2016, pp. 24–25), who distinguished the following types of judgements:

1. A positive and negative general value – for example, *pleasure is good, and pain is bad*
2. Relational, "good-for" value – for example, *drugs are not good for you*
3. Aesthetic value – for example, *this painting by Titian is beautiful*
4. Specific value property – for example, *rescuing the girl was a courageous thing to do*
5. Value relation – for example, *Mozart was a better composer than Salieri*
6. "Attributive" value – for example, *John is a good philosopher*

Value and its perception largely depend on people's individual characteristics. For this reason, the concept of value, drawing on axiology, is also discussed in psychology. From this perspective, the most important issue seems to be what values are common for individuals and what differentiates human attitudes and value systems. In recent years, these questions have been answered by the theory of basic human values, developed by Schwartz (1992), and when it comes to perceiving values from an individual's perspective, the search for features that are common to all values seems to be the primary concern. According to Schwartz (2015, p. 64), these common characteristics are as follows:

1. Values are beliefs linked inextricably to affect.
2. Values affect the goals that motivate action.
3. Values are independent (transcendent) of specific actions and situations, unlike norms and attitudes, which always relate to concrete activities, objects and events.
4. Values serve as standards or criteria. They influence the evaluation of actions, policies, people and events. In other words, they allow for judgements about what is good and what is bad (although these judgements are not always conscious).
5. Values are subject to a hierarchy. One can therefore prioritize values. These characteristics also distinguish values from norms and attitudes.
6. Any attitude or behaviour typically has implications for more than one value. This leads to trade-offs among competing values, which may create contradictions in the perception of values.

As far as differences in the values between people and between communities are concerned, they are conditioned by the fact that different actors pay different attention to the following ten values (Schwartz, 2015, p. 68): Security, Conformity, Tradition, Benevolence, Universalism, Self-direction, Stimulation, Hedonism, Achievement, and Power Grouping. Contrasting these values within a circular form makes it possible to select personality types depending on the link to individual values and the relationships between them (Figure 2.1).

In this way, personality types that place great emphasis on the welfare of all people and nature (universalism), and the preservation of the welfare of those they know personally (benevolence), are, to some extent, diametrically opposed to people who emphasize their own desire to control or dominate people and their self-achievement. This allows us to group these values into two opposing hemispheres, "self-enhancement vs self-transcendence." In turn, individuals who consider tradition and security as important values and who have a tendency to conformism can be classified as conservative and contrasted with individuals who are open to change. The latter group refers primarily to people who value autonomy and independence, and who strive for stimulation based on excitement, novelty, life challenge and hedonism. On the other hand, at a higher level of generalizing basic values, we can identify people with a social focus and contrast them with personal-focused actors. Finally, the outer-most circle relates to two basic

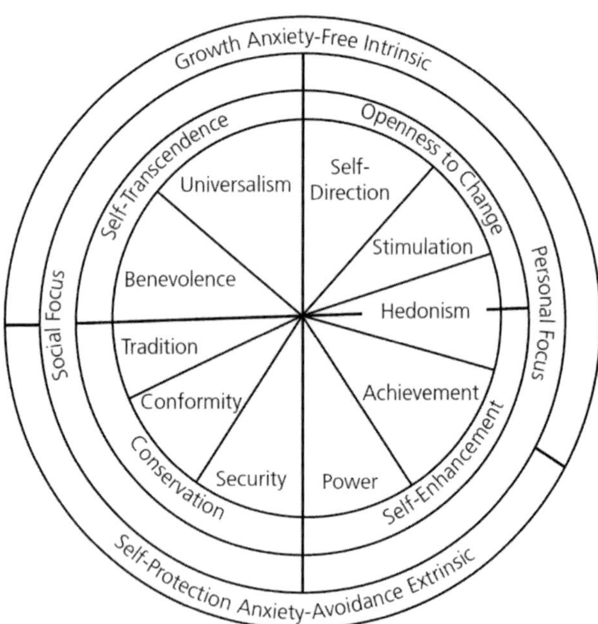

Figure 2.1 Schwartz's theory of basic human values

Source: Schwartz (2015, p. 68).

self-regulation systems: (1) avoiding punishment and preventing loss and (2) the pursuit of rewards and promoting gain (E. T. Higgins, 1997).

Such a deep analysis and classification of values certainly draws attention to the complexity of the concept and makes it possible to realize its connection with the more or less conscious conviction about what is good and what is bad. However, it does not allow or even prevent us from making unambiguous judgements on value. The world of values in the philosophical understanding – initiated by axiology and developed thoroughly by social psychologists – is complex and will remain so. This implies the conviction that many of its key concepts cannot be defined unequivocally, which is typical of social sciences (Kincaid, 2002, p. 291). It is also true of a value that is strongly dependent on human experience and contexts (e.g. historical, economical or geographical).

However, given that one of the important dimensions of value is instrumentality (which should make it helpful in satisfying concrete human needs) and, to some extent, quantifiability, one branch of social science – economics – has been attempting to define value more precisely for several hundred years. Such an attempt can be seen in the writings of Xenophon (Wedderburn et al., 2016), describing the discussion between Socrates and Critobulus (which was later undertaken by Aristotle and then John Locke) (Sedlaček, 2009, p. 227). As with philosophical concepts, in economic science, there are two contrasting positions concerning the sources of values: objective and subjective. Economists who advocate the first notion of value see it mainly as the cost of producing a given good (e.g. Adam Smith, David Ricardo and Karl Marx). The proponents of the subjective viewpoint identify value with consumer benefits in the process of satisfying needs. These concepts combine value with individual and subjective perception (e.g. Étienne de Condillac, Willima Jevons, Léon Walras, Friedrich von Wieser and Eugen von Bohm-Bawerk) (Białynicka-Birula, 2003, pp. 66–67).

It may be surprising to identify work and its effects with value only during the Enlightenment. But previously, philosophical thought did not indicate a direct relationship between them. In ancient times, physical work and economic activity were not even considered a form of human improvement. A worthy occupation or an ethical act were consumption rather than production. This changed in medieval Christianity, although work was still far from instrumental and purely intrinsic. Work was about duty to God and the road to salvation. It was only in Protestantism that the separation of religion and the ethos of work was observed, and there was a slow transition "from theology to mechanics." This turn was particularly noticeable in the nineteenth century – the period when work was being commoditized and became an ethos, not a source of contempt for the leisure class (Sulima, 2015).

The first thinker to attempt to create a comprehensive economic theory of value was Adam Smith. The value considerations he initiated were popularized broadly based on the labour theory of value. Smith (1776, p. 48) distinguished two types of value: use-value (utility) and exchange value.

For both, he claimed that the value can be measured as the volume of labour input for the production and exchange of goods. For this reason, and even today, from an economic point of view, labour input at every stage of the acquisition and production of goods is considered an important carrier of value. From this perspective, historical objects that constitute heritage and works of art can also be interpreted in terms of the (creative) effort needed to produce them.

In turn, the readiness to exchange such goods for something else (exchange value) and the utility and satisfaction of having them (use-value) are nothing more than the readiness to sacrifice the equivalent of one's own work to gain them (whether measured in time or money). In other words, "the real price of everything, what everything really costs to the man who wants to acquire it, is the toil and trouble of acquiring it" (Smith, 1776, p. 50). As Myrdal (2017, pp. 59–60) puts it, "some derive value from an abstract usefulness of objects or from man's estimation of their usefulness (value-in-use). A commodity has economic value to the extent to which it is useful or is held to be useful. Others again emphasize the costs (usually labour costs) incurred in producing the good. Costs, like utility, can be interpreted more or less psychologically. If the psychological aspect is stressed, value stands for the sweat and toil, the sacrifice and pain that have gone into the production of a commodity."[1]

A more in-depth continuation of the labour theory of value is offered by David Ricardo, who also emphasized that the value (i.e. price) of goods produced and sold under competitive conditions tends to be proportionate to the labour costs incurred in producing them. While Smith admitted that the exchange value comprises three components of production costs (wage, profit and land rent), Ricardo pointed out that these factors themselves are not a source of value, but a result of its division between them. Capital and land do not create new value but are paid from the human labour input to the goods. However, Ricardo emphasizes that reducing the value to the workload does not allow for a very simplistic interpretation of this approach. He notes: "Not only the labour applied immediately to commodities affect their value, but the labour also which is bestowed on the complements, tools and buildings, with which much labour is assisted" (sic) (Ricardo, 2001 [1817], p. 16).

As far as the contribution of other production factors to the value is concerned (i.e. capital and rent), it is true that labour bestowed in the production of commodities can be "considerably modified by the employment of machinery and other fixed and durable capital" (Ricardo, 2001 [1817], p. 22), while the value of land – embedded in rent, and understood as "the portion of the produce of the earth paid for the use of the original and indestructible powers of the soil" (Ricardo, 2001 [1817], p. 39), may be increased or decreased depending on the scale of additional inputs of labour and capital (which, after all, is also the result of work) per unit of land. When perceived in this way, value is therefore still dependent on the labour incurred in producing goods, even if labour costs may vary in proportions that depend on other production factors (Table 2.1).

The labour theory of value was later adopted by Karl Marx, who combined it with the theory of surplus value. The latter assumes that human labour alone creates all value and thus constitutes the sole source of profits. Marx does not deviate from the division into use-value and exchange value. He still binds use-value to the usefulness of commodities in satisfying people's needs, and the exchange value as "the proportion in which use-values of one kind exchange for use-values of another kind" (Marx, 1906 [1867], p. 42). However, Marx's approach strongly emphasizes that money is a measure of value, not a carrier. This measurement helps to determine "socially necessary labour," that is, the labour time required to produce any "article under the normal conditions of production, and with the average degree of skill and intensity prevalent at the time" (Marx, 1906 [1867], p. 46). It is apparent that according to the Marxist approach to value, it is very much entrenched in a specific place and time, and more specifically, in human relationships, which determine the meaning attributed to the role of labour in value creation. In Marxism, "value is not a product of nature (although dependent upon it) nor a substance physically embodied in the commodities: value is a social relation between commodity producers that appears as exchange value, a relationship between things. Goods and services possess value only under certain social and historical circumstances (Table 2.1). The value relation develops fully only under capitalism, in tandem with the production of commodities, the use of money, the diffusion of wage labour, and the generalisation of market-related property rights" (B. Fine & Saad-Filho, 2018, p. 28).

In his reflections, Marx drew on the earlier work of utopian socialists, who referred to the labour theory of value, using it paradoxically to criticize capitalism. Looking back, however, this approach seems very simplistic. Using the concept of the labour theory of value only to justify the idea of transferring the entire effect of work to the direct producer ignores the need for economic growth and development and the need to finance the non-productive sphere, which determines the proper functioning of the economy and state (Romanow, 1995, p. 27). It is undeniable, however, that the important achievement of both classical and Marxist economics was a significant advance in capturing its tangible dimension.

It should be stressed, however, that in the case of Marxism, there are problems with and even the impossibility of determining value objectively. As it is based on labour, it is ultimately an abstract category. According to Marx, value consists of various disproportionate elements, constantly changing in various proportions, which cannot be precisely calculated. The situation is different regarding price, which is the expression of an exchangeable value in a specific place and time in the market (as a result of the equilibrium between supply and demand). However, the more the capitalist economy develops, the more the price deviates from the value, becoming an intrinsic figure.

Table 2.1 Evolution of the concepts of value and price in early economic theory

Direction/school	*Proponent*	*Interpreting value*
Classical	Adam Smith	There are two types of values: use-value, understood objectively, and exchange value, which is the ability of a given good to be exchanged for another. The exchange value is independent of the use-value (value paradox). Use-value is determined by the volume of labour contained in the final goods, but it can be divided into three components of the cost of production: wage, profit and land rent.
	David Ricardo	The value of goods includes both the value transferred from production factors used and the newly produced value. As a last resort, value depends on the labour input incurred to produce the good (other production factors affect only the proportions of labour input). In addition to labour input, the value of work is also affected by the scarcity of goods. Market prices that deviate from natural prices (real values) are based on supply and demand in the market.
Marxism	Karl Marx	The only source of value multiplication is human labour. The mechanism of shaping the average profit rate and production price is the basis for market prices, but not value *per se*. Money is a measure of value, not a carrier. Labour, as the only source of value, depends on space and time. It is socially embedded.
Marginalists	William Jevons	The value of a good is understood through the lenses of the subjective perception of individuals.
	Carl Menger	As the consumption of a given good increases, the satisfaction caused by the increased consumption of the good by a unit decreases (marginal utility decreases). The market price is the result of various individual assessments of the value of a good made by buyers and sellers.
Neoclassical	Alfred Marshall	Value is influenced by both supply and demand. Marginal utility is a tool for demand analysis only. Utility constitutes the upper limit of exchange value. The lower limit depends on production costs on the supply side and is understood as the costs of wages of production factors (salary, profit and land rent).

Source: Own study.

The following years shifted the focus to the subjective dimension of value (Table 2.1). In the late nineteenth century, this approach was developed at the same time by Jevons (1871) and Austrian economists, especially Menger (1871). Jevons began by criticizing the distinction between use-value and exchange value, claiming that goods with a high use-value may have a low exchange value and vice versa. What can really bind exchange value with the utility of the good is the so-called marginal utility. The latter means that the actual value depends on the product's utility in its least important use. The key assumption of this approach is the conviction that utility – particularly marginal – varies among people. Jevons, Menger and other marginalists thus believed that value is completely subjective: a product's value is found in its ability to satisfy human wants. Therefore, if the product exists in abundance, it will be used in less-important ways.

On the other hand, when the product becomes scarcer, greater utility will be derived from it, increasing its value. In other words, the subjective view of value connects it with the "ordinariness vs rareness" question. Thus, the subjective theory of value is built upon this simple hedonistic argument. It attempts to use psychological introspection to get behind the observed behaviour of demand, supply and price (Myrdal, 2017, p. 85). This leads to the conclusion that, at first glance, in economics, the term value "carries the association of something solid, homogeneous, and fairly stable, while in reality valuations are regularly contradictory, even in the mind of a single individual, and also unstable, particularly in modern society. Human behaviour is typically the result of compromises between valuations on different levels of generality" (Myrdal, 1974, pp. 33–34).

The development of subjectivism in economic thought also meant popularizing the alternative cost category. It is based on the assumption of the substitutability of goods and results from the fact that human beings function in the context of the simultaneous limitlessness of needs but limited access to the means to satisfy them. Therefore, when making choices, one faces the dilemma of choosing between a set of choices. On a macro-social scale, this means that the resources of production factors are continuously allocated to various applications and sectors of the economy, and individuals continuously compare the effectiveness of these allocations. From the perspective of value considerations, it opens the way to working out methods of valuation, which do not aim at a precise calculation of one value, but at comparing values that depend on different ways of using the available resources.

At the beginning of the twentieth century, the emerging neoclassical school attempted to combine both objective and subjective elements in the understanding of the concept of value (Table 2.1). Marshall (2013 [1890]), in particular, rejected the concept of classical and Marxian economics, which makes value and price dependent exclusively on supply factors (production costs). He also rejected theories that focus only on the demand side of the market and that explain value through usability. His synthetic value theory indicated that value and price are affected to the same extent by both supply and demand in the market. He thus accepts Say's (1880 [1803]: Book II, Chapter 1) earlier assumption that the source of the value of a good is both its utility (which is the upper limit of the exchange value) and the wage costs of the manufacturing factors (which is the lower limit). A good has value because it contains not only the cost of production incurred by the producer but also because it is useful to the consumer. According to Marshall, there is a demand price and a supply price in the market. The demand price, that is, the price that the consumer is willing to pay for a given good, is determined by its marginal utility. The supply price, that is, the price at which the seller is willing to sell the good, is determined by actual production costs, including labour. If the demand price is equal to the supply price, the market is balanced. In short periods of supply, demand has a greater influence on price formation, and in long periods of supply, it depends on production costs. In other words, the value and price of a good are shaped by factors that determine both supply and demand in the market (Białynicka-Birula, 2003, p. 68).

In parallel to the reflections on the concept of value within mainstream economics, this issue also appears in other trends gaining importance in recent years. In particular, institutional, behavioural economists and environmental economics should be mentioned here. Institutionalism assumes that all economic processes – including the perception of values by the public – are socially and institutionally determined. This was pointed out by Polanyi (1944), who distinguished three forms of exchange: 1) reciprocal (usually non-monetary, typical of small communities), 2) redistributive (organized by public institutions) and 3) market. He pointed out that the dominance of the third form is the result of an advanced stage of development, and it depends on a number of historically shaped institutional factors. Institutions are understood as all forms of constraints that man has created in order to shape behaviour, both formal (laws, rules and sanctions for non-compliance) and informal (typical behaviour patterns) (North, 1986). In other words, in economic terms, institutions should be seen as the "rules of the game" in the economy (North, 1997). They are not only rooted in social relations, applicable laws and organizational structures, but they also depend on historically shaped relationships, attitudes and beliefs (see also Granovetter (2017, pp. 17–19). Such broadly perceived institutional factors, therefore, determine values both in instrumental and intrinsic terms. Behavioural economics combines economics and psychology, seeking the psychological and social basis for decision-making. It assumes that people take into account their past experiences, emotions and social relations and make decisions based on psychological, cognitive errors (e.g. individuals tend to assess potential losses more strongly than potential profits), which in human life are not the exception but the norm (Kahneman & Tversky, 2000). In this context, the perceived value of both tangible and intangible goods depends on the specific context in which people make decisions. Behavioural economics refers to the concept of bounded rationality (Simon, 1955), which means that social actors are never fully rational because they: 1) use a simplified picture of reality, 2) are not able to analyze all available solutions (due to incomplete information), and 3) use heuristics instead of in-depth analysis in the decision-making process. Consequently, the perception of values is based on intuition and experience; thus, economic decisions are not based on the best possible solution but on a solution considered most satisfactory by a particular person in a particular place and at a particular time. Behavioural economics emphasizes the individual process of calculating the legitimacy of decisions made and pays particular attention to individual perception of value, albeit affected by the social and institutional environment.

In recent years, the criticism of neoclassical economics has also led to the development of ecological economics. It assumes that economic processes and the valuation of resources cannot be analyzed in isolation from the fact that man exploits resources, much of which are non-renewable. In economic processes, man influences the planet, which is functioning in a situation of growing entropy. Natural resources have value, but a significant part of them are used once, by only one generation. Thus, we cannot ignore that the creation of value for one person generates negative externalities for other people and other species. Economic processes, including value analysis, should therefore be conducted in accordance with the principles of intergenerational and even interspecies equity, and with respect for the rule of sustainable development.

Ecological economics is founded upon the concerns of the 1960s and early 1970s for limits to growth (Meadows et al., 1972) and the study of the flow of energy and materials in the economy based upon the work of Georgescu-Roegen (1976). This subdiscipline was only formally established in the late 1980s and early 1990s, in part due to the growing criticism of and dissension within orthodox environmental economics (Spash & Asara, 2018, p. 120). The importance of ecological economics for value considerations is important inasmuch as it emphasizes its complex epistemology most strongly among other economic trends, especially when compared to mainstream economics. It stresses very clearly that certain aspects of the value of ecological goods can even be measured quite precisely, but many others cannot. It warns against simplifications in the process of value discussion. At the methodological level, it provides tools for capturing the value of complex goods such as heritage, either directly or indirectly. Therefore, from an ecological economics perspective, heritage can be viewed as comparable to nature and other ecological goods because of its complexity, collective character and common conviction of the need to preserve it for future generations.

To conclude, in economic theory, the concept of value has been evolving. Initially, with the birth of this scientific discipline, attempts were made to define value, mainly objectively, as in the natural sciences. However, in an effort to define value more precisely, attempts were made to link value to one fundamental aspect of human activity, especially labour. Thus, even a common distinction between use-value and exchange value showed a tendency to reduce the basic component of value to work units (albeit closely related to other production factors and social context). However, the development of economic theory has led to a return to the subjective aspects of value (that one might say are rooted in cultural, psychological, and axiological factors). It was pointed out again that value has an objective dimension and is also conditioned by individual utility.

Since Marshall, economists have also made it a common assumption that value depends on supply and demand factors equally. In other words, the economic sciences have returned to the conviction that, in the end, people are its main subject. Their needs, aspirations, preferences, values, behaviours and relationships between individuals and groups affect the means of satisfying material and non-material needs. Economics is the science of human beings in their social embeddedness (Granovetter, 2017, p. 14). This social entanglement can take the form of a system, mechanism or drama (Wilkin, 2016, p. 69), and it determines how value is produced and perceived. Therefore, in order to have a full picture of value in economic sciences, following Boltanski and Thevenot (2006), we should see all economies as moral economies. In this context, the concept of value should be extended by the concept of worth. Boltanski and Thevenot (2006) delineate six discrete orders of worth, each epitomized by a particular moral philosopher:

1. Market rationality (the moral philosophy of Adam Smith)
2. Industrial or technological rationality (Henri de Saint Simon)
3. Civic logic (Jean-Jacques Rousseau)
4. Principles of loyalty (Jacques-Bénigne Bossuet)
5. Inspiration (Augustine of Hippo)
6. Renown or fame (Thomas Hobbes)

When satisfying their various material and immaterial needs, people are guided by each of these orders. Thus, if we consider economic processes to be social processes, we cannot limit ourselves to just one (market) order. As an example of weaving each of these orders into the practice of assessing a candidate's value to work, in the world of academia, we can use the one proposed by Stark. If we take letters of recommendation for faculty appointments, we usually find references to multiple evaluation principles. "In fact, a given letter might include performance criteria from each of the six orders of worth. We would not be surprised, for example, to read that a given candidate is 'very creative' (the order of inspiration); that she is incredibly 'productive' (the industrial); and that she is a 'good citizen' (the civic). Moreover, the same letter could note that her work is 'frequently cited' (the order of fame or renown) and that she is fiercely 'loyal to her graduate students' (check off another). Has the letter writer neglected the market order? We are not likely to hear about an academic as the author of a 'best-selling' book. Look through the letter again and you might find that the candidate 'has a strong record of getting grants'" (Stark, 2009, p. 12).

According to Sen (1997, pp. 6–7), modern economics has two separate sources. The first comes from Aristotle and leads through Adam Smith, John Stuart Mill, Henry Sidgwick, Francis Edgeworth, Knut Wicksell, Alfred Marshall and Arthur C. Pigou. It is a tradition of economics as a social science rooted in philosophy, especially ethics. The second comes from such figures as William Petty, Francois Quesnay, Antoine Lavoisier, David Ricardo, Antoine Augustin Cournot and Léon Walras. It is a tradition of linking economics with the natural sciences. While the first source makes it possible to combine economics and psychological elements, that is, the complexity of human behaviour and reflection, the second highlights problems of technology, input–output relationships and seeking precise value measurement techniques. Neither of these options is better, and neither should tend to break with the other. While the second approach focuses on values from the perspective of consequences of human behaviour (and measuring them), the second reaches out to the causes (motives) of human actions and choices (perceiving values from an axiological perspective).

As Gibson et al. (2017, p. 226) pointed out, while traditional research on judgment and decision-making has focused on the role of consequences, centuries ago, the field of normative ethics considered deontology another basic moral orientation in moral decision-making. The latter emphasizes the desirability of obligations, principles or rights, irrespective of the consequences. In other words, value is not only the result of human action but, on an ethical level, it is a condition for it. Influential examples of deontological rules are the Ten Commandments or Kant's (1797) categorical imperative. Thus, we should not treat values in the context of a dichotomous choice between the inefficient moral and the market-based immoral as it is a false dilemma. Markets are never value-free, and so the abstract idea of a "free" market is not practically meaningful. That phrase disguises a particular value-laden version of how markets should operate. "So one challenge now is to ensure that the way markets operate reflect fundamental social norms and values – how to make markets moral" (Coyle, 2011, p. 208).

Value in the theory of monuments

The origins of heritage value theory date back to the beginning of twentieth century, when Alois Riegl published his essay *Der moderne Denkmalkultus: sein Wesen, seine Entstehung* (Riegl, 1903). It is commonly regarded as "the first and the most profound formulation of values-based preservation" (Lamprakos, 2014, p. 419). The pioneering role of Riegl's essay results from the fact that it presented the first coherent system where the value of a monument was defined not only by objective external criteria, but also by the perception of the observer (Lamprakos, 2014; Riegl, 1903, p. 420).

In comparison with earlier attempts to establish a monument's value, the Austrian art historian created a system that was based on reasoned analysis, and although it did not enable unequivocal evaluation, it was free from a negative attitude towards any specific group of assets. Years later, Max Dvorak, Riegl's apprentice, quoted his tutor: "The best art historian is the one who does not have any personal preferences" (Dvořák, 1929, p. 285).

Before, the "transparency" of the observer was not self-evident. The Enlightenment's theory of preserving historical monuments was based on classicist aesthetics, which resulted in ancient Greece being perceived as the crowning achievement of humanity. At the same time, baroque art and architecture were strongly criticized. Alexandre Lenoir, the founder of *Museé des Monuments et Antiquités Francais*, considered early medieval art an example of "bad taste," although he found it appropriate to include selected pieces in the exhibition to present "examples of French sculpture representing most characteristic features and types for a given period" (Poulot, 1997, pp. 10–18). It should be considered one of the first cases when the aesthetic value and the historical value of artefacts were separated, which is the basis of the modern concept of heritage preservation (Frycz, 1975, p. 21).

In the following decades, conservators and theoreticians searched for scientific justification for the supreme position of one style (period) over another. Charles Darwin's theory of evolution had a huge yet often underestimated impact on the preservation of historical monuments. The parallels between architectural heritage and living organisms became a popular way to explain the expiry of a building's life cycle. Soon, the idea of the evolution of the species inspired the minds of architects. Modernist theories of architecture were clearly based on the technical, aesthetic and moral supremacy of the modern movement over nineteenth-century-based eclecticism and historical neo-styles. Combined with Marxist determinism, it led to the phenomenon that Karl Popper (1989) defined as "historicism" – blind faith in linear, predictable development.

Camillo Boito, a direct predecessor of Riegl, tried to formulate a golden mean between the two main schools of monument preservation in the nineteenth century: Viollet-Le-Duc's stylistic restoration and John Ruskin's non-interventionism (Boito & Birignan, 2009). This Italian architect, preservationist and art historian established a synthesis of different perspectives, often described as a critical philological approach, recognized that any intervention must be preceded by value assessment (Boito & Birignani, 2009, p. 69). Although Boito did not create a coherent system of values, he emphasized the need to respect the artistic and historical values of the monument, as well as preserving the marks left by the passage of time (the patina).

A decade after Boito published *Il restauro in architettura* (and two decades after *Prima Carta del Restauro*), Alois Riegl wrote an essay in which he developed the concept of assessing the value of historical monuments. His idea of a monument's value was intended to serve practical aims, as the text was an introduction to a new preservation project (Lamprakos, 2014). He tried to systematize historical monuments, distinguishing three groups:

1. Intentional monuments
2. Unintentional (historical) monuments
3. Age value monuments

Subsequently, he distinguished different categories of values that refer to both the past and present (Riegl, 1903). "Past values" that directly derive from the history of a particular monument are as follows:

1. Commemorative value – the role of the monument as a carrier of social memory
2. Historical value – the monument as a historical document
3. Age value – the monument as a testimony to the passing of time

They often provoke conflicts with what Riegl called "present values" and should be part of the negotiation during any act of preservation. Present values are as follows:

1. Relative artistic value – opinion about a specific style based on changing tastes
2. Use-value – the building should meet users' needs
3. Newness value – the public desire for "newness" (in the nineteenth century, it was closely related to historical reconstruction)

Riegl's theory of values is based on the perception of a monument and refers to its immanent features (past values) and social reception (present values). The essence of preservationists' work should be searching for the balance between them. Although he did not state which group of values is more important, they cannot be interpreted without defining the monument. Riegl extended the existing definitions by adding the category of "unintentional monuments," whose values come from age (Arrhenius, 2013, p. 52). He emphasized that even the simplest assets of everyday use can gain value as time passes, putting fragility over permanence and the values assigned by external observers over the monument's characteristics.

Boito's and Riegl's views on the values and valuation of architectural heritage had an undeniable impact on *The Athens Charter for the Restoration of Historic Monuments* manifesto adopted at the First International Congress of Architects and Technicians of Historic Monuments in Athens in 1931. It is one of the foundations of the modern theory of monument preservation, and its authors clearly stated: "the historic and artistic work of the past should be respected, without excluding the style of any given period" (The Athens Charter for the Restoration of Historic Monuments, 1931). Although Charter did not refer directly to Riegl's theory, the aspect of values' preservation was mentioned as restoration and conservation should be preceded in a way that would "prevent mistakes which will cause loss of character and historical values to the structures" (The Athens Charter for the Restoration of Historic Monuments, 1931).

The tragedy of World War II, thousands of destroyed monuments and pieces of art, as well as post-war reconstruction and rebuilding from wartime devastation, had a significant impact on preservation theory. *The Venice Charter for the Conservation and Restoration of Monuments and Sites* drawn up in 1964 described permitted restoration as a process to "preserve and reveal the aesthetic and historic value of the monument," which "must stop at the point where conjecture begins" (International Charter for the Conservation and Restoration of Monuments and Sites (The Venice Charter 1964), 1965). When the conservation process requires the selection of elements to be preserved (e.g. "when a building includes the superimposed works of different periods"), preservationists are allowed to remove part of it "when what is removed is of little interest and the material which is brought to light is of great historical, archaeological or aesthetic value" (International Charter for the Conservation and Restoration of Monuments and Sites (The Venice Charter 1964), 1965). The Venice Charter, like the Athens Charter, did not provide any definition of "values," although it states that any assessment should not be a matter of individual choice. "Evaluation of the importance of the elements involved and the decision as to what may be destroyed cannot rest solely on the individual in charge of the work" (International Charter for the Conservation and Restoration of Monuments and Sites (The Venice Charter 1964), 1965).

In 1963, Walter Frodl, professor at the Vienna University of Technology, presented a series of lectures on the new interpretation of terms and definitions concerning the preservation of monuments. They were published under the title *Denkmalbegriffe, Denkmalwerte und ihre Auswirkung auf die Restaurierung* (*Notions and Criteria of the Valuation of Historical Monuments. Their Influence on Preservation*) (Frodl, 1963). Although the author openly admitted the fundamental role of Boito's and Riegl's theory in his own research, he emphasized that it was "obsolete." Yet, he added that "the theoretical system of values and notions (...) maintained the relevance to these days" (Frodl, 1963, pp. 12–13). Frodl did not propose his own system; rather, he adapted the value categories invented by Riegl and added new interpretations based on the current state of knowledge. His system consisted of the following categories:

1. Historical value – which refers to the documentary characteristics of the monument:

   a. Scientific value
   b. Emotional value – for example, the value of the symbol

<table>
<tr><th rowspan="4">Values</th><th>Past</th><th colspan="2">Present</th></tr>
<tr><td>Commemorative Value</td><td rowspan="2">Artistic Value</td><td>Relative Artistic Value</td></tr>
<tr><td>Historical Value</td><td>Newness Value</td></tr>
<tr><td>Age Value</td><td colspan="2">Use-value</td></tr>
</table>

Figure 2.2 Values of the cultural heritage according to Riegl's theory

Source: Own study.

2. Artistic value – which consists of:
    a. Historical-artistic value – based on notions of "original form," hypothetical form, a copy of the original form, etc.
    b. Artistic quality
    c. Artistic value – intrinsic artistic value effect (a result of the integral artistic impression) or extrinsic artistic value effect based on external factors (e.g. appearance established by tradition)
3. Use-value – including, for example, usefulness, the role of the monument as a tourist attraction, etc.

In comparison to Riegl's theory (Figure 2.2), Frodl emphasized the aspects related to the social reception of the heritage even more. The relationship between the immanent characteristics of the monument and the values based on its impact on recipients had already been mentioned by Cesare Brandi (1963), but it was Frodl who distinguished the value of appearance established by tradition – a category which indicates that the reception of a monument depends on its spatial context as well as collective memory (Frodl, 1963, pp. 18–24).

The system created by the Viennese professor (Figure 2.3) was widely discussed (Krawczyk, 2013) and became the basis for further research on the historical monuments' valuation. One example of the later interpretations of Frodl's theory is *Monuments' Valuation Analysis*, which transformed it into an axiological query that includes seven basic categories which reflect different reference values (Krawczyk, 2013, pp. 523–524) (Figure 2.4).

Considerations on the valuation of monuments reflected the evolution of thinking in conservation and had a significant impact on both preservation theory and praxis. When comparing *The Venice Charter* and *The*

<table>
<tr><th colspan="7">Values</th></tr>
<tr><th colspan="2">Historical Value</th><th colspan="4">Artistic Value</th><th rowspan="3">Use-value</th></tr>
<tr><td rowspan="2">Scientific Value</td><td rowspan="2">Emotional Value</td><td rowspan="2">Historical-Artistic value</td><td rowspan="2">Artistic Quality Value</td><td colspan="2">Artistic Value</td></tr>
<tr><td>Intrinsic Artistic Value</td><td>Extrinsic Artistic Value</td></tr>
</table>

Figure 2.3 Values of cultural heritage according to Frodl's theory

Source: Own study.

<table>
<tr><th colspan="10">Analysing the Valuation of Monuments</th></tr>
<tr><th colspan="3">Historical Value</th><th colspan="2">Artistic Value</th><th colspan="3">Aesthetical Value</th><th colspan="2">Use-value</th></tr>
<tr><td rowspan="3">Scientific Value</td><td colspan="2">Emotional Value</td><td rowspan="3">Historical-Artistic Value</td><td rowspan="3">Artistic Quality Value</td><td colspan="3">Aesthetical Interaction</td><td rowspan="3">Primary Use-value</td><td rowspan="3">Secondary Use-value</td></tr>
<tr><td rowspan="2">Age Value</td><td rowspan="2">Symbolic Value</td><td rowspan="2">Intrinsic</td><td colspan="2">Extrinsic</td></tr>
<tr><td>Relationship between the monument and its surrounding</td><td>Appearance established by tradition</td></tr>
</table>

Figure 2.4 Analyzing the valuation of monuments

Source: Krawczyk (2013, pp. 523–525).

Nara Document on Authenticity (The Nara Document on Authenticity, 1994), fundamental doctrinal texts, one can easily notice that for three decades, "values" referred to the social reception of a monument rather than its physical characteristics. The authors of *The Nara Document* emphasized the links between values and cultural heritage diversity, stating that "all judgements about values attributed to cultural properties (...) may differ from culture to culture, and even within the same culture." Valuation should not and cannot be considered without the cultural and social context to which the heritage belongs. It implied changes within the theory of preservation, which could no longer be a matter of purely historical and architectural/artistic analysis. "Democratisation of the processes of consultation and assessment of heritage values is not likely to be a threat to the sovereignty of the field, but it still requires a change of attitude and training," wrote Marta de la Torre (2002, p. 4) in the preamble to the Getty Conservation Institute's research report. In fact, values were no longer perceived as an integral part of cultural heritage; rather, they were assigned by those who have an interest in a place. They depend "on the particular cultural, intellectual, historical, and psychological frames of reference held by the particular individuals or groups involved" (Lipe, 1984, p. 2).

The narrative of *The Nara Document* found its continuation in documents devised by international and national organizations, for example, The Australia ICOMOS Charter for Places of Cultural Significance (The Burra Charter, 2013). The Charter defined the significance of cultural heritage through values that are important for past, present or future generations, among which certain categories were mentioned: aesthetic, historic, scientific, social and spiritual. Cultural values referred to "those beliefs which are important to a cultural group, including but not limited to political, religious, spiritual and moral belief" (The Burra Charter, 2013).

Contemporary strategies of heritage valuation are based on the holistic approach. It goes far beyond the material heritage of the past and includes

Table 2.2 Values of cultural heritage according to Affelt's theory

Cultural values	*Socio-economic values*
Social identity *(anthropology, psychology, sociology)*	Social use *(sociology, economy, media)*
Authenticity *(history, archaeology, engineering)*	Maintenance of the function *(history, ethics)*
Integrity *(history, archaeology, engineering)*	Economic potential *(economy, business)*
Uniqueness *(history, geography)*	Educational *(pedagogy, communication)*
Artistic *(history, art)*	Aesthetical *(philosophy, psychology, neurobiology)*
Historical *(history)*	Political *(political sciences)*
Values of special importance, for example, diversity of cultural landscape *(history, geography, philosophy, ethics)*	

Source: Affelt (2012, p. 440).

studies on identity, social awareness and responsibility, environmental issues and sustainability (Szmelter, 2015, p. 267). Waldemar Affelt, who researched post-industrial cultural heritage, identified 13 values of technical monuments which affect the experience of the observer and their valuation by society and individuals. They have been categorized into two groups:

- Cultural values – including social identity, authenticity, integrity, uniqueness, artistic value and historical value
- Socio-economical values – including social usefulness, the preservation of (original) function, economic potential, education, aesthetic value and political value

Affelt also defined "values of special importance," which belong to both categories and can be related to the diversity and attractiveness of the cultural landscape, among others (Affelt, 2012, p. 440). Each can refer to one of four different contexts (social, economic, the natural environment, cultural) and can be evaluated and interpreted against it (Affelt, 2009, pp. 76–77). According to Affelt, a survey on specific values is part of different scientific disciplines, and only when put together do they give a complex valuation of the heritage (Table 2.2).

The development of monument value systems, determined by the evolution of preservation theory, reveals the changes in the role of the cultural heritage within society. The testimony of past periods, the carrier of the collective memory *(lieux de memoire)*, has become subject to negotiations within the process of valuation (Figure 2.5). At the same time, the role of the evaluator has changed – from an objective observer positioned outside

<table>
<tr><th>Riegl (1903)</th><th colspan="2">Frodl (1963)</th><th>Lipe (1984)</th><th colspan="2">Burra Charter (2013)</th><th colspan="2">Affelt (2012)</th></tr>
<tr><td>Age</td><td rowspan="3">Historical</td><td>Scientific</td><td>Economic</td><td colspan="2">Aesthetic</td><td rowspan="6">Cultural</td><td>Social identity</td></tr>
<tr><td>Historical</td><td rowspan="2">Emotional</td><td>Aesthetic</td><td colspan="2">Historic</td><td>Authenticity</td></tr>
<tr><td>Commemorative</td><td>Associative-symbolic</td><td colspan="2">Scientific</td><td>Integrity</td></tr>
<tr><td>Use</td><td rowspan="9">Artistic</td><td>Historical-artistic</td><td rowspan="10">Informational</td><td rowspan="10">Social</td><td>Spiritual</td><td>Uniqueness</td></tr>
<tr><td rowspan="9">Newness</td><td>Artistic quality</td><td>Political</td><td>Artistic</td></tr>
<tr><td rowspan="7">Artistic</td><td>National</td><td>Historical</td></tr>
<tr><td rowspan="7">Cultural</td><td rowspan="6">Socio-economical</td><td>Social use</td></tr>
<tr><td>Maintenance of function</td></tr>
<tr><td>Economic potential</td></tr>
<tr><td>Educational</td></tr>
<tr><td>Aesthetic</td></tr>
<tr><td>Political</td></tr>
<tr><td colspan="2">Use</td><td colspan="2">Special importance</td></tr>
</table>

Figure 2.5 Summary of selected heritage value typologies

Source: Own study.

the system, to an integral part of it. According to Affelt, the links between different elements of the system, which determine the observer's attitude towards the object, imply certain values and, as a consequence, operations (Affelt, 2009, p. 70) (Figure 2.6).

After Boito and Riegl, valuation systems did not differentiate between various types of monuments. On the contrary, preservationists intended to create a universal system that would be applicable to heritage that represents all styles and periods. However, modern theories recognize the specific characteristics of industrial cultural heritage or the heritage of modernist architecture. The valuation and preservation of the heritage of the modern movement raise the issue of the new interpretation of classical tenets and principles. When considering post-war modernist architecture, the criteria are highly selective – local protection laws in many countries reject the criterion of age value (as not relevant), recommending the protection of buildings and assets of "definite quality and character" (Hudson, 2007, p. 53).

Creator ↔ Object ↔ Surroundings ↔ **Observer** ↔ Values ↔ Attitude ↔ Operations

Figure 2.6 The links between the observer, the monument and its context

Source: Affelt (2009, p. 70).

Does the heritage of the modern movement require a new definition of what a monument is and a new valuation theory? Scholars like Kuba Snopek suggest rejecting the paradigm of uniqueness and authenticity, emphasizing that post-war modernism was about typical solutions and their repetitive character. Instead of a traditional aesthetic value, they present intangible values that are inextricably linked to a specific building or site that enforces its significance (Snopek, 2014). The unwanted heritage of yesterday can represent new values for future generations. As William Lipe (1984, p. 2) stated, "The protection of the present significance of heritage, without impairing any other values that might be important for future generations when we do not know what values will be favoured, is considered today one of the biggest conservation challenges."

Architectural heritage as an urban common good

Societies are increasingly diverse, and it is not true that class divisions are disappearing. These divisions still exist in every country, and what is more, the number of social classes is increasing (see, e.g. Domański, 2017; Erikson & Goldthorpe, 1992; Erikson et al., 1979). These diversities have social and economic dimensions (e.g. age, gender, income and its sources, as well as beliefs and values) and a spatial dimension, which applies not only to countries but also to regions and cities within those countries. This makes universal concepts and tools for organizing social and economic life impractical. The diversity of human and, consequently, social needs means that there are no universal solutions to ensure social well-being. Consensus between diverse (often conflicting) interests is difficult or even impossible to achieve. Moreover, because these needs are dynamic, ideas for economies and societies from not only a few hundred years ago, but also even a decade ago – even if they were effective in the past – will not necessarily be effective today. It is difficult today to question the statement formulated by Arrow (1951) a few decades ago about the impossibility of constructing the social function of welfare. It is not possible to develop a model of reaching social agreement (e.g. by voting in elections) that will satisfy everyone.

What is more, as members of society, we simultaneously perform different social roles and function in many "institutional layers" (Grillitsch, 2015, p. 2104). These layers may be not only formal (e.g. public administrative structures such as municipalities, regions or state administration), but also less formal (companies, associations, national or religious groups) or non-formal (friendships, peer groups, neighbourhood groups, etc.). Each institutional layer has particular normative properties such as width (i.e. how many spheres of life are concerned), depth (the level of detail in regulating behaviour in specific situations) and sharpness (to what extent the (re)interpretation of the rules is allowed). Every person is born, grows up and moves between various institutional layers, such as family, schools, professional or interest groups, and individuals have a different ability to distinguish (consciously or subconsciously) between the different institutional layers and to adapt their rules to specific life situations. Therefore, individuals share and belong to different institutional layers with other individuals in an infinite number of combinations (Sokołowicz, 2015, p. 188).

Thus, it is doubtful whether there are societies whose members are guided by an undefined general good. It is not that "there is no such thing as a society" (a saying attributed to Margaret Thatcher) but that the concept of society is abstract. Societies therefore exist, but not as undefined entities. Rather, they are complex structures in which reaching agreements is not the result of discourse around the theoretical idea of society, but a process of concrete negotiations whose participants achieve consensus as a result of their personal endeavours. This was noticed by March and Olsen (1989, p. 198) when they wrote that while social processes are based on the aspirations of individuals and small groups, self-interest is not always the only motive for negotiations.

At the same time, the functioning of societies depends on previous human beliefs, access to knowledge, trust in individuals, etc. In other words, social processes are not free from politics. For this reason, social processes are neither a simple sum of actions taken by individuals, nor can they be effectively controlled top-down, because they are too complex. Nowadays, social sciences aim to find the golden mean in this respect. In terms of value studies, they do not completely give up on the rationality of human choices. Moreover, some economists (who primarily focused on public choice theory, considered today to be one of the most important branches of institutional economics) assume that *homo oeconomicus* acts not only in the sphere of individual choices (regulated by the market), but also in the sphere of collective choices made by the political mechanism. At the same time, however, they assume that not only is human rationality itself bounded (psychologically, axiomatically), but choices and decisions are also limited. In other words, people simultaneously strive to maximize individual satisfaction and are limited (consciously or subconsciously) by:

- The size, structure and quality of their resources (natural, labour, material, etc.)
- Their knowledge of social processes (limitations in perception)
- Institutions

In this respect, economists increasingly agree with most sociologists who, in the normative sphere, propose the development of societies and communities based on intrinsic values (e.g. dignity, loyalty, love, responsibility, diligence, righteousness, friendship, decency, solidarity, justice, respect, honesty, freedom, sensitivity, cooperation, trust and kindness) (Bogunia-Borowska, 2015, p. 40). This involves basing value systems on reciprocity, recognizing instrumental values as secondary to intrinsic ones, or reconciling differences in value systems based on communication, debate and conversation. In the end, therefore, the concept of value is rooted in the idea of the common good.

For this reason, the notion of urban commons has become widespread in urban and regional studies, including research on values and the quality of life. This concept, in turn, is rooted in a common idea, which, although close in meaning, does not mean the same thing. As Dardot and Laval (2019, p. 7) point out, "commune" is used to name a specific, local, self-governing polity, while "commons" refers to a diverse array of objects or resources managed by the activities of individuals and collectives. In other words, "common" is more properly the name of the principle that both animates and guides this activity. This conception refers to the ancient *koinôn* and Aristotle's *koinônein* ("putting or sharing in common"), which occurs when citizens deliberate collectively in order to determine what is appropriate for the city and what constitutes a just course of action. "For Aristotle, 'living together' is not simply a matter of 'sharing the same pasture,' it is more fundamentally based on the 'sharing of conversation and thought': it is to produce, through deliberation and legislation, similar customs and rules of living for all those who pursue the same end" (Dardot & Laval, 2019, p. 15).

Many goods used by dwellers of a given territory are common goods. These goods include not only public spaces and properties, urban transport and infrastructure, but also immaterial elements such as shared urban values and attitudes, urban culture and identity. Today's urban commons are subject to dynamic transformations in the way they are created, supplied and used. They are also used by many entities simultaneously, which generates problems typical of public goods (Sokołowicz, 2018, p. 23). In economic science, goods used to be analyzed through the prism of the division into public and private. However, this division becomes insufficient and is increasingly extended by two intermediate forms: commons and club goods. As a result, economists distinguish four types of goods: private and public, at two extremes, and commons and club goods, as intermediate options. Such a classification is based on two criteria: (1) the excludability of others (apart from the owner) from the consumption and (2) rivalry in consumption (Mankiw, 2009, p. 226). Club goods can be consumed by many people at the same time without affecting their availability to others, but the consumption is limited to a relatively narrow group (e.g. private schools). In turn, commons are goods for which people compete with each other, as access to them is public, by law, or physical properties. However, unlike the case of "pure" public goods, each successive user of commons limits the possibilities for others to use them. As a result, too many people wanting to use a common reduces its utility and value as perceived by others.

In towns and cities, although openly accessible goods (including heritage sites) are popularly considered public, they are actually commons. This category is very broad and includes many urban goods – from parks, squares, streets, gardens and other public spaces (Foster, 2013, pp. 57–58; O'Brien,

2012, pp. 467–468), through the services offered in the city, such as public transport, water supply, health care or energy infrastructure (Iaione, 2012, p. 114), to intangible and difficult to measure urban "resources" such as the urban atmosphere, the culture of diverse communities or urban identity.

In fact, it is not just the law and property rights themselves that define commons, but also human relations and the convictions of why it is worth living in the city (Tims, 2015). In this sense, it is not enough for public goods (e.g. schools, communal housing, public transportation) to be publicly owned to be called urban commons. Commons are, in fact, determined by practices of "commoning" – practices determined not only by law, but also (perhaps most importantly) by the relationships between the users and their attitude towards these goods. These relationships determine the specific conviction that prevails in the urban community as to what should and should not be considered a common good (Susser & Tonnelat, 2013, p. 8). It is the urban community that determines the extent to which the urban environment, parks and public spaces or culture in the city should be private, public, club goods or commons. Such decisions are complex processes, which result from confronting various interests that arise from the diversity of views and needs, and the bargaining power of city users (Sokołowicz, 2017). The process of commoning is understood as a social practice of managing shared resources for the common benefit (Bollier, 2014, p. 20). This practice manifests itself in encouraging collective action through bottom-up, personal participation, the results of which are shared by the community as a whole, but which can also be partly or fully accessible to others. The creation and use of collective goods do not use market mechanisms and are not subject to market valuation (Harvey, 2012).

Common goods, in addition to being placed in the taxonomy as intermediate between purely public and purely private, are also defined by the impossibility of excluding third parties from consumption and by being the subject of commoning. These two conditions are considered necessary, but two more are needed to be sufficient. Firstly, commons are the subject of specific norms and rules established within a community regarding such resources. They form specific and territorially rooted institutional conditions that are both formal and informal (including trust between group members). Secondly, the effective sharing of commons needs the awareness of joint, collective benefits among community members. It is the latter that motivates actual action in favour of commons. Such benefits are assessed from the perspective of the values that commons and the process of commoning bring.

Initially, researchers were primarily concerned with traditional common resources, known as the "Big Five," which consisted of forestry, fishing, pastures, water management and irrigation systems (van Laerhoven & Ostrom, 2007, p. 8). Such resources are natural, renewable and located mostly in non-urbanized areas. Their spatial range is usually local, and they are co-managed by communities, for which they are the main source of livelihood. Over time, scientific research on common goods has grown in scale. Attempts are now being made to adapt the principles formulated for the "Big Five" to the conditions for commons, such as global (usually environmental) common goods (Stern, 2011), virtual common goods, which refers to the open software communities (Kollock & Smith, 1996) and urban common goods (Foster & Iaione, 2019). The range of new common goods is very large. C. Hess (2009, p. 13) classified them based on a very extensive literature review, creating and describing a map of new common goods in which she distinguished the following categories:

- Cultural commons
- Neighbourhood commons
- Knowledge commons
- Infrastructure commons
- Medical and health commons
- The market as commons
- Global commons

Architectural heritage can be seen as a specific form of urban commons, also from the perspective of the above classification. Heritage is inscribed into a group of material cultural goods that function in the urban community by the historical context and the provenance of the monuments. Monuments are also a form of neighbourhood commons because of their intrinsic value and the willingness to preserve them for future generations, and also – in the case of the most recognizable landmarks that determine the image of a city – their utility value. Through the mechanism of pecuniary externalities, their location in the vicinity of other properties often translates directly into an increase in their market value. Thus, they also acquire the characteristics of market commons. Urban heritage perception also depends on the level of knowledge about material culture inherent in architecture and urban structure, and thus it can be indicated as a form of knowledge commons. As heritage also consists of technical urban monuments (e.g. old streetcars, funiculars, aqueducts, bridges, monumental sewage systems, underground railroads, etc.), some of them possess the features of the infrastructure commons group. Finally, historical green complexes contribute to good health, quality of life, and the state of the environment, generating value as health and environmental commons.

The benefits for societies and communities of heritage understood as urban common goods are generally acknowledged. However, the methodological and, to some extent, political challenge is to determine the scale of such benefits and to value them. Some externalities can be measured, provided they are precisely defined; therefore, economic theory can be a source of inspiration here. Externalities are defined as the effects of individuals' actions affecting the utility of others who cannot directly influence the strength or direction of those actions. They arise when a person engages in an activity that influences the well-being of a bystander and yet neither pays nor receives any compensation for that effect (Mankiw, 2009, p. 204). As such, they are not directly calculated, although they affect the economic account within society. One of the main sources of externalities remains the concentration of people and businesses in a relatively small physical space. Such externalities are called agglomeration economies, and they are defined as a form of external benefits that result from the concentration of populations, buildings, production, services, commercial activities, etc. Thanks to such agglomeration benefits, urban dwellers gain access to benefits such as more clients, the possibility to function in a better-developed labour market, diverse consumer choices, or economies of scale in the use of infrastructure and attractively built-up spaces (O'Sullivan, 2007, pp. 46–47). In macroeconomic terms, agglomeration economies are the most fundamental form of explaining the concentration of human activity in space.

However, the traditional view on the benefits of agglomeration highlights, above all, those types of externalities that are relatively easily measurable and related to business. Therefore, classical economics has primarily studied externalities related to how, through the physical proximity and associated availability of co-operators, subcontractors and qualified employees, the concentration of businesses in a small area has translated into economic profits or growing land rent (Marshall, 2013). With time, however, it became apparent that agglomeration economies are brought not only by economic specialization but also by the diversity of human activity and social diversity, as well as the role of tangible and intangible heritage in the perception of the town or city as a whole. The first to draw attention to this was Jane Jacobs (1969), who claimed that the diversity of social and economic structures typical of large cities is their unique value. This value is therefore influenced by urban density, the quality of urban architecture (including the presence of historic buildings), and by filling spaces with activities that enable social interaction.

Later, in the framework of urban studies, the benefits of agglomeration started to be revealed, not only from the point of view of business and entrepreneurs, but also consumers and other users of urban spaces. Therefore, Glaeser et al. (2001) stressed that next to production advantages, the role of the urban environment in facilitating consumption is also extremely important, albeit understudied. There are four particularly critical urban amenities that fundamentally influence how the value of living in a particular city and its districts are perceived (Glaeser et al., 2001, p. 28): (1) the presence of a rich variety of services and consumer goods, (2) good public services, (3) transport infrastructure availability and (4) aesthetics and physical setting. Also, "diversity in itself is often an urban amenity, since urban consumers are attracted to cities with ethnic restaurants, international cultural offering, and a lively street scene" (Glaeser et al., 2001, p. 48). A city's quality of life and the perception of its parts as valuable or not is therefore influenced by what Gehl called "the life between buildings." Such life constitutes the functions of public and common urban spaces, which thus provide: (1) contact at a modest social level, (2) a possible starting point for contact at closer social levels, (3) the possibility of maintaining established contacts, (4) a source of information about the social world outside and (5) a source of inspiration and experience (Gehl, 2011, p. 15).

When determining the value of space in the approach outlined above, it suggests adopting the perspective of the actual sources of value (i.e. buildings, facilities, infrastructure and other objects constituting the material heritage) and their surroundings. The latter consists of physical (public spaces), social (e.g. demography and class structure of the neighbourhood) and economic elements (facilities for entrepreneurs and consumers, and the attractiveness and accessibility of the offer in trade and services, etc.). Such an environment constitutes all the urban amenities that should be considered in terms of urban commons as a complex good that consists of many components (Galster, 2003; Lancaster, 1966). Some of these goods are also abstract, as apart from material amenities, they also include non-material elements, for example, the atmosphere created within the social relations built in the urban neighbourhood (local culture).

Overall, urban commons create bundles of spatial attributes of both material and non-material character, which comprise the following urban amenities (Galster, 2003, p. 154): (1) the structure of buildings (the scale and density of buildings, quality of design, maintenance and architectural and landscape values), (2) infrastructure (the presence and quality of roads, pavements, installations, etc.), (3) the availability of public services (the quality of public schools, health care, cultural and recreational facilities, etc.), (4) accessibility to places of work, leisure, culture and consumption, conditioned by the proximity and availability of means of transport, (5) environment: noise levels, air, water and soil pollution, topographical characteristics, climate, etc., (6) demographic and socio-economic characteristics of the population living in the neighbourhood (age, gender, origin, income, occupation, etc.) and (7) type and density of social relations (network of contacts, interpersonal relations, level of participation in local social institutions, possibility to influence the local authorities' political decisions, identifying the community with a given place, etc.). Such urban common amenities are characterized by strong location dependency, non-transferability to other locations, its exogenous nature in relation to individual choices, complexity, variability over time, and difficulty in valuing such goods precisely (Diamond & Tolley, 1982, pp. 5–10; Galster, 2003, p. 156).

Architectural heritage as a territorial capital

For two decades, social sciences have shown a growing interest in the territorial development paradigm, which has substantially changed the interpretation of space and its role in social and economic development. According to this approach, a territory is not just a place where strategically valuable resources are located and cumulated; it is seen as a place where resources are created together with the growth capacity of local entities. Understood this way, territory ceases to be a physical space distinguished based on an administrative criterion; rather, it becomes a historically shaped space with a specific social, institutional and organizational framework. This space is created by local actors who are brought together not just by mere physical proximity and common history and culture but, above all, by relationships and shared values (Torre, 2015). A territory is a space that should not be "taken for granted," as it is built by local actors, social and economic networks, the history and culture of the place, trust, as well as local values and norms.

From a territorial perspective, growth is presented as a process that creates the resources that give a place its unique character. Arguably, through a dense network of relationships, a territory can create resources, such as knowledge, innovation, social values and norms or heritage and tradition, which generate potentials that make the territory a specific and unique place. The diversity and unique combinations of these potentials build up the distinctiveness of the place (Camagni, 2012). The physical proximity of local actors within a territory helps build direct interactions and create other forms of social, institutional and cognitive closeness (Torre & Rallet, 2005). Cooperation emerges, together with the identification of common goals pursued by local actors who create and stimulate the territorial growth dynamics. The evolutionary way in which territorial resources are generated is vital for the process, together with "inheritance" and "attachment" to the development path dictated by the past of the place. This is how transformation/evolution takes place when we proceed from a space based on the simple physical concentration of resources to the active space built by actors, generating unique resources and conditions for living or pursuing economic activity (Colletis & Pecqueur, 2005; Lévesque, 2008).

The idea of territorial development makes strong reference to the notion of the localized nature of actors. It underscores the embeddedness of local entities in space, their cooperation and the reciprocity of actions. Here, development is seen not as an effect of market exchange only, but as a result of a complex set of social relations between entities operating within a given space (Jewtuchowicz, 2005). These entities are localized, engaged actors – anchored in both geographic space and a network of mutual relations that are conditional to their economic and social success. This is how a territory becomes a meeting place for market and social relations and economic conditions with an institutional and cultural framework that, together, create unique trajectories of space development (Nowakowska 2018; Torre 2018).

The territorial paradigm has paved the way for the notion of *territorial capital* to be introduced to social sciences as a term that captures public and private goods, as well as tangible and intangible resources (Camagni, 2019;

Camagni & Capello, 2013). Territorial capital is defined as a combination of localized natural, human, organizational, relational and cognitive assets that, taken together, represent the competitive potential of a given territory (Camagni, 2008). It also includes the ability to cooperate, creativity, business climate, know-how and innovation capabilities (Capello et al., 2009). Territorial capital transforms an abstract space into a place where localized competencies, knowledge, skills, relationships, values, principles and local practices can be found (Camagni, 2008; Tóth, 2015). Understood as such, territorial capital is viewed as an endogenous resource anchored within a given territory that depends on the qualities and development path of a given place. In addition, the potential is highly diversified across territories. It is widely recognized that the development capacity of territorial units and individual actors lies more than ever in the strength of the deeply rooted and unique resources. And thus, the resources that make up territorial capital are seen as far more strategically valuable than the relatively widely available financial, in-kind capital or infrastructure.

From the above-presented perspective, cultural heritage, including architectural heritage, acquires a new meaning. It is a relevant component of territorial capital as it brings in the value and uniqueness of the place at multiple levels (Camagni et al., 2020). Traditionally, architectural heritage mainly covers the material growth potential and provides a background for the life and activities of municipal and regional communities. The territorial approach highlights the role it plays in creating a place's intangible assets, such as identity, social bonds or the source of economic value. The classical approach sees architectural heritage primarily as monuments, the legacy left by previous generations that experts have assessed as valuable. It depicts the past of a place; it is also a testimony of old times and evidence of the standards of beauty, value and sensitivity or technological progress and innovation of the time (Ashworth, 2013; Vecco, 2010). At a territorial level, architectural heritage goes beyond the affiliation with the past or specific material values. In this case, architectural heritage bears a powerful social load and provides the context for interactions and social engagement. Consequently, it also generates a place's intangible resources, such as social bonds and relationships, its atmosphere, or the local *milieu*, which triggers innovative ideas and new social and economic activities (Camagni, 2012; Saquet, 2016). This is how the past, encoded in architectural heritage, becomes a catalyst for increasing interdependencies between local actors as well as between them and the territory.

From the territorial perspective of development, the value of heritage is articulated not only by experts who provide scientific justification for its source. It is co-created by the community that inhabits a particular territory, which self-develops the awareness of the heritage and shapes its new meaning. That is true mostly of relatively young components of architectural heritage, which are often sources of powerful emotions and are viewed by many actors as "difficult" or even "unwanted" heritage.

On the other hand, such heritage is an opportunity for vivid discussions to be held across the community on the history, culture and identity of the place. Thus, architectural heritage becomes an impulse and a unique social "glue," a foundation on which relationships and bonds, local anchoring, or the historical awareness of a place can develop. Many examples can be given to demonstrate how local communities that reside in what is seen as "unwanted" and forgotten architectural heritage, or heritage that went unnoticed and underappreciated by experts, have successfully created new social values. Through a bottom-up process, they have given value to such places, making them "places to visit" or generating demand for new local attractions. London's brutalist Barbican Centre project is an example of turning a fiercely contested architectural legacy into value for the local community, where a highly criticized residential district has been transformed into a lively centre of culture and entertainment recognizable by the residents.

Meanwhile, the modernist van Nelle factory in Rotterdam, until quite recently associated with the collapse of the food processing industry, is known today for the revitalization project that transformed it into a residential and office complex inscribed in the list of The 25 Most Beautiful Factories in the World. Nowa Huta [New Steelworks], the industrial district of Krakow built under communist rule in the 1950s as a counterbalance for the conservative historic city centre, is today re-discovered by its inhabitants and urban activists as an interesting example of socialist realism architecture, hosting re-emerging economic and cultural activities. Warsaw's modernist Powiśle railway station is also an interesting case. The place has retained its transportation function, but the opening of the Art Café in its space has introduced new economic and artistic functions, making it one of the icons of Polish urban movements and urban social activism in the capital of Poland. These examples provide evidence of two parallel and synergistic processes taking place: the social creation of architectural value and the building of a cultural community. Architectural heritage becomes a territorial bond, the principal link around which social capital develops.

The local embeddedness of social and economic activity in the territorial tissue is the key analytical category in the territorial development paradigm (Granovetter, 1985; Grzesiuk, 2015). For architectural heritage, it means not only the physical anchoring of a monument in space but, above all, its embeddedness in social and economic relations. The connection between territory and heritage is highlighted, in which the latter shapes and is shaped by relationships, as well as the social, economic, institutional or cultural conditions (M. Hess, 2004). This is how architectural heritage and its value become a strongly territorialized resource, "tied" to the place, difficult to transfer and reproduce anywhere else.

The perception of architectural heritage evolves together with the social and economic challenges faced by a given territory. It is a reflection of the historical accumulation of values, traditions and experiences or the piling up of values cherished by past and contemporary cultures. One might say that the legacy that results from a territory's past and present social and economic development undergoes endogenous and continuous revitalization. In this case, we are dealing with a value that is generated and which then constantly evolves following the transformation pattern of territorially rooted social relations and the status and dynamics of economic development, which ultimately translate into changes in the system of values.

Architectural heritage may become territorial capital as a result of well-thought-out decisions and actions undertaken within the framework of a development policy. It may also happen unintentionally, through bottom-up, spontaneous processes and social interactions oriented at building a place's resources. In the second case, the value and relevance of architectural heritage are co-created by local actors, who create and give a new social and economic dimension to the heritage. In the territorial approach, it is not only experts who decide what constitutes heritage and is decisive for the identity of a place (e.g. to include a structure in the official register of monuments or to cover it with another formal protection measure). Increasingly, actors within the territory co-decide about the value of architectural potential and the possibilities to exploit it in development processes. This is how space is created at the social level, and the value of architectural heritage is estimated through a process whose sense is awarded and identified by the local community, where new users are redefined together with new ways of using it (Poulios, 2014). As a result, architectural heritage contributes to the increasing interdependencies between the local community and the territory, where local entities co-create the architectural territorial capital and, at the same time, use it for their own development.

Architectural heritage turns an indifferent and valueless space into a concrete place that stirs emotions, bonds and social relationships and generates local values and development capabilities. In the territorial approach, architectural heritage provides an impulse and catalyst for development, becoming an integral component of the local economic system. Architecture creates the economic tissue, unleashes creativity and stimulates the emergence of new economic activities (Bowitz & Ibenholt, 2009). Within the local economic environment, it acts as a base for triggering mechanisms that co-create new values and valuable resources. It may inspire both individual entities and the entire local community to act. As a result, it creates the "*genius loci*" (the spirit of the place), as well as its transformational capacities and unique competitive advantages (Camagni et al., 2020; Cerisola, 2019b). Perceived in this way, architectural heritage fosters synergy mechanisms and opens up opportunities to trigger positive externalities (through identity, the atmosphere of the place or business climate), determining the development of the place and strengthening its competitive position (Capello & Perucca, 2017; Cerisola, 2019a).

In the territorial approach, architectural heritage is viewed as a resource that may provide exceptionally beneficial conditions for unusual and sophisticated economic activities that seek rare and unique location factors (Gospodini, 2004). Old post-industrial sites in Lodz, second Polish largest city, transformed into lofts, sophisticated office spaces, artists' studios, institutions of culture, or first-rate meeting spaces are excellent examples. This post-industrial architecture has not only created the uniqueness of the city, but has also enriched the offer of the real estate market. Lodz's unique architectural heritage, strengthened by the activity of the local community, has become the basis for revising ways of thinking about the territory's past and creating its future. In this case, the post-industrial architectural heritage has become an impulse and catalyst for the city's development, creating opportunities for new economic activities and setting new trajectories for the city. It performs inspirational functions for local economic entities and attracts new specific users of urban spaces (e.g. the creative class) (Nowakowska & Walczak, 2016). As indicated by the analyses of the OECD and European Union, mobilizing unique territorial capital by aligning economic or social activities with the uniqueness and resources of a given place generates higher profits and fosters synergy mechanisms in the local environment (EU, 2011, pp. 12–13; OECD, 2001, p. 16).

The active involvement of the local community in defining how a territory is organized and functions also leads to a new model of territorial interaction and heritage management, called territorial governance (Davoudi et al., 2008). It implies not only the decentralization of management and the cooperation of public, private and non-governmental sector organizations, but above all, the inclusion of local actors in a continuous process of defining and managing heritage. As a result, a new way of creating visions and objectives and organizing and coordinating heritage conservation policies is emerging in the local environment. The ongoing shift in thinking about architectural heritage highlights the need to include society and its recognized values in holistically perceived cultural heritage (UNESCO, 2013).

Recognizing architectural heritage as a particular territorial capital significantly changes the way local development policies are shaped. In the territorial approach, architectural heritage is a resource that requires an out-of-the-box development policy, tailored to the place (Pratt, 2004). Consequently, activities should focus not so much on protecting architectural monuments as on creating a place-based capital with its own specificity and identity.[2] This implies the need to apply a place-based approach to heritage management and integrate local institutions and actors who co-determine strategic actions for urban development (multilevel governance).

The skilful integration of architectural heritage elements into the territory becomes a stimulator of economic development and contributes to a better understanding of the value of the architectural heritage itself and the place in which it is located. This, in turn, impacts the sense of stability and the attachment/embeddedness of the actors and community involvement in development activities (Brown et al., 2003; Vorkinn & Riese, 2001). This new view of heritage – moving from looking at a single architectural monument from an expert perspective to thinking in terms of territory and the social production of heritage values – is a *sine qua non* condition for effective urban management (Ripp & Rodwell, 2016).

Heritage surroundings and its value from the societal and spatial order perspective

Axiological and economic considerations do not directly touch on the role of place and space in the creation and perception of value. However, the impact of spatial disparities on economic processes, including value differentiation, although not always explicitly, is of interest to socio-economic geography and regional economy. Contemporary spatial analyses, in particular, increasingly focus on the notion of "territory" – the essence of which boils down to combining the physical, cognitive and social dimensions of a space. The last two dimensions refer both to the inhabitants' attitudes to the area they inhabit and to the relationships between the inhabitants, which make up the place specificity.

The first works of economic geographers and regional economists referred directly to the intellectual achievements of classical economics. These studies can be divided into three main groups:

1. Theories that refer to the concept of land rent, looking for reasons for the diversification of the value of land as a production factor (Hoover, 1937; Ricardo, 2001; von Thünen, 1826);
2. Location theories that identify the prerequisites for the placement of production and other business activities (Launhardt, 1882; Palander, 1935; Predöhl, 1925; Weber, 1909). They concentrate on identifying the value in space from the perspective of its impact on the profitability of production and, consequently, the transformation of the built-up landscape as a human environment;
3. Theories that explain mechanisms of how settlement systems are formed (Christaller, 1933; Isard, 1960; Lösch, 1940; Perroux, 1950; Zipf, 1949), which explain both the causes and consequences of the different sizes and spatial distribution of human activity places – from the smallest settlements and villages to the largest metropolises.

Among the first economists to strongly emphasize the complexity of the issue of space and the need to abandon its simplified interpretation was Perroux (1950). He distinguished between the geonomic space and the economic space. The former is "banal" and may be defined by the geonomic relationships between points, lines and sizes; the latter, on the other hand, should be defined through the lenses of various economic relations

(Perroux, 1950, p. 92). The "banal" geonomic space is also interpreted in terms of the availability of labour and material resources and thus in terms of classically understood location factors. As such, it has more of a technical than economic dimension. The economic space, on the other hand, should be interpreted more abstractly (Perroux, 1950, pp. 95–96):

- As a space where the economic actors' decisions, plans, and strategic behaviour can be observed
- As an area of continuous interaction between various centripetal and centrifugal economic processes
- As a specific homogeneous aggregate, separated from the environment in terms of production conditions, sales, costs, etc.

This issue was later developed by Tuan (1977), who distinguished between "space" and "place." While the former is treated as a blank card, the latter is the centre of established specific values. Thus, "'Space' is more abstract than 'place.' What begins as undifferentiated space becomes place as we get to know it better and endow it with value" (1977, p. 6). In other words, while "space" is, to a great extent, similar to the "banal" geonomic space in the meaning of Perroux, "place" is an effect of its valuation from the experiential human perspective. "Human beings not only discern geometric patterns in nature and create abstract spaces in the mind, they also try to embody their feelings, images, and thoughts in tangible material. The result is sculptural and architectural space, and on a large scale, the planned city" (1977, p. 17).

The complexity of the notion of space and place was also stressed by Soja (1971, p. 7), who pointed out the need to analyze spatial issues from three perspectives: (1) control over the distribution, allocation and ownership structure of rare resources, among which he considered land, as a production factor, to be the most important; (2) the maintenance of order and the exercise of power in a given territory, which arises from the trajectory of its development and (3) the legitimacy of power for social integration.

As a consequence of the above considerations, a conceptual distinction is proposed between the notions of land as a factor of production, space, place and finally, territory; as a factor of production, it can be interpreted in terms of a scarce resource for which various economic actors compete. The allocation and distribution of land is the result of a specific political and economic system that defines the structure of property rights. Space, on the other hand, is linked to a power structure that is capable of maintaining order within it and establishing a particular administrative system to maintain its authority.

However, space can also be understood in a variety of other contexts: mathematical, in the sense of the metric that defines it; physical, as a characteristic property of matter; geographical – as a result of the evolution of nature outside human influence, real space meant the entire surface of the earth, or parts of it; social (relational), defined by relative distances (or inversed proximity) produced by human communities in the course of history (Nijkamp & Ratajczak, 2015, p. 19). In the last meaning, interpreting space comes close to the notion of place, as Tuan (1977) meant it. On the one hand, territory is a combination of the above concepts, but on the other hand, it is something more. It should be defined by "territoriality," understood as a specific relationship to the land and space. However, the key issue is to stress that apart from its interdependence with concepts such as "land," "area," "space" and "place," it is proposed that "territory" be considered in the context of the relationships within it (Elden, 2010, p. 807).

Therefore, when searching for the essence of value in space, we cannot abstract from either the economic considerations or the axiological and psychological ones. Space and place are sources of geographic differentiation of the axiological and cultural conditions of value perception; they are also sources of the social and economic differences in values of different goods in the eyes of different actors. Therefore, it is necessary to talk about the different perspectives of looking at value. Spaces are inhabited by particular groups of people with particular interests, while resources of all kinds are not spread evenly throughout space (B. Higgins, 2018 [1988], p. 40). For instance, economic development does not spread itself evenly throughout space; therefore, there is a spatial trend for the formation of growth poles (Perroux, 1955). In other words, human activity (economic activity, in particular) shows a tendency to agglomerate, while value tends to vary spatially.

Consequently, considerations around value in territorial units should treat territory as both a geographical unit (e.g. a spatial variation of value at different scales of analysis) and the playing field for economic, social, technological, institutional or regulatory forces that affect value. Such an approach, not unfamiliar and actually quintessential for regional scientists, requires interdisciplinarity and a willingness to build conceptual and methodological bridges between philosophy, psychology, economics, geography, demography, planning, political science and so on (see Nijkamp & Ratajczak, 2015, p. 16). Therefore, "economists are interested in value as a construct that allows modelling choices, cognitive psychologists and neuroscientists investigate the mechanisms that explain how an individual ascribes value, sociologists and social psychologists focus on concepts of value that can be shared within a social group, philosophers address a vast array of conceptual questions concerning the properties of value at all these different stages" (Brosch & Sander, 2016, p. 398).

In the face of the diverse values in terms of differences within the humanities and social and geographical disciplines, standardizing them does not seem possible. Research seems to be "condemned to diversity" but also to deliberation in terms of research methods and procedures in valuation studies. This "value pluralism" results in variability in social, cognitive and motivational needs, interests and tendencies. What is more, such differences in value prioritization are psychologically (and perhaps even physiologically) embedded (Jost et al., 2016, p. 370).

For this reason, the discussion of value cannot be objective, as in the natural sciences. There is no single value, as it is the subject of political discussion, understood as the effect of deliberation and agreeing on common positions at various (including geographical) levels of societal organization. It requires an approach known in political science as procedural justice (Tyler, 2007), as well as non-coercive forms of communication and deliberation (see also Habermas, 1987). When the process of creating rules is based on discussion, it leads to a greater sense of justice and, therefore, greater acceptance of political decisions. In this process, research on valuation and communicating its results (often presented in the form of alternative and comparative solutions) is not intended to provide evidence that can unequivocally indicate the validity of certain decisions. It is more a starting point that presents the distribution of a set of social preferences regarding the value of certain goods, on the basis of which deliberation can take place.

Communities, along with the spaces and places they inhabit, are evolving, and they are constantly deliberating values. Society consists of both *communitas* and *societas*. The first is built on the values that connect people in a symbolic and cultural dimension. The second, on the other hand, refers to institutions. It includes everything that organizes social life in the formal dimension (Bogunia-Borowska, 2015, p. 17). However, modern society is not integral, but disjunctive (Bell, 1972). Its various segments (and localities) have a different rhythm of change and are governed by different rules and norms. This sometimes gives rise to tensions, including conflicts of values, which is why it is so important to make society more cohesive, and why an institutional mechanism of conciliatory deliberation around values is necessary. This is not possible, however, if certain actors understand values as fundamentally absolute and unquestionable. Fundamentalisms cannot be reconciled. What remains is peaceful coexistence and ecumenism or open war (Hausner, 2017, p. 26).

Finally, values are components of cultural heritage, and are thus handed down to successive generations and communities, which reinterpret and multiply them. This makes it possible to maintain continuity and change at the same time. While existential values are experienced, instrumental ones are exploited. Communities need both types of values. The balance between the creation of existential values and instrumental values means that individualism does not destroy the community (Hausner, 2017, pp. 70–71). Creating and deliberating values require a social space.

At the same time, it is worth noting that acceptance of the diversity of sources of value was also reflected in economic thought in the second half of the twentieth century. In countries with market economies, it resulted from the emergence of the neoclassical synthesis (Samuelson, 1955, p. 212). It was an attempt to combine previously competing approaches – the Keynesian

(Keynes 1936) macroeconomic income theory explaining sources of value by the demand for goods, and the classical economic theory, analyzing value primarily from the perspective of the supply of production factors.

A synthesis in the considerations of value can also be found in the wider spatial macroscale on both sides of the Iron Curtain. It is visible in the convergence of some assumptions in two completely opposite economic blocks: real socialism and modern capitalism. In the former, the works of the Polish economist Lange (1971), in particular, emphasized that even in a nationalized socialist economy, within the social ownership of the means of production, there is freedom of choice of profession and place of work, as well as goods on the consumer goods market. So, there is a labour market and a market for consumer goods. Official and non-market price formation concern production goods, which comprise the framework for the functioning of the whole economy.

In this understanding of how the economy functions, we can therefore see compromises between market and central control. Such compromises were also noticed by Stark (1985, 1989), who studied the organizational structures of socialist enterprises in the 1980s. He noted that in state-owned enterprises, small groups of employees were allowed to organize a specific form of microenterprise within larger organizations, where part of the production took place outside the planning process, and its effects could be sold on consumer goods markets. This demonstrates that in the late stages of socialism, the development of intermediate solutions between the market and the centralized, hierarchical structures was allowed.

By contrast, in capitalist countries after World War II, the concept of the welfare state developed. Under pressure from left-wing parties and trade unions, apart from monetary and fiscal policy measures and forms of direct state intervention (the nationalization of certain branches, antitrust laws, etc.), policy tools such as income control through progressive taxation, universal education, medical care, municipal housing and public investment, among others, appeared. Thus, a compromise can also be seen here, with state interference in market processes being accepted (Romanow, 1995, pp. 66–67). In this synthesis, however, one can perhaps look for the reasons for the popularity of modernism in architecture, which, after all, often concerned investments made by the state, on both sides of the Iron Curtain.

An important thread of research into the value of historic buildings is the analysis of the relationship between them and their surroundings. The analysis focuses on the impact of a historic site on its neighbourhood and vice versa. The impact of a historic building on its surroundings – urban environment, landscape, socio-economic growth or sustainable development is relatively well recognized and described in the literature (Affelt, 2008; Philokyprou & Michael, 2021; Rudokas et al., 2019). A less well-researched relationship is the impact that the neighbourhood in which a historic site is located has on its value. Although this issue has long been recognized and postulated in many works (including Throsby 2001, 2012), it remains poorly operationalized because there is still a lack of an explicit conceptual framework and an identification of the cause and effect relationships between architectural heritage and its urban environment.

Meanwhile, the neighbourhood and its quality in social sciences are perceived as a resource that is reflected in economic value. The impact of the surroundings on the value of a historic site is confirmed by, among others, numerous studies on the effect of green areas on the value of property or the influence of landscape on the value of spa facilities (Czembrowski et al., 2016; Fleischer, 2012; Ruijgrok, 2006; Spahr & Sunderman, 1999).

In the field of research on heritage value, this problem was recognized by Rudokas et al. (2019), who highlighted that one of the challenges in valuing heritage sites is the need to take into account the diverse urban environment. They pointed out that "[architectural] heritage objects are inseparably linked with their context including adjacent heritage and non-heritage buildings and by co-existing create synergetic effects on values" (Rudokas et al., 2019, p. 236). Similarly, van der Hoeven (2018) proposed a holistic understanding of urban heritage that focuses not only on isolated architectural heritage sites and objects but also on their wider physical, cultural and social context.

The discussion on the relationship between a heritage site and its neighbourhood mainly focuses on the issue of integrity. Integrity means wholeness, complementarity and inviolability, and refers to the state in which architectural heritage is understood as the sum of tangible and intangible elements, including the urban environment, which should form a harmonious unity (Taher Tolou Del et al., 2020). The integrity of architectural heritage can determine the value of the heritage, and it can even be considered a separate value – the value of the physical, functional, cultural and spiritual integrity (genius loci) of the architectural heritage and its urban environment (Rudokas et al., 2019). Integrity (e.g. the landscape or natural assets) is also seen as a prerequisite that must be met in order to inscribe a heritage site on the World Heritage List (Taher Tolou Del et al., 2020). The interaction and integrity of a heritage site with its neighbourhood in the context of sustainable urban development were also highlighted by researchers from Kaunas University of Technology. Based on an analysis and synthesis of the literature, they formulated a theoretical model that demonstrates the links between a historic building, a historic urban landscape and sustainable development (Grazuleviciute-Vileniske et al., 2021). Their insights laid the foundations for planning and heritage-based sustainable urban development policy recommendations.

One way to assess the value of architectural heritage in the context of the urban environment is to refer to the idea of spatial order and its dimensions, that is, architectural, aesthetic, social and functional order. Such an analytical approach was proposed by Nowakowska et al. (2020). It relies on the assumption that the value of a historic site is not created solely by the features and values of the site itself; it significantly depends on the quality of the surrounding areas. The neighbourhood strongly impacts the perception of a historic site and determines its value and qualities. The value of a historic site or building may be weakened or strengthened by the composition and quality of the development of its surroundings. Making a monument clearly visible and ensuring its harmony with its surroundings may positively affect the perception of its aesthetic, architectural, social or functional value.

An experiment carried out on the example of the Warszawa Ochota railway station illustrates this analytical approach. The results of the study showed that the value of a historic building assessed according to the four dimensions of spatial order differs significantly depending on the assessment of its neighbourhood. Thus, the study confirms that the spatial order in the surroundings influences the way people perceive and evaluate the value of a historic site. These findings are of fundamental importance for urban development policy, especially spatial planning. They point to the need to apply a place-based approach to shaping policies designed to protect architectural heritage.

The ambiguity and complexity of valuing (architectural) heritage are related to, among others, the dual nature of the relationship between historic buildings and their surroundings. The valuation of modernist architecture, like any architecture, is influenced by the time factor on the one hand, and by the space factor on the other. Every architectural monument is defined by its location in a specific space, which provides the "context" in which its values are assessed. The neighbourhoods of historic sites evolve over time prompted by natural factors, technical and civilizational progress, new ideas and social sensitivity. This process reflects various ideological and cultural influences; it also reflects society and its needs, including those in the realm of aesthetics. The neighbourhood may become degraded or regenerated; both processes redefine the relevance of a historic site and foster or erode its significance and value.

Against this backdrop, our study is based on the assumption that a historic site or building, together with its neighbourhood, should be viewed as one functional system. The historic site becomes an element that creates the urban landscape and shapes the spatial order, while the neighbourhood adjacent to the historic site dictates the perception of its value (Birdsall et al., 2021; Grazuleviciute-Vileniske et al., 2021) which can be either undermined or strengthened by the neighbourhood's quality and layout. Ensuring a heritage site's visibility and harmonious integration with the neighbourhood may positively impact the perception of its multidimensional value.

The novelty of the approach proposed for this research involves linking values that are pertinent to architectural heritage with the idea of spatial order, which considers social, economic, environmental, cultural, political, moral and aesthetic aspects of space management. In urban planning, the concept means aesthetic, coherent and harmonious urban space management (Boeing, 2019; Carmona, 2016; Hatuka & Forsyth, 2005; Mikołajczyk & Raszka, 2019). Spatial order refers to the compatibility or mutual complementarity of components and their properties. The key dimensions of spatial order can be described as follows (Różycka-Czas et al., 2019; Szczepańska & Pietrzyk, 2019) (Figure 2.7):

- Social order, which is linked with social relations, the symbolism of a place, and its importance for identity building
- Functional order, linked with the usefulness of a given space, its filling with service facilities, comfort of use and accessibility to users
- Aesthetic order, connected with the beauty of a space, its attractiveness, cleanliness and tidiness, as well as its positive or negative impact upon our senses
- Architectural order, expressed by the composition of the space, its clarity, the logic of the arrangement of its components and their shapes, sizes, diversity, how well they fit into the image of the city, and the uniqueness of the place
- Ecological order, linked to the value of the natural environment in a given space

The assessment of architectural heritage carried out in accordance with the aspects of spatial order is therefore based on the perceived harmony and integrity of the components of architectural heritage with

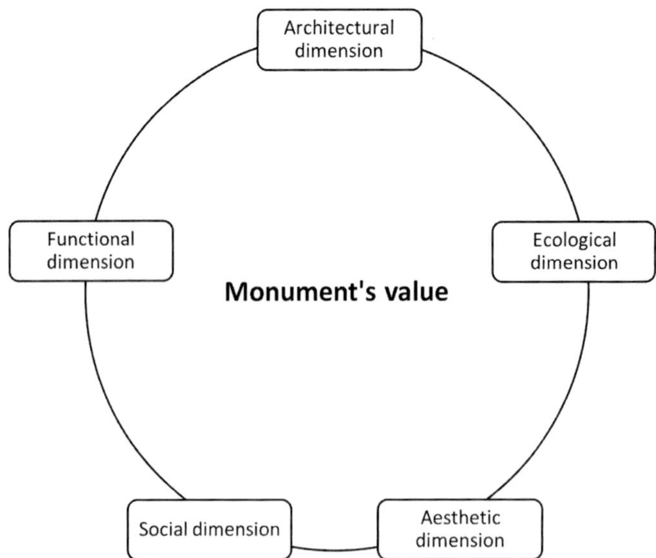

Figure 2.7 Aspects of spatial order in the context of the value of a historic site

Source: Own study based on Różycka-Czas et al. (2019) and Szczepańska and Pietrzyk (2019).

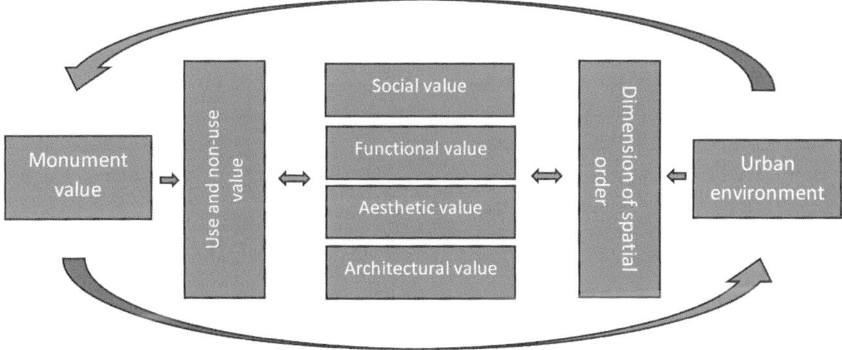

Figure 2.8 Relationship between a historic site and its neighbourhood in the context of spatial order

Source: Own study.

its urban neighbourhood. This approach highlights a move away from exploring the attributes of a single historic site to seeing it as an integral part of a larger unit. In other words, we assume that a heritage site being well integrated into the surroundings, and its harmony with the urban neighbourhood may positively influence the assessment of its utility and non-utility values. At the same time, we assume the reverse, that is, that the heritage site co-creates the neighbourhood and becomes an important element shaping the spatial order in the city (Figure 2.8). This means that the users of urban space may experience a symbiosis between a historic site and its urban neighbourhood (Rasmussen, 1964; Stephenson, 2008), which translates into an assessment of the site's value.

Notes

1 Although Smith initially based the value of goods almost exclusively on the labour needed to produce them, he gradually changed his position and developed a theory based on production costs. He eventually claimed that as the capitalist economy develops, the value of a good consists of the costs of three production factors: wage (as compensation for work), profit (income from capital) and land rent (the effect of disposing of land).

2 This approach to shaping development policy coincides with the directions in which conservation doctrines contemporarily evolve, giving preference to integrated and territorial protection. They point to the social dimension of architectural heritage, which should become an integral component of territorial development. It is also highlighted in relevant documents that provide the definitional framework and directions for the development of heritage protection and conservation, such as the Council of Europe's Faro Convention on the Value of Cultural Heritage for Society (2005) or the UNESCO Recommendation on the Historic Urban Landscape, Including a Glossary of Definitions, 2011, adopted in Paris in 2011.

References

Affelt, W. J. (2008). Dziedzictwo techniki w kontekście rozwoju zrównoważonego. W. B.. Szmygin (Ed.), *Współczesne problemy teorii konserwatorskiej w Polsce* (Międzynaro, pp. 7–16). http://bc.pollub.pl/Content/629/PDF/wspolczesneproblemy.pdf

Affelt, W. J. (2009). Dziedzictwo techniki, jego różnorodność i wartości. *Kurier konserwatorski*, *5*, 5–20.

Affelt, W. J. (2012). Moc i niemoc estetyczna – Rozważania o zabytkach techniki. In W. E. Szmit-Naud, B. J. Rouba, & J. Arszyńska (Eds.), *Wokół zagadnień estetyki zabytku po konserwacji i restauracji* (pp. 435–452). Narodowy Instytut Dziedzictwa.

Arrhenius, T. (2013). The fragile monument: On Alois Riegl's modern cult of monuments. *Nordisk Arkitekturforskning/Nordic Journal of Architectural Research*, *16*(4), 51–55. http://arkitekturforskning.net/na/article/download/296/256

Arrow, K. J. (1951). *Social choice and individual values*. Yale University Press.

Ashworth, G. J. (2013). Heritage and local development: A reluctant relationship. In *Handbook on the economics of cultural heritage* (pp. 367–385). Edward Elgar Publishing. https://econpapers.repec.org/RePEc:elg:eechap:14326_18

Bell, D. (1972). The cultural contradictions of capitalism. *Journal of Aesthetic Education*. https://doi.org/10.2307/3331409

Białynicka-Birula, J. (2003). Wartość dzieła sztuki w kontekście teorii estetycznych i ekonomicznych. *Zeszyty Naukowe Akademii Ekonomicznej w Krakowie*, *640*, 63–75.

Birdsall, C., Halauniova, A., & van de Kamp, L. (2021). Sensing urban values: Reassessing urban cultures and histories amidst redevelopment agendas. *Space and Culture*, *24*(3), 348–358. https://doi.org/10.1177/12063312211000654

Boeing, G. (2019). Urban spatial order: Street network orientation, configuration, and entropy. *Applied Network Science*, *4*(1), 67. https://doi.org/10.1007/s41109-019-0189-1

Bogunia-Borowska, M. (2015). *Fundamenty dobrego społeczeństwa. Wartości*. Znak.

Boito, C., & Birignani, C. (2009). Restoration in architecture: First dialogue. *Future Anterior*, 6(1), 68–83. https://doi.org/10.1353/fta.0.0026

Bollier, D. (2014). *Think like a commoner. A short introduction to the life of the commons*. New Society Publishers.

Boltanski, L., & Thevenot, L. (2006). *On justification: Economies of worth*. Princeton University Press.

Bowitz, E., & Ibenholt, K. (2009). Economic impacts of cultural heritage – Research and perspectives. *Journal of Cultural Heritage*, *10*(1), 1–8. https://doi.org/10.1016/j.culher.2008.09.002

Brandi, C. (1963). *Teoria del restauro*. Edizioni di Storia e Letteratura.

Brosch, T., & Sander, D. (2016). From values to valuation: An interdisciplinary approach to the study of value. In W. T. Brosch & D. Sander (Eds.), *Handbook of value. Perspectives from economics, neuroscience, philosophy, psychology, and sociology* (pp. 397–404). Oxford University Press.

Brown, B., Perkins, D. D., & Brown, G. (2003). Place attachment in a revitalizing neighborhood: Individual and block levels of analysis. *Journal of Environmental Psychology*, *23*(3), 259–271. https://doi.org/10.1016/S0272-4944(02)00117-2

Camagni, R. (2008). Regional competitiveness: Towards a concept of territorial capital. In *Modelling regional scenarios for the enlarged Europe: European competiveness and global strategies* (pp. 33–47). Springer.https://doi.org/10.1007/978-3-540-74737-6_3

Camagni, R. (2012). Creativity, culture and urban milieux. In W. T. Baycan, L. F. Girard, & P. Nijkamp (Eds.), *Sustainable city and creativity: Promoting creative urban initiatives* (pp. 183–197). Routledge.

Camagni, R. (2019). Territorial capital and regional development: Theoretical insights and appropriate policies. In W. R. Capello & P. Nijkamp (Eds.), *Handbook of regional growth and development theories* (2nd ed., pp. 124–148). Edward Elgar.

Camagni, R., & Capello, R. (2013). Regional competitiveness and territorial capital: A conceptual approach and empirical evidence from the European Union. *Regional Studies*, *47*(9), 1383–1402. https://doi.org/10.1080/00343404.2012.681640

Camagni, R., Capello, R., Cerisola, S., & Panzera, E. (2020). The cultural heritage – Territorial capital nexus: Theory and empirics. *Capitale Culturale*, *11*, 33–59. https://doi.org/10.13138/2039-2362/2547

Capello, R., Caragliu, A., & Nijkamp, P. (2009). *Territorial capital and regional growth: Increasing returns in cognitive knowledge use* (Nr 09-059/3; Tinbergen Institute Discussion Papers). https://www.econstor.eu/bitstream/10419/86826/1/09-059.pdf

Capello, R., & Perucca, G. (2017). Cultural capital and local development nexus: Does the local environment matter? In W. H. Shibusawa, K. Sakurai, T. Mizunoya, & S. Uchida (Eds.), *Socioeconomic environmental policies and evaluations in regional science* (pp. 103–124). Springer. https://doi.org/10.1007/978-981-10-0099-7_6

Carmona, M. (2016). *Public places urban spaces. The dimensions of urban design* (3rd ed.). Routledge.https://doi.org/10.4324/9781315158457

Cerisola, S. (2019a). A new perspective on the cultural heritage–development nexus: The role of creativity. *Journal of Cultural Economics*, *43*(1), 21–56. https://doi.org/10.1007/s10824-018-9328-2

Cerisola, S. (2019b). *Cultural heritage, creativity and economic development*. Edward Elgar.

Christaller, W. (1933). *Die Zentralen Orte in Süddeutschland. Eine ökonomisch-geographische Untersuchung über die Gesetzmässigkeit der Vorbereitung und Entwicklung der Siedlungen mit städtischen Funktionen*. Fischer.

Colletis, G., & Pecqueur, B. (2005). Révélation de ressources spécifiques et coordination située. *Économie et Institutions*, 6–7, 51–74. https://doi.org/10.4000/ei.900

Coyle, D. (2011). *The economics of enough: How to run the economy as if the future matters*. https://doi.org/10.1177/0094306112468721f

Czembrowski, P., Łaszkiewicz, E., & Kronenberg, J. (2016). Bioculturally valuable but not necessarily worth the price: Integrating different dimensions of value of urban green spaces. *Urban Forestry & Urban Greening*, *20*, 89–96. https://doi.org/10.1016/j.ufug.2016.07.010

Dardot, P., & Laval, C. (2019). *Common. On revolution in the 21st century*. Bloomsbury Academic.

Davoudi, S., Evans, N., Governa, F., & Santangelo, M. (2008). Territorial governance in the making. Approaches, methodologies, practices. *Boletín de la Asociación de Geógrafos Españoles*, 46, 33–52.

de la Torre, M. (2002). *Assessing the values of cultural heritage: Research report.* https://www.getty.edu/conservation/publications_resources/pdf_publications/pdf/assessing.pdf

Dewey, J. (1922). *Human nature and conduct: An introduction to social psychology.* Holt.

Dewey, J. (1939). Theory of valuation. *Philosophy of Science*, 6(4), 490–491. https://books.google.pl/books?id=ZUOwAQAACAAJ

Diamond, D. B., & Tolley, G. S. (1982). The economic roles of urban amenities. In W. D. B. Diamond & G. S. Tolley (Eds.), *The economics of urban amenities* (pp. 3–54). Academic Press.

Domański, H. (2017). Stratyfikacja klasowa Polsce: 1982–2015. In W. M. Gdula & M. Sutowski (Eds.), *Klasy w Polsce. Teorie, dyskusje, badania, konteksty* (pp. 15–29). Instytut Studiów Zaawansowanych.

Dvořák, M. (1929). Alois Riegl. In J. Wilde & K. M. Swoboda (Eds.), *Gesammelte Aufsätze zur Kunstgeschichte* (pp. 279–299). R. Piper & Co.

Elden, S. (2010). Land, terrain, territory. *Progress in Human Geography*, *34*(6), 789–806. https://doi.org/10.1177/0309132510362603.

Erikson, R., & Goldthorpe, J. H. (1992). *The constant flux: A study of class mobility in industrial countries.* Oxford University Press.

Erikson, R., Goldthorpe, J. H., & Portocarero, L. (1979). Intergenerational class mobility in three Western European societies: England, France and Sweden. *The British Journal of Sociology*, *30*(4), 415–441. https://doi.org/10.2307/589632

EU. (2011). *Territorial state and perspectives of the European Union.* https://ec.europa.eu/regional_policy/sources/policy/what/territorial-cohesion/territorial_state_and_perspective_2011.pdf

Faro Convention on the Value of Cultural Heritage for Society. (2005). https://www.coe.int/en/web/conventions/full-list/-/conventions/treaty/199?module=treaty-detail&treatynum=199

Fine, B., & Saad-Filho, A. (2018). Marxist economics. In W. L. Fischer, J. Hasell, J. C. Proctor, D. Uwakwe, & Z. Ward-Perkins (Eds.), *Rethinking economics: An introduction to pluralist economics* (pp. 19–32). Routledge.

Fine, S. H. (1992). *Marketing the public sector. Promoting the causes of public & nonprofit agencies.* Transaction Publishers.

Fleischer, A. (2012). A room with a view—A valuation of the Mediterranean sea view. *Tourism Management*, *33*(3), 598–602. https://doi.org/10.1016/j.tourman.2011.06.016

Foster, S. R. (2013). Collective action and the urban commons. *Notre Dame Law Review*, *87*(1), 57–134.

Foster, S. R., & Iaione, C. (2019). Ostrom in the city: Design principles and practices for the urban commons. In W. H. Blake, J. Rosenbloom, & D. H. Cole (Eds.), *Routledge handbook of the study of the commons.* Routledge.

Frodl, W. (1963). *Denkmalbegriffe, Denkmalwerte und ihre Auswirkung auf die Restaurierung.* Institut für Österreichische Kunstforschung.

Frycz, J. (1975). *Restauracja i konserwacja zabytków architektury w Polsce w latach 1795–1918.* Wydawnictwo Naukowe PWN.

Galster, G. C. (2003). Neighbourhood dynamics and housing markets. In W. K. Gibb, D. MacLennan, & A. O'Sullivan (Eds.), *Housing economics and public policy. Essays in honour of Duncan MacLennan* (pp. 153–171). Blackwell Science.

Gehl, J. (2011). *Life between buildings: Using public space* (6th ed.). Island Press.

Georgescu-Roegen, N. (1976). *Energy and economic myths*. Pergamon Press.

Gibson, R., Tanner, C., & Wagner, A. F. (2017). In Brosch, Tobias Sander, David (Eds.), Protected values and economic decision-making. In *Handbook of value: Perspectives from economics, neuroscience, philosophy, psychology and sociology* (pp. 223–241). Oxford University Press.

Glaeser, E. L., Kolko, J., & Saiz, A. (2001). Consumer city. *Journal of Economic Geography*, *1*(1), 27–50. https://doi.org/10.1093/jeg/1.1.27

Gospodini, A. (2004). Urban morphology and place identity in European cities: Built heritage and innovative design. *Journal of Urban Design*, 9(2), 225–248. https://doi.org/10.1080/1357480042000227834

Granovetter, M. S. (1985). Economic action and social structure: The problem of embeddedness. *American Journal of Sociology*, *91*(1), 481–510. https://doi.org/10.1086/228311

Granovetter, M. S. (2017). *Society and economy: Framework and principles*. The Belknap Press of Harvard University Press.

Grazuleviciute-Vileniske, I., Seduikyte, L., Daugelaite, A., & Rudokas, K. (2021). Links between heritage building, historic urban landscape and sustainable development: Systematic approach. *Landscape Architecture and Art*, *17*(17), 30–38. https://doi.org/10.22616/j.landarchart.2020.17.04

Grillitsch, M. (2015). Institutional layers, connectedness and change: Implications for economic evolution in regions. *European Planning Studies*, *23*(10), 2099–2124.

Grzesiuk, K. (2015). *Zakorzenienie społeczne gospodarki. Koncepcja Marka Granovettera*. Wydawnictwo Katolickiego Uniwersytetu Lubelskiego.

Habermas, J. (1987). *The theory of communicative action*. Beacon Press.

Harvey, D. (2012). *Rebel cities. From the right to the city to the urban revolution*. Verso.

Hatuka, T., & Forsyth, L. (2005). Urban design in the context of glocalization and nationalism: Rothschild Boulevards, Tel Aviv. *URBAN DESIGN International*, *10*(2), 69–86. https://doi.org/10.1057/palgrave.udi.9000142

Hausner, J. (2017). Value economics vs. economic value. In W. B. Biga, H. Izdebski, J. Hausner, M. Kudłacz, K. Obłój, W. Paprocki, P. Sztompka, & M. Zmyślony (Eds.), *Open eyes book* (pp. 23–75). Fundacja Gospodarki i Administracji Publicznej.

Hess, C. (2009). Mapping the new commons. *SSRN*.

Hess, M. (2004). 'Spatial' relationships? Towards a reconceptualization of embedded ness. *Progress in Human Geography*, *28*(2), 165–186. https://doi.org/10.1191/0309132504ph479oa

Higgins, B. (2018). Francois Perroux. In W. B. Higgins & D. J. Savoie (Eds.), *Regional economic development. Essays in honour of Francois Perroux* (2nd ed., pp. 31–47). Routledge. (Originally published 1988)

Higgins, E. T. (1997). Beyond pleasure and pain. *American Psychologist*, *52*, 1280–1300. https://doi.org/10.1037//0003-066x.52.12.1280

Hoover, E. M. (1937). *Location theory and the shoe and leather industries*. Harvard University Press. https://doi.org/10.2307/359958

Hudson, J. (2007). Conservation values, climate change and modern architecture. *Journal of Architectural Conservation*, *13*(2), 47–67. https://doi.org/10.1080/13556207.2007.10784995

Iaione, C. (2012). *City as a commons*. http://dlc.dlib.indiana.edu/dlc/bitstream/handle/10535/8604/Iaione_prelversion.pdf

International Charter for the Conservation and Restoration of Monuments and Sites (The Venice Charter 1964). (1965). https://www.icomos.org/charters/venice_e.pdf

Isard, W. (1960). *Methods of regional analysis: An introduction to regional science*. John Wiley & Sons.

Jacobs, J. (1969). *The economy of cities*. Random House.

Jevons, W. S. (1871). *The theory of political economy*. Macmillan.

Jewtuchowicz, A. (2005). *Terytorium i współczesne dylematy jego rozwoju*. Wydawnictwo Uniwersytetu Łódzkiego.

Jost, J. T., Basevich, E., Dickson, E. S., & Noorbaloochi, S. (2016). The place of values in a world of politics: Personality, motivation, and ideology. In W. T. Brosch & D. Sander (Eds.), *Handbook of value. Perspectives from economics, neuroscience, philosophy, psychology, and sociology* (pp. 351–374). Oxford University Press.

Kahneman, D., & Tversky, A. (2000). *Choices, values, and frames*. Cambridge University Press.

Kant, I. (1797). *Die Metaphysik der Sitten* [The metaphysics of morals]. Nicolovius.

Keynes, J. M. (1936). *The general theory of employment, interest and money*. Palgrave Macmillan.

Kincaid, H. (2002). Social sciences. In W. P. Machamer & M. Silberstein (Eds.), *The Blackwell guide to the philosophy of science* (pp. 290–311). Blackwell Publishing.

Kollock, P., & Smith, M. A. (1996). Managing the virtual commons. In W. S. Herring (Ed.), *Computer-mediated communication: Linguistic, social, and cross-cultural perspectives* (pp. 109–128). John Benjamins.

Krawczyk, J. (2013). Dialog z tradycją w konserwatorstwie – Koncepcja zabytkoznawczej analizy wartościującej. *Acta Universitatis Nicolai Copernici. Zabytkoznawstwo i Konserwatorstwo*, *XLIV*, 507–529. https://doi.org/10.12775/AUNC_ZiK.2013.021

Lamprakos, M. (2014). Riegl's 'modern cult of monuments' and the problem of value. *Change Over Time*, *4*(1), 418–435.

Lancaster, K. J. (1966). A new approach to consumer theory. *Journal of Political Economy*, *74*(2), 132–157. https://doi.org/10.1086/259131

Lange, O. (1971). *Political economy*. Pergamon Press.

Launhardt, W. (1882). Die Bestimmung des Zweckmäßigsten Standortes einer gewerblichen Anlage. *Zeitschrift des Vereins Deutschen Ingenieure*, *XXVI*, 105–116.

Lévesque, B. (2008). Contribution de la «nouvelle sociologie économique» à l'anlayse des territoires sous l'angle de l'économie plurielle. In W. G. Massicotte (Ed.), *Sciences du territoire. Perspectives québécoises* (pp. 231–258). Presses de L'Universite du Quebec.

Lipe, W. D. (1984). Value and meaning in cultural resources. In W. H. Cleere (Ed.), *Approaches to the archaeological heritage* (pp. 1–11). Cambridge University Press.

Lösch, A. (1940). *Die räumliche Ordnung der Wirtschaft. Eine Untersuchung über Standort, Wirtschaftsgebiete und internationalem Handel*. Fischer.

Mankiw, N. G. (2009). *Principles of microeconomics* (5th ed.). South-Western Cengage Learning.

March, J. G., & Olsen, J. P. (1989). *Rediscovering Institutions. The organizational basics of politics*. Simon and Schuster.

Marshall, A. (2013). *Principles of economics*. (Originally published 1890). https://doi.org/10.1057/9781137375261

Marx, K. (1906). *Capital. A critique of political economy*. The Modern Library. (Originally published 1867)

Meadows, D. H., Meadows, D. L., Randers, J., & Behrens, W. W. III (1972). *The limits to growth*. Pan.

Menger, C. (1871). *Grundsätze der Volkswirtschaftslehre*. Braumüller.

Mikołajczyk, M., & Raszka, B. (2019). Multidimensional comparative analysis as a tool of spatial order evaluation: A case study from Southwestern Poland. *Polish Journal of Environmental Studies*, *28*(5), 3287–3297. https://doi.org/10.15244/pjoes/91944

Myrdal, G. (1974). *Against the stream. Critical essays on economics*. Palgrave Macmillan.

Myrdal, G. (2017). *The political element in the development of economic theory*. Routledge.

Nijkamp, P., & Ratajczak, W. (2015). The spatial economy: A holistic perspective. In W. P. Nijkamp, A. Rose, & K. Kourtit (Eds.), *Regional science matters. Studies dedicated to Walter Isard* (pp. 15–26). Springer.

North, D. C. (1986). The new institutional economics. *Journal of Institutional and Theoretical Economics*, *142*(1), 230–237.

North, D. C. (1997). *Institutions, institutional change and economic performance*. Cambridge University Press.

Nowakowska, A. (2018). Od regionu do terytorium – reinterpretacja znaczenia przestrzeni w procesach rozwoju gospodarczego. *Gospodarka Narodowa*, *3*, 5–22.

Nowakowska, A., Guz, J., & Łaszkiewicz, E. (2020). How is the multidimensional perception of modern architectural objects associated with their surroundings? An example of Warsaw Ochota urban railway station. In W. Z. Gál, S. Z. Kovács, & B. Páger (Eds.), *Proceedings of the 7th CERS Conference* (pp. 323–336). European Regional Science Association. http://real.mtak.hu/116284/7/cers-kotet-2020.pdf

Nowakowska, A., & Walczak, B. (2016). Dziedzictwo przemysłowe jako kapitał terytorialny. Przykład Łodzi. *Gospodarka w Praktyce i Teorii*, *4*(45), 45–56. https://doi.org/10.18778/1429-3730.45.04

O'Brien, D. (2012). Managing the urban commons: The relative influence of individual and social incentives on the treatment of public space. *Human Nature*, *23*(4), 467–489.

OECD. (2001). *Territorial outlook*. https://doi.org/10.1787/9789264189911-en

O'Sullivan, A. (2007). *Urban economics*. McGraw Hill-Irwin.

Palander, T. (1935). *Beitrdge zur Standortstheorie*. Almqvist and Wiksells.

Perroux, F. (1950). Economic space: Theory and applications. *Quarterly Journal of Economics*, *64*(1), 89–104.

Perroux, F. (1955). Note sur la notion de pôle de croissance. *Économie Appliquée*, *8*, 307–320.

Perry, R. B. (1926). *General theory of value*. Harvard University Press.

Philokyprou, M., & Michael, A. (2021). Environmental sustainability in the conservation of vernacular architecture. The case of rural and urban traditional settlements in Cyprus. *International Journal of Architectural Heritage*, *15*(11), 1741–1763. https://doi.org/10.1080/15583058.2020.1719235

Polanyi, K. (1944). *The great transformation the political and economic origins of our time*. Beacon Press.

Popper, K. (1989). Creative self-criticism in science and in art. *Diogenes*, *37*(145), 36–45. https://doi.org/10.1177/039219218903714503

Poulios, I. (2014). *The past in the present: A living heritage approach*. Ubiquity Press. https://www.jstor.org/stable/j.ctv3s8tpq

Poulot, D. (1997). *Musée, nation, patrimoine, 1789–1815*. Gallimard.

Pratt, A. C. (2004). The cultural economy: A call for spatialized 'production of culture' perspectives. *International Journal of Cultural Studies*, *7*(1), 117–128. https://doi.org/10.1177/1367877904040609

Predöhl, A. (1925). Das Standortsproblem in der Wirtschaftstheorie. *Weltwirtschaftliches Archiv*, *21*, 294–321.

Rabinowicz, W., & Rønnow-Rasmussen, T. (2016). Value taxonomy. In W. T. Brosch & D. Sander (Eds.), *Handbook of value. Perspectives from economics, neuroscience, philosophy, psychology, and sociology* (pp. 23–42). Oxford University Press.

Rasmussen, S. E. (1964). *Experiencing architecture* (2nd ed.). MIT Press.

Recommendation on the Historic Urban Landscape. (2011). http://portal.unesco.org/en/ev.php-URL_ID=48857&URL_DO=DO_TOPIC&URL_SECTION=201.html

Ricardo, D. (2001). *On the principles of political economy and taxation*. Batoche Books. (Originally published 1817)

Riegl, A. (1903). *Der moderne Denkmalkultus: Sein Wesen und seine Entstehung*. Verlage von W. Braumüller.

Ripp, M., & Rodwell, D. (2016). The governance of urban heritage. *The Historic Environment: Policy & Practice*, *7*, 81–108. https://doi.org/10.1080/17567505.2016.1142699

Rokeach, M. (1973). *The nature of human values*. Free Press.

Romanow, Z. (1995). *Teorie wartości i ceny w rozwoju myśli ekonomicznej*. Wydawnictwo Akademii Ekonomicznej w Poznaniu.

Różycka-Czas, R., Czesak, B., & Cegielska, K. (2019). Towards evaluation of environmental spatial order of natural valuable landscapes in suburban areas: Evidence from Poland. *Sustainability*, *11*(23). https://doi.org/10.3390/su11236555

Rudokas, K., Landauskas, M., Gražulevičiūtė-Vilneiškė, I., & Viliūnienė, O. (2019). Valuing the socio-economic benefits of built heritage: Local context and mathematical modeling. *Journal of Cultural Heritage*, *39*, 229–237. https://doi.org/10.1016/j.culher.2019.02.016

Ruijgrok, E. C. M. (2006). The three economic values of cultural heritage: A case study in the Netherlands. *Journal of Cultural Heritage*, *7*(3), 206–213. https://doi.org/10.1016/j.culher.2006.07.002

Samuelson, P. (1955). *Economics* (3rd ed.). McGraw-Hill.

Saquet, M. A. (2016). Territory, geographical indication and territorial development. *DRd - Desenvolvimento Regional em Debate*, 6(1), 4–21. https://doi.org/10.24302/drd.v6i1.1106

Say, J.-B. (1880). *A treatise on political economy, or the production, distribution, and consumption of wealth.* Claxton, Remsen & Haffelfinger. (Originally published 1803)

Schwartz, S. H. (1992). Universals in the content and structure of values: Theoretical advances and empirical tests in 20 countries. *Advances in Experimental Social Psychology.* https://doi.org/10.1016/S0065-2601(08)60281-6

Schwartz, S. H. (2015). Basic individual values: Sources and consequences. In W. T. Brosch & D. Sander (Eds.), *Handbook of value. Perspectives from economics, neuroscience, philosophy, psychology, and sociology* (pp. 63–84). Oxford University Press.

Sedlaček, T. (2009). *Economics of good and evil: The quest for economic meaning from Gilgamesh to wall street.* Oxford University Press.

Sen, A. (1997). *On ethics and economics.* Blackwell Publishing.

Simon, H. A. (1955). A behavioral model of rational choice. *Quarterly Journal of Economics*, 69(1), 99–118. https://doi.org/10.2307/1884852

Smith, A. (1776). *An inquiry into the nature and causes of the wealth of nations.* W. Strahan and T. Cadell.

Snopek, K. (2014). *Bielajewo: Zabytek przyszłości* [Bielajewo: Monument of the future]. Bęc Zmiana.

Soja, E. (1971). *The political organization of space.* Commission on College Geography Resource Paper 8.

Sokołowicz, M. E. (2015). Rozwój terytorialny w świetle dorobku ekonomii instytucjonalnej. Przestrzeń - bliskość - instytucje. In *Rozwój terytorialny w świetle dorobku ekonomii instytucjonalnej. Przestrzeń – Bliskość – Instytucje.* Wydawnictwo Uniwersytetu Łódzkiego. https://doi.org/10.18778/8088-785-4

Sokołowicz, M. E. (2017). The urban commons from the perspective of urban economics. *Studia Regionalne i Lokalne*, 70(4). https://doi.org/10.7366/1509499547002

Sokołowicz, M. E. (2018). Urban amenities - An element of public dimension of housing stock. *Acta Universitatis Lodziensis. Folia Oeconomica*, 6(332), 125–143.

Spahr, R., & Sunderman, M. (1999). Valuation of property surrounding a resort community. *Journal of Real Estate Research*, 17(2), 227–243. https://doi.org/10.1080/10835547.1999.12090974

Spash, C. L., & Asara, V. (2018). Ecological economics. From nature to society. In W. L. Fischer, J. Hasell, J. C. Proctor, D. Uwakwe, Z. Ward-Perkins, & C. Watson (Eds.), *Rethinking economics: An introduction to pluralist economics* (pp. 120–132). Routledge.

Stark, D. (1985). The micropolitics of the firm and the macropolitics of reforms: New forms of workplace bargaining in Hungarian enterprises. In W. P. B. Evans, D. Rueschemeyer, & E. Huber (Eds.), *States vs. markets in the world-system* (pp. 247–273). Sage Publications.

Stark, D. (1989). Coexisting organizational forms in Hungary's emerging mixed economy. In W. V. Nee & D. Stark (Eds.), *Remaking the economic institutions of socialism* (pp. 137–168). Stanford University Press.

Stark, D. (2009). *The sense of dissonance. Accounts of worth in economic life.* Princeton University Press.

Stephenson, J. (2008). The cultural values model: An integrated approach to values in landscapes. *Landscape and Urban Planning*, *84*(2), 127–139. https://doi.org/10.1016/j.landurbplan.2007.07.003

Stern, P. C. (2011). Design principles for global commons: Natural resources and emerging technologies. *International Journal of the Commons*, *5*(2), 213–232. https://doi.org/10.18352/ijc.305

Sulima, R. (2015). Pracowitość. In M. Bogunia-Borowska (Ed.), *Fundamenty dobrego społeczeństwa. Wartości* (pp. 121–145). Znak.

Susser, I., & Tonnelat, S. (2013). Transformative cities: The three urban commons. *Focaal*, *66*, 105–132. https://doi.org/10.3167/fcl.2013.660110

Szczepańska, A., & Pietrzyk, K. (2019). A multidimensional analysis of spatial order in public spaces: A case study of the town Morąg, Poland. *Bulletin of Geography. Socio-Economic Series*, *44*(44), 115–129. https://doi.org/10.2478/bog-2019-0020

Szmelter, I. (2015). Społeczna strategia wielokryterialnego wartościowania w ochronie dziedzictwa kultury. In W. B. Szmygin (Ed.), *Ochrona wartości w procesie adaptacji zabytków* (pp. 265–277). Politechnika Lubelska-Polski Komitet Narodowy ICOMOS. http://bc.pollub.pl/dlibra/docmetadata?id=12729

Taher Tolou Del, M. S., Saleh Sedghpour, B., & Kamali Tabrizi, S. (2020). The semantic conservation of architectural heritage: The missing values. *Heritage Science*, *8*(1), 70. https://doi.org/10.1186/s40494-020-00416-w

The Athens Charter for the Restoration of Historic Monuments. (1931). https://www.icomos.org/en/167-the-athens-charter-for-the-restoration-of-historic-monuments

The Australia ICOMOS Charter for Places of Cultural Significance (The Burra Charter). (2013). https://australia.icomos.org/wp-content/uploads/The-Burra-Charter-2013-Adopted-31.10.2013.pdf

The Editors of Encyclopaedia Britannica. (2015). *Encyclopaedia britannica*. https://www.britannica.com/

The Nara Document on Authenticity. (1994). https://www.icomos.org/charters/nara-e.pdf

Throsby, D. (2001). *Economics and culture*. Cambridge University Press.https://doi.org/10.1017/CBO9781107590106

Throsby, D. (2012). Heritage economics: A conceptual framework. In W. G. Licciardi & R. Amirtahmasebi (Eds.), *The economics of uniqueness* (pp. 45–74). World Bank Group.

Tims, C. (2015). A rough guide to the commons: Who likes it and who doesn't. In *Build the city: Perspectives on commons and culture* (pp. 19–31). European Cultural Foundation - Krytyka Polityczna.

Torre, A. (2015). Territorial development theory. *Géographie, Économie, Société*, *17*(3), 273–288. https://doi.org/10.3166/ges.17.273-288

Torre, A. (2018). Les moteurs du développement territorial. *Revue d'economie Regionale et Urbaine*, *4*, 711–736. https://doi.org/10.3917/reru.184.0711

Torre, A., & Rallet, A. (2005). Proximity and localization. *Regional Studies*, *39*(1), 47–59. https://doi.org/10.1080/0034340052000320842

Tóth, B. I. (2015). Territorial capital: Theory, empirics and critical remarks. *European Planning Studies*, *23*(7), 1327–1344. https://doi.org/10.1080/09654313.2014.928675

Tuan, Y.-F. (1977). *Space and place. The perspective of experience*. University of Minnesota Press.

Tyler, T. R. (2007). *Psychology and the design of legal institutions*. Wolf.

UNESCO. (2013). *Managing cultural world heritage*. https://whc.unesco.org/document/125839

van der Hoeven, A. (2018). Valuing urban heritage through participatory heritage websites: Citizen perceptions of historic urban landscapes. *Space and Culture*, *23*(2), 129–148. https://doi.org/10.1177/1206331218797038

van Laerhoven, F., & Ostrom, E. (2007). Traditions and trends in the study of the commons. *International Journal of the Commons*, *1*(1), 3–28. https://doi.org/10.18352/ijc.76

Vecco, M. (2010). A definition of cultural heritage: From the tangible to the intangible. *Journal of Cultural Heritage*, *11*(3), 321–324. https://doi.org/10.1016/j.culher.2010.01.006

von Thünen, J. H. (1826). *Der isolierte Staat in Beziehung auf Landwirtschaft und Nationalekonomie*. Perthes.

Vorkinn, M., & Riese, H. (2001). Environmental concern in a local context: The significance of place attachment. *Environment and Behavior*, *33*(2), 249–263. https://doi.org/10.1177/00139160121972972

Weber, A. (1909). *Über den Standort der Industrien: Teil 1: Reine Theorie des Standorts*. J. C. B. Mohr.

Wedderburn, A. D. O., Collingwood, W. G., & Ruskin, J. (2016). *Bibliotheca pastorum. Vol. I. The economist of xenophon*. Leopold Classic Library.

Wilkin, J. (2016). *Instytucjonalne i kulturowe podstawy gospodarowania. Humanistyczna perspektywa ekonomii*. Wydawnictwo Naukowe SCHOLAR.

Zipf, G. K. (1949). *Human behavior and the principle of last effort*. Addison-Wesley.

3 Towards a methodology of valuating ambiguous heritage

The review of research on valuating soc-modernist architecture

The UNESCO Recommendation on the Historic Urban Landscape (Recommendation on the Historic Urban Landscape, 2011) advocates treating heritage as being integrated into broader urban contexts. Moreover, it calls for the promotion of practices that allow community participation as a tool to elicit values attributed to diverse stakeholders. It thus contrasts this approach to some extent with practices in which elicitation is an expert-driven process that follows value typology frameworks (Chen & Li, 2021, p. 3). Thus, we are observing a dynamically growing number of heritage valuation studies. The dynamic rise in value research commenced with the seminal work of Throsby (1999, 2001), who developed the "cultural capital" framework to better understand the economics of cultural heritage conservation. To a significant extent, this framework refers to the "total economic value" framework, adapted from environmental economics to cultural heritage.

In the following years, subsequent studies of this type appeared. Choi et al. (2010) investigated the average acceptance for a tax increase to protect Old Parliament House in Canberra, as well as the willingness to pay (WTP) for extra exhibitions in its facilities. Báez and Herrero (2012) conducted a study on the perceived value of the old town in Valdivia (Chile). By asking the contingent valuation question on a price for a hypothetical guided walking tour, they obtained a bid at a specific price for the good. Ferretti et al. (2014) studied the value of former woollen and paper mills and silk factories located in the municipality of Caselle (northern Italy). They found that the level of value attributed to the mills varies among different actors (e.g. public government representatives, architects, architectural historians, developers and owners). They also confirmed the presence of various types of value (historical, artistic, cultural and economic). Langemeyer et al.'s (2015) study of the Montjuïc Park in Barcelona revealed divergent results on its value, and they advocated the need to apply combined, hybrid or integrated assessments of different value dimensions.

DOI: 10.4324/9781003299172-4

Appalardo et al.'s (2020) study revealed that the publicity of the value of dry-stone walls in the terraced vineyards of Mt Etna through their inscription on the UNESCO heritage list had a significant effect on public perceived value (measured by asking WTP in a survey). They called it the effect of appealing to the authorities to evaluate environmental goods. A stated preference non-market valuation approach was also applied to determine the direct use value of the Pearl Harbor National Memorial in Hawaii (Sinclair et al., 2020). Using a contingent valuation method (CVM), visitors to the site were asked about their maximum willingness to accept increased travel and admission costs. The study showed that for such a highly acclaimed attraction, the individual consumer surplus value was $148.43 per day, leading to an immense aggregate annual value of $270 million.

An economic landscape valuation method based on the WTP declared in questionnaires was also conducted in Iran, in the thirteenth-century tomb of Sheikh Zahed (Jahandideh-Kodehi et al., 2021). Among the most important factors affecting this site's value were religion, tourists and nature-friendly motives, as well as relatively easy accessibility. As in previous studies, a factor that significantly increased perceived value was knowledge about this heritage site, supported by programmes to increase public awareness.

In 2002, Garnett (2002) presented a meta-analysis of over 180 publications which revealed that 87% of the impact of science centres and museums concerned personal utilities, while only 9% examined societal value, and 4% focused on the economic value of the institutions. Subsequently, Provins et al. (2008) concentrated solely on studies that directly applied CVM and choice modelling (CM) methods (see Figure 3.11). This meta-analysis considered the broader scope of heritage assets, such as single monuments, groups of buildings and heritage sites. It also listed specific questions that are asked in surveys designed to capture attitudes to monuments and their value perception. This catalogue includes the following queries:

- Travel costs to the heritage sites
- Declared intensification (or reduction) of planned individual journeys to the heritage sites
- The WTP to enter heritage sites (also as an alternative to compulsory entry fees)
- The WTP to establish entrance fees to heritage sites to prevent them from closing
- The WTP to shorten how long it takes to clean a monument
- Choices between various intervention strategies after presenting their costs (e.g. a restoration option vs a preservation option)
- The maximum length of time that visitors were willing to wait until the improvements to a heritage site have been completed
- The level of acceptance of a potential tax increase for the restoration of buildings

- The willingness to accept a voluntary fund for the maintenance of historical buildings
- The level of acceptance of a compulsory hotel fee for tourists that would finance a rehabilitation plan
- Accepting new taxes to cover the investment costs of protecting heritage (e.g. road tunnels or re-routing)

Another meta-analysis of 63 monetary valuation studies of heritage using combinations of the search terms "cultural" and "heritage" with "value" and "valuation" in the Thomson Reuters Web of Science and Google Scholar was carried out by Wright and Eppink (2016). They revealed a steady increase in the number of heritage valuation studies, with contingent valuation methods used most commonly, while choice modelling and hedonic pricing were used less frequently. This meta-analysis referred to a very diverse number of individual cases, which necessarily leads to diversity and the difficulty or impossibility of formulating universal conclusions. Nevertheless, the common denominator was the strong positive impact of conservation practices on the value of historic buildings. The authors also revealed the positive impact of adaptive reuse on the perceived value. Finally, country-grouping effects were significant across the studies, suggesting that preferences and drivers for the conservation of heritage sites are structurally different between countries (Wright & Eppink, 2016, p. 281).

Chen and Li (2021) conducted a systematic review based on research conducted between 2010 and 2020 from both qualitative and quantitative perspectives. Using the SCOPUS database to search for the "heritage" and "value" keywords, they found 58 papers devoted to genuine and explicit studies on the built heritage value, providing new insight into the discipline. Their study also revealed a clear trend over time (a significant multiplication of the number of published studies just between 2010 and 2020) and the continued dominance of the Western world in value research (prominently the UK, Italy and Spain), albeit with an increasing number of studies from China.

Strikingly, many of these studies dealt with built heritage that is strongly recognized nationally and internationally (through the UNESCO list). However, the vast majority dealt with heritage recognized only locally (Chen & Li, 2021, p. 4). An important contribution of this review was the combination of quantitative and qualitative approaches. The former revealed the diversity of sources of heritage values, with a clear dominance of historical, followed by architectural factors and the observation that values revolve around identity and memory. In turn, the qualitative research showed that heritage experts asked to define values have a different understanding of values than local communities and local activists. It clearly indicates that heritage values are locally embedded, "as intertwined with the local ethnic, cultural, religion characteristics and collective memories"

(Chen & Li, 2021, p. 6). They concluded that research on heritage value is moving away from a static approach (based on genuine authenticity) to the so-called dynamic authenticity, understood as a differentiated perception, action, experience and social practice, dependent on time and place (see also L. Gibson & Pendlebury, 2009, pp. 8–10). It means seeking a holistic approach to perception and identifying value, and replacing rigid professional typologies of value with a set of interlocking themes, for example, the authors' proposed surroundings, architectural/urban/landscape, affiliation, emotional, and economic (Chen & Li, 2021, p. 10).

The above studies are increasingly based on a combination of methods and scientific approaches. Usually, integrated monetary and non-monetary valuation approaches provide a more comprehensive picture as they capture different and often complementary values attached to heritage. Also, to obtain different perspectives on heritage value, sophisticated methods based on both quantitative and qualitative attributes, involving experts from various fields, are applied. However, a review of the research allows for an attempt to group the drivers responsible for influencing the perception of heritage values. These factors – according to the order and frequency of appearance in the studies – include the following:

1. Income – the higher the respondents' income, the greater their declared WTP to protect heritage
2. Knowledge and information about heritage sites – heritage education increases its perceived value by the individuals and by the public
3. Heterogeneity of heritage – the growing complexity of heritage sites leads to a more ambiguous determination of its value
4. Timing – the heritage age, the moment of valuation, as well as discounting mechanism significantly affect valuation procedures
5. Accessibility of heritage sites – facilities that are easier to reach and easier to discover are perceived as more valuable
6. Conservation level and flexibility in terms of adapting buildings to new functions – the adaptive reuse of heritage, in particular, positively affects economic and cultural values
7. Physical context – the spatial order and aesthetics of the surrounding environment, population density, and the presence or absence of economic activities in the vicinity strongly affect the perceived value
8. Institutional context – the drivers of heritage value vary between countries, regions and cities because of legal regulations (e.g. the structure of property rights) and different sensitivities to non-use value among different communities

Despite the growing number of empirical studies concerning heritage valuation and assessment, there are still too few to generalize the research results. The same applies to comparing the results of these studies from the perspective of monument types and their geographical location.

For example, studies from the UK and, to a lesser degree, from other Western European countries dominate, while studies from Central and Eastern Europe (CEE) are visibly lacking. For example, in Poland, these methods have been applied to some regionally recognisable tourist attractions (Nowacki, 2009) and the cellars of Warsaw's Saski Palace (Śleszyński & Wiewiórski, 2011). Additionally, Merciu et al.'s (2021) recent study devoted to estimating the value of Bucharest's historic centre is worth mentioning. They attempted to value the historical centre using the travel cost method. Their study also pointed out the multifactorial nature of value. Distance and cost of accessing the heritage were essential but not the only factors that influence value. Satisfaction with the tourist experience and the tourists' income and motivations were also significant.

Also, there are almost no studies devoted to the value of modernist objects of the socialist era of concrete construction (Sokołowicz & Przygodzki, 2020, p. 1). Consequently, expanding the scale and scope of empirical studies on heritage valuation is highly desirable for further comparisons. As far as modernist architecture is concerned, it is still widely criticized for its mechanistic treatment of man and his lifestyle (Flint, 2018; Levine, 2015). This is also the case with modern architecture in post-communist countries, where highly negative emotions and associations with the previous socio-economic system are observable. In CEE countries, modernist architecture is still strongly associated with the communist regime. For this reason, it can be treated as a dissonant heritage. The social and economic changes that followed the collapse of the regime first led to a strong contestation of the legacy of the second half of the twentieth century in this part of Europe.

However, the opposite phenomenon then emerged, called "a fashion for the neo-vernacular" (Murzyn, 2008, p. 323). This meant that attempts were made to expose the earlier material legacy from before World War II, which the authorities of communist Poland, the Czech Republic, Hungary or Slovakia, as well as the former republics of the USSR (Ukraine, Lithuania, Latvia and Estonia), had wanted to forget. If post-socialist dissonant heritage was exhibited, it was done in the architectural objects of the period, but in the context of criticizing the regime that created them (cf. the Stasi Museum and Checkpoint Charlie in Berlin, or the House of Terror Museum in Budapest, among others). Yet another wave of activities, such as the growing popularity of Nowa Huta (New Steel Mill) quarter in Krakow as a tourist attraction, along with the organization of tours around it "in the traces of ordinary life in a socialist country," moved the vector in a slightly different direction (Murzyn, 2008).

Research on modernist architecture and its value has so far been carried out mainly in the USA (Benton-Short, 2006; Dwyer, 2002), the United Kingdom and France (Fée et al., 2020; While, 2006). Among the studies on the value of modernist architecture, one may also include the Headquarters Building of the Turkish Republic's 17th Regional Directorate of Highways

Complex in Istanbul (Durusoy Özmen & Omay Polat, 2021). The study of this unit – a spatial landmark and a remarkable example of modernism in Turkey's capital city – pointed to the ambiguity of the perceived value. It highlighted the variation of values for different stakeholders and the changeability of their perceptions. The study is also a case study without monetary valuation applied and was addressed to professionals and not public stakeholders.

In CEE, the discussion of heritage that is not difficult but worth remembering (e.g. because it is related to the history of the Holocaust) and ambiguous – where the question of its preservation itself comes to the fore – is relatively recent. The work of Merta-Staszczak (2018) is an example of a comprehensive study on the controversial "post-German" legacy in Lower Silesia in Poland. Ciarkowski (2016) wrote about the historical narrative of the Litzmannstadt Ghetto – on one hand, a memorial to the Holocaust, but on the other hand, a deprived district of Lodz. Concerning modernist architecture specifically, Ciarkowski also signalled a growing awareness of the potential of communist Poland's architecture as cultural heritage (Ciarkowski, 2017d) and zoomed in on the spa architecture of the period in a similar context (Ciarkowski, 2017b).

An interesting study of Estonian collective farm administrative buildings was conducted by Ingerpuu (2018). "These prosaic buildings, which used to play important role in the Soviet-time rural life, have become a dissonant heritage today, although their controversial nature lies in the complicated contemporary environment they fell into after the collapse of the socialist regime, rather than in the fact that they were constructed for ideological purposes" (Ingerpuu, 2018, p. 954). However, that study was based on a non-strict quality method, using open interviews with purposively selected respondents. Numerical valuation methods were not used here either, treating the value of the heritage as difficult to measure and referring mainly to the decision on whether or not it makes sense to enter the described objects in the state's register of monuments.

Polish studies concerning heritage are also rare. One of the latest studies revealed that 92% of Poles aged over 55 consider heritage to have an important social role. However, on the other hand, 22% of people aged 65 claim it is not worth investing public money to protect it (in the age groups 18–24 and 35–44, these shares were lower – 14% and 15%, respectively) (NID, 2013). That study made no effort to monetize the perceived heritage value.

Ochkovskaya and Gerasimenko (2018) also studied a few architectural sites erected in Warsaw during socialist times: the Palace of Culture and Science, the SMYK Toy Store, the building of the Ministry of Agriculture and Rural Development and the former headquarters of the Polish Communist Party. Their study revealed that buildings connected to the era of the Polish People's Republic might attract different groups interested in this historical period and architecture. Apart from being potential tourist attractions, these buildings are being re-evaluated and restored to become integrated into the urban environment and more "pleasing" for the local inhabitants. However, today, people tend to adopt a pragmatic attitude to the former landscapes of socialism, and they mainly associate socialist buildings and public spaces with their contemporary uses. Ochkovskaya and Gerasimenko's study also did not employ valuation methods; it asked for opinions without asking the respondents for an expression of the monetary value.

Finally, Sokołowicz and Przygodzki (2020), who proposed a three-stage valuation procedure to capture the value of the twentieth-century Post-Socialist Train Stations in Warsaw, presented the results of a pilot study of the value perception of a small Warszawa Ochota modernist object. Constructed in the 1960s as a part of the Polish capital's commuting system, this station serves as part of one of the biggest urban transportation nodes in Poland. Its historical value as an architectural object seems to be of secondary interest, although more and more experts and architecture enthusiasts appreciate its modernist legacy. Conducting the first stage of a study – a public survey with CVM – Sokołowicz and Przygodzki revealed that this kind of post-socialist architecture is not perceived as heritage by the wider public, and its non-use value dominates over its use value. They also reported that monetary valuation methods are more relevant for commercial forms of use. Interestingly, their survey of 222 respondents revealed that knowledge and type of use affect the heritage value more than the population's age. The latter proved not to be statistically significant as an element affecting value perception. For the above reasons, the WTP approach to heritage is valuable from a cognitive point of view but requires further development. In other words, surveying should be, at most, the first step and thus a starting point for further research involving experts in subsequent, more qualitative steps of the study.

A small number of studies on post-socialist modernist architecture have resulted in the unambiguous assessment and acceptance of modernist architectural heritage. On the other hand, despite the original foundations and genesis of modernism, which by definition was to focus on universality and functionality rather than respect for history, "ill born" modernist architectural objects – as one Polish journalist called them (Springer, 2011) – find more and more advocates (Łukasik, 2014).

Whole towns and cities are already becoming objects of appreciation. An interesting example is Chandigarh in India, a thoroughly modernist city designed by Le Corbusier (Chalana, 2015; Chalana & Spragu, 2013; Ghosh, 2016). The review of the state-of-the-art confirms that trying to capture the value of the heritage of post-socialist architecture is not an easy task. While an increasing number of heritage management specialists and scholars regard modernist architecture as an important legacy, a significant group of non-specialists consider such buildings to be, at best, utilitarian objects. However, new valuation methods make it possible to determine their hypothetical value in monetary terms.

In a situation of value ambiguity, there is a desire to "measure the unmeasurable," that is, to estimate both use and non-use value, for the needs of decision-makers or to convince public stakeholders to undertake specific actions. It requires interdisciplinarity and a combination of different approaches. In particular, the achievements of economic and social sciences should be combined with heritage studies for this purpose (Fredheim & Khalaf, 2016, p. 470), especially since it is difficult for heritage stakeholders and local, regional and national authorities to make clear decisions about what to protect first and what the appropriate level of spending on heritage should be (Ready & Navrud, 2002). This argument is also becoming more important given the research being conducted, which increasingly reveals that non-experts do not recognize built heritage values according to the typology set created by experts. For example, research to provide insights into the perceived landscape based on data from photos posted on Flickr shows significant differences between experts' and users' perspectives (Ginzarly et al., 2019b). As a result, a stakeholder-oriented approach to public value has become a central focus of attention. An example of such a study is the attempt to capture the values of Austrian museums (Grüb & Martin, 2020). An online survey confirmed that citizens perceive museums as valuable from the individual, societal and economic perspectives. The study also revealed that citizens are less often passive recipients (consumers) of cultural institutions' activities; increasingly, they are active stakeholders, and their perception of value significantly determines the public value of cultural heritage.

However, this does not obviate the awareness that from an axiological point of view, values have a hierarchy – from the lowest placed hedonic values, through utilitarian and vital values, to cultural, spiritual and religious values (Gadacz, 2010, p. 21). Thus, the deliberately simplified division of heritage values into use and non-use is helpful for analysis and research. However, at the stage of interpreting the valorization results obtained, an awareness of its simplifying character is crucial.

Ambiguous heritage and architecture

Heritage is important – for societies but also for economies. From both the axiological and utilitarian points of view, it has value. However, heritage value differs significantly due to the heterogeneity of peoples' perceptions and values but also due to the heterogeneity of the heritage itself. Heritage can be seen as an aggregation of myths, values and inheritances determined and defined by the needs of societies in the present (McDowell, 2008, p. 38). Individuals, groups or communities all tend to remember different aspects of the past. So, an evolution of definitions in heritage can be noticed: from a traditional view, which focuses on material aspects and basic social needs, towards the inclusion of immaterial aspects, such as intangible heritage and well-being (Guzmán et al., 2017, p. 193). The interpretation of heritage value is predetermined by the social, economic, political and/or local context, and this context is inseparable from culture. Therefore, in heritage economics, the notion of cultural capital appears, defined as an asset that embodies, stores or provides cultural value in addition to whatever economic value it may possess. At the same time, cultural value is interpreted as a combination of aesthetic, spiritual, social, historical, symbolic and authentic circumstances (Throsby, 2001, pp. 84–85).

Cultural heritage refers to single monuments, such as architectural works, sculptures, and paintings, as well as groups of buildings and sites, considering, for example, areas that include archaeological sites (*Convention Concerning the Protection of the World Cultural and Natural Heritage*, 1972, article 1). However, this initial definition has been enlarged, and nowadays, cultural heritage also includes territorial systems, landscapes, itineraries and intangible legacy (Ferretti et al., 2014, p. 645). From an economic point of view, heritage can be perceived as a common good that is unique, cannot be reproduced and is maintained over time (Hutter & Rizzo, 1997; Throsby, 1999). It can also be defined as "a contemporary product shaped from history" (Tunbridge & Ashworth, 1996, p. 20). As Harvey (2001) points out, this concise definition conveys that heritage is subjective and filtered with reference to the present, whenever that "present" actually is. It is a value-laden concept, related to commodification, but intrinsically reflective of a relationship with the past; however, that "past" is perceived and defined (Harvey, 2001, p. 327). This definition stresses the important role of society in shaping the perception of heritage. In a nutshell, the value of heritage depends heavily on what people treat as heritage. Dalmas et al. (2015) define urban heritage as being inseparable from its multidimensional nature, including four closely interlinked elements:

1. The economic dimension, which incorporates physical assets represented by economic infrastructure (transport), networks, buildings and collective equipment
2. The social dimension, which incorporates the main characteristics (qualifications and conditions of social life) of the "human capital" of the resident population, which designates all physical and intellectual aptitudes of labour that are conducive to economic production
3. The environmental dimension comprises natural capital, in the form of parks, landscapes and water as constituent elements of urban heritage
4. The cultural dimension, which consists of the historic buildings and cultural events in the territory

In this definition, different combinations of these four dimensions characterize the nature of each territory's urban heritage, and all of these elements are interdependent. This interdependence is an essential characteristic of urban heritage that must be taken into consideration in the economic evaluation of any heritage-related activity and decision

(Dalmas et al., 2015, pp. 682–683). However, the perception of heritage is also influenced by the views of others. The value – especially its intrinsic value – is determined by the strength of the beliefs of fellow citizens, which certainly vary over time. Thus, "heritage is often defined by a dominant group within a particular society which, in many cases, tends to be national governments" (McDowell, 2008, p. 44). "Heritage is political and often territorial, serving certain agencies and groups through communicating narratives of inclusion and exclusion, continuity and instability" (McDowell, 2008, p. 49). "[It] is a dynamic and negotiable process, subject to contestation and malleable to the needs of societies and cultures in the present" (McDowell, 2008, p. 50). In other words, notions of power are central to the construction of heritage, and consequently identity, giving weight to the argument that heritage "is not given; it is made" (Brett, 1996; Harvey, 2001, p. 336). "Those who wield the greatest power, therefore, can influence, dictate or define what is remembered and consequently what is forgotten" (McDowell, 2008, p. 444).

As a result, the process of using heritage objects (e.g. historical buildings) can be seen as a complex decision problem because of the presence of different objectives to be pursued, the existence of many types of values (historical, artistic, cultural, economic, etc.), the presence of different stakeholders (public government representatives, architects, architectural historians, developers and owners) and the reality of both private and public nature of heritage goods (Ferretti et al., 2014, p. 644). This issue is gaining significance, especially in the urban environment, where the economic, social and spatial complexity, and the versatility of the surrounding area in which heritage objects are located, are particularly noticeable. As Mitchell (2003) noticed, the landscape itself is an active agent in constituting heritage perception and valuation. Therefore, the urbanistic view on heritage implies an integral approach, which includes many different perspectives on heritage: the spatial and urban planning perspective, the landscape perspective, the architectural perspective, the cultural and historical perspective, the technical and infrastructural perspective, the legal perspective, the economic perspective and the ecological perspective (Šćitaroci, 2019, p. x).

So, as Babić et al. (2019, p. 1) noted, "Heritage management tends towards ensuring tangible (as well as intangible, or more precisely indirect) benefits for local communities and in this way towards the development of society in general. Critical heritage studies over the last few years have significantly influenced the perception of heritage, and consequently the essence of heritage management and heritage interpretation. Stress on the participative and inclusive approach has become crucial, where multi/polyvocality is (almost) self-evident." Also, "heritage literacy stands for the idea that every community has the undisputed right to shape and define its heritage and to manage it in the way that the (local) community understands and recognizes that it will best shape its progress and development as well as contribute to the common good. Reaching a level of heritage literacy is demanding but necessary if we want to democratize heritage and to put heritage practically on a pedestal concerning human rights" (Babić et al., 2019, p. 8).

According to Fredheim and Khalaf (2016, p. 470), interactions between heritage professionals and cultural economists have highlighted that not only do they describe and measure the value of heritage differently but also what they mean by the word "value" is different. While economists suggest that value is generated through interacting with heritage, as the benefits generated by use, most heritage professionals speak of heritage having value also when it is not in use.

Heritage can also be perceived as a part of the so-called cultural ecosystem services (TEEB, 2011). The latter is understood as the contribution of the living environment to the wider human well-being, which consists of

1. provisioning services (providing, e.g. food, raw materials, medicinal resources),
2. regulating services (e.g. wastewater treatment, carbon sequestration, biological control, moderation of extreme events),
3. supporting services (ensuring habitat for species, genetic diversity), and last but not least, and
4. cultural services.

Therefore, ecosystem services include elements of human culture that provide opportunities for recreation, aesthetic appreciation and inspiration, spiritual experiences and sense of place, tourism and consequently social cohesion. These cultural ecosystem services enrich human life with meanings and emotions, and they help enhance the physical and mental health of city inhabitants Langemeyer et al. (2015, p. 178).

Over time, human value systems, individual and social needs, as well as social and economic systems and power relationships change, and this has an impact on the relationship between tangible and intangible heritage. Particularly since the birth of modernism, in which culture and economic processes have been massified, and the complexity of societies and their internal diversity have grown significantly, it is increasingly difficult to reach a consensus as to what heritage is considered valuable and worth preserving for future generations. Some elements of heritage are becoming ambiguous or even dissonant. In these cases, controversy and public discussion about the heritage emerge.

The number of studies on dissonant and contested heritage has significantly increased in recent years (Rampley, 2012; Silverman, 2011). The pioneers of the conceptualization of controversies in heritage studies are Tunbridge and Ashworth (1996), who claim it is intrinsic to the nature of all heritage. Dissonance arising around some heritage sites is a wider social process that should not be reduced to site-specific management (Smith, 2008), as today's world is "loaded with conflicts and intolerance but is simultaneously undergoing constant change and evolution" (Ingerpuu, 2018, p. 959).

Consideration of the nature of such ambiguous heritage is also associated with the concept of "unwanted heritage" (MacDonald, 2009), used primarily in the studies of post-war, post-conflict and post-catastrophe societies, mostly in the context of tourism management. These studies refer to the ideological context of architecture raised under the dictatorship of the Nazis, communists (Light, 2000; Logan & Reeves, 2009) or fascists (Ciarkowski, 2017a). Disagreement arises mainly over the question of whether such undesired and painful objects and sites should be demolished or, if preserved, how they should be presented and exhibited (Ingerpuu, 2018, p. 959).

However, undesired heritage need not refer only to the darkest episodes of the past but also to all the legacy left behind by aggressors or invaders (Ingerpuu, 2018, p. 960). To some extent, this is the case of socialist realism architecture, imposed in the countries of CEE, which in the middle of the twentieth century were dominated politically and economically by the Union of Soviet Socialist Republics. Although such architecture is increasingly viewed as interesting and somewhat rehabilitated from the cultural heritage point of view by specialists in architecture, urban planning and art theory, in general, it is still not fully accepted by "ordinary" people. "Modernist buildings, with undecorated and modest facades, and often with robust and box-like characters, are not (yet?) perceived as beautiful or aesthetically pleasing by many people" (Ingerpuu, 2018, p. 962). It also does not help see such architecture as valuable, as it was very often made with significant cost-cutting and substandard materials, and today it functions in a very bad technical and aesthetic condition.

This kind of legacy, therefore, originates both in modernization as a process and in modernism as a social phenomenon. Modernity interpreted in such a way means as follows: (1) autonomy of thought (as beliefs and ways of doing things as they were done before are massively questioned), (2) industrialization and (3) a general expectation of progress (Despland, 1969, pp. 167–168). The first feature that constitutes modernity refers primarily to the massive participation of citizens in public life, including general education. Industrialization means mechanizing and standardizing many aspects of human activity, which includes not only constructing both representative and utilitarian architecture but also standardizing culture and art, at least to some extent (which become mass and popular).

The last element that constitutes modernism seems to be the most vulnerable today. Individuals' independence and the democratization of access to knowledge and information are growing in times called postmodernism, and industrialization, although dominated by services, is still crucial for building prosperity (after all, there is no software without innovative hardware). However, the belief in continuous progress is increasingly being challenged. That is why a significant dissonance between supporters of progressive and conservative thought (which results in different attitudes towards heritage) is becoming increasingly evident. It is partly because modernity had the ambition to offer humankind a better life and a better world from a moral point of view. Thus, it seems that from the very beginning, modernity has been characterized by a sharp division between opponents and supporters of this direction of social change. "Some [used] the adjective 'modern' to describe everything good under the sun that they would like to see realised in the country. On the other hand, 'modern' [meant] for others everything new and evil of which they disapprove. (...) [Beside] the presence of the two groups, is the fact that apparently few people see modernity as an ambiguous affair; most are either for it or against it in a global undifferentiated way" (Despland, 1969, p. 167).

Ultimately, modernity's achievements are ambiguous, as the promise of modernity was "not at all fulfilled in the contemporary world" (Despland, 1969, p. 173). Nor did the achievements of various "modernisms" in reality lead only to good. Often yes, but sometimes not. Accordingly, the heritage of modernism is often considered valuable but sometimes not. It depends on the far-reaching diversity of value systems between different continents, countries and regions. In other words, just as institutional bases of the economy are culturally diverse (Amable, 2003; Hofstede, 1997), so too are the perception of values – especially those perceived ambiguously or contradictorily

It is quite easy to appreciate a heritage that is commonly regarded as valuable, and protecting it is then usually a function of the availability of financial resources. But what if heritage elements are poorly recognized? Then, the question arises: Is the legacy a legacy if it is ambiguously assessed and not universally accepted? We should bear in mind that legacy does not always have to be old. It is not always monumental. It is often a testament to a history that is judged not unequivocally. A legacy is often overlooked because of gaps in collective memory or simply its poor physical condition. It is often not appreciated until years have passed, as are those affected by a difficult history.

In effect, valuating ambiguous architecture concerns relatively new premises, and it currently concerns the modernist legacy. In Europe, in particular, where the twentieth century was exceptionally turbulent, components of heritage are assessed unequivocally, and in European culture, more ancient monuments is valued much more than the latest. European modernism is also controversially assessed for its machine-like treatment of man and his life (cf. the concept of a living machine used by Le Corbusier (1923) to describe modern residential buildings). Moreover, it should be borne in mind that modernism flourished when both Nazi and communist regimes dominated. Hence, many architectural objects of that period are directly or indirectly associated with those times, even if they were not directly related to such ideologies. Additionally, many modernist buildings, already recognized as unique and significant by specialists, serve as residential, transport, recreational or ordinary (i.e. not representative) public buildings, such as basic medical health clinics, libraries, community centres or public transport stops. Finally, their uniqueness is obscured not only by their associations with history and mundane use but also by the "ordinary" surroundings.

Therefore, we admire such buildings as the Centennial Hall and Market Hall in Wroclaw, the Spodek Hall in Katowice (Poland), the A1 and A2 Halls of the Brno Exhibition Center and the Ještěd Hotel in Liberec (Czech Republic), the SNP Museum in Banská Bystrica (Slovakia), the Sports Hall in Bacau (Romania) or the Bauhaus Archives (Design Museum) in Berlin (Germany), without losing our confidence in their value.[1] However, it is more difficult to find and determine the value for objects that are less significant both in terms of physical scale and meaning for the collective imagination, including everyday use spaces.[2] A particular challenge is to determine the proportion between use and non-use value. The first refers to the possibility of generating income (direct use value), or aesthetics and quality of life affecting the possibility of generating it or providing inspiration for creative processes (indirect use value). The other stresses the intangible and symbolic facets of value (the so-called existence value), historical legacy (bequest value) and the possibility of deriving use values in the future (option value) (Murzyn-Kupisz, 2015, p. 157; The Allen Consulting Group, 2005, p. 5).

When the use value of heritage exceeds its non-use value, the economic pressure can lead to its over-exploitation and destruction, although it generates resources for its maintenance. When use value is perceived by contemporaries as lower than non-use value, heritage is perceived as a public or common good, and its value is mainly perceived as a bequest and non-tangible. In this case, most of society feels the need to protect heritage for future generations due to its historical legacy and the willingness to keep it for future generations (Figure 3.9).

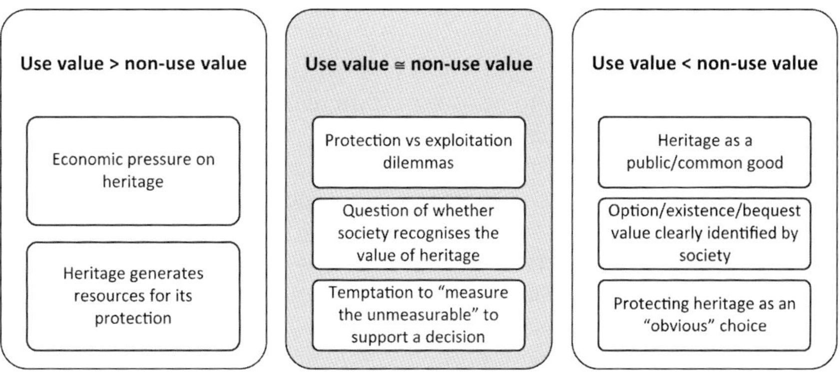

Figure 3.9 Use value vs non-use value – Dilemmas

Source: Own study.

The biggest challenge occurs when the difference between the use and non-use value of heritage is minor or difficult to identify. In this case, dilemmas concern whether heritage should be protected with no intervention, leading to it being exploited economically, or if it should be transformed significantly to contemporary needs. Also, there is a reflection on whether something that is not perceived as valuable today may become valuable from the perspective of the next several decades. For these reasons, there is a temptation to "measure the unmeasurable." Thus, there is a readiness to monetize (e.g. for decision-makers, needs or to convince the public) both the use and non-use heritage value, which, in turn, affects political and economic decisions in the real world.

While searching for appropriate heritage valuation methods, building a consensus and cognitive bridges between the different specialists that deal with these issues is more than desirable. According to Fredheim and Khalaf (2016, p. 470), interactions between heritage professionals and cultural economists have highlighted that not only do they describe and measure the value of heritage differently but also what they mean by the word "value" is different. While economists suggest that value is generated through interacting with heritage (i.e. as the benefits generated by use), most heritage professionals speak of heritage having value also when it is not in use. However, there is a lack of consensus among the latter on the valuation methodologies, and the criteria used for this purpose are still subjective and intuitive. This opens up the opportunity to structure the considerations on the methodology of heritage valuation.

The classification of heritage valuation methods

The most widely used approach to express value in monetary terms is economic. It results from adopting restrictive assumptions about values, and, in practice, it is primarily concerned with the real estate market. Any good or service to be valuated as an asset must possess at least four economic features (Blackledge, 2009, p. 5):

1. Utility – the possibility to be used for different purposes; the greater the perceived utility, the greater the value
2. Scarcity, which is greater when current and potential needs are larger
3. Demand, which has to be effective so that there are potential buyers or users of the asset
4. Transferability – ownership or the possibility of using it must be able to be transferred in technical and legal terms

The complexity of the issue of economic valuation makes a profession od chartered surveyors highly institutionalized (formalized). In practice, the principles of such valuation are the subject of deliberation among specialists, and they are agreed upon in the form of universally applicable standards. The most well-known and longest functioning association of such specialists in Europe – the Royal Institution of Chartered Surveyors – has been establishing valuation standards for over 150 years to ensure consistency and the application of "best practices" within the profession (RICS, 2015, 2019). Similar standards and philosophy of real estate valuation have been adopted in other market economies and, since the 1990s, also in CEE (Kucharska-Stasiak, 2016a, 2016b; PFSRM, 2011). According to the International Valuation Standards, the basis of a valuation typically refers to the following categories (Parker, 2016, p. 59):

1. The valuation should, in principle, lead to the most probable price that would be achieved in a hypothetical exchange in a market. This is a basic category for professional property valuators, whose primary occupation is based on the assumption that the first step is to search for the *market value*. In practice, it means that as long as there is a market (i.e. a willingness and opportunity to exchange) for a certain type of resource, it is necessary to search for value based on observing previous exchange behaviours.
2. If it is not possible to search for market value (i.e. there is no transaction data or the assets are not subject to this type of exchange), one should search for a more specific type of value. It can be specific to a given person or entity and indicates the benefits that a person or an entity enjoys from owning an asset. Based on this category, professionals determine the *investment value*. This category can be broadly interpreted, and according to the International Valuation Standards, it may also refer to the *special value*. This is an amount that reflects particular attributes of an asset, that is, that are valuable only to the special user (e.g. of historic properties) and not necessarily available to other buyers (Parker, 2016, p. 70).
3. The last category refers to the price that would be reasonably agreed between two specific parties for the exchange of an asset, even if the asset is not necessarily exposed in the market. This approach is a prerequisite for identifying the proper value, based on the conviction that the parties are not acting under pressure, either reciprocal or time based. This condition is called *fair value*.

Based on the above categories, one can differentiate five principal approaches to property valuation: comparative, investment, profit, residual and contractor's (cost) methods (Scarrett, 2008). The first is based on comparisons derived from current market evidence to "find value" directly (e.g. based on prices of properties, rent or lease levels, etc.). The investment method compares evidence of previous developments for similar purposes, comparing the investment expenditures with expected income flows within the assumed time frame to find rates of return and thus capital value.

The profits method can be used if the previous two methods cannot be used. It is primarily utilized when a property is used for business purposes, and the receipts and expenditure accounts can be analysed to find the rental value. The residual method is used to analyse development or redevelopment proposals to discover whether they are viable and to determine the price that can be paid to acquire the site or existing premises. Elements of this method, with some reservations (primarily related to a purpose other than pure economic profit), may be used in valuating heritage properties to consider the profitability of a special purpose investment (e.g. using parts of historic buildings for services that will be subject to at least a partial charge in the form of entrance tickets). The cost method is often considered the "method of last resort" and used when none of the above approaches can be utilized or to supplement a valuation from one of the other methods. Such value is based on the costs of constructing the building on the site plus the value of non-developed land on which it is located (Blackledge, 2009, p. 134).

Hence, as basic property valuation methods, the comparable and investment methods are considered appropriate where transactional evidence of sales and lettings is readily available (Scarrett, 2008, p. 115). However, according to the International Valuation Standards, a "fundamental consideration in the application of the cost approach is whether that asset being valued would be recreated exactly as it exists at the date of valuation or replaced by a modern version which offers the same usefulness as a building or something in between – being the concepts of reproduction, replacement, modern equivalent asset and utility which underpin the application of the cost approach (…)" (Parker, 2016, p. 201).

In practice, it is often necessary to provide a valuation of undeveloped land or land with obsolescent or unwanted buildings. In such cases, new development or redevelopment methods are taken into account, including the possibilities of reproduction or replacement. It occurs particularly when assets are classified for historic preservation in their entirety or their design and features are recognized by owners and users as a source of additional benefit or utility (e.g. iconic buildings) (Parker, 2016, p. 201). In such a situation, appraisal very often combines investment, residual and cost methods, and the following valuation scenarios are then taken into account (Parker, 2016, p. 201):

- Calculating a reproduction cost, that is, the current cost of recreating a replica of the asset
- Calculating a replacement cost, that is, the current cost of a similar asset that offers equivalent utility
- Consideration of the valuation of a modern equivalent asset – an asset that provides a similar function and equivalent utility to the asset being valued, but which is of a current design and constructed or made using current materials and techniques
- Utility – an expression of the degree of an asset's usefulness

In each of the above scenarios and valuation procedures (including for historical sites), both the intrinsic features of the buildings themselves and the surroundings in which they operate are of key importance. The valuation itself should take account of the age, type, size, aspect, amenities, fixtures and features of the property, the tenure of the legal interest, and other significant environmental factors within the locality (Wyatt, 2007, p. 104). The surroundings is thus broadly understood not only in the physical, legal and economic sense but also in the institutional or cultural meaning (e.g. the general public's perception of the asset's value).

In the case of attempts to capture the value of heritage, more and more studies combine various methods and approaches. They increasingly combine the monetary and non-monetary valuation methods to provide a more comprehensive picture and secure different and often complementary values attached to heritage. Sophisticated methods based on both quantitative and qualitative attributes, involving experts from various fields, are applied to obtain different perspectives on heritage value (Sokołowicz & Przygodzki, 2020). In this context, cultural heritage assessment methods very often refer directly to natural capital methods, elaborated and tested within the framework of ecological economics. The sustainability issue remains important, as cultural capital, like the natural environment, should be part of the wealth for today's and future generations. Thus, in this context, there is a similarity between the notions of "heritage" and "capital."

There are two competing theories about sustainability. One refers to the weak sustainability approach, and the other to the strong sustainability approach (Pearce & Atkinson, 1993). In terms of strong sustainability, to a certain extent, the authenticity value makes any loss irreversible (Dalmas et al., 2015, p. 683). Any heritage losses cannot be replaced by substitutes. For example, even if a destroyed monument is rebuilt, the value of its legacy will never be the same again, the materials used for its reconstructions will never perfectly replicate the genuine ones, and so on. Thus, "strong sustainability" proposes protecting heritage in its fully authentic state, while the possibilities of monetizing the cultural, social and environmental dimensions, as well as the substitutions between the different dimensions, will be limited (Dalmas et al., 2015, p. 683).

However, bearing in mind that heritage is the subject of transformation and that attitudes towards heritage are changing over time, the concept of "genuine savings" can be adopted here. Often called "weak sustainability," it represents a first-approximation numeric indicator of the degree to which a nation satisfies the *Hartwick-Solow rule* (Hartwick, 1977). It finally aims to capture all capital investment and depreciation flows to obtain an overview of the evolution of total value and wealth.

In the case of heritage, since the 2000s, the classification of values based on decreasing tangibility of value to individuals has become more popular (The Allen Consulting Group, 2005, p. 5). It is based on the aforementioned subdivision into use and non-use values (Figure 3.10). The former corresponds to the nature of instrumental values and the latter to intrinsic value proposed by Dewey (1922, 1939). In the first case, the value of the legacy is associated with the possibility of translating it into economic benefits. In the direct aspect, the heritage value will result in rental income or

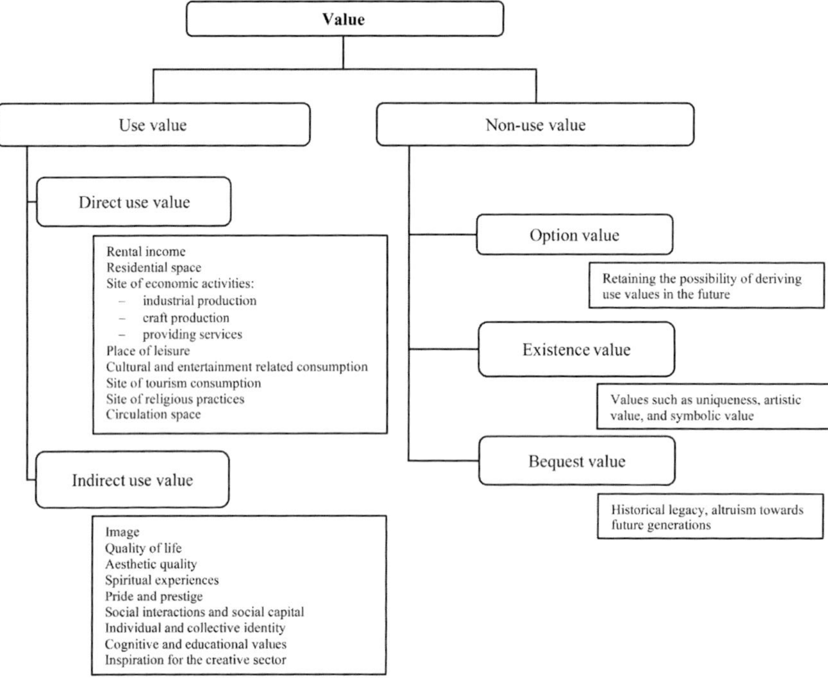

Figure 3.10 Categories of values attributed to built heritage

Source: Murzyn-Kupisz (2015, p. 157) and The Allen Consulting Group (2005, p. 5).

utility resulting from living in places purchased in the neighbourhood or even in the heritage objects themselves. From the most traditional perspective, direct use value results from the use of heritage as a tourist destination, a source of recreation, entertainment and leisure, religious practices or the provision of services based on cultural connotations (e.g. craft production). All activities of this type usually constitute a source of tangible cash inflow for the owner of these assets.

For this reason, direct use value can be identified using classic real estate valuation methods, which are consistent with the International Valuation Standards. The challenge, in this case, remains that in the vast majority of cases, the direct use value is provided to the owner's budget. However, it does not cover the costs of maintenance and preservation for future generations (which are usually higher than in the case of non-historic properties). Moreover, the estimated potential cash revenue may be limited due to the historical nature of the sites (e.g. significantly limiting the possibilities of typical use of heritage sites for profitable purposes).

The possibilities of capturing value in the monetary dimension also refer to indirect use value. It is connected with agglomeration economies and assumes that the positive influence of heritage objects on the image of the place, quality of life, aesthetics of the surroundings, the sense of pride and prestige, or positive sensory experiences, and social interactions can be interpreted as positive externalities. Thus, the property's value will increase due to its proximity to material heritage. Although the latter will be an urban common good, today, modern valuation techniques make it possible to capture the correlation between such commons and their influence on property prices. For this reason, heritage also has a positive impact on the actual use value.

The situation is different when quantifying non-use value. There are often deeply hidden human and collective value systems, and non-use value has no instrumental dimension, at least not at the moment of valuation. There are three types of values in this group: option, existence, and bequest. The first is based on the assumption that a heritage asset that is not considered usable today may be a source of use value tomorrow. Although it is difficult to predict whether and when it will occur, there is a belief that the value of heritage is a function of time. This category of value is often important in the public discourse on the future of relatively recent objects, whose value today is ambiguous. However, there is a growing group of people who predict an increase in its intrinsic value in the future.

Meanwhile, the existence value refers to uniqueness, and artistic and symbolic meaning, which is already visible to a certain community today. However, this feeling is intangible and does not translate into economic benefits. This type of value is associated with the conviction that a monument is valuable because of its history, aesthetic value and (national or local) identity, which must be maintained "at all costs" and "whatever the price is." This type of value is difficult to convert into money explicitly. However, one can try to capture it using indirect methods, for example, by asking in surveys about the WTP and the scale of declared payment for maintaining the monument as a heritage asset. In such a situation, however, the monetary value is auxiliary (i.e. it should not be interpreted directly). It is used primarily for comparative research, for example, to benchmark the readiness to pay for different objects or for the same objects but for alternative uses.

The last and least tangible type of heritage value is bequest value. It refers directly to the historical legacy, and the strongly declared desire to preserve the heritage for future generations comes to the fore. For this type of value, any discussion on alternative applications or economic benefits is usually irrelevant, and if there is a need to invest in such monuments, the main goal is to maintain them according to a strong sustainability approach.

When estimating and capturing heritage value, there is usually a combination of use and non-use values. For this reason, classical valuation techniques, based on market, investment or cost approaches, are of limited use. More often, indirect value-seeking methods are applied, where the main approach refers to questioning the public about its WTP. There are two basic ways of asking people about their WTP in relation to environmental resources, heritage protection, but also other decisions concerning the

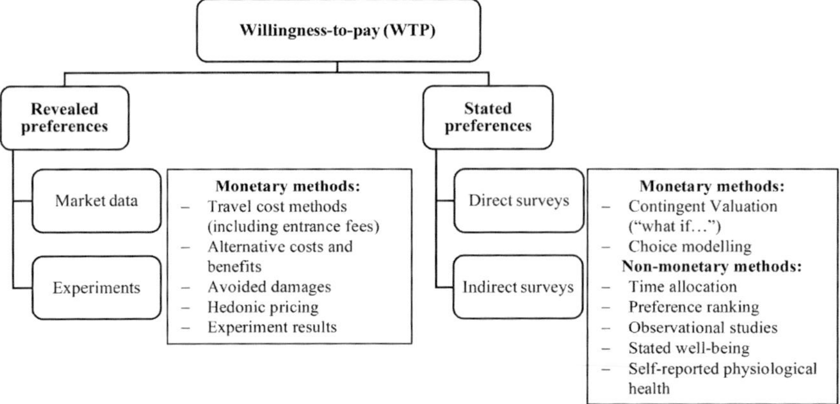

Figure 3.11 Classification framework for methods to measure willingness to pay (WTP)

Source: Breidert et al. (2006, p. 10) and Langemeyer et al. (2015, p. 178).

public interest. The first is based on the possibility of revealed preferences of respondents, while the other concerns situations where the released data do not exist (or is difficult to access). Therefore people are asked about their potential valuation when presented with a hypothetical situation and asked to decide under "what if..." conditions (Figure 3.11).

Revealed preference methods are applicable only when data on market transactions or activities are present. In such cases, a few methods can be applied. First, the cost of travel incurred in visiting a site and paying entrance fees can be calculated (as in the case of travel cost methods). Additionally, the cost to avoid an inconvenience or hazard (averting behaviour or market prices) may be considered (Choi et al., 2010, p. 214). It is also possible to design a field experiment in real life in which, for example, the manipulation of entrance fees for certain attractions, or the targeted facilitation (or restriction) of access and reduced transport costs through infrastructure investments, can be examined in terms of their impact on changes in the behaviour of "consumers" of heritage sites. Finally, an increasingly popular method of value elicitation in the spirit of revealed preferences is the hedonic valuation method. It is based on econometric models in which the explained variable is the price of the purchased (rented) property, while the explanatory variables are the selected characteristics of the surroundings, including the proximity of heritage sites. Such models are interpreted as the extra prices paid to enjoy such proximity (Choi et al., 2010, p. 214).

However, hedonic studies are not capable of providing estimates of the full range of open space benefits, for example, they tend to overestimate coefficients on central (dis)amenities and underestimate coefficients on peripheral (dis)amenities in the urban areas (Schläpfer et al., 2015, p. 38). This is a general problem of valuation studies based on revealed preferences. While this approach deals with the availability of real-world data, we are not always able to isolate from this data the factors that directly refer to the exact aspect of the value that interests us. Thus, stated preference methods are often an alternative. Although their results are more dependent on study design and implementation, they make it possible to capture a more comprehensive set of benefits that affect the heritage value. In other words, when reliable market data are not available, or the problem of heritage valuation is compound, researchers may need to create a hypothetical market to elicit consumer preferences. Then, stated preference methods are used, when respondents are asked (in direct or indirect surveys) to directly express how much they are willing to pay (or accept) for a given good or to choose their preferred option from a set of choices (Choi et al., 2010, p. 214).

There are two monetary methods to elicit stated preferences: the contingent valuation method (CVM) and choice modelling (CM). In the former, respondents are presented with a detailed scenario of delivering a specific good (e.g. renovating a monument or setting up a museum within it), including the cost that would have to be spent. Then they are asked whether, if such a scenario arose, they would vote for or against it, remembering that it will incur personal costs, for example, in the form of tax. The CVM uses surveys to elicit the value individuals or households place on a resource such as heritage sites. The surveys ask respondents about their WTP for a carefully defined public good or service (McConnell & Walls, 2005, p. 29). However, the ways of asking about WTP are crucial in this case. The most commonly used methods include the following: (1) dichotomous choice (when respondents are asked to say "yes" or "no" to a given proposition), (2) payment cards (when respondents are asked to choose from a list of prices the one that best reflects their WTP) and (3) auction bidding (when respondents are asked to say "yes" or "no" to escalating or descending stated prices) (Choi et al., 2010, p. 214). CVM is a method that, in contrast to the revealed preferences method, risks imperfections that result not only from the significant complexity of the valued subject but also from the significant subjectivity of assessments. The most common biases of contingent valuation include the following (Bateman et al., 2002; Venkatachalam, 2004):

- Hypothetical or strategic bias – an unreal/hypothetical scenario setting in which respondents may overstate or understate their true preferences
- Embedding or scope effect – depending on whether a valued good is presented as a separate unit or as a part of aggregate goods
- Information or "framing" effect – how information is given to respondents in surveys and whether alternative choices are provided
- The tendency to say "yes" (yea-saying)
- Starting point bias – depending on whether respondents are asked to pay a high or low amount
- Payment vehicle bias – caused by the payment method presented to the respondents

Conversely, CM is an extension of the method of conditional valuation, in which respondents are presented with a wider range of hypothetical scenarios. In this case, instead of asking questions about approval for a specific programme, respondents are presented with a set of variants and asked to choose the one they think is best. This approach also employs surveys to elicit preferences, but it offers respondents much clearer choices among the alternative options and, based on the results, it estimates values (McConnell & Walls, 2005, p. 30).

From an analytical point of view, this method is more complicated, but it offers a more readable classification of elicited values. From a quantitative perspective, the starting point when applying it is usually the random utility model (Louviere, 2001). In the CM technique, a good is viewed as a bundle of component attributes and their levels, and to capture the value of heritage, a series of questions called "choice sets" are presented to survey respondents. Technically, for each question, respondents are asked to choose one preferred option from several alternatives. One of the choice options is usually given as a "status quo" or "no action" policy, while other "change" options are designed using variations in the levels taken by constituent "characteristics" or "attributes." Finally, one attribute typically represents a monetary variable (known as a "payment vehicle"), which makes it possible to derive implicit prices (Choi et al., 2010, p. 215). Apart from analytical rigour, an important feature of this method is the scenario approach. In this methodology, there is no ambition to capture the "only right" value, but to compare different values for different scenarios using the same heritage object. Therefore, this method allows researchers to compare the respondents' propensity to value different types of use and different types of values – including use vs non-use types. Despite the scientific stringency, the CM method is essentially marked by a certain subjectivity of responses. However, by enabling quantification and comparison, it can be helpful for decision-makers, especially when referring to an ambivalent heritage.

All of the above-presented methodologies differentiate between monetary and non-monetary evaluation techniques. In particular, in the context of stated preference methods, which take into account a considerable proportion of the subjective aspect of value, non-monetary valuation methods are a useful extension of monetary methods. Although the latter provides a valuation of legacies with a considerable amount of objective charge (i.e. the possibility of comparing multiple quantified variants of possible decisions), they are not free from subjective assessments. When applying the quantitative elements of the analyses, the evaluators should be at least aware of subjective evaluations, as well as the complexity of decision-making problems concerning heritage.

When addressing the challenge of the complexity of decision-making problems, the quantitative elements of the analyses should be complemented by multi-criteria elements, at least trying to capture the subjective diversity of attitudes towards the valuated objects. Usually, non-monetary methods focus on techniques, such as allocating time (e.g. devoted to visiting or taking care of monuments), ranking preferences on possible scenarios for future heritage development, stated well-being or physiological health that results from the possibility of experiencing the heritage and, last but not least, observational studies on the behaviour of users and contemplators of heritage in urban spaces (e.g. counting users, behavioural mapping and tracking) (Madden & Schwartz, 2000, pp. 145–165).

However, there is a growing tendency to combine data from different sources and thus capture the multifacetedness of the problem of heritage valuation. In this case, techniques are used that combine various aspects into one model, such as multi-criteria analysis (MCA) (Nesticò & Sica, 2017; Nesticò et al., 2018). Such techniques aim to provide a holistic and integrated evaluation of the cultural–historical assets under investigation. In the model, they include the specific opinions of experts, stakeholders and policy makers (Ferretti et al., 2014, p. 654).

Cost–benefit analysis as a response to the complexity of heritage development

Public projects, including those that require "interfering" with heritage, especially in the form of investment activities, are complex. They involve both the ambivalent attitudes of different stakeholder groups towards heritage, as well as a variety of ways its value is perceived. Such interventions have a multifaceted impact (emotional, social, economic, environmental, spatial, etc.). Therefore, the most common and increasingly widespread ex-ante assessment of the legitimacy of public interventions is based on cost–benefit analysis (CBA). The popularity of this method is also reinforced by the fact that in a growing number of countries, its application is mandatory to justify the establishment of new regulatory solutions in various aspects of socio-economic life – from tax policy, through health policy, to allowing the implementation of large publicly funded investment megaprojects (Sunstein, 2019).

CBA is a method of assessing the legitimacy of legislative measures, developments and other projects. It has its roots in the works of the French engineer and economist Jules Dupuit, who first applied it in the 1930s (Mind Tools Content Team, 2021). It considers all expected benefits and costs, including alternatives and externalities (e.g. environmental, agglomeration, social). Unlike traditional methods of analysing investment profitability, which consider only directly incurred costs and revenues from a given project, this method makes it possible to compare the value of virtually all resources (costs) used in the implementation of a given project with the value of any positive results (benefits) (Niżankowski et al., 2002, p. 20).

CBA takes into account both direct expenditures on the project and indirect costs, usually treated as alternative costs. The latter is defined as a cost of lost opportunity (Buchanan, 1991) resulting from the fact that directing the sources to a given project reduces the possibility of spending them on other, substitute undertakings. Similarly, in the case of benefits, CBA aims to identify revenues that come directly and indirectly from a given project. In this context, CBA, in its essence, refers to the theory of externalities.

Decisions on heritage planning are political in the sense that they appeal to values. And in such a situation, arguments about public policy are often expressive (Sunstein, 2019, p. 7). Among other things, the CBA-based approach is intended to limit this expressiveness and replace it with argument-based discussion. On the one hand, it requires decision-makers to avoid overly controversial decisions and assume explicitly that no action may be taken unless the benefits justify the costs. On the other hand, it assumes that officials will not rely on intuitions, interest groups, polls, or dogmas (Sunstein, 2019, p. 40).

An occasional criticism of the CBA, that is, that it takes a technocratic approach, can, in fact, be deemed its merit. Such analysis requires a specific, well-established procedure to consider specific categories of costs and benefits. It also monetizes the value, even if it refers to intangible and timeless aspects. All this to compare alternative decisions and their consequences for the public domain. Therefore, CBA also uses increasingly advanced analytical methods. All this results in cost–benefit analyses having the characteristics of a foreign language (Sunstein, 2019, p. 48). This foreignness distances us from our intuitions and immediate, automatic reactions. It is replaced by analytical thinking, based not on emotions but on rational premises. Because when people use a language other than their first, they are less likely to make some of the most important errors found in decades of work in behavioural science (Costa et al., 2014; Hayakawa et al., 2016). In other words, people are more likely to be rational when using a foreign language – they think less automatically and more deliberatively (Sunstein, 2019, p. 60). Thus, from a psychological point of view, the analytical and technical language of CBA seems to work like a foreign language.

Other advantages of cost–benefit analysis as a method of evaluating socio-economic measures include its versatility and enrichment with qualitative elements. Moreover, CBA makes it possible to consider the social aspects of implementing various undertakings, which remains important for projects implemented from public funds. Finally, the flexibility of the method allows the user to combine it with other techniques for evaluating the effectiveness of the projects. Typical problems encountered when implementing CBA in practice include difficulties in determining all the benefits and costs associated with the project and in expressing them in monetary terms. Moreover, this method remains time-consuming and costly, and it requires expert knowledge (Table 3.1). However, the elimination of some CBA limitations in public project evaluation, including heritage projects, may lend credibility to decisions on strategic choices.

Table 3.1 Advantages and disadvantages of cost–benefit analysis

Advantages	*Disadvantages*
1. Comprehensiveness 2. Possibility of including the qualitative aspects of the analysis 3. Makes it possible to define a wide range of costs and benefits for society as a whole 4. Possibility of combining other techniques for evaluating the effectiveness of the projects	1. Difficulty in determining all benefits and costs 2. Difficulty in expressing all of the components in monetary values 3. The need to collect large data volumes 4. The need for high expertise and experience of the executors 5. Time-consuming and expensive 6. High risk of errors

Source: Trocki and Grucza (2007, p. 199).

Two features significantly differentiate cost–benefit analysis from other methods of evaluating the effectiveness of investments and public projects – expressing costs and benefits in monetary terms and taking into account the time value (Figure 3.12). Therefore, monetization and discounting are key steps of the CBA procedure. Firstly, this method seeks to capture all benefits and costs in monetary terms. It makes it possible to answer whether, in a measurable sense, the benefits are worth the costs incurred and which of the compared programmes gives higher net benefits (Niżankowski et al., 2002, p. 12). In this respect, CBA utilizes an alternative decision rule with much greater feasibility than the Pareto efficiency rule. The latter assumes that effectiveness occurs when it is not possible to improve the situation

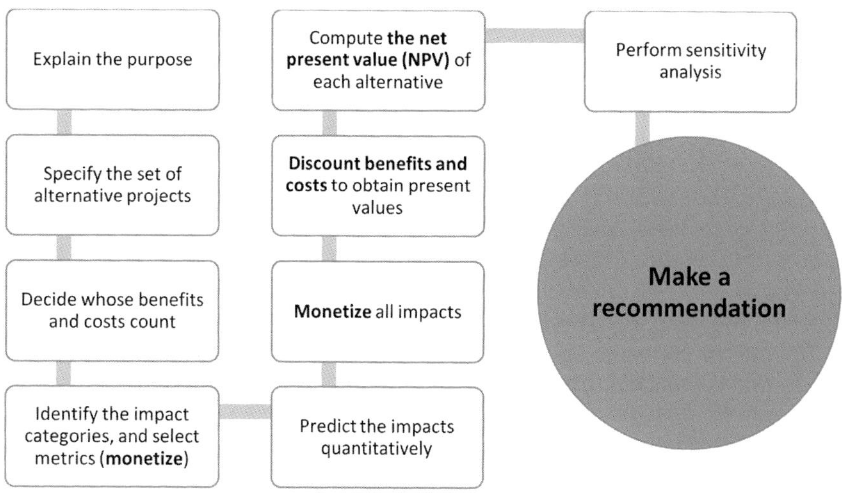

Figure 3.12 The major steps in CBA

Source: Boardman et al. (2018, p. 5).

(satisfaction) of one member of society without worsening the situation of others. In this sense, its guidance refers to the aforementioned "strong sustainability" approach. Cost–benefit analysis, meanwhile, is based on what is known as the Kaldor–Hicks criterion. It states that a policy should be adopted if and only if those who will gain could fully compensate those who will lose and still be better off (Hicks, 1940; Kaldor, 1939). In this approach, we see a reference to the "weak sustainability" approach. The Kaldor–Hicks criterion means adopting those policies that have positive net benefits. As long as the net benefits are positive, the losers could be compensated, so potentially, the policy could be Pareto improving (Boardman et al., 2018, p. 33).

Second, in the CBA (which usually assumes that costs and benefits will occur over several years), the decrease in the value of monetary assets over time is taken into account (through a discounting mechanism). Hence, the inseparable elements of the CBA are the estimation of the Net Present Value (NPV) and the Internal Rate of Return (IRR) – key financial mathematics' concepts. The benefits, together with the costs of the project, must then be pinpointed and quantified, and a reasonable schedule for the introduction of the plan must be estimated (e.g. ten years) (Báez & Herrero, 2012, p. 241). Discounting the viability of actions over time for public projects, including those concerning heritage, requires the determination of the so-called social discount rate (SDR). The techniques for its calculation are analogous to concepts found in corporate finance. What is different, however, is that social aspects must be taken into account more strongly, but they cannot be clearly valued.

Three approaches are used in the SDR calculation process: the social time preference rate (STPR), the social opportunity cost rate (SOCR) and the synthetic or weighted average cost rate (Addae-Dapaah, 2012, p. 72). The first refers to the relative value that society as a whole assigns to present as opposed to future consumption. Here, referring to the risk of death theory, people usually prefer to enjoy benefits today than tomorrow for fear that they may not be alive tomorrow. This implies that people of different ages will have different time preferences, which are all subject to probabilities. Logically, the older you are, the higher your time preference rate will be. The social opportunity cost rate refers to the aforementioned alternative cost approach (Buchanan, 1991). It assumes that public investment involves withdrawing resources from alternative investment opportunities in the private sector or, more broadly, from other applications, including public ones. The last approach attempts to merge SDR with shadow prices of capital to confuse the two issues. Such prices express a monetary value assigned to currently unknowable or difficult-to-calculate costs in the absence of correct market prices (Kanbur, 1987).

Finally, the SDRs used in practice vary from country to country and even within countries. For example, US government agencies use SDRs ranging from 0 to 12%, while an SDR of 8% has been used by the Australian government. In the United Kingdom, the HM Treasury Green Book recommends an SDR of 3.5% for projects with an economic life of up to 30 years, after which a declining schedule of discount rates is recommended. Using one SDR for a public project that may have repercussions on future generations is problematic as the SDR is likely to change with time, if it can be realistically estimated at all (Addae-Dapaah, 2012, p. 73).

Warsaw Ochota railway station, Poland – Valuating soc-modernism in the daily life

An example of valuating the heritage of modernism that is ambiguous is a study carried out in Warsaw between 2019 and 2021. If architecture is controversial and relatively young, its valuation raises ambiguities. Unconventional valuation methods can then help resolve them by helping decision-makers make more accurate decisions. The study presented in this paper combines different valuation methods, different perspectives (both expert and non-expert) and types of values (economic, social and cultural; both use and non-use). The study also considers the perspective of the object itself as well as its physical surroundings.

Warsaw Ochota train station is an element of the Warsaw Cross-City Railway *(Warszawska Kolej Średnicowa)*, sometimes called by journalists “the pearls of post-war modernism” in Warsaw (Poland) (Florencka, 2018). In the 1940s and 1950s, the Polish Communist party approved socialist realism as the only accepted architectural style. For this reason, modernist design was rejected as “too Western” for the country (Ciarkowski, 2017c). Nevertheless, the changes in party leadership that started after Stalin’s death led to an openness to other architectural styles. That is why it was possible to realize the idea of building several minor commuter stations in the modernist style in the 1960s. This endeavour was a kind of manifesto to loosen the communist regime. Consequently, three modernist objects among the four suburban stations of the Warsaw Cross-City Railway were constructed: Stadion – in 1955, Ochota – in 1963, and Powiśle – in 1963. Only one – Warszawa Śródmieście (1963) – remained in the socialist realist style (to match the Palace of Culture, an urban landmark in the immediate vicinity), receiving only a small, roofed, underground entrance designed in a modernist style (see Picture 1.10 in Chapter 1). All these stations still operate, and their functional and architectural solutions, based on modernist rules, can today be considered interesting examples of railway architecture (see Pictures 3.17 and 3.18).

The procedure to determine the value of the concrete architecture of the Warsaw railway station consisted of three stages. The first took the form of a questionnaire survey using techniques to identify the WTP to implement the presented station development scenarios. It used an online survey of 222 respondents recruited through cultural institutions and universities, as well as non-governmental organizations and circles that focus on

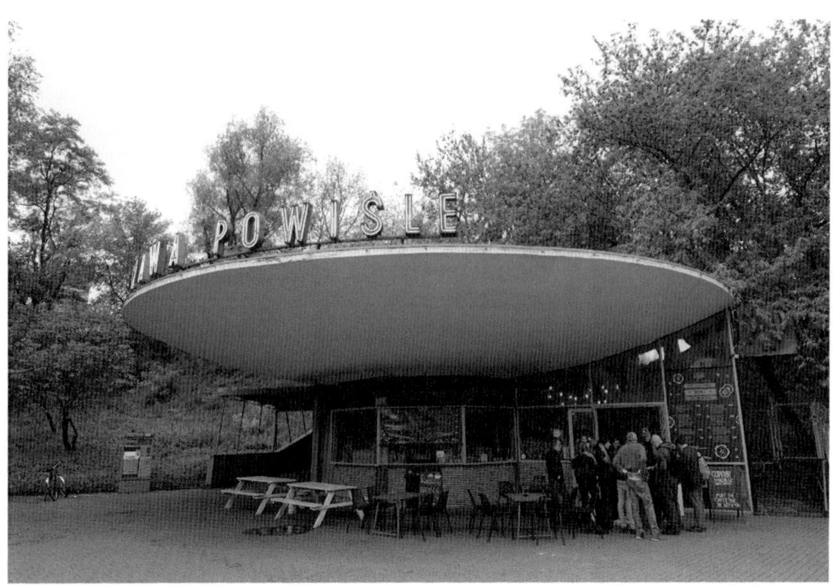

Picture 3.17 Warszawa Powiśle Station consists of two pavilions of different forms and structures. The lower pavilion, in a characteristic shape of a "flying saucer," is one of the modernist icons of the Polish Capital. Warszawa Powiśle Cross-City railway station in Warsaw (Poland), designed by A. Romanowicz, P. Szymaniak, 1963. © Błażej Ciarkowski.

promoting modernist architecture in Poland. The results provided data for the following two stages of the study: a self-conducted cost–benefit analysis (CBA) and a Delphi expert panel (Figure 3.13). The survey was conducted at the turn of 2019 and 2020, the cost–benefit analysis in 2020, while the two-round Delphi study was carried out in January 2021 and March 2021.

The starting point in our methodology was to borrow from the CVM, as the most relevant for the first stage of the study. The respondents included members of public and academic institutions and NGOs, as well as communities oriented towards promoting modernist architecture in Poland. In order to avoid the bias of reaching only the most active people in these social circles, half a year before the survey, we created a profile on a social network devoted to the gloss and shadows of the concrete architecture of the socialist period in Poland. This profile promoted the study and attracted a broader spectrum of potential respondents. They completed an online survey after receiving a link to the questionnaire via instant messaging or email. Finally, our survey response database contained 222 valid records that became the subject of inquiry.

The survey's main questions helped obtain information on the respondents' attitudes to the proposed hypothetical scenarios on the future use of this station. Existing studies let us extract several options regarding the

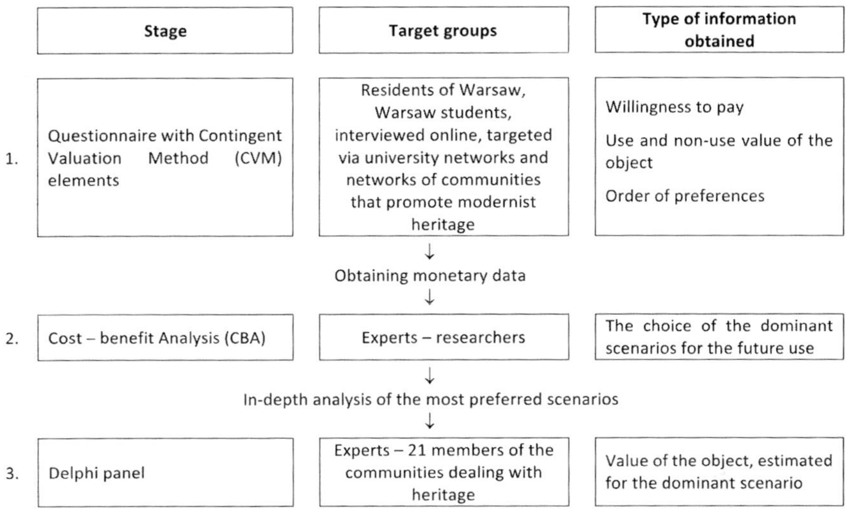

Figure 3.13 A methodological model to valuate twentiethth-century post-socialist train stations

Source: Own study.

development of the existing heritage of post-socialist modernism and identify eight possible adaptive reuse scenarios for the station (Table 3.2).

In the second stage of the study, the cost–benefit analysis captured the broad context of possible station use scenarios. It is considered an intermediate solution between a "market" and a conservationist approach to heritage. The former focuses on the objectification of values, although some scholars criticize it as being too simplistic. The latter reveals the non-monetary aspects of value, but at the expense of appealing to more subjective factors. Another significant value of CBA is that it is based on specialized and universal terminology. Therefore, its use makes it possible to universalize the language of communication between people with different experiences and knowledge. Subsequently, more reliable comparisons of various cases are feasible (Costa et al., 2014; Hayakawa et al., 2016; Sunstein, 2019).

The CBA adopted a "public sector perspective," that is, the costs and benefits borne directly by the public owner of the station (the railway company) were analysed first. For example, if a scenario involved leasing part of a station for commercial purposes, the benefits side took into account the revenue from the lease rent but ignored the potential business income of the tenant. On the direct costs side, we included the costs borne by the public sector but ignored those borne by the tenants (e.g. the costs of electricity consumption for the common parts of the site were included, while the electricity charges borne by the tenants were not). Secondly, we also analysed the costs and benefits of public entities other than the entity that directly owns the facility. For example, in the scenario

Table 3.2 Potential scenarios of station development

Scenario code	*Scenario name*	*Description*
S1	The station is thoroughly renovated	The railway station undergoes a significant refurbishment but retains its original style. It undergoes technological modernization (i.e. intelligent transport systems and services). Efforts are made to improve the aesthetics of the station's surroundings. The station remains an important transport node integrating different transport modes. The facility is adapted to the needs of people with disabilities.
S2	A club cafe is created at the station	The railway station hall is open to the public for cultural and catering activities as a meeting place over lunch and drinks. Despite the introduction of new functions, the platforms and passageways are still used for rail traffic needs.
S3	The area of the station undergoes a general reconstruction into an interactive museum	The station undergoes a substantial reconstruction into an interactive museum. The trademark silhouette of its hall is "encapsulated" inside a new building but still visible in the urban landscape through the glass structure. Platforms and passageways still serve rail traffic.
S4	A small art gallery opens in the station building	The platforms and passageways still fulfil their transport function, but the station's interior acts as a small art gallery. Exhibitions are also displayed on platforms. External exhibitions are free of charge, while events inside the station may be ticketed.
S5	The railway station is liquidated for new buildings	The station is demolished, the real estate is sold and new buildings are constructed on the site.
S6	The area of the station undergoes a general reconstruction into a shopping mall	The upper part of the station undergoes a noticeable reconstruction and development into a shopping facility, albeit it preserves its trademark silhouette. The historical look is retained but dominated by a large-scale commercial function. The ground level of the station still serves urban transport purposes.
S7	A shop is located in the station building	A grocery store opens in the station hall, while platforms and passageways still serve the rail traffic. The construction elements and the silhouette of the building are still identifiable. The object serves as a utilitarian space and attracts more users, some of whom have a chance to see its legacy.
S8	Nothing changes	The station remains unchanged and still serves transport purposes. Guided tours of all the modernist Warsaw Cross-City Railway stations are organized here occasionally.

Source: Sokołowicz and Przygodzki (2020, p. 9).

involved transforming the station into a museum, we assumed a public entity (e.g. a museum company) would operate it. Thus, we included the monetized costs and benefits of its operating costs. On the other hand, in the "club café" scenario, we assumed that a private company would operate it directly and did not include its operation costs into the CBA.

In addition, we considered the facility's value as a common good, using methods to approximate the non-use value of the station. We based these estimates on the assumption that the more an object's cultural value is exposed in a given scenario, the greater it is recognized. It would then involve a WTP for artefacts associated with the image of the facility (e.g. posters and marketing gadgets) and attending events held there (e.g. exhibitions, tours, meetings with famous people). We also approximated recognition based on the so-called advertising equivalent (the amount of money that would be spent on publishing a message if it were an advertisement).

We included five of the eight station development scenarios in the CBA. We selected those that the respondents in the first stage of the study (survey) indicated as their first or second choice. In contrast, the fifth scenario was the least popular (cf. Table 3.3).

For each of the five scenarios, a five-year analysis period was assumed, and each item on the cost–benefit side was monetized. In addition, a triangulation of price and cost data sources was applied, using a wide range (Table 3.4).

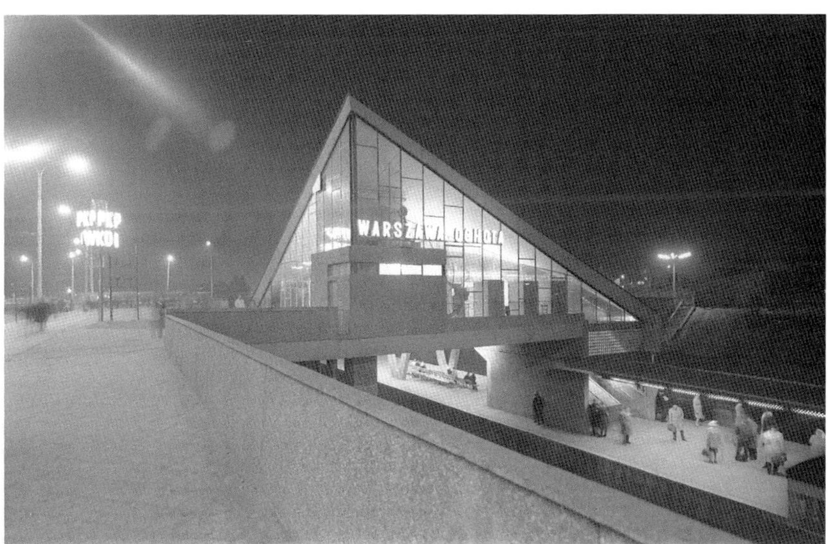

Picture 3.18 Despite its modest scale, the modernist form of the Warszawa Ochota Station pavilion makes it an urban landmark due to the unique shape of the concrete roof. Warszawa Ochota Cross-City railway station in Warsaw (Poland), designed by A. Romanowicz, P. Szymaniak, 1963. © Zbyszko Siemaszko – NAC.

Table 3.3 Development scenarios for Warszawa Ochota railway station selected for cost–benefit analysis (second stage of the study) as a result of a survey (first stage of the study)

Ranking of responses (first stage of the study)	*Scenarios presented to respondents in the questionnaire (first stage of the study)*		*Scenarios subjected to CBA (second stage of the study) and presented to the respondents during the Delphi panel (third stage of the study)*
S1:	The station is thoroughly renovated		STATUS QUO – RENOVATION ONLY
S2:	A club cafe is created at the station		"CLUB CAFÉ OCHOTA"
S3:	The area of the station undergoes a general reconstruction into an interactive museum	–>	"MUSEUM WKD OCHOTA" – INTERACTIVE MUSEUM
S4:	A small art gallery opens in the station building		"ART OCHOTA" – SMALL ART GALLERY
S8:	Nothing changes		-
S5:	The railway station is liquidated for new buildings		-
S6:	The area of the station undergoes a general reconstruction into a shopping mall		-
S7:	A shop is located in the station building		"OCHOTA MARKET" – SHOP

Source: Own study.

We considered the initial investment and running costs for the first year of the analysis and included the discounted running costs for the remaining four years. The social discount rate captured the value decline over time. It was presumed to be as follows:

- 2.8% (average of the currently proposed recommendations for the evaluation of public projects proposed by Fields et al. (2020) and Hultkrantz (2021)) for the scenarios that assume no or a low level of commercialization of the activities: "renovation only," "small art gallery" and "interactive museum" (S1, S3 and S4);
- 5% for scenarios that are assumed to make a profit – "club-café" and "shop" (S2 and S7) and
- for comparison purposes, the NPV was also estimated for a discount rate of 0%, following the proposal of Stern (2007), who advocated thinking about climate change in terms of economic necessity and treating the future equally with the present. This approach is increasingly popular with a paradigm shift towards the so-called zero-growth or post-growth ideas.

Table 3.4 Data sources used in the CBA

Costs and benefits	*Data sources*
Construction and renovation costs	Poland's national price database for investment costing (per 1 m2 of space) (Sekocenbud)
Energy costs	Price of 1 kWh of electricity in public buildings as an average of costs incurred in 2018–2020 in similar public buildings in Warsaw and Lodz
Salary costs	Employment costs of personnel who maintain public buildings as an average of costs incurred in 2018–2020 in Warsaw public institutions (offices) and higher education institutions (per 1 m2 of space)
Insurance costs	Overview of insurance offers for public buildings in Warsaw, as an average insurance rate (per 1 m^2 of area)
Costs of technical wear and tear	Value of annual depreciation write-off of the facility for tax purposes under accounting regulations
Staff costs of organizing events	Review of information on rates and allowances for artists between 2018 and 2020, as average remuneration (per event)
Costs of technical support of events	Review of pricing rates for such services in Warsaw, as an average cost (per event)
Promotional costs	Review of public tender awards between 2018 and 2020 for promotional services, as the average annual cost of such activities
Lease of space revenue	Average market rental rate in similar facilities in Warsaw Ochota district between 2018 and 2020
Non-commercial revenues (non-use value)	• Data on the annual number of passengers at Warsaw Ochota station, • Data on the average number of visitors to museums in 2018, from the National Institute for Museums and Public Collections
Non-use value approximation	• Average market prices for promotion gadgets, posters and thematic literature and albums • Average prices of guided tours held in Warsaw • Prices of social media advertisements • Prices of nationwide newspaper advertisement

Source: Own study. For the Polish version, see Sokołowicz (2022).

We confronted the results of the CBA in the last stage with the opinions of experts in a Delphi panel. This method ensures the mutual reconciliation of answers between the experts (in subsequent rounds, they decide whether they agree with the majority or would stay with their opinion if it was different), but with the assurance of their anonymity (Linstone & Turoff, 1975, p. 3). This method is used to predict the future and evaluate alternative directions of action (Reilly, 1973, p. 188; Williamson, 2002, p. 213). On one hand, its purpose is to obtain expert opinion (the respondents are specialists in a specific field) and, on the other hand, to conduct at least two rounds of surveys or interviews (Sproull, 1988, p. 240). In other words, Delphi provides the expertness of the opinions and the anonymity of the judgements. Finally, its multi-stage procedure allows participants to agree by referring anonymously to previous opinions (Krupowicz, 2005, p. 207).

Thirteen male and eight female experts (21 people in total) participated in this phase, representing the following experiences:

- Architects and town planners (9 people)
- Urban planning and revitalization civil servants (4 people)
- Specialists in urban economics and real estate markets (3 people)
- University staff from main academic towns in Poland who specialize in urban planning, urban geography, urban regeneration, urban economics and sociology, architecture and cultural studies (11 people)
- Cultural institution employees (Warsaw museums, National Heritage Institute) (5 people)
- Journalists involved in architectural criticism (3 people)
- Activists of urban movements in Warsaw (5 people)

Some experts declared that they represent more than one background (e.g. an architect who is also a university employee, an entrepreneur who is an urban activist). After familiarizing themselves with the scenarios in the first Delphi round, the participants ranked them from the most to the least preferred. The juxtaposition of these scenarios, together with the monetary values obtained in the CBA procedure, provided an opportunity to base reasoning and judgment on their own experience, knowledge and monetary values. In the second round, the panellists compared their answers with the other 20 panellists. After reviewing the results, the participants had the option to stay with their previous answer or change it and re-order the scenarios. Both answers could be justified in a written comment in the second round. There were 18 participants in the second round (three participants declined to answer again).

As our studies on railway stations in Warsaw have shown, when properly asked, the public can provide experts with knowledge on the desirable forms of development of this type of architecture and show where its biggest value is. In the survey questionnaire, the respondents valued the station in monetary terms depending on the development scenarios presented (Figure 3.14). At this stage, they attributed the highest value to the most commercial (and therefore cost-intensive) scenarios for the future use of the facility. Thus, they associated the highest average WTP with turning the station into a shop or bar. Lower values appeared for less commercial but still paid activities (e.g. events that involve an entrance fee or paid guided tours). Interestingly, the scenario of not demolishing the station and preserving it for future generations (respondents' WTP 11.72 PLN in the form of willingness to pay extra tax) was comparable to scenarios generating much higher costs, that is, building a museum in the facility (12.52 PLN for willingness to contribute to investment costs, and 10.53 PLN to pay the entrance fee). The least attractive scenario, as can be inferred from the low declared WTP, was the facility's conversion for residential purposes.

The development scenarios were strongly influenced by the following:

1. The suggestion that was "hidden" in the question itself, as we honestly indicated the cost per inhabitant of the scenario that results from our calculations of Warsaw
2. Knowledge about the station (tested by recognition of silhouettes and knowledge about the period when the station was constructed)
3. The presented development direction (with three statistically significant scenarios – renovation, housing and commercial purposes)

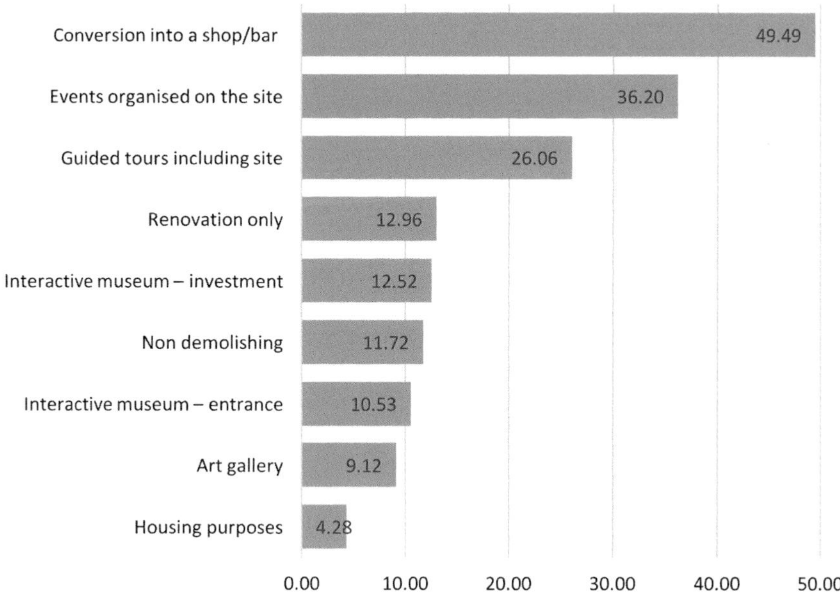

Figure 3.14 Willingness to pay (WTP) depending on site use (in PLN)

Source: Own study.

Interestingly, valuation was not significantly affected by age. The first stage also revealed that non-use value dominates over use value, and monetary valuation methods are more relevant for commercial forms of use (Sokołowicz & Przygodzki, 2020).

The costs and benefits described in monetary terms at the CBA stage allowed the Delphi expert panel participants to familiarize themselves with all scenarios. Also, the possibility of comparing the NPV calculated during the CBA allowed them to make clear comparisons (Table 3.5). The NPV is one of the primary methods of estimating the feasibility of actions, both in classic investment projects and more complex activities. It juxtaposes the present value of cash inflows and outflows over a period of time, taking into account the mechanism of the decline in the value of money over time.

From a financial perspective, the least profitable scenario was the simple renovation of the station (S1), while the most beneficial was opening a small art gallery in the facility (S4). However, the S4 scenario brought the highest level of investment risk, which the very high IRR (63%) reflects. The middle scenarios are opening a café (S2) and a museum (S3). Meanwhile, calculating the NPV assuming a zero discount rate offered interesting results. At this level, the only "positive" scenario was a small art gallery (S4). The assumption that today's benefits should not be accrued at the expense of future generations (as in the "zero growth" concept) was not reflected in almost any scenario.

The differences in the response distribution of the respondents in the survey (the first stage of the study) with the preferences of the Delphi panel

Table 3.5 Results of cost–benefit analysis for specific development scenarios for Warsaw Ochota railway station

Scenario	*NPV for the discount rate of 0%*	*NPV for the discount rate of 2.8%*	*NPV for the discount rate of 5%*	*Internal rate of return – IRR (risk level)*
S1: STATUS QUO – RENOVATION ONLY	−1,077,250.4	−354,250.5	-	18%
S2: "CLUB CAFÉ OCHOTA"	−37,115.3	-	2,867,270.0	18%
S3: "MUSEUM WKD OCHOTA" – INTERACTIVE MUSEUM	−5,595,622.9	2,571,875.0	-	5%
S4:"ARTOCHOTA"– SMALL ART GALLERY	4,088,452.5	13,437,003.9	-	63%
S7: "OCHOTA MARKET" – SHOP	−493,087.6	-	840,968.09	22%

Source: Own study.

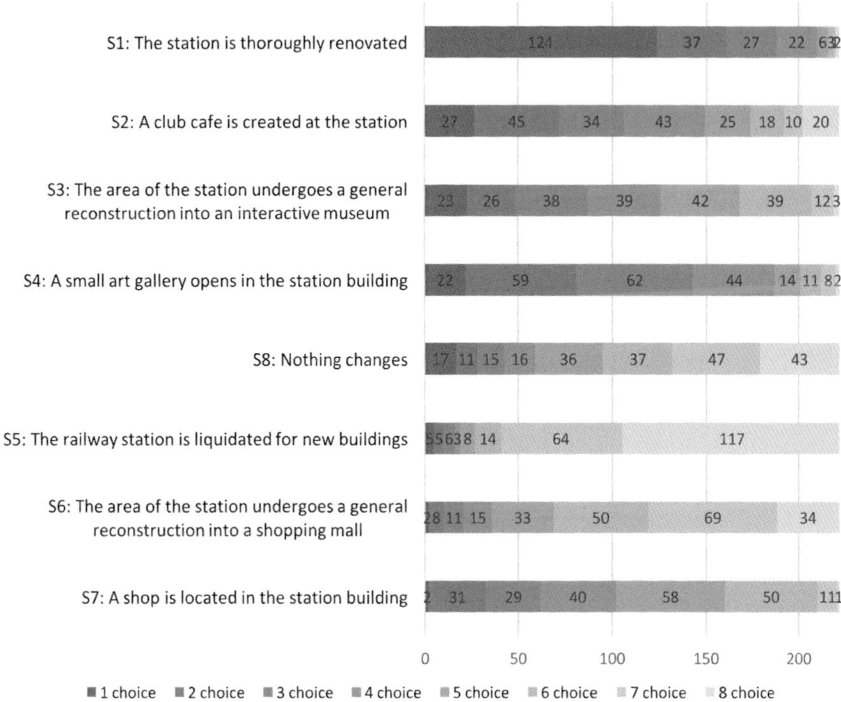

Figure 3.15 Preference structure of development scenarios for Warsaw ochota station in the surveys (first stage of the study)

Source: Sokołowicz and Przygodzki (2020).

experts are also worth noting. In the first case, the respondents indicated renovating the facility as the most preferred scenario – over 55% of respondents (Figure 3.15). In contrast, the least preferred scenarios included locating a store there, converting it to a large shopping centre, and demolition. In the first round of the Delphi survey, the "club café" scenario dominated firmly as the first choice. Twelve out of the 21 people participating in the panel indicated this scenario as the most preferred (Figure 3.16). The least preferred scenario, analogous to the distribution of survey responses, was locating a store location within the building. The medium scenarios were opening a club cafe, creating a museum and opening an art gallery. In these scenarios, the survey's distribution of preferences was similar to those declared in the two rounds of the Delphi expert survey.

The non-use value took on greater importance with the Delphi participants than the survey respondents in the first stage of the study. The relatively high popularity among the experts of the scenarios of developing the station for cultural purposes confirms this observation. However, among survey respondents, the "status quo" and "club café" scenarios

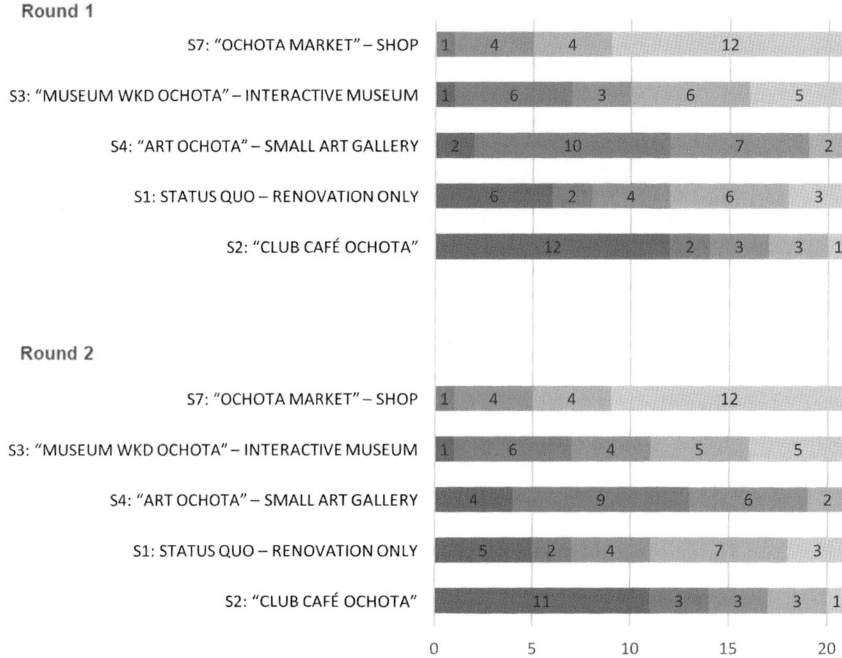

Figure 3.16 Preference structure of development scenarios for Warsaw ochota station in Delphi (final stage of the study)

Source: Own study.

were relatively frequently indicated when adding commercial functions to some extent in the scenario description. In contrast to the experts, the respondents in the first round of the study – confronted with a precise cost–benefit calculation – were more susceptible to the financial consequences of their choices. However, this "advantage" of use value over non-use value was not strong enough to point to most commercial scenarios (e.g. store or shopping mall) as the most popular. Finally, even when indicating the doing nothing ("status quo") scenario as the most preferred choice, some renovation to preserve the object for future generations was still welcomed.

The Delphi experts were also not extreme in their views, strongly preferring non-commercial scenarios over use value. Instead, they were looking for the "golden mean" of the station's development in their hypothetical decisions. Finally, when confronted with the first round results, Delphi experts strongly insisted on their opinion.

Comparing the surveys with the Delphi panel results shows a convergence of responses, despite the differences in perception of the heritage of modernism between experts and non-experts. Both groups balance the need to preserve Ochota station as a heritage for the future with the need

Picture 3.19 Nowadays, Warszawa Ochota station serves its original function (communication), but its surroundings evolved. Warszawa Ochota Cross-City railway station in Warsaw (Poland), designed by A. Romanowicz, P. Szymaniak, 1963. © Błażej Ciarkowski.

for solutions to generate income from it. When presented with alternative scenarios for the development of the facility, the survey respondents also tended to see it as valuable and historic. On the other hand, in the Delphi study, the experts interpreted the financial indicators from the CBA correctly but not technocratically and did not blindly follow them. In other words, the numerical representation of the scenarios serves not so much to objectify them as to allow comparisons with each other in a broader context. Monetary values as outcomes of CBA were not a factor that convinced individuals to make specific choices. Instead, they were a factor that supported the choice rather than determining it. This argument is particularly highlighted by an analysis of statements from the Delphi panel, which were logically consistent and convincing in each case (Lyons, 1989, p. 382).

This case study shows that combining an opinion survey with a cost–benefit analysis and Delphi study may be helpful when investigating the value of ambiguous modernist twentieth-century architecture. While it bears the characteristics of a qualitative and comprehensive study, it also has the characteristics of a quantitative study, as it monetizes the value of many possible consequences of each scenario (Boardman et al., 2018; Vickerman, 2007). However, although CBA seeks to quantify designed actions, it should only be considered an approximation to evaluate their financial consequences (Sunstein, 2019, p. 314). Its use allows various scenarios to be compared with each other, and it provides a general orientation of the anticipated costs and benefits.

Nevertheless, it is not devoid of subjectivity. The different categories of benefits and costs are, in fact, the consequence of a discretionary choice made by the authors of the study. The value of heritage, especially ambiguous heritage, will always remain difficult to capture objectively. Despite this, the objectification of valuation methods through the use of monetary indicators seems justified for both comparative and cognitive purposes.

At the end of the study, the relationship between the Warszawa Ochota railway station and the heterogeneous urban neighbourhood adjacent to it was tested. The surroundings of the railway station are filled with diverse architectural forms and urban layouts. The station neighbours mainly new developments (e.g. high-rise office buildings or hotels). Far from providing a coherent and harmonious urban landscape, they overshadow it (see Picture 3.19).

Our analysis focused on the relationship between the value of a heritage site and the quality of its urban neighbourhood. For this purpose, we conducted a field survey using a standardized questionnaire in which the respondents were asked to value a heritage site from three different spatial "angles." The selection of sites was determined by two criteria: (1) the diversity of neighbourhood components (the sites were chosen to properly capture the diversity of landscape components which make up the surroundings of the heritage site), and (2) there must be a similar distance between the evaluated site and the object so that a similar scale of the station was maintained. Based on these criteria, three angles were selected (Figure 3.17):

1. Angle A – from this perspective, we can see the rooftops of Ochota railway station. The urban environment has metropolitan qualities. Despite powerful architectural structures, the railway station building is not overshadowed. Although this heritage site is surrounded by "younger" and massive buildings, it looks the most modern and "light" among them.
2. Angle B – from this perspective, the body of the station, in particular, the unique hyperbolic curvature of the roof, is most visible. The station dominates the neighbourhood; however, the immediate surroundings are chaotic, distracting attention from the historic site.
3. Angle C – from this perspective, the architectural qualities of the station and its building are hardly visible. We can see only the rooftops of the station. The urban neighbourhood of the building is chaotic, with a great variety of components. From this perspective, no building clearly dominates the view.

Purposive sampling was used to select the respondents. The respondents were students aged 20-25 years. We decided to deliberately select a

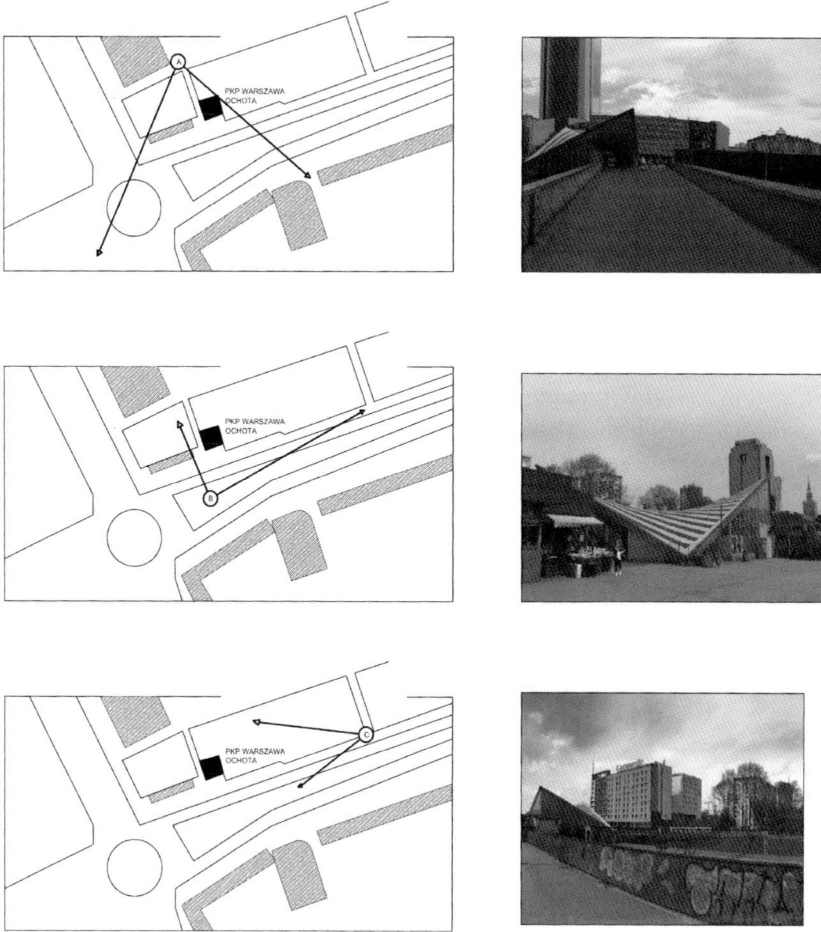

Figure 3.17 Views and angles for the valuation of Warszawa Ochota railway station

Source: Nowakowska et al. (2020, p. 330).

homogeneous age group to the evaluation of the monument. We made this decision following a pilot study conducted in May 2018 on a sample of 22 respondents. Based on this, we adjusted the clarity and understanding of the research tool and the scope of the features evaluated for a particular site, and we calibrated the final selection of the examined group.

Ultimately, the relationship between the valuation of the railway station and its neighbourhood was examined in May 2019 on a sample of 119 respondents. Having validated the collected material, 30 answers were rejected (due to being incomplete), and further analysis covered data for N=89.

The respondents were asked to assess the value of a historic site while actually being there on the spot. Although the method is time-consuming and less popular than the photographic method (Schirpke et al., 2016; Sikorska et al., 2020; Urbis et al., 2019), it eliminates the significant weaknesses of that method (Subiza-Pérez et al., 2021). It allows people to experience the space, offering the whole spectrum of sensations of a site, that is, it takes into account what the respondent feels or hears.

The values of the heritage site were described by categories decomposed in accordance with the four dimensions of spatial order (Łaszkiewicz et al., 2022):

- The social context/dimension of the value of a heritage site – safe/dangerous, with/without historical value, to be left/demolished, builds/does not build the identity of the place, a good/unfavourable place for recreation
- The functional dimension of the value of a heritage site – convenient/inconvenient, a good/unfavourable place for doing business, accessible/inaccessible, useful/useless, modern/obsolete
- The aesthetic dimension of the value of a heritage site – pleasant/irritating, clean/dirty, attractive/unattractive
- The architectural dimension of the value of a heritage site – human/inhuman, fading/dominates the neighbourhood, matches/does not match the image of the city, unique/typical

In the survey, the value of the heritage site was assessed on a ten-point numerical scale. Each respondent evaluated 17 features of the site by scoring them from 1 (most negative features, e.g. unattractive, dirty, dangerous) to 10 (the most positive features, e.g. attractive, clean, safe).

The respondents' mean values were mostly negative. Only 4 of the 17 features earned an average score higher than zero. This confirms that the historic building has an "ambiguous architecture," which rarely elicits positive associations and is generally perceived as having little value to the community (Orszag et al., 2010). However, the respondents described the site as unique rather than typical (0.41), dominating the urban landscape rather than fading into it (0.09), accessible rather than inaccessible (0.61) and useful rather than useless (0.38). The remaining categories, which represented different dimensions of value, were generally rated negatively. The respondents described most negatively those elements that comprise the aesthetic value of the historic site. In particular, they perceived the structure as visually unattractive, dirty and irritating (the lowest value in the aesthetic dimension (–1.75)). In the social dimension, the low value is mainly due to the negative perception of the heritage site as a recreational area (Nowakowska et al., 2020).

The value of the historic building was best assessed from angle B. This perspective provides the best view is what is characteristic and noticeable at first sight, that is, the silhouette of the Warszawa Ochota railway station and its most obvious assets – the curvature of the hyperbolic roof and glazed walls. Apart from the good visibility of the structure itself, the highest score could have been influenced by both its immediate and further surroundings. This is the most "human" perspective, where there are service establishments in the immediate vicinity of the station, and we can see the entrance to the railway station. Further in the background of the station are contemporary buildings of the centre of Warsaw as well as one of the best-known buildings of the capital – the Palace of Culture and Science, one of the landmarks that dominate the landscape of Warsaw. From this perspective, the station is not overwhelmed by other structures that are strong dominants (Nowakowska et al., 2020).

In contrast, the station view seen from angle C is rated the worst. Its value in the social, functional, aesthetic and architectural-urban dimensions is lower than for angles A or B. One might assume that the negative perception of this perspective may have been influenced mainly by the development of the area in front of the station, which includes neglected elements of the railway infrastructure and an inaesthetic concrete wall. This negative impression is reinforced by the chaos in the further neighbourhood of the facility. The fact that angle C was the first to be assessed by the respondents may also be significant as it was their first contact with the building. The halo effect (the automatic attribution of positive or negative characteristics based on the first impression) may have been at work here (Łaszkiewicz et al., 2022).

However, comparing angles A and B, it can be observed that the respondents assigned lower social and architectural value to the heritage site in the first case. In angle A, the body of the building is not so prominent, and its immediate surroundings do not represent high architectural or urban values. Similarly, the lower rating for the social dimension in this perspective may be the result of virtually no development of the building's immediate surroundings, which only perform connective functions (a passage to the entrance to the station over the railway tracks) (Nowakowska et al., 2020).

The research revealed that of all the respondents' characteristics, only the education profile and the frequency with which they use the station are factors that differentiate the assessment of the historic building. However, that is true only for the social (impact of education profile) and architectural aspects (impact of the frequency of use) of value. This confirms that education and actual experience of architecture are important in perceiving the value of a heritage site.

The research has therefore shown that the neighbourhood of Warszawa Ochota railway station impacts the assessment of its value. The assessment of the value of the heritage site is higher for those angles where architectural values of the structure are visible (e.g. roof curvature and glazed walls). In addition, the coherence and harmony of the development in the neighbourhood of the historic building, that is, spatial order, affect the perception of its value. The value of a historic site depends on its features and values, and it is conditioned by its integration into the surrounding urban tissue. The good visibility of the historic building and its harmony with the neighbourhood positively change the perception of the building and significantly determine its social, aesthetic, functional or architectural value.

This may mean that the idea of spatial order is not only a theoretical framework that is useful for architects and urban planners but also a determinant of people's preferences regarding the place or assessing the value of a historic site. Our study showed that people are able to perceive spatial order in visual and aesthetic terms, and also more broadly, for example, as the harmony or spatial cohesion of a heritage site's social or functional features. We have demonstrated that such a wide range of experiences related to a historic site may be manifested in its valuation, which cannot be reduced to a single, standardized value as it is a complex and multidimensional category.

The results of the study provide practical recommendations for shaping urban development policies. They highlight the need for an integrated and holistic view of a heritage site and its neighbourhood (Cilliers et al., 2015; Della Spina, 2018). Urban order should be shaped in such a way that a heritage site's value is reinforced through the composition and quality of the development of its neighbourhood. Additionally, the protection awarded by the conservation authorities and the assessment of the heritage site's value should go beyond a one-dimensional analysis of the very idea, form or function of a historic site and be replaced by a multidisciplinary approach that also takes into account the quality of the space around it. In this context, a place-based policy approach, which emphasizes the place and understanding its development mechanisms, is becoming increasingly important. The challenge becomes to shift from looking through the prism of a single historic site to thinking in terms of a place with its own identity, building a relationship with history, and its embeddedness in the local space (Camagni et al., 2020; Ginzarly et al., 2019a). The focus should be not so much on actions oriented towards eliminating the dysfunctions of the historic site itself, but on undertakings focused on creating the capital of the place. The favourable location of a historic site in space and its integration into the urban environment contribute to a better understanding of not only the value of the site itself but also of the place in which it is located. This, in turn, affects the sense of stability, embeddedness and social involvement in local activities (Brown et al., 2003; Historic England, 2008; Rudokas et al., 2019; Vorkinn & Riese, 2001). This approach implies the need for a holistic and integrated approach to heritage management. These proposals are in line with the thinking about heritage and its protection outlined by, among others, the Faro Convention (Faro Convention on the Value of Cultural Heritage for Society, 2005) and the UNESCO Recommendation (Recommendation on the Historic Urban Landscape, 2011).

Our research confirms that valuing cultural heritage requires a complex approach to capture the multidimensional nature of such value. The proposed analytical approach responds to the call for the need to integrate different valuation methods, especially across disciplines, as a way to explore more deeply the different determinants and dimensions of value (Kronenberg & Andersson, 2019; O'Brien, 2010). The advantage of our research approach lies in its interdisciplinary nature and the combination of the achievements of multiple research streams/disciplines. The study that we carried out is at the borderline between the economics of value (value of a historic site), socio-economic geography (environment and its development), the psychology of perception (perception of urban space) and architecture and urban planning (protection of cultural heritage).

Notes

1 The most valuable heritage sites in Western Eastern Europe are listed, among others, in the Innova Concrete Selection of Significant Twentieth-Century Heritage Sites in Europe.

2 Such facilities are listed within the Socialist Modernism initiative by the Bureau for Art and Urban Research (BACU).

References

Addae-Dapaah, K. (2012). Appraisal and cost-benefit analysis. In S. J. Smith (Ed.), *International encyclopedia of housing and home* (pp. 70–75). Elsevier. https://doi.org/10.1016/B978-0-08-047163-1.00607-X

Amable, B. (2003). *The diversity of modern capitalism*. Oxford University Press.

Appalardo, G., Toscano, S., & Pecorino, B. (2020). Assessing the effects of 'appeal to authority' in the evaluation of environmental goods. Evidences from an economic experiment in Mt Etna, Italy. *Aestimum*, *77*, 113–125. https://doi.org/10.13128/aestim-8365

Babić, D., Kaptan, M. V., & Esquerra, C. M. (2019). Heritage literacy: A model to engage citizens in heritage management. In *Cultural urban heritage development, learning and landscape strategies* (pp. 1–18) https://link.springer.com/chapter/10.1007/978-3-030-10612-6_1

Báez, A., & Herrero, L. C. (2012). Using contingent valuation and cost-benefit analysis to design a policy for restoring cultural heritage. *Journal of Cultural Heritage*, *13*, 235–245. https://doi.org/10.1016/j.culher.2010.12.005

Bateman, I., Carson, R., Day, B., Hanemann, M., Hanley, N., Hett, T., Jones-Lee, M., & Loomes, G. (2002). *Economic valuation with stated preference techniques. A manual*. Edward Elgar. https://doi.org/10.4337/9781781009727

Benton-Short, L. (2006). Politics, public space, and memorials: The brawl on the Mall. *Urban Geography*, *27*(4), 297–329. https://doi.org/10.2747/0272-3638.27.4.297

Blackledge, M. (2009). *Introducing property valuation*. Routledge.

Boardman, A. E., Greenberg, D. H., Vining, A. R., & Weimer, D. L. (2018). *Cost-benefit analysis. Concepts and practice* (5th ed.). Cambridge University Press.

Breidert, C., Hahsler, M., & Reutterer, T. (2006). A review of methods for measuring willingness-to-pay. *Innovative Marketing*. https://doi.org/10.3111/13696998.2011.644408

Brett, D. (1996). *The construction of heritage*. Cork University Press.

Brown, B., Perkins, D. D., & Brown, G. (2003). Place attachment in a revitalizing neighborhood: Individual and block levels of analysis. *Journal of Environmental Psychology*, *23*(3), 259–271. https://doi.org/10.1016/S0272-4944(02)00117-2

Buchanan, J. M. (1991). Opportunity cost. In J. Eatwell, M. Milgate, & P. K. Newman (Eds.), *The new Palgrave: The world of economics* (pp. 520–525). Palgrave Macmillan.https://doi.org/10.1007/978-1-349-21315-3_69

Camagni, R., Capello, R., Cerisola, S., & Panzera, E. (2020). The cultural heritage – Territorial capital nexus: Theory and empirics. *Capitale Culturale*, *11*, 33–59. https://doi.org/10.13138/2039-2362/2547

Chalana, M. (2015). Chandigarh: City and periphery. *Journal of Planning History*, *14*(1), 62–84. https://doi.org/10.1177/1538513214543904

Chalana, M., & Spragu, T. S. (2013). Beyond Le Corbusier and the modernist city: Reframing Chandigarh's 'world heritage' legacy. *Planning Perspectives*, *28*(2), 199–222. https://doi.org/10.1080/02665433.2013.737709

Chen, D., & Li, J. (2021). Process-led value elicitation within built heritage management: A systematic literature review between 2010 and 2020. *Journal of Architectural Conservation*, 27(1–2), 1–16. https://doi.org/10.1080/13556207.2021.1909900

Choi, A. S., Ritchie, B. W., Papandrea, F., & Bennett, J. (2010). Economic valuation of cultural heritage sites: A choice modeling approach. *Tourism Management*. https://doi.org/10.1016/j.tourman.2009.02.014

Ciarkowski, B. (2016). Trudne dziedzictwo łodzi – Historyczna narracja w przestrzeni dawnego Litzmannstadt Ghetto. *Przegląd Kulturoznawczy*, *1*(27), 49–59. https://doi.org/10.4467/20843860PK.16.004.5044

Ciarkowski, B. (2017a). Dissonant heritage: Decoding the historical narrative of rationalist architecture in fascist Italy. *Acta Academiae Artium Vilnensis*, *86–87*, 319–328.

Ciarkowski, B. (2017b). Harmonia czy dysonans – Rozwój architektury uzdrowiskowej w Karpatach i Sudetach w latach 60. i 70. XX wieku. *MAZOWSZE Studia Regionalne*, *20*, 13–24. https://doi.org/10.21858/msr.20.01

Ciarkowski, B. (2017c). *Odcienie szarości. Architekci i polityka w PRL-u* [Shades of grey. architects and politics in the Polish People's Republic]. Wydawnictwo Uniwersytetu Łódzkiego.

Ciarkowski, B. (2017d). Unwanted heritage and its cultural potential. Values of modernist architecture from the times of the Polish People's Republic. *MAZOWSZE Studia Regionalne*, *22*, 71–83. https://doi.org/10.21858/msr.22.05

Cilliers, E. J., Timmermans, W., van den Goorbergh, F., & Slijkhuis, J. S. A. (2015). Designing public spaces through the lively planning integrative perspective. *Environment, Development and Sustainability*, *17*(6), 1367–1380. https://doi.org/10.1007/s10668-014-9610-1

Convention concerning the protection of the world cultural and natural heritage. (1972) (testimony of UNESCO). https://whc.unesco.org/archive/convention-en.pdf

Costa, A., Foucart, A., Arnon, I., Aparici, M., & Apesteguia, J. (2014). 'Piensa' twice: On the foreign language effect in decision making. *Cognition*, *130*(2), 236–254. https://doi.org/10.1016/j.cognition.2013.11.010

Dalmas, L., Geronimi, V., Noël, J. F., & Tsang King Sang, J. (2015). Economic evaluation of urban heritage: An inclusive approach under a sustainability perspective. *Journal of Cultural Heritage*. https://doi.org/10.1016/j.culher.2015.01.009

Della Spina, L. (2018). The integrated evaluation as a driving tool for cultural-heritage enhancement strategies BT - Smart and sustainable planning for cities and regions. In A. Bisello, D. Vettorato, P. Laconte, & S. Costa (Eds.), *Smart and sustainable planning for cities and regions* (pp. 589–600). Springer International Publishing.

Despland, M. (1969). The moral ambiguity of modernity. *Islamic Studies*, *8*(2), 167–184.

Dewey, J. (1922). *Human nature and conduct: An introduction to social psychology*. Holt.

Dewey, J. (1939). Theory of valuation. *Philosophy of Science*, *6*(4), 490–491. https://books.google.pl/books?id=ZUOwAQAACAAJ

Durusoy Özmen, E., & Omay Polat, E. (2021). Assessing the values-based context of conservation for modern architectural heritage: A study on the headquarters building of the T.R. 17th Regional Directorate of Highways Complex, Istanbul. *Journal of Architectural Conservation*, *27*(1–2), 84–103. https://doi.org/10.1080/13556207.2021.1930714

Dwyer, O. J. (2002). Location, politics, and the production of civil rights memorial landscapes. *Urban Geography*. https://doi.org/10.2747/0272-3638.23.1.31

Faro Convention on the Value of Cultural Heritage for Society. (2005). https://www.coe.int/en/web/conventions/full-list/-/conventions/treaty/199?module=treaty-detail&treatynum=199

Fée, D., Colenutt, B., & Schäbitz, S. C. (Eds.). (2020). *Lessons from British and French new towns: Paradise lost?* Emerald Publishing Limited.https://doi.org/10.1108/9781839094309

Ferretti, V., Bottero, M., & Mondini, G. (2014). Decision making and cultural heritage: An application of the multi-attribute value theory for the reuse of historical buildings. *Journal of Cultural Heritage*, *15*, 644–655. https://doi.org/10.1016/j.culher.2013.12.007

Fields, L., Slomka, M., & Shepherd, M. (2020). *A formula for success: Reviewing the social discount rate*. https://www.oxera.com/insights/agenda/articles/a-formula-for-success-reviewing-the-social-discount-rate/

Flint, A. (2018). *Modern man: The life of Le Corbusier, architect of tomorrow*. Amazon Publishing.

Florencka, K. (2018). *Warszawa/Rozpoczęto badania architektury stacji WKD Śródmieście* [Warsaw. A study on the WKD Śródmieście station architecture has been started]. Nauka w Polsce [Science in Poland]. https://naukawpolsce.pl/aktualnosci/news%2C30441%2Cwarszawa-rozpoczeto-badania-architektury-stacji-wkd-srodmiescie.html

Fredheim, L. H., & Khalaf, M. (2016). The significance of values: Heritage value typologies re-examined. *International Journal of Heritage Studies*, *22*(6), 466–481. https://doi.org/10.1080/13527258.2016.1171247

Gadacz, T. (2010). Wartości w czasach zamętu. In M. Madurowicz (Ed.), *Wartościowanie współczesnej przestrzeni miejskiej* (pp. 17–30). Wydział Geografii i Studiów Regionalnych Uniwersytetu Warszawskiego – Urząd Miasta Stołecznego Warszawy.

Garnett, R. (2002). *The impact of science centers/museums on their surrounding communities: Summary report*. Association of Science-Technology Centers, Questacon. https://www.ecsite.eu/sites/default/files/impact_study02.pdf

Ghosh, N. (2016). Modern designs: History and memory in Le Corbusier's Chandigarh. *Journal of Architecture and Urbanism*, *40*(3), 220–228. https://doi.org/10.3846/20297955.2016.1210048

Gibson, L., & Pendlebury, J. (2009). Introduction: Valuing historic environments. In J. Pendlebury & L. Gibson (Eds.), *Valuing historic environments* (1st ed., pp. 1–16). Routledge. https://doi.org/10.4324/9781315548449

Ginzarly, M., Houbart, C., & Teller, J. (2019a). The historic urban landscape approach to urban management: A systematic review. *International Journal of Heritage Studies*, *25*(10), 999–1019. https://doi.org/10.1080/13527258.2018.1552615

Ginzarly, M., Pereira Roders, A., & Teller, J. (2019b). Mapping historic urban landscape values through social media. *Journal of Cultural Heritage*, *36*, 1–11. https://doi.org/10.1016/j.culher.2018.10.002

Grüb, B., & Martin, S. (2020). Public value of cultural heritages – Towards a better understanding of citizen's valuation of Austrian museums. *Cultural Trends*, *29*(5), 337–358. https://doi.org/10.1080/09548963.2020.1822142

Guzmán, P. C., Pereira-Roders, A. R., & Colenbrander, B. J. F. (2017). Measuring links between cultural heritage management and sustainable urban development: An overview of global monitoring tools. *Cities*, *60*, 192–201. https://doi.org/10.1016/j.cities.2016.09.005

Hartwick, J. M. (1977). Intergenerational equity and the investing of rents from exhaustible resources. *American Economic Review*, *67*(5), 972–974.

Harvey, D. (2001). Heritage pasts and heritage presents: Temporality, meaning and the scope of heritage studies. *International Journal of Heritage Studies*, *7*(4), 319–338. https://doi.org/10.1080/13581650120105534

Hayakawa, S., Costa, A., Foucart, A., & Keysar, B. (2016). Using a foreign language changes our choices. *Trends in Cognitive Sciences*, *20*(11), 791–793. https://doi.org/10.1016/j.tics.2016.08.004

Hicks, J. R. (1940). The valuation of the social income. *Economica*, *7*(26), 105–124. https://doi.org/10.2307/2548691

Historic England. (2008). *Conservation principles: Policies and guidance for the sustainable management of the historic environment*. English Heritage. https://historicengland.org.uk/images-books/publications/conservation-principles-sustainable-management-historic-environment

Hofstede, G. (1997). *Cultures and organizations: Software of the mind*. McGraw-Hill.

Hultkrantz, L. (2021). Discounting in economic evaluation of healthcare interventions: What about the risk term? *The European Journal of Health Economics*, *22*(3), 357–363. https://doi.org/10.1007/s10198-020-01257-x

Hutter, M., & Rizzo, I. (1997). *Economic perspectives on cultural heritage*. Palgrave Macmillan. https://doi.org/10.1007/978-1-349-25824-6

Ingerpuu, L. (2018). Socialist architecture as today's dissonant heritage: Administrative buildings of collective farms in Estonia. *International Journal of Heritage Studies*, *24*(9), 954–968. https://doi.org/10.1080/13527258.2018.1428664

Jahandideh-Kodehi, G., Kavoosi-Kalashami, M., & Motamed, M. K. (2021). Landscape valuation of historical tourism site in Northern Iran: A case study from Sheikh-Zahed Tomb. *GeoScape*, *15*(1), 79–89. https://doi.org/10.2478/geosc-2021-0007

Kaldor, N. (1939). Welfare propositions of economics and interpersonal comparisons of utility. *The Economic Journal*, *49*(195), 549–552. https://doi.org/10.2307/2224835

Kanbur, R. (1987). Shadow pricing. In J. Eatwell, M. Milgate, & P. K. Newman (Eds.), *The new Palgrave: A dictionary of economics. Volume IV* (2nd ed., pp. 316–317). Palgrave Macmillan.

Kronenberg, J., & Andersson, E. (2019). Integrating social values with other value dimensions: Parallel use vs. combination vs. full integration. *Sustainability Science*, *14*(5), 1283–1295. https://doi.org/10.1007/s11625-019-00688-7

Krupowicz, J. (2005). Metody heurystyczne. In M. Cieślak (Ed.), *Prognozowanie gospodarcze. Metody i zastosowania* (4th ed., pp. 201–222). Wydawnictwo Naukowe PWN.

Kucharska-Stasiak, E. (2016a). *Ekonomiczny wymiar nieruchomości.* Wydawnictwo Naukowe PWN.

Kucharska-Stasiak, E. (2016b). Wycena nieruchomości w gospodarce globalnej. *International Business and Global Economy*, *35*(1), 429–440.

Langemeyer, J., Baró, F., Roebeling, P., & Gómez-Baggethun, E. (2015). Contrasting values of cultural ecosystem services in urban areas: The case of park Montjuïc in Barcelona. *Ecosystem Services*, *12*, 178–186. https://doi.org/10.1016/j.ecoser.2014.11.016

Łaszkiewicz, E., Nowakowska, A., & Adamus, J. (2022). How valuable is architectural heritage? Evaluating a monument's perceived value with the use of spatial order concept. *SAGE Open*, *12*(4), 21582440221142720. https://doi.org/10.1177/21582440221142720

Le Corbusier. (1923). *Vers une architecture.* L'Esprit nouveau.

Levine, N. (2015). *The urbanism of frank Lloyd Wright.* Princeton University Press.

Light, D. (2000). An unwanted past: Contemporary tourism and the heritage of communism in Romania. *International Journal of Heritage Studies*, *6*(2), 145–160. https://doi.org/10.1080/135272500404197

Linstone, H. A., & Turoff, M. (1975). *The Delphi method. Techniques and applications.* Addison-Wesley Publishing Company.

Logan, W., & Reeves, K. (2009). *Places of pain and shame. Dealing with 'difficult heritage'.* Routledge.

Louviere, J. J. (2001). Choice experiments: An overview of concepts and issues. In J. Bennett & R. Blarney (Eds.), *The choice modelling approach to environmental valuation* (pp. 13–36). Edward Elgar.

Łukasik, M. (2014). Redefinition of modernist architecture in the context of creating "the social". *SGEM 2014 International Multidisciplinary Scientific Conferences on Social Sciences and Arts*, 939–946.

Lyons, J. (1989). *Semantyka.* Państwowe Wydawnictwo Naukowe.

MacDonald, S. (2009). *Difficult heritage: Negotiating the Nazi past in Nuremberg and beyond.* Routledge.

Madden, K., & Schwartz, A. (2000). *How to turn a place around: A handbook for creating successful public spaces.* Project for Public Spaces.

McConnell, V., & Walls, M. (2005). *The value of open space: Evidence from studies of nonmarket benefits*. Resources for the Future. https://media.rff.org/documents/RFF-REPORT-Open20Spaces.pdf

McDowell, S. (2008). Heritage, memory and identity. In *The Ashgate research companion to heritage and identity* (pp. 37–53). Ashgate Publishing.

Merciu, F.-C., Petrişor, A.-I., & Merciu, G.-L. (2021). Economic valuation of cultural heritage using the travel cost method: The historical centre of the municipality of Bucharest as a case study. *Heritage*, *4*(3), 2356–2376. https://doi.org/10.3390/heritage4030133

Merta-Staszczak, A. (2018). *Niechciane Dziedzictwo. Nieruchomości zabytkowe na Dolnym Śląsku w latach 1945–1989*. Wydawnictwo Naukowe SCHOLAR.

Mind Tools Content Team. (2021). *Cost-benefit analysis. Deciding, quantitatively, whether to go ahead*. Mind Tools. http://www.mindtools.com/pages/article/newTED_08.htm

Mitchell, D. (2003). *Cultural geography: A critical introduction*. Blackwell Publishing.

Murzyn, M. A. (2008). Heritage transformation in Central and Eastern Europe. In B. J. Graham & P. Howard (Eds.), *The Ashgate research companion to heritage and identity* (pp. 315–345). Ashgate Publishing.

Murzyn-Kupisz, M. (2015). Values of cultural heritage in the context of socio-economics. In B. Szmygin (Ed.), *Heritage value assessment systems. The problems and the current state of research* (pp. 147–164). Lublin University of Technology-Polish National Committee of the International Council on Monuments and Sites (ICOMOS).

Nesticò, A., Morano, P., & Sica, F. (2018). A model to support the public administration decisions for the investments selection on historic buildings. *Journal of Cultural Heritage*, *33*, 201–207. https://doi.org/10.1016/j.culher.2018.03.008

Nesticò, A., & Sica, F. (2017). The sustainability of urban renewal projects: A model for economic multi-criteria analysis. *Journal of Property Investment and Finance*, *35*(4), 397–409. https://doi.org/10.1108/JPIF-01-2017-0003

NID. (2013). *Społeczno-kulturowe oddziaływanie dziedzictwa kulturowego. Raport z badań społecznych*.

Niżankowski, R., Bała, M., Dubiel, B., Hetnał, M., Kawalec, P., Łanda, K., Plisko, R., & Wilk, N. (2002). *Analiza opłacalności*. Uniwersyteckie Wydawnictwo Medyczne VESALIUS.

Nowacki, M. (2009). Skłonność do zapłaty a cena wstępu do atrakcji turystycznej. *Zeszyty Naukowe Uniwersytetu Szczecińskiego. Ekonomiczne Problemy Turystyki*, *568*(13), 101–114.

Nowakowska, A., Guz, J., & Łaszkiewicz, E. (2020). How is the multidimensional perception of modern architectural objects associated with their surroundings? An example of Warsaw Ochota urban railway station. In Z. Gál, S. Z. Kovács, & B. Páger (Eds.), *Proceedings of the 7th CERS Conference* (pp. 323–336). European Regional Science Association. http://real.mtak.hu/116284/7/cers-kotet-2020.pdf

O'Brien, D. (2010). *Measuring the value of culture: A report to the Department for Culture, Media and Sport*. https://www.gov.uk/government/publications/measuring-the-value-of-culture-a-report-to-the-department-for-culture-media-and-sport

Ochkovskaya, M., & Gerasimenko, V. (2018). Buildings from the socialist past as part of a city's brand identity: The case of Warsaw. *Bulletin of Geography*, *39*(39), 113–127. https://doi.org/10.2478/bog-2018-0008

Orszag, P. R., Barnes, M. C., Douglas, D., & Summers, L. (2010). *Developing effective place-based policies for the FY 2012 Budget*. https://obamawhitehouse.archives.gov/sites/default/files/omb/assets/memoranda_2010/m10-21.pdf

Parker, D. (2016). *International valuation standards. A guide to the valuation of real property assets*. John Wiley & Sons.

Pearce, D. W., & Atkinson, G. D. (1993). Capital theory and the measurement of sustainable development: An indicator of 'weak' sustainability. *Ecological Economics*, *8*(2), 103–108. https://doi.org/10.1016/0921-8009(93)90039-9

PFSRM. (2011). *Międzynarodowe standardy wyceny* (M. Trojanek, J. Konowalczuk, & T. Ramian (Eds.)). Polska Federacja Stowarzyszeni Rzeczoznawców Majątkowych.

Provins, A., Pearce, D., Ozdemiroglu, E., Mourato, S., & Morse-Jones, S. (2008). Valuation of the historic environment: The scope for using economic valuation evidence in the appraisal of heritage-related projects. *Progress in Planning*, *69*(4), 131–175. https://doi.org/10.1016/j.progress.2008.01.001

Rampley, M. (2012). *Heritage, ideology, and identity in Central and Eastern Europe. Contested pasts, contested presents*. The Boydell Press.

Ready, R. C., & Navrud, S. (2002). Why value cultural heritage? In *Valuing cultural heritage. Applying environmental valuation techniques to historic buildings, monuments and artifacts* (pp. 3–9). Edward Elgar Publishing.https://doi.org/10.4337/9781843765455.00009

Recommendation on the Historic Urban Landscape. (2011). http://portal.unesco.org/en/ev.php-URL_ID=48857&URL_DO=DO_TOPIC&URL_SECTION=201.html

Reilly, K. D. (1973). The Delphi technique: Fundamentals and applications. In H. Borko (Ed.), *Targets for research in library education* (pp. 187–199). American Library Association.

RICS. (2015). *Code of measuring practice* (6th ed.). Royal Institution of Chartered Surveyors.

RICS. (2019). *RICS valuation – Global standards. Incorporating the IVSC international valuation standards*. Royal Institution of Chartered Surveyors.

Rudokas, K., Landauskas, M., Gražulevičiūtė-Vilneiškė, I., & Viliūnienė, O. (2019). Valuing the socio-economic benefits of built heritage: Local context and mathematical modeling. *Journal of Cultural Heritage*, *39*, 229–237. https://doi.org/10.1016/j.culher.2019.02.016

Scarrett, D. (2008). *Property valuation. The five methods* (2nd ed.). Routledge.

Schirpke, U., Timmermann, F., Tappeiner, U., & Tasser, E. (2016). Cultural ecosystem services of mountain regions: Modelling the aesthetic value. *Ecological Indicators*, *69*, 78–90. https://doi.org/10.1016/j.ecolind.2016.04.001

Schläpfer, F., Waltert, F., Segura, L., & Kienast, F. (2015). Valuation of landscape amenities: A hedonic pricing analysis of housing rents in urban, suburban and periurban Switzerland. *Landscape and Urban Planning*, *141*, 24–40. https://doi.org/10.1016/j.landurbplan.2015.04.007

Šćitaroci, M. O. (2019). Preface: The heritage urbanism approach and method. In M. O. Šćitaroci, B. Bojanić, O. Šćitaroci, & A. Mrđa (Eds.), *Cultural urban heritage development, learning and landscape strategies* (pp. v–xiv). Springer.

Sikorska, D., Macegoniuk, S., Łaszkiewicz, E., & Sikorski, P. (2020). Energy crops in urban parks as a promising alternative to traditional lawns – Perceptions and a cost-benefit analysis. *Urban Forestry & Urban Greening*, *49*, 126579. https://doi.org/10.1016/j.ufug.2019.126579

Silverman, H. (2011). *Contested cultural heritage. Religion, nationalism, erasure, and exclusion in a global world*. Springer.

Sinclair, W., Huber, C., & Richardson, L. (2020). Valuing tourism to a historic World War II national memorial. *Journal of Cultural Heritage*, *45*, 334–338. https://doi.org/10.1016/j.culher.2020.04.007

Śleszyński, J., & Wiewiórski, R. (2011). Wycena ekonomiczna dóbr kultury na przykładzie piwnic Pałacu Saskiego w Warszawie. *Ekonomista*, *2*, 283–295.

Smith, L. (2008). *Uses of heritage*. Routledge.

Sokołowicz, M. E. (2022). Wartościowanie niejednoznacznego dziedzictwa modernizmu w mieście na przykładzie stacji kolejowej Warszawa Ochota [Valuating the ambiguous heritage of modernism in cities based on the case of the Warsaw Ochota train station]. *Studia Regionalne i Lokalne*, *1*(87), 86–107. https://doi.org/10.7366/1509499518706

Sokołowicz, M. E., & Przygodzki, Z. (2020). The value of ambiguous architecture in cities. The concept of a valuation method of 20th century post-socialist train stations. *Cities*. https://doi.org/10.1016/j.cities.2020.102786

Springer, F. (2011). *Źle urodzone. Reportaże o architekturze PRL-u*. Karakter.

Sproull, N. L. (1988). *Handbook of research methods: A guide for practitioners and students in the social sciences*. Scarecrow Press.

Stern, N. (2007). *The economics of climate change. The Stern review*. Cabinet Office – HM Treasury. https://webarchive.nationalarchives.gov.uk/ukgwa/20100407172811/https:/www.hm-treasury.gov.uk/stern_review_report.htm

Subiza-Pérez, M., Korpela, K., & Pasanen, T. (2021). Still not that bad for the grey city: A field study on the restorative effects of built open urban places. *Cities*, *111*, 103081. https://doi.org/10.1016/j.cities.2020.103081

Sunstein, C. R. (2019). *The cost-benefit revolution*. MIT Press. https://doi.org/10.7551/mitpress/11571.001.0001

TEEB. (2011). TEEB manual for cities: Ecosystem services in urban management. In *The economics of ecosystems and biodiversity*. United Nations Environment Programme-European Commission.

The Allen Consulting Group. (2005). *Valuing the priceless: The value of heritage protection in Australia*.

Throsby, D. (1999). Cultural capital. *Journal of Cultural Economics*, *23*, 3–12. https://doi.org/10.1023/a:1007543313370

Throsby, D. (2001). *Economics and culture*. Cambridge University Press.

Trocki, M., & Grucza, B. (2007). *Zarządzanie projektem europejskim*. Polskie Wydawnictwo Ekonomiczne.

Tunbridge, J. E., & Ashworth, G. J. (1996). *Dissonant heritage. The management of the past as a resource in conflict*. John Wiley & Sons.

Urbis, A., Povilanskas, R., & Newton, A. (2019). Valuation of aesthetic ecosystem services of protected coastal dunes and forests. *Ocean & Coastal Management*, *179*, 104832. https://doi.org/10.1016/j.ocecoaman.2019.104832

Venkatachalam, L. (2004). The contingent valuation method: A review. *Environmental Impact Assessment Review*, *24*(1), 89–124. https://doi.org/10.1016/S0195-9255(03)00138-0

Vickerman, R. (2007). Cost-benefit analysis and large-scale infrastructure projects: State of the art and challenges. *Environment and Planning B: Planning and Design*, *34*(4), 598–610. https://doi.org/10.1068/b32112

Vorkinn, M., & Riese, H. (2001). Environmental concern in a local context: The significance of place attachment. *Environment and Behavior*, *33*(2), 249–263. https://doi.org/10.1177/00139160121972972

While, A. (2006). Modernism vs urban renaissance: Negotiating post-war heritage in English city centres. *Urban Studies*, *43*(13), 2399–2419. http://10.0.4.56/00420980601038206

Williamson, K. (2002). The Delphi method. In K. Williamson (Ed.), *Research methods for students, academics and professionals. Information management and systems* (pp. 209–220). Woodhead Publishing.

Wright, W. C. C., & Eppink, F. V. (2016). Drivers of heritage value: A meta-analysis of monetary valuation studies of cultural heritage. *Ecological Economics*, *130*, 277–284. https://doi.org/10.1016/j.ecolecon.2016.08.001

Wyatt, P. (2007). *Property valuation in an economic context*. Blackwell Publishing.

4 The protection of ambiguous legacy in CEE countries

Case studies

Modernism was a movement in architecture and urban planning that, as an "international style," took over the whole world in the twentieth century. Nevertheless, in different parts of the world, it has its local manifestations, reflected both in the aesthetic and visual layers and in the attitude of nations and local communities to specific objects in particular locations. This ability to create local variations and the propensity to interpret through the spirit of place and time constitutes the international character of the modern movement in architecture (Basista, 2001, p. 56). In this context, it is possible to distinguish modernism's uniqueness in the post-socialist (socialist modernism – soc-modernism) bloc of Central and Eastern Europe (CEE) against the rest of the world, but also to see the specifics of individual countries, cities and regions within the bloc.

The term soc-modernism was coined by Adam Miłobędzki (1994, pp. 122–123), who referred to the domestic construction of 1956–1989 in Poland. In recent years, however, both the term and its definition have begun to raise some doubts and attract critics. Researchers and journalists (mainly from CEE) still use it. In *The Guardian*, Naomi Larsson (2018) defined it as the architecture of the former Eastern Bloc countries from 1955 to 1991, citing Dumitru Rusu, a Romanian architect and founder of the B.A.C.U. Studio (B.A.C.U., 2019) and websites that promote the architecture of "socialist modernism" (B.A.C.U., 2021). However, the term is not reserved only for post-communist construction in CEE countries. Jelena Janković-Beguš, for example, wrote about soc-modernism in Serbian music as a combination of modernist form and socialist idea (Janković-Beguš, 2017, p. 149). This short definition seems accurate and, importantly, universal – it can be successfully applied to architecture.

A means of capturing soc-modernism's peculiarities against the background of world modernism and the search for local differences within the Eastern Bloc is to adopt a methodological approach based on case studies (Blatter, 2008). For such investigations, choosing a subject of study is complicated based on rigorously objective criteria. It is because such a choice depends on the researcher's conviction that selecting a particular subject is justified from the perspective of the research goals.

DOI: 10.4324/9781003299172-5

We do not consider this a flaw but an advantage of the study, taking into account the ambiguity of soc-modernist concrete heritage. The value of this approach is the possibility of a deeper understanding of specific, territorially embedded phenomena. The proximity to the local reality that the case study brings, and the opportunity to learn from the study during the investigation are conducive to further research. The kind of intensive observation made possible by a case study differs from quantitative research based on the statistical study of large groups, where the researcher decomposes cases into anonymized variables which remain "hidden" in the mass of other cases (Flyvbjerg, 2006, p. 236). In the humanities and social sciences, absolute research objectivity does not exist – knowledge always remains context dependent. For this reason, "sometimes we simply have to keep our eyes open and look carefully at individual cases – not in the hope of proving anything, but rather in the hope of learning something!" (Eysenck, 1976, p. 7) Or, as Bent Flyvbjerg (2006, p. 224) writes, "predictive theories and universals cannot be found in the study of human affairs. Concrete, context-dependent knowledge is, therefore, more valuable than the vain search for predictive theories and universals."

Referring to the classification of case studies proposed by Stake (1994), our approach is a collective case study, as, within a single research exercise, we study the same phenomenon (i.e. the ambiguous heritage of soc-modernism) and its territorially embedded conditions. We have chosen our cases to understand better or create better theoretical generalizations while referring to the context of CEE countries. On the other hand, we propose descriptive cases in this chapter regarding Robert Yin's classification (Yin, 2003, p. 5). Thus, we developed a preliminary theoretical description of the phenomenon before the research project. We based it on the classification of value with a general division into use and non-use value and a more detailed classification, including (in the non-use dimension) option, existence and bequest value (Murzyn-Kupisz, 2015, p. 157; The Allen Consulting Group, 2005, p. 5) (cf. Section 3.2). Therefore, in covering each case, we explicitly refer to this classification, each time attempting to assess which type of value prevails according to this classification.

The cases for our analysis come from different post-communist countries: Poland, Bulgaria, Lithuania (formerly part of the USSR), and two countries that emerged from the breakup of Yugoslavia – Slovenia and Macedonia (Table 4.1). It provides a geographically diverse distribution – from one of the largest countries of the bloc, such as Poland, to a mid-sized country (Bulgaria), a country heavily dependent on the "core" of the Soviet bloc (Lithuania as a small peripheral republic of the USSR), to countries that, since the 1990s, have built their national identity basically from scratch and, for this reason, have had to redefine their relationship to the Yugoslav legacy of the socialist era.

Table 4.1 The protection of ambiguous legacy in CEE countries – Comparing the case studies

	The Railway station in Katowice	*Buzludzha Monument (The Monument of the Bulgarian Communist Party)*	*Telecommunications Centre (Current name: Macedonian Telecom, Post Head Office of Macedonia HQ, MEPSO)*	*Concert and Sports Palace (Sporto rūmai)*	*Republic Square in Ljubljana, Slovenia*
Location	Katowice, Poland Maria and Lech Kaczyński Square 2, 40-098 Katowice, Poland	Hadji Dimitar, Buzludzha mountain Stara Zagora 6140 Shipka, Bulgaria www.buzludzha-project.com	Marko Cepenkov 40, Skopje 1000, North Macedonia	Rinktinės Street 1 17400 Vilnius, Lithuania	Republic Square 1 Ljubljana, Slovenia
Authors	**Architects:** **Engineers:**	**Architect:** Georgi Stoilov **Engineer**: Dobromir Kolarov **Artists:** Vladislav Paskalev, Kuncho Kanev, Velichko Minekov, Valentin Starchev, Hristo Stefanov, Ioan Leviev, Dimitar Boykov, Mihail Benchev, Ivan Kirkov, Toma Varbanov, Alexander Terziev, Georgi Trifonov, Ivan Stoilov – Bunkera, Ivan B. Ivanov, Grigor Spiridonov, Dimitar Kirov, Stoimen Stoilov, Stoyo Todorov	**Architects:** Janko Konstantinov (with Dušanka Balabanovska, Lenka Janeva, Kostadinka Pemova and Mimora Kapsarova), Zoran Štaklev **Artist:** Borko Lazeski	**Architects:** Eduardas Chlomauskas, Jonas Kriukelis, Zigmantas Liandzbergis **Engineers:** Henrikas Karvelis, Algimantas Katiulius, Sofija Kovarskaja **Artists:** Tadas Baginskas (interior design), R. Kavaliauskas	**Architects:** Edvard Ravnikar Anton Bitenc, Miloš Bonča, Jože Koželj, Anton Pibernik, Franc Rihtar, Vladislav Sedej

(*Continued*)

Table 4.1 The protection of ambiguous legacy in CEE countries – Comparing the case studies (*Continued*)

	The Railway station in Katowice	*Buzludzha Monument (The Monument of the Bulgarian Communist Party)*	*Telecommunications Centre (Current name: Macedonian Telecom, Post Head Office of Macedonia HQ, MEPSO)*	*Concert and Sports Palace (Sporto rūmai)*	*Republic Square in Ljubljana, Slovenia*
Dates of commission	…	1959 (1971)	1968–1969	1960	1960
Dates of completion	…	1974–1981	1972–1981 1987–1989	1964–1971	1961–1974 1975–1982
Prevailing heritage value	Use value + Option value	Option value	Use value + Option value	Existence value	Use value + Existence value
Use vs non-use value	Use value > non-use value	Use value < non-use value	Use value > non-use value	Use value >< non-use value	Use value >< non-use value

The cases are also functionally diverse – the chosen sites and places serve different roles and functions that have changed over the years. Thus, our case studies cover transportation functions (the railway station and its surroundings in Katowice, Poland), representational objects, such as the Communist Party "palace" on top of Mount Buzludzha in Bulgaria, or the palace of sports and culture in the Lithuanian capital. The cases from the Balkans concern a building with primarily office functions, erected as part of the reconstruction of the city after the earthquake (the Central Post and Telecommunication Office in Skopje, Northern Macedonia) or the representative and complex public space of the main square in the capital of the new state, Republic Square in Ljubljana, Slovenia. The sources of knowledge used in our research were primary and secondary materials. For the former, we based the research on six conversations and interviews with local experts who deal with issues of modernist architecture in their countries and cities. They work either in academia or in NGOs involved in protecting and promoting the heritage of modernism. We also used scholarly and journalistic studies published in English and the native languages. From the perspective of deepening the knowledge of soc-modernism in CEE, this selection seems appropriate, providing valuable material to reflect on the ambiguous legacy of soc-modernism.

The railway station in Katowice, Poland – From destruction to value discourse

Historical background and evolution of object's functions

The Railway Station in Katowice was one of those investments that were part of a wide-ranging cross-sector modernization programme of the whole region. In the first years after World War II, the communist authorities initiated a strategy to develop the Upper Silesian Industrial Region (Pol. *Górnośląski Okręg Przemysłowy* – GOP). It included expanding heavy industry, building coal mines and steelworks, and increasing the number of new housing estates, schools and public-use buildings. There was also an increase in communication and transport networks, which were also modernized. Starting with a complex inventory of the existing situation, as well as analyses and preliminary forecasts, architects and urban planners created visions of the region's development (Żmudzińska-Nowak, 2017, p. 145).

Silesia was a region of special importance because of the key role its heavy industry played in the economic development of socialist Poland. From the late 1950s, the Silesian local authorities wanted to create an image of a dynamic, modern region. First, there was Edward Gierek, the first secretary of the Katowice Voivodeship Committee of *Polska Zjednoczona Partia Robotnicza* (PZPR; the Polish United Workers' Party). After Gierek left Silesia to become the First Secretary of the PZPR at the national level, he was replaced by General Jerzy Ziętek. For many years, he was the charismatic leader of the region who, among other achievements, became a patron of architecture (Żmudzińska-Nowak, 2017, pp. 182–183).

The development of architecture in communist Poland was similar to that in other socialist countries of the Eastern Bloc. The years between 1945 and 1948 were a time when the communist authorities were only laying the groundwork for their regime in Poland. The unification of the Polish Socialist Party and the Polish Workers' Party into the Polish United Workers' Party in 1948 allowed for a tougher course in external policy. In the middle of the following year, the doctrine of socialist realism was officially implemented. The National Council of Party Architects proclaimed a resolution that defined the directions of development of socialist architecture (National Party Meeting of Architects, 1949, p. 162). The Stalinist vision of architecture was applied until 1956, when advocates of moderate reforms came to power. From then, Polish architecture developed somewhat freely, and the limitations were not a result of ideology but economic factors and technical and executive possibilities.

The communist authorities considered modernist (soc-modernist) architecture an important means of creating an image of a modern, progressive country. In the architectural landscape of *Polska Rzeczpospolita Ludowa* (PRL; the Polish People's Republic), there was a special place reserved for "icons" or, as Andrzej Basista named them, "prestigious investments" (Basista, 2001, pp. 101–102). They were considered by politicians to be a priority, resulting in bigger budgets, better quality building materials and technologies, and, last but not least, a wider range of possibilities for architects. The railway station in Katowice was, without doubt, one of the "prestigious investments" of its time.

The first railway station was built in the 1840s, but due to the rapid growth and development of the Silesian agglomeration, and ambitious plans for the future, it was too small. In 1957, the Regional Headquarters of Polish State Railways in Katowice commissioned four versions of a preliminary project of the new station, which would be much larger than the existing one and capable of servicing 200,000 passengers a day (Borowik, 2019, p. 252). The competition was finally announced in 1959. The task was not only to design a railway station in Katowice but also to its surroundings, which comprised an additional, temporary pavilion of the railway station and an office building. The jury awarded first prize to a team of Warsaw-based architects: Wacław Kłyszewski, Jerzy Mokrzyński and Eugeniusz Wierzbicki, supported by Wacław Zalewski and Zenon Zieliński (construction engineers) (Borowik, 2019, pp. 253–254). Their concept, in addition to the functions included in the competition programme, included a 60-metre high hotel – a visible landmark and spatial dominant, which would emphasize the importance of the new complex. The jury noted in the verdict that the project combined the values of an economical yet aesthetically satisfying building (Minorski, 1960, p. 138) (see Picture 4.20).

Picture 4.20 The new railway station in Katowice was constructed in the early 1970s. It was one of the architectural symbols of the power of the whole region and the prosperity of Gierek's times. Railway station in Katowice (Poland) designed by W. Kłyszewski, J. Mokrzyński, E. Wierzbicki, 1966–1972. © Kazimierz Seko PAP.

Kłyszewski, Mokrzyński and Wierzbicki were recognized architects, designers of several important buildings (e.g. the headquarters of the Central Committee of the Polish United Workers' Party in Warsaw and the University of Social Sciences in Warsaw) and winners of multiple competitions. Professional successes were the reason why their team was nicknamed "The Tigers," architectural predators who ruthlessly defeated any competitors (Barucki, 1987, pp. 24–25). Meanwhile, Zalewski, who was responsible for the structural engineering part of the project, became known as the most talented engineer in post-war Poland, involved in designing multiple iconic structures (e.g. the "Supersam" department store in Warsaw or the "Spodek" sports hall in Katowice) and, later, professor at Massachusetts Institute of Technology).

In 1963, the new platforms were ready, and the construction of the "southern pavilion," which was supposed to serve travellers until the main building was completed, started. It was completed in 1964. The construction of the main part of the project, the new railway station, started in 1966 and lasted six years. The new structure was raised 300 metres above the location of the old railway station. To make it possible, various styles of tenements in the vicinity of the station had to be demolished. Although nowadays, one might regard it as cultural barbarity, it was a natural result of negative attitudes towards the nineteenth-century aesthetics that most modernist architects represented. Particular parts of the whole complex were completed in phases, and the local media praised the efficiency of the construction works because they did not stop the train traffic. Finally, the official inauguration took place in 1973. Despite the relatively long time from the very beginning to the grand finale, the original concept of functional and structural solutions, created in 1959, remained almost unchanged (Barucki, 1987, p. 39).

The new building had the shape of a huge rectangle (144 × 54 metres) and was 14.5 metres high. The extensive functional aspects were split over two levels connected by escalators. On the ground floor, there were ticket offices, a lounge, luggage storage, an office and a restaurant. Meanwhile, on the first floor, the architects provided space for ticket offices, a waiting room, a cafeteria, a social room, a post office and a kiosk (Architektura, 1973, p. 370). Kłyszewski, Mokrzyński and Wierzbicki designed an innovative functional system based on separating arrivals and departures, with an expected capacity of 25,000 passengers per hour.

The form of the building was determined by its structure, which comprised 16 reinforced concrete pillars that supported a thin-shell vault (8 cm thin) (Kozina, 2019, p. 298). Their surface had visible traces of the wooden formwork, emphasizing the features of the structure and the material, which was characteristic of brutalism in architecture (Jencks, 1975, 1980). Mokrzyński, one of the designers, stated: "In the architectural composition of the object and its interiors, the number of means of artistic expression was limited, and only strived to preserve the authentic texture and colour of the materials used" (Mokrzyński, 1979, p. 518).

The uniqueness of the building's structure lies not only in its aesthetics but also in how it was constructed. Although it was Zalewski who came up with the general concept, the final result was a team effort, a result of the cooperation of several engineers: Zalewski, Jerzy Lindeman, Tadeusz Woźniak and Tadeusz Zajączkowski (Borowik, 2019, p. 259). They created a unique system that allowed them to raise a massive structure in a zone of mining disasters. Due to the difficult ground conditions, they designed a system in which every pillar had independent monolithic foundations (Gzowska, 2012, p. 36). The shape of mushroom columns that smoothly passed into vaults was an innovative solution used abroad by architects, like Felix Candela, but in socialist Poland, it was almost unknown (Gzowska, 2012, p. 35) (see Picture 4.21).

Picture 4.21 The unique characteristic of the railway station in Katowice is derived from the innovative reinforced concrete structure comprising massive mushroom pillars. Railway station in Katowice (Poland) designed by W. Kłyszewski, J. Mokrzyński, and E. Wierzbicki, 1966–1972. © Kazimierz Seko PAP.

The architecture of the railway station was widely commented on, and the reactions of architectural critics were positive. The building was compared to the best examples of modernist architecture in the world. Commentators described the mastery in design and the "Niemeyer-like use of reinforced concrete" (Borowik, 2019, p. 268). According to one of the most recognized architects in post-war Poland, Aleksander Franta, the station was an example of architectural design at a high level. Tadeusz P. Szafer, architect and architecture historian, noted that the shape of the railway station in Katowice distinguishes itself with the scale and the form of beautiful proportions, with dominating reinforced concrete construction of the sculpture-like vaultsn (Szafer, 1979, p. 245). In 1974, Kłyszewski, Mokrzyński and Wierzbicki were awarded the first-degree state prize for their outstanding achievement in the category of public-use building.

The fate of the brutalist railway station after the collapse of the communist system in 1989 is a portrait of the change in attitudes to soc-modernism. In 2010 the building was demolished. The negative social reception of the architecture of the railway station was mostly a result of negligence and lack of day-to-day maintenance and conservation (Gzowska, 2012, p. 122). The rough concrete surfaces were covered with dirt, and the once elegant composition of the building was distorted by kitschy, colourful advertisements and signboards. However, no major modifications were made, and the building designed by "The Tigers" preserved its functionality and structural quality till the end. It could easily have been adapted to the needs and expectations of contemporary users and visitors (Gzowska, 2012, p. 123). Unfortunately, one of the stakeholders, Polish Railways, decided not to adapt and reuse the old structure. Instead, in 2000, together with the municipality, they announced a tender to redeveloping the station and its surroundings. It was the first time that the reinforced concrete structure had been earmarked for demolition and replaced with a multi-functional complex. In 2009, a contract with Neinver was signed, and a Spanish company was supposed to build a new multi-functional centre, including bus and train stations, offices and a shopping mall.

However, when the plans for the demolition were revealed, prominent architects, architecture historians as well as international organizations (Docomomo, Europa Nostra) protested. Nonetheless, the Voivodship Monuments' Conservator decided not to protect the building and recognize it as a part of its cultural heritage. Ultimately, however, the reinforced concrete structure, with its characteristic mushroom columns, was reconstructed and became part of a new station and shopping mall. Wacław Zalewski, who designed the construction, criticized the idea. "The columns were part of a rational entity. They can rebuild them – maybe using plaster? Or paper? There will be a theatre set instead of a building," he said ironically (Zalewski, 2013).

Before that, in 1999, prominent Silesian architect, Aleksander Franta, wrote that the railway station in Katowice was "his favourite building." He appreciated the brutalist structure and openly criticized the slow decay of the building. "The deterioration of this building is a loss for society – less for its owner" (Franta, 1999, p. 77). However, society had a different opinion of the station. Journalists quoted people who were tired of the old, dirty, unrenovated concrete behemoth whose form they did not understand. Concepts of preserving the building were called "an outright mockery of the architects' lobby" (Smolorz, 2006, p. 12). One can easily notice the rift between the voice of the professionals (architects, conservators) who appreciated the architectural value of the Katowice building and the opinions of its users, who focused on their everyday negative experiences (Grotowska, 2016, p. 38). The activists who called for the building to be preserved focused on raising social awareness and promoting knowledge. However, the stakeholder and local authorities avoided any substantial discussion with their adversaries and had already started negotiations with selected developers (Malkowski, 2007a, 2007b).

The only visible result of the protest was the above-mentioned reconstruction of the concrete-based mushroom pillars, which have very little in common with the authentic ones (see Picture 4.22). Hidden inside the shopping mall, with a surface imitating *béton brut*, they look much more like a set than a real brutalist structure. Only two remains of the soc-modernist building were preserved: the underground passage on the southern side of the railway station and the reinforced concrete canopy on *Plac Oddziałów Młodzieży Powstańczej* (Insurgent Youth Troops Square) (Kozina, 2019, p. 298).

Dominant value and impact of the surroundings

The new railway station in Katowice was opened in October 2012. An underground bus station with a tunnel under the station was commissioned a few months later, followed by the opening of the Galeria Katowicka shopping centre in September 2013. This is one of the largest investment projects in Katowice in the last two decades, with a total cost of €240 million (Jedlecki, 2020).

Today, this new development has a predominantly utilitarian value. The railway station, together with Galeria Katowicka, makes up an integral unit in which the retail component dominates. It is an important site in the centre of Katowice with dual functions. For local residents, it is first and foremost a shopping centre and a place for leisure activities, with catering and cultural services. These functions and values are reinforced by the presence of a large car park located in the city centre. For those from outside Katowice, the place is, above all, a railway station and an important transport hub. It performs transport functions at a regional level, serving the traffic of residents of the Górnośląsko-Zagłębiowska Metropolis. Users of the station appreciate this new functionality.

The modern railway station no longer carries any significant non-utility value in architectural and aesthetic terms. It is overshadowed and dominated by a shopping centre. The restored concrete goblet-like pillars are integrated into the structure of the new building so much that they are hardly visible. Today, it is no longer the station but the adjacent shopping centre that dominates the perception of this space and strongly determines how it is perceived. This is due to the scale of the shopping centre, which is where the retail and catering offer of this part of the downtown area of Katowice is concentrated.

Despite attempts to regenerate the space around the station, a plan to highlight the preserved qualities of the station has failed. Immediately outside the station is a concrete square, which has been developed with new structures in recent years. In addition, new public spaces have been created on the north side of the station, such as the pedestrianized 3 Maja Street, Maria and Lech Kaczyński Square, and Dworcowa Street, a little further away. However, they are not relevant to the perception and exposure of the preserved architectural qualities of the station.

The local community commonly believes that there is a clear inconsistency between the (only two) visible goblet-like pillars and the building, which gives the overall impression of a caricature. The argument for demolishing the old station was that its shape was not in harmony with its surroundings – the neighbouring tenements. Today, it is not only poorly integrated into the surrounding space, but above all, it is not in harmony with itself, that is, the body of the railway station and the shopping centre.

Socio-economic embeddedness and local uniqueness

The decision to demolish the railway station and create new functions for this downtown area evoked strong public resistance. The demolition of the railway station was a top-down decision made by the local authorities, public sector institutions and the investor without any consultations with

Picture 4.22 The reconstructed mushroom pillars are supposed to create a connection between the old, modernist railway station and the new structure. © Aleksandra Nowakowska.

social partners. In the first phase of the investment, heritage protection institutions (such as the Municipal and Provincial Heritage Conservation Officers) also adopted a passive attitude. Their reaction and active stance only built under pressure from the local community.

The decision to demolish the station and build a shopping centre on the site sparked opposition not only from urban planners, architects and art historians but, above all, from the inhabitants. It provided the impulse for a broad spontaneous and grassroots civic/social movement. Local leaders, NGOs and the local media were the *spiritus movens* of the actions. A "Brutal from Katowice" profile was created on Facebook, which became very popular (over 7,000 followers). The Facebook campaign "Let's save the goblet-like pillars of the Katowice railway station," which was supported by several hundred people, also played an important role. Numerous demonstrations and events took place in front of the station (including "We love you" and "Let's say no!"), during which candles were symbolically lit. Discussions and exhibitions on the uniqueness of the station's construction were organized locally. Artists created works inspired by the station's architecture, and "railway station" gadgets appeared on the market, for example, T-shirts, mugs, and bags with images of the railway station hall (Borowik, 2020).

The grassroots protests of the urban community were accompanied by numerous campaigns initiated by academics and the Silesian community of architects and urban planners. On one hand, their activities were oriented towards influencing the local authorities to change their decision and refrain from demolishing the station. On the other hand, they were trying to build local awareness and demonstrate the multifaceted value of the railway station. As a result, the Katowice railway station has won many supporters, at home and abroad, with its defenders receiving numerous letters of support from around the globe. The *Napraw Sobie Miasto* (Fix Your City) foundation came up with the initiative to symbolically sell the goblet-like pillars of the Katowice railway station to nationally and internationally renowned architects. This idea was successful and also helped bring international circles into the discussion.

The local discourse revealed two clashing points of view. The public authorities and the developer emphasized the practical and commercial side of the project, that is, building a modern and multi-functional space in the city centre. The introduction of a commercial function and the construction of a shopping centre were not only intended to raise external funds for the renovation of the station but also to bring back the attractiveness of the traditional city centre. Defenders of the railway station, on the other hand, prioritized the artistic and emotional value of the building (Grotowska, 2016; Molecki, 2014).

The social movement that was created around defending the railway station was a phenomenon not only in Poland, but also across Central and Eastern Europe. The local battle for the railway station, which lasted for almost a year, had a significant impact on integrating the local community and building its awareness and identity. The local press wrote at the time, "A wall of civic apathy collapsed in Katowice" (Malkowski, 2010). The impetus for this was precisely the mobilization and integration around the defence of the station's architecture (see Picture 4.23).

Protests and bottom-up community actions helped to educate and build understanding and acceptance of socialist modernist architecture, which remains a significant component of the contemporary landscape. The demolition of the railway station awakened local discussion and sensitivity to modernist buildings, and many bottom-up educational and cultural actions were organized in the city. Additionally, several articles on the value of Zalewski's construction were published in the local press.

As a result, although the railway station no longer exists in its original form, it undoubtedly remains one of the best-described and documented examples of modernist architecture in Poland in publications and scientific research. Against the backdrop of grassroots protests, academic circles (art historians, architects, sociologists) produced many research papers and organized events demonstrating the station's qualities. For example, Professor Irma Kozina and her students prepared extensive photographic

Picture 4.23 The new railway station in Katowice does not resemble the brutalist building created by Kłyszewski, Mokrzyński and Wierzbicki. Instead of individually designed architecture, visitors can rather see the generic aesthetics of a modern "non-place." ©Aleksandra Nowakowska.

documentation of the station, while the Association of Architects of the Republic of Poland organized an exhibition in its headquarters and in the station's restaurant. Monographs, expert reports and numerous academic articles have also been produced (Gzowska, 2012; Jasiński et al., 2010; Jaśniok et al., 2010; Załuski & Rzepnicka, 2018).

This is how the Katowice railway station became a symbol of modernist architecture in Poland. This example shows that the widespread social dislike and a misunderstanding of modernist architecture from the communist era can, through local discussion and educational activities, be transformed into new values that build up the strength of the city. Paradoxically, despite its demolition, Katowice's railway station, neglected and unwanted by many, has been successfully turned into an architectural icon, and it has become an impulse for social mobilization. Although the station was almost completely demolished, the sentiment and memory of its architecture remain strong in the local community. This is confirmed by the celebration of anniversaries of the station's demolition, or the entries and discussions in the media that still follow every newspaper article about it. A kind of social capital has been created around the old railway station, and memories of it are firmly rooted in the local consciousness, revitalizing and animating the local community (e.g. in recent months, an event was organized to demonstrate that the escalators at the railway station do not work properly).

The Buzludzha Monument, Bulgaria – The struggle of soc-modernism heritage with nature and political controversies

Historical background and evolution of object's functions

The monument on Buzludzha Peak was once described as a "Sistine Chapel of Socialism" by the New York Times journalist Andrew Higgins. He recalled the words of Nikifor Haralampiev, a conservator from Bulgaria's National Academy of Art, who described the building and said that despite the difference in the quality of the artwork, "the idea was the same," that is, "the glorification of an all-powerful system of faith" (Higgins, 2022). Indeed, the location, the architectural form and the socio-political context build the complex narrative of this outstanding example of the dissonant heritage of the communist system.

The location on the top of Buzludzha Peak was chosen not only because of its landscape values, as the mountain overlooks Stara Planina and is visible from a great distance, but also because of its great historical significance. In 1891, at the foot of the mountain, the Bulgarian social democrats held a secret meeting (known as the Buzludzha Congress) at which the Bulgarian Social Democratic Party was established. The *Balgarska Komunisticheska Partiya* (BKP; Bulgarian Communist Party), which ruled from 1946 to 1989, considered itself its heir.

However, that was not the only historical event witnessed by Mount Buzludzha. In 1868, Hadzhi Dimitâr, the Bulgarian national hero, fell in battle against the Ottoman forces. A decade later, a nationwide uprising erupted. One of its most important episodes took place just 10 kilometres from the peak, at the Shipka Pass, where in January 1878, Russian and Bulgarian troops defeated the Turkish army. In the twentieth century, during World War II, communist partisans fought and defeated fascist units on Buzludzha. Therefore, the summit's symbolic and historical meanings are undisputable.

On 29 January 1959, a competition was announced, inviting design proposals for four new monuments to celebrate the history of the birthplace of the Bulgarian socialist movement. Three of them, which honoured, respectively, the founders of the Bulgarian Social-Democratic Party (authors: architects Kalin Boyadzhiev and Boris Nenkov, and sculptors Dimitâr Daskalov, Georgi Gergov and Ivan Kesyakov), Hadzhi Dimitâr (authors: architect Lyuben Dimitrov and sculptor Petko Tsvetkov) and the fallen partisans of the Gabrovo regiment (authors: architect Ivan Tatarov, and sculptors Stella Raynova and Ivan Ivanov) were completed in 1961. The execution of the last one, a monumental tower on top of the mountain, surrounded by six columns and bearing the five-pointed red star, was postponed. It was only at the beginning of the 1970s that its architect, Dimitri Stoilov, received a commission directly from the communist party leaders, asking him to revise the primary concept. Finally, the construction of the Memorial House started in January 1974.

The overall pace of the evolution of architecture in post-war Bulgaria was similar to that in other socialist countries, but the local characteristics should not be omitted. After the introduction of the doctrine of Socialist Realism in 1948, modernist aesthetics were officially rejected as "non-socialist." However, after the April Thaw in 1956, "the language of post-war modernism started to prevail in the country, maintaining its leading role in the decades to come" (A. Vasileva, 2019, p. 43). Like communist parties in other countries of the Eastern Bloc, the Bulgarian Communist Party followed the Soviet example and proclaimed de-Stalinisation and the end of the "cult." However, it did not mean an openness to Western ideas.

The architecture of socialist Bulgaria is often considered a relatively closed system, isolated from foreign influence. The national reception of modernism was far from "the monotony of flat facades and plain surfaces"; it favoured artistic values and sculptural forms (Metalkova-Markova, 2008, p. 179). In the late 1960s and 1970s, the relationship between economic and cultural development was stressed by the Bulgarian Communist Party, resulting in a great number of new cultural facilities. The development became even more rapid after 1975, when Lyudmila Zhivkova, daughter of Todor Zhivkov, the long-time Chairman of the State Council and Leader of the Bulgarian Communist Party, became Chair of the Arts and Culture Committee (equivalent to the Ministry of Culture). She concentrated on celebrating several anniversaries to "prove ancient cultural roots, and on deliberately exporting Bulgarian culture to define a national identity in a global context" (Kaleva & Vasileva, 2018, p. 130). Even after the socialist realism doctrine was rejected, modernist aesthetics were criticized as manifestations of technicism and cosmopolitism. At the same time, "the ideas of organic architecture fitted into the local nationalistic-ideological narrative by searching for the spirit of the place in a natural or traditional architectural environment" (Stoilova, 2018, p. 126). Thus, the construction of the Buzludzha Monument fell during times of "architectural prosperity."

Initially, the investment was supposed to be financed by the state. However, the architect Georgi Stoilov, who held the position of the Minister of Architecture and Public Works between 1971 and 1973, suggested that the "monument of the people" should be constructed with people's donations. A total of 16 million leva was raised among Bulgarians, who gave donations and bought commemorative postage stamps.[1] It exceeded the budget of the monument (estimated at 14 million leva), and the surplus was spent on infrastructure related to Buzludzha (www.buzludzha-monument.com). When analysing the investment budget, the input of volunteers' work of the brigades organized by DKMS – Dimitrov Communist Youth Union must be considered. They worked on the extraordinary initiative along with the professionals and the Construction Troops, a paramilitary organization subordinate to the Ministry of Construction, led by general Delcho Delchev. The concept of volunteer work on public investments, termed "subbotnik" in the Soviet Union, where it was invented in 1919, was popular in the Eastern Bloc. It provided significant savings in the budget, but at the same time, it was supposed to create a spirit of cooperation and sacrifice for the common good (Kaplan, 1968).

On 23 August 1981, Todor Zhivkov, the Bulgarian communist leader, inaugurated the Monument "built in honour of the accomplishments of Dimitar Blagoev and his associates, who 90 years ago laid the foundations for the revolutionary Marxist Party in Bulgaria" (Bell, 1986, p. 22). The main part – a saucer-shaped body covered with a 60-metre diameter dome, was placed on a high pedestal, making the structure look like it was hovering. The pedestal was designed on a Y-shape plan, with staircases in each of the branches leading to the great auditorium and the tower. The auditorium was planned as a set of concentric rings with a circular central space surrounded by rows of seats for the audience and a passage above them. It was surrounded by an open gallery (the outer ring of the structure), allowing visitors to admire the picturesque yet formidable panorama of the Stara Planina mountain chain.

At the same time, the interior of the building, its "heart," was totally separated from those magnificent views, as though the architect wanted visitors to remain focused on the ideology and not be disturbed by nature. The "battlefield" between nature and (modern) architecture was not limited to the visual aspects of the composition of the two. To make the construction of the Buzludzha Monument possible, extensive construction and earthworks were necessary. The height of the Peak was reduced by nine metres, and 15,000 m^3 of rock was removed to prepare the foundations. Seventy thousand tonnes of concrete and 3000 tonnes of steel were used to create the "Sistine chapel of socialism," built in pristine scenery.

The steel structure of the flattened copula of the monument was covered with copper plates, and the external walls, as well as an inverted dome (the bottom part of "the saucer"), were constructed in reinforced concrete and left uncovered. Stoilov claimed that it was done because of his desire to achieve purity and honesty (Grekov, 1981), which sounds much like Le Corbusier's description of the *béton brut* of Unité d'Habitation in Marseille (Jencks, 1975, p. 142). Years later, in 2013, the architect said that it was used "for being a durable, indestructible material" (N. Vasileva, 2013, p. 18). The 68-metre-high tower was designed as a double pylon, a concrete wedge slightly tapering to the bottom, located on the western side of the summit and connected with the main part of the building by the elongated part of the pedestal. On the top, there was a five-pointed star-shaped opening filled with ruby red tinted glass. The decision to place the tower offset was not only a purely aesthetical matter but also structural, as it provided greater stability for the whole Monument (the construction of the Memorial was designed by a team led by Dobromir Kolarov).

The complex consisted not only of the monumental building on the top of the mountain, but there was also a composition of paths, piazzas and viewpoints. Visitors were welcomed by a reinforced concrete and granite sculpture depicting two enormous fists holding burning torches ("Torches" by Stoyu Todorov). The path led through the tree-less slope of Buzludzha mountain so that the target of the visit (or, rather, the pilgrimage) was always visible. A few hundred metres before the destination was a large rectangular piazza paved with stone. It preceded the "gate" made of symmetrical monumental waving flags made of concrete which flanked the way to the monumental stairs that led directly to the steel gate of Buzludzha. The artistic layout was not limited to the exterior. For those who entered the building, even more impressive works of monumental and decorative art awaited them, created by 60 renowned Bulgarian artists.[2] The monumental mosaics depicted the history of the Bulgarian Communist Party ("The Birth of the Party," "The 5th congress of the BKP," and portraits of Dimitar Blagoev and Todor Zhivkov). There were also scenes that were characteristic of international socialist iconography, for example, a composition entitled "Proletarians of all countries, unite!" with the emblem of the hammer and the sickle in the centre of the ceiling of the auditorium, "The woman in the socialist society," as well as portraits of Karl Marx and Friedrich Engels. The staircases were decorated with white crystal glass compositions created by the Czechoslovakian sculptor Stanislav Libensky (see Picture 4.24).

Picture 4.24 The interiors of the Buzludzha Monument were covered with mosaics which were supposed to attract visitors' attention on the history of Bulgarian socialist party rather than picturesque landscapes of Stara Planina outside. The Buzludzha Monument (Bulgaria) designed by Georgi Stoilov et al., 1971–1981.

Source: © "Arhitektura" 1981, no. 10.

Everything in Buzludzha, from the general concept of the whole complex, through the form of the Monument, to its interior decorations, was a unique mixture of monumental realism (the "Two Generations. Shipka-Buzludzha" sculpture of Stoho Todorov, and the popular "Torches"), expressionism (sculptures entitled "The Party" by Valentin Starchev and "The Victory" by Velitchko Minekov), neo-traditionalism (the mosaics that were vaguely reminiscent of Orthodox ones) and brutalism. Georgi Stoilov himself described the sources of his inspiration differently, depending on when he made his comment. Once, he recalled a fascination with astronautics, UFOs and flying saucers, which was typical of the 1970s (N. Vasileva, 2013, p. 16). Another time, he mentioned the impact of his architectural gurus – Gropius and Le Corbusier (Spassov & Morten, 2022). In the early 1980s, when the monument had been erected, Stoilov explained the circular shape as a reference to the Thracian tombs and, in this way, a visible sign of historical continuity (Grekov, 1981).

On the other hand, Emilia Kaleva noted that the architect admitted to "observations from the Roman Pantheon dome of Brunelleschi,[3] the dome of St. Sofia and the domes of Pier Luigi Nervi" (Kaleva, 2014, p. 84).

However, regardless of the interpretative path one follows, Buzludzha was a manifestation of the architectural zeitgeist. The modernist concept of modern "culture" as a contrast to "nature," visible in numerous buildings erected in natural landscapes (Ciarkowski, 2018), was apparently the essence of Stoilov's design. Simple but powerful forms resemble primitive structures of primary cultures or the monumental architecture of Louis Kahn. At the same time, the futuristic shape could be considered a socialist version of the Googie architecture of the United States and, further, the effect of worldwide fascination with space discovery programmes (Hatherley, 2012). Due to its bold form and ideological meaning, the memorial house fully deserved a name given by architecture historian Nedyalka Vasileva, who called it simply "A Symbol" (N. Vasileva, 2013).

Stoilov designed a building-monument, a communist shrine, which was more a place of a cult than a piece of architecture with a specific functional programme. It can be compared with the communist mausoleums, for example, Georgi Dimitrov's Mausoleum in Sofia, designed by Georgi Ovcharov and Racho Ribarov in 1949. They would become active ideological tools – a centre of cyclical solemn rituals (Vladova, 2012, p. 133). The structure erected on the Buzludzha Peak had representative, educational and symbolic functions. As the authorities requested a memorial house with interior spaces to protect visitors and attendees of special events from the elements outside, the architect replaced the circular colonnade with a saucer-shape volume. The original idea of the tower, with the red star symbol on the top, remained, although the shape and composition changed.

The communist system collapsed in Bulgaria on 10 November 1989. Before then, more than two million people had visited Buzludzha. Entry was free of charge as society had paid for the construction of the Memorial House. Visits were often arranged by schools and enterprises, who had to book them in advance due to the great demand. When it was not open to the public, Buzludzha served as a venue for BKP events (see Picture 4.25). When Zhivkov was deposed as the first secretary of the Central Committee of the Communist Party, his former comrades took down the portrait of the former leader. In 1992, the monument was nationalized under the Law on the Nationalisation of the Property of the BKP, and the entrances were sealed.

Despite that, the shrine to Bulgarian socialism soon became dilapidated. Looters stole equipment, furniture and even marble plates from the interior and copper roof panels. Some of the decorations which had strong ideological communist meanings were destroyed. Apparently, the authorities did not consider Buzludzha worth protecting, like dozens of other carriers of "bad memory." "This silent inaction allows the weather and looters to destroy the monuments "naturally," wrote the experts from ICOMOS (Machat & Ziesemer, 2017, pp. 32–37). The location on the remote mountain, away from the centre of political actions, resulted in a lack of heated discussion on the monument's future, as there had been regarding Dimitrov's Mausoleum.

Its situation after 1989 should be considered representative of the public debate about the dissonant heritage of socialism in Bulgaria, as, during the research, two-thirds of the interviewees wanted the structure to be preserved (Vladova, 2012, p. 141). Among them, a relatively large number of respondents suggested that the building should be adapted for a new functional programme. It was the same idea that inspired Georgi Stoilov. During an interview in 2013, he suggested that the Buzludzha Memorial "should be transformed into a pantheon of Bulgarian heroes; their images in granite should replace the murals on the circular wall, and a lion replace the ruby star on top of the pylon" (N. Vasileva, 2013, p. 21). Fortunately for the authenticity of the object, his proposal was ignored by the authorities.

The desire to preserve the facility for subsequent generations came from the bottom up, especially in the art, art historian and conservationist communities. Initially, it took the form of open discussions about the site's future, where, for example, proposals to commercialize the building, as a casino, appeared. Such commercial projects, however, were never considered by the broader public as an actual transformation course. The growing interest from modernist architecture and art enthusiasts channelled the discussion into more actionable action. Websites began to spring up, publishing present-day photos of the building, sometimes compared with old photographs. The photographers were probably the first to be interested in the building, making their pictures recognisable and appreciated. Soon, other artists, performers and even skating enthusiasts followed them in the 2000s. These years thus brought inspiration for different milieus and renewed discussion about the future of the building.

In 2011, the Bulgarian Government decided to transfer Buzludzha to the Bulgarian Socialist Party, the successor to the BKP.[4] However, the State Property Law from 2017 undermined the earlier decisions and Buzludzha, among other properties, was passed back into the possession of the state. Four years later, in 2021, the Buzludzha was included on the register of national heritage. In the meantime, multiple initiatives to preserve the monument and stop further deterioration were undertaken. It was not easy due to the location, the building's condition and political reasons. "With a few exceptions, buildings constructed after 1944 are generally not officially listed as cultural monuments in Bulgaria," wrote Aneta Vasileva and Emilia Kaleva in 2017, a few years before the Memorial became officially protected by the law (A. Vasileva & Kaleva, 2017, p. 172).

Founded in 2015 the Buzludzha Project Foundation has continuously worked on preserving Stoilov's work, building social awareness of its value, preparing recommendations and applying for external funding. The effects of their activities are already visible. In 2018, the monument was recognized as one of the seven most endangered heritage sites in Europe by Europa Nostra. One year later, the Getty Foundation in Los Angeles, which praised it as "a masterpiece of architectural engineering," established a $185,000 grant to create a Conservation Management Plan. In 2020, the same institution provided $60,000 to stabilize existing mosaic panels (Buzludzha Project Foundation, 2022).

Picture 4.25 Thodor Zhivkov, the leader of the People's Republic of Bulgaria, laid the capsule addressed to the future generations in the foundations of the Buzludzha. The structure was supposed to serve people for many years as a monument depicting the history of Bulgarian socialism.

Source: © "Arhitektura" 1981, no. 10.

Dominant value and impact of the surroundings

Several ideas emerged in the debate over the possible future use of the Buzludzha site. However, the possibility of using it as an object to glorify the communist era (which is forbidden by law in Bulgaria) was rejected quickly. Ideas from the opposite side of the spectrum of possibilities, such as commercialization (hotels, restaurants and casinos), were also rejected for political reasons or because they were not cost-effective. What is considered more seriously is the possibility of developing the heritage site in a form that would somehow tell its history, that is, make it a form of a museum, but critically approaching Bulgaria's socialist history. In that case, it would be in the form of developing it as a cultural object that would tell the visitors a multi-layered story. It could also be a place of art, where the artist could make different critical interpretations of the building and foster further discussion. It could also host educational and cultural events or conferences. It leads to the conclusion that, at this stage, the non-use value outweighs the use value among the wider public, and we think the option value is dominant.

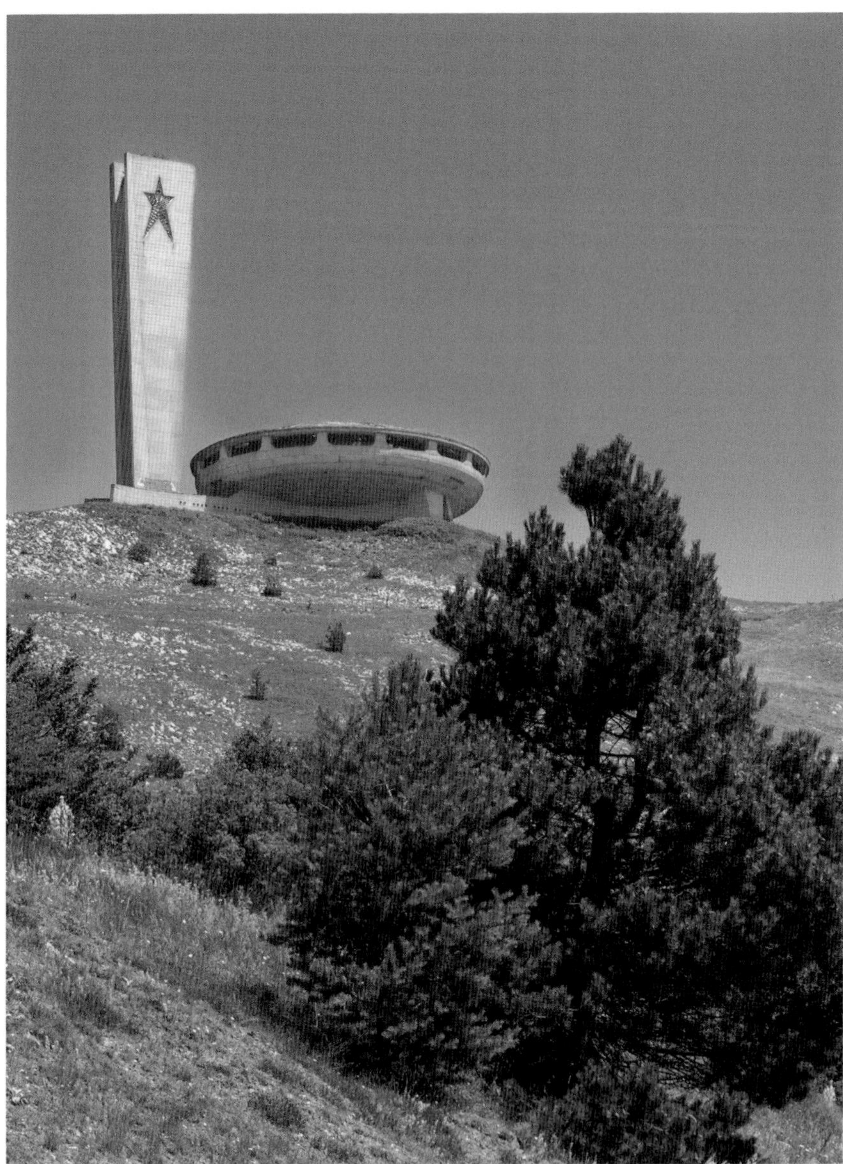

Picture 4.26 The monumental ruins on Buzludzha Peak became an inspiration for urbex fans, who drew the attention of the broad international audience to the socialist modernist masterpiece. The contrast between the natural landscape and massive brutalist structure makes the site unique. © kennethving (CC BY-SA 4.0).

The monument's location on Buzludzha Peak is crucial for its visual and social perception. The peak, which was called Hadzi Dimityr (Bulgarian: Хаджи Димитър, after the Bulgarian national hero) after the fall of communism, is 1,441 metres high. Although it is one of the lowest in the Old Planina mountain range, the massive monument's location here makes it a significant spatial landmark. The former Communist Party of Bulgaria House-Monument would not have the same character if not located in such a physical setting. Conversely, locating an object of modernist architecture of such a large scale in the high mountains renders this previously natural space into a completely different perspective than the pristine one for the perceiver. The critical question that arises is whether, indeed, the monument is a foreign body to nature (see Picture 4.26).

On one hand, it seems that as a civil engineering object, it certainly is. Nevertheless, if we said that this building is destroying nature, then we would have to say that every building in the world is destroying nature. Meanwhile, architectural researchers from Bulgaria who have studied this building precisely from the perspective of its integration into its surroundings have said from the beginning that its creators designed it to be integrated into nature, although it is undoubtedly a man-made work. Nature dictated its scale, position and orientation. Likewise, its infrastructural elements – the paths, roads, seats and water fountains – are all well suited to nature. Therefore, there seems to be a harmony between the whole complex and nature. First-time visitors to Buzludzha are surprised that it is not a single building but a vast ensemble of the entire mountain. In other words, combining the qualities of the building and the natural elements make it an extraordinary asset.

Recent years have also changed how the site is perceived in its surroundings. The mountainous nature of the site and the favourable winds have led to the installation of wind farms in the vicinity. These renewable energy sources change the landscape from several angles and negatively affect the perception of the monument, whose value as a dominant feature decreases in relation to the windmills. This issue has not yet been debated, but it has undoubtedly quite permanently changed the relationship between the object and its physical surroundings.

Socio-economic embeddedness and local uniqueness

The site's uniqueness is undoubtedly discernible by professionals, the general public and tourists. However, apart from its location, it is not easy to regard it as a local peculiarity. This object is unique on at least a national, if not European or even worldwide scale. As such, it can be considered a landmark, but it also has the potential to build Bulgaria's recognition internationally.

Picture 4.27 The concept of preservation of the Buzludzha monument and its adaptive reuse aims at conserving the existing remains of the original tissue and creating a multi-layered narrative about the recent history and its dissonant heritage. © Stanislav Traykov (CC BY 3.0).

For these reasons, territorial embeddedness is not limited to the vicinity; it refers to Bulgaria's national identity and culture. Therefore, it is unsurprising that journalistic discussion of the site's future is not limited to local media. It arouses emotions on a national scale, and the uniqueness of this heritage site has also been mentioned by international specialists. Notwithstanding, the bottom-up initiatives have primarily helped rethink the place as heritage, a place of art or a multi-functional venue. The resumption of discussion about the future of a declining monument of modernism – a symbol of former socialist power – would not have happened without activists and enthusiasts of this type of architecture. The general attitude to the building has changed thanks to these grassroots initiatives. Thus, we are increasingly seeing support from local and central public institutions. In June 2022, a specially created organization – the Buzludzha Foundation – received its first funding from the Bulgarian state. Before that, since 2019, the foundation had worked only with private donations and international funding. In 2022, the Ministry of Culture funded a project to secure the monument and open it to visitors. Further activities planned for the monument are the joint initiative of many stakeholders – the municipality, the regional governments and the Ministry of Culture (see Picture 4.27).

Central post office in Skopje – The memory of the socialist reconstruction in the process of oblivion

Historical background and evolution of object's functions

On 26 July 1963, an enormous earthquake of 6.1 on the Richter scale turned three-quarters of Skopje into rubble. More than a thousand people were killed, and around 150,000 lost their homes. The capital of the Socialist Republic of Macedonia was almost completely destroyed within just fifteen seconds.

News of the tragedy spread worldwide, resulting in support and aid. The Warsaw municipality, with Warsaw's Chief Architect, Adolf Ciborowski, declared that Poland would offer help. It was said that the experience that Warsaw's urban planners gained while reconstructing the capital that had been destroyed after WW2 would be particularly useful (Wyporek, 2009, p. 25). The general concept was prepared and sent to the Macedonian authorities, as well as the United Nations commission (as an alternative for a similar project prepared by a team led by Constantinos Doxiadis). They were not the only ones who, led by an impulse of sympathy, answered Josip Broz-Tito's appeal and offered help. The communist leader of Yugoslavia was aware that Skopje's reconstruction was beyond the country's capabilities, and he decided to turn it into a collective, world effort – a symbol of international solidarity and empathy.

The project for the centre of the city was the subject of an international competition. The winner, Japanese architect Kenzo Tange, presented an astounding composition of public-use buildings joined by transport infrastructure. The forms of the new buildings were closely related to the aesthetics of Japanese Metabolism, with functional modules set between a fixed grid of horizontal and vertical communication (Jencks, 1980). Their monumentality and scale were supposed to indicate the direction for the city's future development; however, they evoked the criticism of those who indicated the inadequacy of the new complex' magnitude and possible functional problems in the future (Nettmann-Multanowska, 2022, pp. 290–291). Eventually, Skopje's new centre combined Tange's vision with the bold creativity of Macedonian architects who filled the urban tissue with concrete-based brutalist structures at the end of the 1960s and 1970s. Nevertheless, it was the Japanese architect whose name has become associated with the construction of the new Skopje, outshining local designers and Polish urban planners (Nettmann-Multanowska, 2022, p. 292) (see Picture 4.28).

One of the Macedonian architects who had a great impact on the image of the rebuilt capital was Janko Konstantinov. Born in 1926 in Bitola, he was one of the most intriguing designers of his generation. Konstantinov graduated from the Faculty of Architecture at the Technical College in Belgrade in 1952. He soon left his country, heading first to Copenhagen,

Picture 4.28 The reconstruction of Skopje after the earthquake in 1963 was a gesture of international solidarity and, on the urban and architectural level, a unanimous victory of brutalism and metabolism. A team led by Japanese architect Kenzo Tange created the masterplan of the city centre. Later it was filled with buildings designed by architects who, like Janko Konstantinov, presented a local interpretation of the international style. © Osamu Murai.

Source: Museum of the City of Skopje.

where he simultaneously continued his education and worked, and later to Stockholm, Sweden and Juveskula, Finland. Finally, he moved across the Atlantic to the United States of America. From 1958, Konstantinov worked in Los Angeles in the atelier of architect Victor Gruen. When he received the tragic news about the catastrophe in Skopje, he had already settled his position, but immediately decided to return and help with the city's reconstruction effort. Compared with most of the young Yugoslavian professionals involved, Konstantinov had broad experience, which he had gained alongside renowned architects. The *Telekomunikaciski centar* project (Telecommunication Centre) demonstrates not only his skills but also his deep knowledge of the latest trends in modern architecture.

Although Konstantinov's close relationships with the Western world's architecture should be considered an exception rather than a common practice, Yugoslavia's version of socialism was not exactly the same as in other Eastern Bloc countries. After WWII, tensions between the Soviet Union, ruled by Stalin, and Tito's Yugoslavia increased. Its origins came from the latter's aspirations to pursue an independent foreign policy and, therefore, act as a local leader. Stalin first accused the Yugoslav Communist Party of nationalism and betraying Marxist-Leninist ideology. Most Eastern Bloc countries then suspended contact with Yugoslavia, and the Communist Party of Yugoslavia was expelled from the Cominform (the Information Bureau of the Communist and Workers' Parties). Facing a political and economic crisis, Tito turned to the West, requesting assistance from the United States. As a result of the Soviet-Yugoslav split in 1948, in the early 1950s, a series of fundamental reforms began. They led to the liberalization and decentralization of the political system and the implementation of a diplomacy policy of non-alignment that was non-confrontational with the West. In the 1960s American journalists even called Yugoslavia "the most autonomous, open, idiosyncratic and unCommunist Communist country," emphasizing that "[alone] among Red peoples, Yugoslavs may freely travel to the West" ("Yugoslavia: Socialism of Sorts," 1966). This had a great impact on Balkan architecture. Vladmir Kulić (2017) identified several different paths of transfer, among them the international effort of Skopje's reconstruction.

The dynamics and chronology of the architectural evolution in post-war Yugoslavia are different than in other socialist countries. Just after World War II, architects searched for individual interpretations of the socialist realism doctrine, and Josip Broz Tito openly suggested that they visit the Soviet Union in search of inspiration (Živančević, 2012, p. 281). In 1950, a year after the proclamation of the "Third Way," the Council of Yugoslav architects declared that they were open to Western influences and rejected Socialist Realism which, in fact, remained just "an unpleasant episode in the history of Yugoslavian architecture" (Putnik, 2017, p. 349). Just like in politics and the economy, Yugoslavia searched for its own way in the field of architectural design. Instead of thoughtlessly copycatting the West, the architects searched for a national spirit, expressed using modern means, designing uniquely local assets. The "Socialist Aestheticism," as some scholars call Yugoslav architecture designed after 1950, was based not solely on functionalism but primarily on its aesthetic and artistic quality (Perović, 2003).

The Telecommunication Centre in Skopje was based on Tange's masterplan of the city centre, along with several public-use buildings, including the Museum of Macedonia by Mimoza Nestorova-Tomik and Kiril Muraotvski, Ss. Cyril and Methodius University by Marko Music, and the Museum of Contemporary Art by Wacław Kłyszewski, Jerzy Mokrzyński and Eugeniusz Wierzbicki. The project was the result of a contest announced in 1968 and won by a team led by Konstantinov. Before the construction works started in 1972, the architects prepared several different versions of the complex, trying to meet the expectations of the governmental and urban authorities. Each design contained three separate buildings with different functions: a Telecommunication Centre, a Post Office (with the Main Counter Hall) and an Administrative Building. They were "placed on a unifying platform, a public square, generously equipped with greenery, water, and sculptures" (Deskova et al., 2019, pp. 208–209). The buildings created a U-shaped composition surrounding a public square that was supposed to connect all three parts of the complex. The descending platforms of the piazza facing the bank of the Vardar river and the citadel were never realized, and the space was left empty (Pedio, 1976, p. 92).

The first concept of the complex was a powerful vision of the Metabolist megastructure. The massive solid vertical cylindrical communication shafts supported a bridge-like construction hovering above the large piazza. It was "inspired by an original Japanese approach, then further developed as a national form of architecture" (Weiss, 2010, p. 93). Konstantinov soon developed a new design proposal, "considerably rationalised and simplified in its expression" (Deskova et al., 2019, p. 210). The three units became separate buildings of differentiated sizes and forms. The PTT (Пошта, телеграф и телефон; Post, Telegraph and Telephone) Telecommunication Centre was designed as a vertical dominant that comprized a rectangular slab and a tower, the Administrative Building had a form of a floating square lump, and the Post Office with the Main Counter Hall was located in a sculptural rotunda. "The design project for the Telecommunication Centre is one of the most discussed projects in Skopje," wrote Konstantinov in 1970. "Committees of experts and the wider public have been meeting for more than a year, and the final decision has not yet been taken. The unusual sculptural treatment of the building, intended to be built at an important and highly sensitive location in the city, has resulted in a wide range of views that are difficult to reconcile into a single, common position" (Konstantinov, 1970).

The construction finally started on 19 October 1972. The first stage ended in 1979, with the unveiling of the 54-metre high PTT tower connected with the 29-metre high block. The structure was very similar to the primary concept prepared by Konstantinov, with rounded corners and massive walls clad with prefabricated concrete panels pierced with circular and semi-circular windows.

The second phase of the investment began in 1979 and involved constructing the Post Office and Counter Hall. The official inauguration of the building took place at the end of December 1981. The circular structure, with a large open space containing a spacious counter for postal services, was more sculptural than a rational composition of the PTT tower, yet created a stylistic unity. Eight reinforced concrete wedges supported the rotunda, and, at the same time, they determined the general outlook of the structure with its curved, decorative shapes. Their raw concrete surface, as well as the massive reinforced concrete cornice, created a contrast with the glazed curtain walls. The interior of the Counter Hall was illuminated with dim natural light falling from the radiating skylights and decorated with five large murals painted by Macedonian artist Borko Lazeski, depicting the history of the local community and its fight for liberation.

The third and final phase of the PTT Complex did not begin until 1987. The Administrative Building designed by Konstantinov was a floating structure supported on massive triangular reinforced concrete pillars. Despite its visual attractiveness, the local authorities deemed it too expansive and complicated. This resulted in the disagreement between Konstantinov and the investor, who handed over the design of the building to architect Zoran Štaklev. Štaklev created an object based on the concept of his predecessor, ensuring that the whole complex would remain a unity. However, in place of the demanding structural system, he proposed a simple volume with glazed curtain walls shaded by soaring curved cornices supported by rows of slender reinforced concrete columns. Construction was completed in 1989 (see Picture 4.29).

The massive complex of the Telecommunication Centre became a new value added to the city landscape and was supposed to create a new public space. Unfortunately, however, this was not realized. Its concrete-based futuristic buildings drew a subtle analogy to the historical landmarks of Skopje – the Stone Bridge and the Citadel. It indicated a new approach

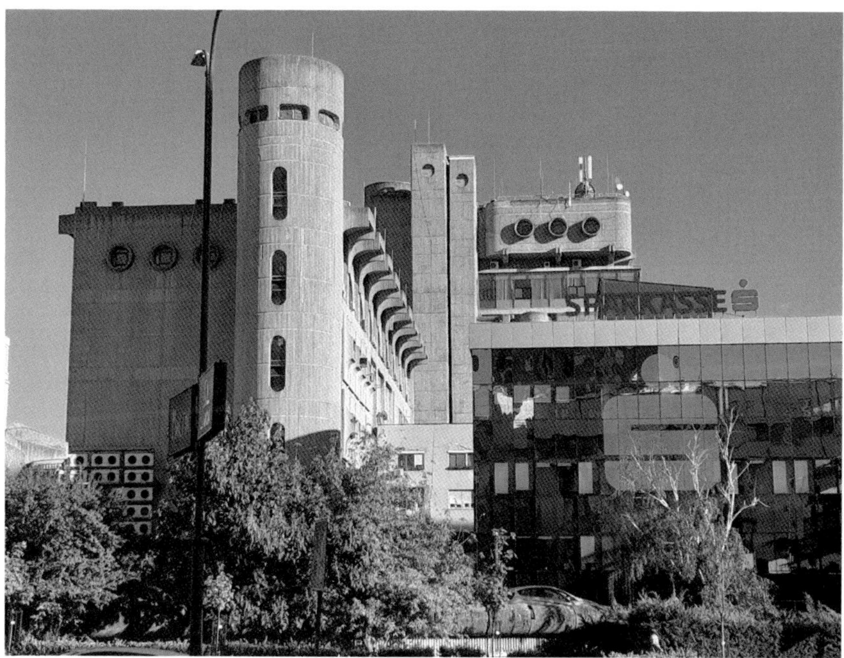

Picture 4.29 The Telecommunication Centre was supposed to become a modernist complex with a large public square in front. The architect, Janko Konstantinov, paid great attention to the spatial context and created a futuristic structure which drew subtle analogies to the historical landmarks of Skopje. Telecommunication Centre in Skopje (North Macedonia), designed by Janko Konstantinov, 1968–1981. © Aleksandra Nowakowska.

to architectural design, much closer to the postmodernist idea of pluralism and the concept of a metaphor than purely modernist simplicity (oversimplicity). It provides further evidence of Konstantinov's awareness of the latest trends in world architecture (Jencks, 1977).

The Telecommunication Centre in Skopje should be considered a "document" of a complicated history, which is not limited to the multi-phased construction of the complex. The site, situated on the southern bank of the Vardar River, where Konstantinov designed his project, was the location of the previous post office edifice, as in 1936, the modernist building created by the architect Jovan Ranković was erected there. After the earthquake and the partial collapse of the old structure, the authorities decided to replace it with the new PTT Complex, according to the Skopje centre master plan.

The developed functional programme of the new structure included communication services (served in PTT Tower), postal services and a communication dispatch centre connected with offices of the "Electricity of Macedonia" (ESM – Електростопанство на Македонија) state enterprise. The post office building is now partially abandoned, but other parts of the complex serve functions similar to the original ones. The administrative building became the headquarter of the North Macedonian Electricity System Operator, set up in 2005 after the split of ESM (MEPSO – Македонски електропреносен систем оператор), while the PTT Tower is an administrative building of Makedonski Telekom. In the late 1990s, the new building for the Makedonski Telekom was erected on the corner of the plot. A simple, rectangular lump was clad with bluish mirror glass and did not follow the general principles of the composition of the PTT Complex. In 2013, the Post Office building survived a massive fire, which destroyed most of the interior decorations, custom-made furnishing and lighting, and the original glazing of the rotunda's dome.

The growing interest in the PTT Complex in Skopje should be considered in the broader context of the transformation of the whole city. The urban reconstruction, which lasted until the early 1980s, was a part of the policy of the Yugoslav and Macedonian authorities, who reimagined Skopje as a "City of solidarity," a symbol of cross-bloc cooperation, a strategic move "made necessary by the Cold War context" (Trajanovski, 2021). With the Kenzo Tange idea, Skopje developed a successful planning system that could have been an example of the future urban shaping of the public space. However, the idea was never completed, and instead, the city moved towards an unfinished utopia (Mrduljaš & Kulić, 2012). The situation became even more complicated at the beginning of the 1990s with the breakup of Yugoslavia. The chaotic transition to capitalism, common for most of the former socialist countries, resulted in a new attitude to city planning as well as recent history. The result of those changes was the "Skopje 2014" project.

Instead of "modernization," "Baroque-isation" started, as the post-war modernist buildings changed their aesthetics. In terms of constructing a new narrative, the look of the city changed, as did the public space

(Janev, 2017). The authorities decided to replace "international" with "national" and to recall Macedonian history by promoting "true" cultural references (Amiot, 2018, p. 8). New buildings were constructed in "neo-baroque" or "neo-classicist" style, with a number of elements inspired by antiquity like monumental colonnades, pilasters, frontons or Italian baroque (e.g. the balconies of the National Theatre) (Amiot, 2018, p. 15). The transformation of the city's character has not only been limited to new investments. Reinforced concrete brutalist structures have been covered with historical detailing; the Administrative Building of the Telecommunication Complex is one of the most striking examples of this strategy. Today, there is little left of Zoran Štaklev's original design. The concrete cornice supported by slender pillars was turned into a classical entablature supported by squat Doric columns, while the glazed curtain walls were covered with pilasters and cornices. The "Skopje 2014" project is a part of an initiative to create a new identity for the country and recast the national profile (Brsakoska, 2021, p. 2). Unfortunately, one of the brightest examples of post-war concrete-based architecture became victim to this "war on collective memory."

Vladimir Kulić called the architecture of "Skopje 2014" ultra-nationalistic, an "invented tradition" and a parody (Kulić, 2017, pp. 95–96). The costly makeover has provoked international attention, as well as criticism from architects and scholars in Macedonia and strong reactions from Skopje's citizens. Although they express anti-government sentiments, not contempt for the architectural kitsch, their actions have a visible impact on the buildings as angry people target the new facades with paint-filled balloons. Nevertheless, the anti-communist policy has resulted in the progressive destruction of brutalist architecture, considered by the authorities to symbolize the socialist past.

Thus, in 2021, Europa Nostra nominated the Central Post Office in Skopje for inclusion in the 7 Most Endangered programme. The submission was prepared by the Institute for Research in Environment, Civil Engineering and Energy (IECE), supported by the Skopje division of Macedonian Post, the Ministry of Culture of North Macedonia, Fraunhofer Institute for Building Physics from Germany, and the heritage and sustainability consultant, Dr Georgi Georgiev. "The Central Post Office represents everything the 7 Most Endangered Programme is about: a heritage site of extraordinary significance that is a bold symbol of the rebirth of a city post-earthquake. This site needs to be reborn a second time," the Board of Europa Nostra stated (Europa Nostra, 2013).

Dominant value and impact of the surroundings

Today, the Konstantinova building complex is primarily seen through its utility function. One of the buildings still houses the administrative offices of the post office, while the other has become the office building of a global

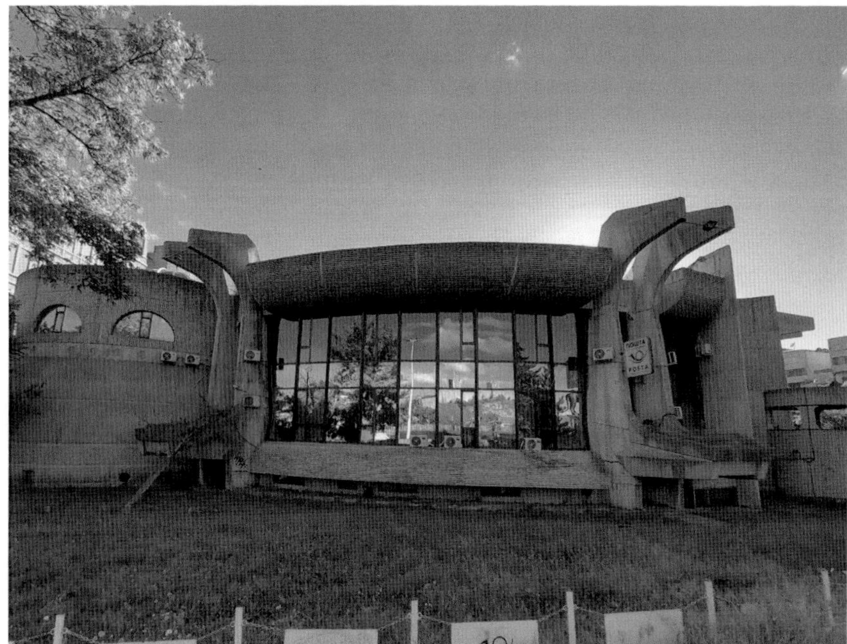

Picture 4.30 The derelict and abandoned rotunda building attracts attention with its sculpture-alike form and inspires artists who use its empty interior as a scenography. © Aleksandra Nowakowska.

telecommunications corporation. The most distinctive part of the complex, the rotunda (which used to be the main hall of the post office), has remained abandoned since a fire broke out there in 2013. Its future functions are not clearly defined, giving it a high option value and opening up multiple possibilities to derive utilitarian values in the future.

The entire Skopje Telecommunications Centre has experienced progressive degradation. This refers to the body, the surroundings and the interior of the buildings. The buildings require a thorough refurbishment to stop further degradation of the concrete structure and to maintain their functional attractiveness (see Picture 4.30).

Assessing how the surroundings impact the perceived qualities of the buildings depends on the spatial distance from which the building complex is viewed. On one hand, the north-western perspective (from the Vardar River and the traffic artery) allows the complex to be seen from a distance, making it possible to grasp the composition and the entire complex. It sharpens the vision of the architectural qualities and allows the architect's intention to be understood. This perspective makes the building intriguing and recognisable.

On the other hand, seeing the buildings up close reveals the degradation and the spatial chaos that surrounds them, weakening the perception of

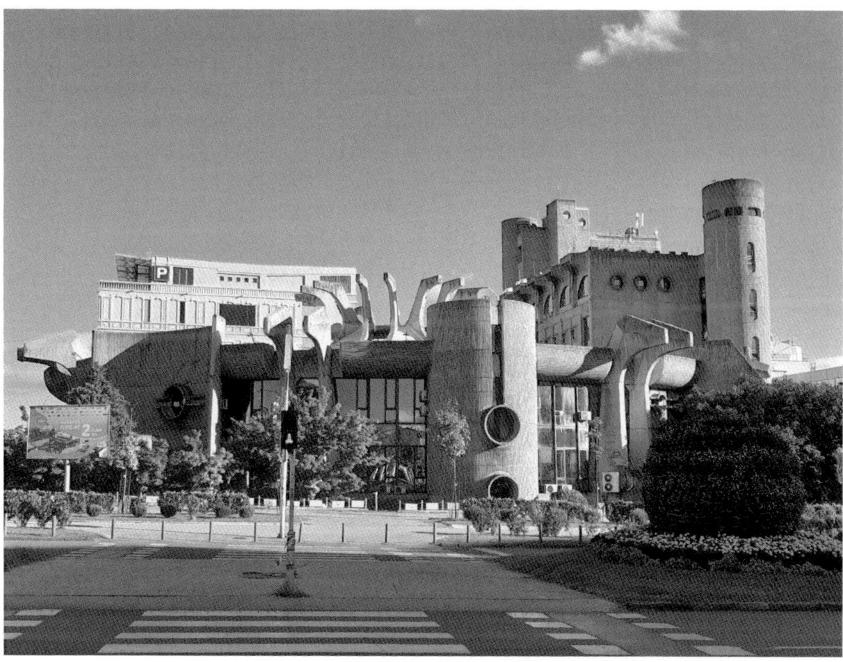

Picture 4.31 The view of the brutalist complex from the western side reveals the nuances involved in Janko Konstantinov's design. The architect played with different forms and scales, presenting the great potential of concrete as a material. © Aleksandra Nowakowska.

the value of the buildings. They give the impression that they have been squeezed in between other structures (e.g. a modern office building), and the narrow passages between them (packed with parked cars) make it impossible to assess their architectural values. This unfavourable impression is not changed by the patches of green around the complex, which are heavily neglected and "grow into" the facades of the buildings. The lack of order and spatial coherence within the complex undoubtedly have a negative impact on the perception of the value of this soc-modernist architecture. Building a harmonious space in close proximity to the complex provides an opportunity to highlight values other than those related to its utility function, not only in the eyes of experts but also of the general public.

Socio-economic embeddedness and local uniqueness

Recent years have seen a growing interest in Konstantinov's architecture. Brutalist-style buildings are gaining attention and are seen as extremely attractive, especially in artistic circles. Their artistic value and "dormant/silent" potential are highlighted, which is particularly true of the abandoned rotunda-shaped building. The uniqueness of its body and its original construction have made it an inspiration and a desirable setting for many cultural events. In 2013, the renowned fashion designer Irina Tosheva chose the place as the location for the "Memento Mori" photo session. Seven years later, in 2020, the promotional video for the Skopje fashion weekend was set there. At the same time, scholars, researchers and visual artists have focused their attention on Konstantinov's architecture. In 2020, Erina Bogoeva, with the collaboration of Natalija Teodosieva, created The Brutalist Music Box, and one year later, Martin Dimitrijev prepared the REACT/OR light installation. Earlier, in 2018, the Telecommunication Centre was included in the "Towards Concrete Utopia. Architecture in Yugoslavia, 1948–1980" exhibition presented in New York at MoMA, the Museum of Modern Art.[5]

Skopje's citizens have general knowledge of the origins and significance of this heritage. However, the vast majority remain indifferent to its architecture, which no longer stirs up as much emotion and discussion as it did in the past when it was built. The complex of post-modern buildings has grown into the local consciousness and is perceived as neutral. Even those who work in these buildings and directly experience this architecture mostly have an indifferent attitude towards it.

This is probably due to the scale of architectural and urban changes in the heart of the city that have been implemented in the last decade. The attention of the authorities and the local community is drawn to implementing the Skopje 2014 Programme, which involves the renewal of the city centre and giving it new functions and meanings. The Programme (officially announced during the celebrations of the 20th anniversary of the independence of Macedonia in 2010) provides for the construction of almost 20 new public utility buildings (museums, theatres, and philharmonics) and more than fifty huge monuments and fountains. At the heart of this project is the assumption that through the production of material culture (i.e. monuments and architecture) and the production of symbolism with clear historical references, the national identity of the Macedonian capital and community will be strengthened. In reality, the antique-baroque styling of the new buildings did not win the approval of either the professional circles (architects, urban planners, cultural studies experts or historians) or the local community. As a result, the city centre became an alien and alienating urban form, imposed in a top-down manner (Katerina et al., 2013). In view of such a large scale of investment activities undertaken close to the Konstantinov complex, it has become a somewhat overwhelmed and forgotten heritage of the city (see Picture 4.31).

In addition, the hostile attitude of the local authorities and the actions taken under this programme undermine the potential of soc-modernist architecture. They have consolidated academics, architects and conservationists around the idea of preserving the artistic and historical qualities of this heritage. This is confirmed by the inclusion of the Central Post Office in the 7 Most Endangered Programme 2021. It is commonly believed that it is not so much the physical existence of the complex and its utilitarian values that are endangered, but the non-utilitarian, primarily aesthetic and symbolic values.

Palace of concerts and sports in Vilnius, Lithuania – Sports utility vs difficult history and dissonant heritage

Historical background and evolution of object's functions

Modernization in the post-war Soviet Union was not limited to industrialization and the development of infrastructure. Of course, they were the priorities for communist authorities, but in the 1960s, increasing attention was given to developing leisure and cultural facilities. It led to the growing number of new theatres, cinemas and sports stadiums built in important cities across the country. Vilnius, the fast-growing capital of the Lithuanian Soviet Socialist Republic, was no exception. As the city suffered from a lack of large modern leisure complexes, in 1960, an architectural competition for a sports and event hall in the Piromontas area in Vilnius was announced. It was supposed to become part of a large entity that included the existing Żalgris Stadium.

Rather than an open competition, the commission was given to the State Urban Construction Design Institute, where an internal contest, which included three groups of designers, took place (Dremaitė, 2017, pp. 291–293). The project by architects Eduardas Chlomauskas and Zigmantas Liandzbergis (Jonas Kriukelis joined the team later), which took second place, was chosen for construction (Mačiulis, 2002).

After the death of Joseph Stalin in 1953, but before Nikita Khrushchev's "On the Cult of Personality and Its Consequences" speech, Soviet architecture rejected the ideology of socialist realism (the "Stalinist Empire"). Khrushchev signed a decree entitled "About elimination of unnecessary extravagance in architecture," which was a clear sign of the turn towards modern aesthetics and technologies. "Russia gave priority to engineers, discovered concrete and adopted the International Style and all its plainness" (Chaubin, 2011, p. 14). The licenses purchased abroad, in capitalist countries, supported the technological development, especially in the field of prefabrication. At the same time, architects established contacts with Western architecture, through study visits or, more frequently, books and papers. The brutalist tendencies in Western architecture influenced Soviet designers, as journals (e.g. "Sowriemiennaja arhitiektura") published photos and descriptions of the latest constructions from not only socialist countries, like Poland, but capitalist ones as well (e.g. Japan and Sweden).

Both architects and politicians emphasized the advantages of prefabrication over construction in situ (Cooke & Reid, 2007, p. 175), suggesting that construction sites should become assembly sites. Along with the promotion of repeatable "typical" projects, it resulted in a certain unification of the built environment in the Soviet Union (Kotkin, 2007, p. 520).

Construction of the new sports facility in Vilnius started in 1964 and was completed seven years later. The Sports Palace was a universal, multipurpose arena whose size was determined by the dimensions of the ice hockey rink (although it never hosted a single ice hockey game). The brutalist edifice was praised for its construction, designed by engineers Henrikas Karvelis and Algimantas Katiulius. The effective, single-curvature, suspended roof structure, 1.5 times lighter than a reinforced concrete thin-shell construction of the same size, was recognized as an innovation. The prestressed cables were suspended every three metres, with concave steel trusses hanging beneath to provide the necessary rigidity of the structure and its endurance to wind loads (Černauskienė, 2020, p. 28).

The roof was clad with lightweight asbocement plates. The external walls were originally supposed to be left in sheer concrete. However, due to the poor quality of the casting concrete, many improvements had to be made; for example, the wall and roof plates were sprayed with "cement milk" (Mikučianis, 1972). Additionally, different types of plaster were used. Its scratched and furrowed surface resembled the aesthetics of brutalist architecture, but it was much easier to achieve than similar effects in concrete. In addition to the concrete imitations, the architects designed *béton brut* surfaces, with visible traces of the wooden framework (see Picture 4.32).

The Sports Palace was considered one of "the brightest examples of implemented experimental design projects" (Černauskienė, 2016, p. 10). Its prestressed cable structure "at the time (...) equalled the world's best construction projects" (Parasonis, 2007, p. 1). Architecture historian, Liutauras Nekrosius, recognized it as a reflection of the architectural trends of its

Picture 4.32 The variety of details and fractures made the form of Sports Palace in Vilnius unique, although its typology and structure were very much like sports halls in other socialist countries. © Błażej Ciarkowski.

times, and compared the Palace in Vilnius to the Soviet Union's Expo pavilion in Montreal (architect Mikhail Posokhin, 1967) and Dulles Airport in Washington (architect Eero Saarinen, 1962) (Nekrošius, 2020, p. 34). However, despite the formal resemblance, what made the architecture of the Sports Palace special was the construction based on prestressed cables, which made it possible to create a roof with a 60-metre span without any internal support. The final shape of the sports hall was a result of a long design process supervised by the authorities.

Chlomauskas and his associates were given as a reference for the Minsk Sports Arena (architects Sergey Filimonov and Valentin Malyshev, 1962–1966) (Drėmaitė, 2018). The similarities in form and spatial distribution are clearly visible (Kistyakovsky, 1973, pp. 145–146). However, they can also be distinguished in other sports halls, in Chelyabinsk or Volgograd, as this specific typology of the multipurpose arena was very popular in the Soviet Union in the 1960s. It was also implemented abroad, in countries of the Eastern Bloc, where there are many local interpretations of the scheme (e.g. the Olivia sports hall in Gdańsk, Poland, architects Maciej Gintowt and Maciej Krasiński). However, the Palace in Vilnius differs from its "brothers" in the sculptural way it shapes the architectural form, rich with detail and textures. The dominance of straight lines, right angles and "mechanical" aesthetics was replaced by expression and the dynamics of composition.

The spatial concept was based on a scheme of a sports hall with stands of a total capacity of between 2800 and 4400 people located on one side of the arena. Opposite them, the auxiliary rooms were designed. Visitors to the Palace entered the spacious lobby created under the stands with a large, fully glazed curtain wall. The massive concrete structure soaring over the void and contrasted with transparent glazing was a typical formal solution one can find, for example, in the Palace of Sports in Minsk. The interiors of the building, designed by architect Tadas Baginskas, emphasized the extraordinary position of the project with a wide range of expensive materials and high-quality finishing. Marble and granite in the lobby, mahogany veneer, natural leather and the stained-glass composition in the bar and lounge of the lodge were implemented.

In the vestibule, a large wooden sculptural panel made by Kavaliauskas was installed (Reklaite & Leitanaite, 2011, pp. 126–127). "The Sports Palace was a very serious object," said Baginskas, who was working in the Experimental Construction Bureau (EKB) at the time (Auškalnytė, 2012, p. 18). The project and the building were widely presented by the press and in literature. In 1973, the architects and engineers were honoured with the prize of the Soviet Socialist Republic of Lithuania Award. In addition to the words of appreciation, the Palace was also subject to criticism. Renowned architect Vytautas Landsbergis-Žemkalnis pointed out the dissonance of the brutalist structure and the nearby Gediminas Hill, suggesting that the location was wrongly chosen (Nemeikaitė, 2006, p. 46). By contrast, Jonas Minkevičius claimed that at the time of its construction, the Sports Palace could evoke the feeling of "dissonance" as "there was a lot of unfilled space around it, in contrast to the present time." However, as the new buildings were constructed, "the dissonance disappeared" (Auškalnytė, 2012, p. 22). Considering its functionality, the location of the Sports Palace, which was built close to the city centre, was good. The building was an integral part of the sports and leisure area, with indoor and outdoor swimming pools, a skating rink and the "Žalgris" stadium (built in 1950) (Jackiewicz, 2018, p. 108), where people who lived in the housing estates spent their free time (Štelbiene, 2019, pp. 74–75).

However, it was not the sheer architectural quality or functional aspects that made the Sports Palace in Vilnius special. It was the collective memory that mattered most. From the national revival in the 1980s, when basketball games of the Lithuanian national team became a political manifestation, through the Congress of the Lithuanian Reform Movement in 1988, to the funerals of the victims of the Soviet attack on the Radio and Television Broadcasting Centre in 1991 – the Sports Palace was the scene of events that could be called turning points of the country's recent history. Despite this, the edifice shared the fate of many soc-modernist structures. After the collapse of the communist system, it was considered "unwanted heritage."

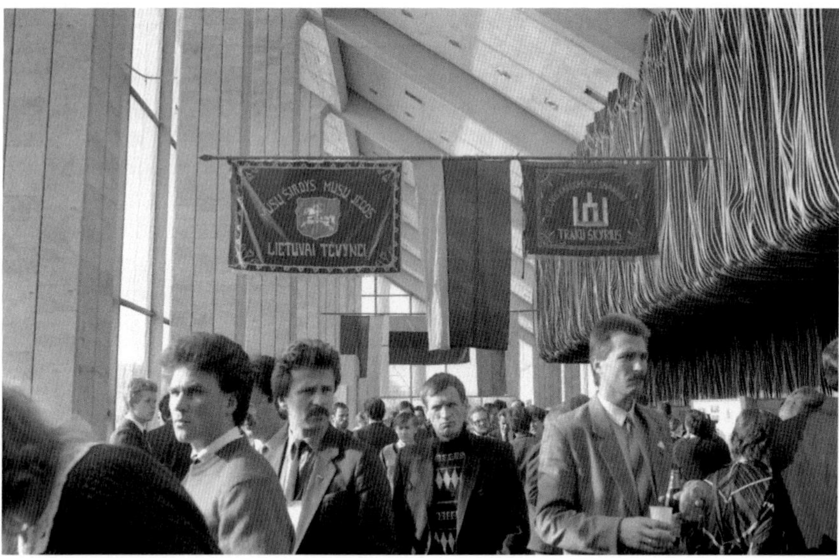

Picture 4.33 The founding Congress of the Lithuanian Reform Movement took place in the Vilnius Concert and Sports Palace in 1988. On the right-hand side, above the crowd, one can see the composition by R. Kavaliauskas in the lounge. © Roma Beliajeviene/Lietuvos centrinis valstybės archyvas (LCVA).

Picture 4.34 The Sports Palace became an integral part of the history of Lithuanian independence and the place of farewell to the victims of 13 January 1991. © Raimundos Šuikas/Lietuvos centrinis valstybės archyvas (LCVA).

The facility was finally closed in the early 2000s due to safety concerns. In August 2004, most of the company shares in the Vilnius Concert and Sports Hall were bought by a private enterprise from the Confederation of Lithuanian Trade Unions. The new owner's idea was to demolish it to get a prestigious building plot in the very heart of the city. However, less than a year later, the transaction was deemed illegal, as the law by which the property was sold contradicted the Lithuanian Constitution (Trilupaitytė, 2017, p. 354). The protests of Lithuanian architects and social resistance resulted in the Palace being included in the heritage register in 2006. The decision was justified due to its engineering and memorial value rather than its architectural quality (Nekrošius, 2020, p. 35). The atmosphere around the building resulted in a loss of interest in it from private capital. The government then repurchased the building with the intention of developing it as a conference facility. When the decision to refurbish the building and convert the building into a congress centre was made in 2008, the local Jewish community protested, complaining that the Palace was built on an old Jewish cemetery (which closed in 1817). Finally, as a compromise and result of negotiations, the cemetery was included on the Register of Archeologic Values. The plans to expand the congress centre were limited, so it would not expand further into the former cemetery (Nekrošius, 2020, p. 35).

The language of the narrative changes depending on the circumstances. When there was a strategic interest in demolishing and replacing the Palace with a new structure, it became another victim of "architectural dehumanisation" (see: Petrulis, 2007). The term "socialist legacy" was used in a negative way, and Chlomauskas' building was called a "Soviet Concrete Monster." The situation changed when it was listed. The authorities decided to include it in the project of a new congress centre as "an architecturally and technologically interesting building from the 1960s" (Drėmaitė, 2018, p. 37), and in 2015, the Government announced that the restoration of the Sports Palace in Vilnius was a project of national importance.

The current status of the Sports Palace is somewhat unclear. Although plans to redevelop the palace were announced in 2015, construction did not start due to legal issues and possible corruption. Two years later, the leaders of the Jewish community presented a petition against the reconstruction and appealed to the authorities to save the old Vilna Jewish Cemetery from further development of the Convention Centre (Norwilla, 2022).

The facility has served sporting and cultural purposes from the beginning, but what attracted attention from the outset was its functional flexibility in this respect. It was designed with a transformable stage (it was foldable like a book, and the transformation only took 20 minutes). Therefore, a wide variety of events were held here, such as sports competitions (basketball, handball, boxing, ice dancing and ice hockey (there was a system for producing artificial ice in the cellar, and it used to take 24 hours to cover the rink)), concerts (e.g. folk, pop, and rock, including world-class stars of that time), circus and drama performances, the Miss Lithuania competitions, political events (e.g. communist party meetings or celebrations, the first meeting of the Reform Movement of Lithuania) (see Picture 4.33) and even funerals (including, ironically, both the first communist state secretary and the victims killed by the Soviet army in January 1991) (see Picture 4.34). The lack of a new functional programme is not simply the result of technical faults or the building being unsuitable for modern needs. On the contrary, sports facilities of an almost identical structure are still in use in Gdańsk (Poland) or Minsk (Belarus), serving their original purpose.

Dominant value and impact of the surroundings

The Concerts and Sports Palace case in Vilnius proves that the value of the building does not always lay only in its architectural quality. Moreover, the historical events for which the edifice was the scene defined its identity much larger than the innovative structure or impressive brutalist aesthetics. According to Pierre Nora's concept, a site of memory *(lieu de memoire)* is "any significant entity, whether material or non-material in nature, which by dint of human will or the work of time has become a symbolic element of the memorial heritage of any community" (Nora, 2009). Apparently, since the communist system collapsed, the site's materiality has been a carrier of collective memory rather than a value on its own.

Thus, one can conclude that the perception of an object as having both use value and non-use value (primarily existence value) is currently competing. In other words, an ambiguous attitude towards its valuation can be observed. On the one hand, the wider public sees that the facility can still serve sporting and cultural purposes and monetize itself as it did less than two decades earlier. On the other hand, people do not want to devote it entirely to commercialization, bearing in mind that it has hosted events that are important to the modern history of Lithuania. Adding to the controversy concerning the function of this site in the nineteenth century (a Jewish cemetery), the historical value of the site and the desire to preserve it for future generations (bequest value) also matter. What comes to the fore here is not the brutalist architecture of the building, which reinforces its current non-use value, but its functionality and how the building has been used so far. If one looks for a fascination with the architectural style itself, its manifestations are more likely to appear among the youngest generation. The site was long regarded as a soviet monster. Still, opinions have changed over the last decade: the older generation has many memories and a feeling of nostalgia, and there is some respect due to the nationally significant events (e.g. the Reform movement or the funeral of January 1991). Meanwhile, the younger generations, especially architects, consider it exotic, intriguing or even beautiful.

At the time of its construction, the building was in an area that lacked dense development. It was an architectural landmark for it, favourably located in an urban fringe, with its façade facing the river Neris, but separated by a strip of sparse green area. Progressive suburbanization resulted in the expansion of sporadic new developments. The situation changed after the fall of communism. In the 1990s and 2000s, new development, mainly office buildings, was built around the site. At present, it is surrounded primarily by this type of development, so its function as a landmark has decreased, although its location opposite the river boulevard still makes it exceptionally advantageous (see Picture 4.35).

It can be said that the most favourable view of the monument is from the southern (river) and western sides. The dilapidated surroundings of the

Picture 4.35 The Concerts and Sports Palace was in the centre of the sports and leisure area in Vilnius. Nowadays, the potential of the building and its surrounding remains untapped. © Błażej Ciarkowski.

facility (e.g. small barracks buildings) on the eastern side and the neglected buildings and large parking area on the northern side create a much worse, even unfavourable, impression. Plans to maintain the facility's function as an events centre require that the surroundings be improved from these angles. The space around the facility has already been used to organize small, social, open-air events. Keeping this space public and improving its quality, with particular attention to the needs of pedestrians, seems to be the best solution. However, it certainly requires considerable investment and design creativity. Transforming the physical surroundings would also require marking the memory of the former cemetery. A promising direction would be not to build new structures in this area, as this would further limit the Palace's exposition to the surroundings. Any new development should be regarded with caution to avoid damaging the integrity of the site, which has already been partially lost. The stadium and several other buildings that formed the vast sports complex were demolished and replaced with offices and housing.

Socio-economic embeddedness and local uniqueness

The uniqueness of the building is due, on one hand, to the fact that it is an essential spatial dominant feature of Vilnius, and on the other hand, to its somewhat central importance in Lithuania's recent history. Considering its architecture and the construction technology used, it is difficult to say that the building is unique to the city. These aspects are related to many other objects in Soviet architecture mentioned above. However, given the relatively scarce pool of such facilities in general, the uniqueness of the brutalist architecture is present, especially as it is the only one of its kind in the country's capital. Moreover, it is not the physical features of the object itself, but the history associated with it that is embedded in the collective memory of the people of Vilnius and Lithuanians. Even if it is not a critical object for the uniqueness of Lithuanian architecture, its removal will create a gap.

Initially, the idea to protect the building and include it in the heritage list was bottom up. It started with the organization of a specific NGO, Protest-LAB, with artists Nomeda and Gediminas Urbonas as its leaders. There were several social events, a protest, a video and campaigning to publicize the initiative. Simultaneously, the Jewish community campaigned for the former cemetery to be preserved. These activities brought the issue of preserving the deteriorating site back into the public debate loud enough that it could not be passed over in silence by decision-makers. As a result, today, the object appears important for the city and the national government authorities. The formerly grassroots initiatives have opened the way for the value and heritage of other entities of Soviet modernist architecture to be discussed. Today it is the government's responsibility to ensure that the Palace's technical design for its reconstruction – by adapting it to the activities of a conference centre and arranging the surrounding cemetery area – is completed and approved.

Republic Square in Ljubljana, Slovenia – The beginnings of statehood and every day of the capital's civic life

Historical background and evolution of object's functions

The history of twentieth-century Slovenian architecture is similar to that in most CEE countries – determined by a search for its own national identity and attempts to set its own place between East and West. After World War I, in all the countries that reclaimed their independence, architecture was one of the means of doing this. However, the whole process did not start in 1918. The symptoms of the Czech or Polish cultural renaissance were already visible at the end of the nineteenth century, when artists and architects tried to establish a "national style." It resulted in the new image of Prague in the First Czechoslovak Republic, Budapest in Hungary and Krakow in Poland – modern yet bound with local tradition. Slovenia was no exception.

The origins of the idea of Ljubljana as a European capital go back to the beginning of the twentieth century, when Slovenian architect, Josef Plečnik, implemented several prestigious and visionary projects that had a great impact on the cityscape. The National and University Library of Slovenia building, insurance company offices and bridges over the Ljubljanica River became visible signs of the metropolitan aspirations of the local authorities and citizens. At the same time, Plečnik himself was a role model, the archetype of the versatile architect. Not only did he lay the foundation of the "national style" in Slovenian architecture, but he was also a mentor for younger generations of architects. One of Plečnik's most recognized apprentices was Edvard (Edo) Ravnikar. Born in Novo Mesto in 1907, he studied in Vienna and worked in Le Corbusier's studio shortly before WWII. After the war, he settled in Ljubljana, where he soon became known as a skilled designer, an extraordinary personality and a leader of the new generation of Slovenian architects.

The Slovenian capital is often described as "Plečnik's Ljubljana." However, Ravnikar can rightfully be called Plečnik's heir, and not only because he was his most successful student. Ravnikar's projects in the city were probably as important as Plečnik's, and he was also an influential teacher at the Ljubljana School of Architecture. Vladimir Kulić noted:

> The chief difference between the master and the disciple, however, was Plečnik's inherent conservatism, both aesthetic and political. Despite great freedom with which he transformed the canons of classicism, Plečnik was deeply suspicious of modernism, particularly of Le Corbusier. In contrast, Ravnikar was not only willing to engage with evolving modernism, but he also embraced the goals of the Yugoslav socialist revolution, which allowed him to assume a prominent position on the architectural scene of the new state as soon as World War II was over.
>
> (Kulić, 2013, pp. 804–805)

Ravnikar praised Plečnik and his ideas, but, at the same time, he made a step forward and pushed Slovenian architecture in a new direction "in order to construct not only a local modernism, but also a local version of modernity that would be cosmopolitan, yet also all its own" (Kulić, 2013, p. 803). Concerning his undeniable role in the development of Slovenian late-modernist architecture, it is not surprising that Nataša Koselj called Edvard Ravnikar "the father of regionally tempered Slovene structuralism" (Koselj, 2018a, p. 36). The idea of modernist architecture in post-war Slovenia developed with the openness to the West combined with the search for a local identity and elements of "national style" that were characteristic of the whole of socialist Yugoslavia. Rather than pathos and the overblown monumentality of socialist realism, architects developed a different, more creative formula of official representation. Ravnikar was one of the first to succeedin combining traditional elements with the spirit of modernity.

Republic Square (named Revolution Square between 1947 and 1991) was one of the greatest achievements of Edo Ravnikar's career. His first project for the site where a monastery was once located was made in 1960 as a winning competition entry. Four years later, due to the changes of developers, the concept was transformed (Koselj, 2018a, p. 38). Finally, in the mid-1970s, the complex was developed and changed once again. Nevertheless, from the very beginning, Ravnikar answered the competition task, which was to shape a new city centre, by creating two towers, the "Ljubljana gate," a symbolic entry to the city. As the square was supposed to become a "political space," the architect added "a certain degree of aggression" embodied in a pair of massive, 20-storey high skyscrapers, and turning a former convent garden into "a concrete wilderness" (Koselj, 2018a, p. 38). The monumental symmetrical composition included a site for the memorial to the National Liberation War located in the central place between the two towers (E. Ravnikar, 2010, pp. 158–159) (see Picture 4.36). Ravnikar reduced the height of the tower blocks and differentiated the forms of their tops. The monument to the revolution was moved to the western side of the square, disturbing the original symmetry of the composition.

Construction started in 1961 and took more than a decade; it was completed in 1974. The twin towers, located in the southern part of the square, have an identical triangular-shaped layout, arranged so that the cantilevered bevelled points of the equilateral triangles are set opposite each other, creating a relatively narrow pass. The high-rise buildings, named TR2 and TR3, had, respectively, 14 and 17 storeys. Their vertical bodies, which overhung the ground floor and were topped with expressive "crowns" of different shapes and sizes, were a strong dominant of the composition of the square.

The eastern frontage of the square is determined by Maximarket – a large commercial building completed in 1971. Its elongated, solid, stone-clad body creates an architectural boundary preceded by a partially open underground commercial passage. The multi-level composition not only

Picture 4.36 Edvard Ravnikar designed a pair of monumental, triangular towers on the Republic Square as a landmark, an actual "gate to the capital." © Błażej Ciarkowski.

extended the usable area of the whole complex, but also gave the spatial composition of the square a certain dynamic. Ravnikar, a child of his time, believed that architecture and urbanism were aimed at creating a stage for life. He wrote in 1974:

> We should look upon a city as a large group of things – objects, buildings, sometimes as a sequence of images, as an "urban design" with a system of sequences and aesthetic exclusivity, which is often the way in which we try to replace the missing space of the social energies by contacts and harmony. In this case a city is not only an exterior appearance, although this is very important and necessary, but also a place where things happen.
>
> (E. Ravnikar, 1974)

The western part of Republic Square is the opposite of its eastern frontage. Instead of an architectural frontier, there is a park which creates a "green wall." Close to the Revolution Monument is a large bronze statue created in 1975 by sculptor Drago Tršar and architect Vladimir Brac Mušič.

Once most of the square had been completed, major changes in the design were required. Despite the original plans, the complex was not supposed to serve only as a political centre, but as a mixed-use heart of the capital. In 1977, the construction of a large cultural, convention and congress centre, later named after the Slovenian writer and politician Ivan Cankar (Cankarjev Dom), began. The inauguration of the new building took place in 1983 as the whole process had been very demanding at the organizational, architectural and structural engineering levels. Part of the complex, which comprises four large auditoria and vast auxiliary spaces, had to be built under an existing structure. Visitor access was provided from the central shopping passage on the basement level or through the large reception hall above ground (Vodopivec, 2010, p. 25).

Ravnikar's deep devotion to structuralism in architecture was reflected in the project's ability to accommodate functional changes. "The existing content of a bank, office areas, shops, restaurants and special services is already taking shape in the form of an interesting social environment that the further construction of the Revolution Square Complex will enhance with further new content," he stated, saying that Cankarjev Dom "[would] expand opportunities to mingle, through the organization of exhibitions of industrial production, by offering many opportunities for fine arts exhibitions and ever more open-air events, from theatre to every kind of social gathering. All this creates an entirely new basis for a very necessary higher level of life in our city that stems from its environment" (E. Ravnikar, 1974, pp. 81–83) (see Picture 4.37).

Ravnikar's vision of modernist architecture was, to a certain extent, based on the ideas of his teacher, Jože Plečnik, and the concept of a "national style." The complex structure of different parts of Revolution Square allowed him to use a "rich vocabulary of forms, structures, and textures, while still creating a cohesive whole" (Kulić, 2013, p. 807). The architect decided to use local materials and building technologies that were available in and appropriate for Slovenia. The reinforced structures are clad with thin stone plates, joined to the reinforced concrete structure with metal bolts, which are a particular kind of technical "ornament" (similar to those used by Otto Wagner in Österreichische Postsparkasse in Vienna). At the same time, the white marble cladding of the Cankarjev Dom pavilion distinguishes it from the rest of the complex, giving it a solemn character.

Ravnikar wanted to create an interplay between new, modernist architecture and the existing building structures, not only by using different materials (e.g. natural stone and raw concrete) but also by using different scales, oscillating between the monumental and the intimate. Therefore, the square became a living space of representation; however, at the same time, it does not overwhelm its visitors. The architect often spoke about the city as a process and warned against considering it as a set of picturesque views. "It is necessary to strive for the city as a process, not the city as a view," he wrote. "Fullness of content develops on its own, in the flow of time, during the process" (cited by Koselj, 2018b, p. 56; orig. E. Ravnikar, 1974). According to Ravnikar, the main role of the designer was to find a suitable architectural vocabulary, "rich and exciting," understandable for people and capable of having an impact on their psyche and not only serving a specific functional programme.

The design and realization of Republic Square were conferred the Plečnik Award in 1975 and the Prešeren Award three years later. Nevertheless, it was not protected until 2002, despite suggestions from professionals who emphasized its uniqueness and need for preservation as a whole (V. Ravnikar et al., 2000, p. 16). In 2014, the complex was listed as a cultural heritage of national importance. Unfortunately, due to the lack of awareness of architectural and historical values, during the refurbishment works which took place in 2000, some parts of the buildings were irreversibly destroyed, including the interiors of the Nova Ljubljanska Banka, which architects considered some of Ravnikar's finest works (Koselj, 2020, pp. 67–68).

The role of Revolution Square within the urban tissue of the Slovenian capital goes far beyond its functional programme. Located in the heart of Ljubljana, on the ruins of the Roman settlement of Emona, it is "the symbolic centre of Slovenian statehood, defined largely by three structures designed by Ravnikar" (Kulić, 2013, p. 807). The most characteristic are the twin towers, the monumental "gate" to the city.

The skyscrapers were originally intended for state administration, together with the National Assembly building, which encloses the square from the north and was designed by architect Vinko Glanz and built between 1954 and 1959. The economic reform in the mid-1960s in Yugoslavia led to a change of developers – it was no longer the state, but the Ljubljanska Banka (after 1991 reformed as Nova Ljubljanska Banka – NLB) and the Iskra Company. Consequently, the construction of the project came to a standstill for some time, and the urban plan and architectural concept had to be changed (Koselj, 2018b, p. 55).

Ravnikar described the origins of the project as follows:

> We started only with an uncertain wish to prepare the environment for an important national monument. In this way, the initial brief was but a symbolic record of still unknown functions, only a starting point for little active building masses. The initial ambition, however, already pointed to the need for a large central public space, a component that remained unchanged till the end.
>
> (E. Ravnikar, 1974, p. 82)

The architect was overcome with the idea of movement, so he designed a space where the flow of visitors could be really free thanks to the entrances, passages, underground passages, staircases and galleries. One of his aims was to create a place for shopping, meeting without disturbance, relaxing and observing – every kind of activity related to urban life. A space that would be a substitute for the street – a carrier of life within the city. An exterior that attracts people with many things they are used to inside buildings (E. Ravnikar, 2010, pp. 157–158) (see Picture 4.38).

Picture 4.37 The complex of the Republic Square intends to stimulate people to many different activities – among them cultural, which centre is Cenkarjev Dom. © Błażej Ciarkowski.

Revolution Square is not only a manifesto of Ravnikar's concept of architecture and urban planning based on the concept of the free placement of large buildings in space. It also reveals the transformation in Yugoslav politics, which shifted from socialist dogmatism to pragmatism. Rather than a monumental "political space," the architect provided the Slovenian capital with a "space of freedom" (at least to some extent) where people could wander through the labyrinth of passages.

After the collapse of socialist Yugoslavia and Slovenia's proclamation of independence, the square secured its role as a scene of important political events. It changed in 2005 when, due to a High Court decision, the once public space owned by the municipality of Ljubljana was handed over to the BSL company, which owned the underground garage under the square. It was a result of several operations that started in 1988 when the Republic Square Construction Institute transferred the underground garage and the square, which from the technical point of view, is the roof of the garage, to the Park-hiša Šubičeva company free of charge. After two resales, in 2003, both the garage and the market became the property of BSL, which the court confirmed in July 2005. Six years later, in 2011, according to the agreement between the local authorities and BSL, the city of Ljubljana became the owner of Trg Republike once again, while the company remained the owner of the garage under the square (Pahor, 2011). In 2014, the square was cleared of parked cars and renovated as a representative pedestrian area.

Picture 4.38 Variety of forms and different scales of particular objects designed by Edvard Ravnikar were meant to create a “living space.” Nowadays, socialist modernist aesthetics can appear a little “overwhelming.” © Błażej Ciarkowski.

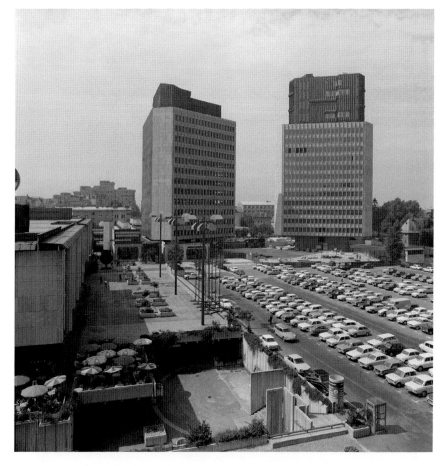

Picture 4.39 The Republic Square in Ljubljana was a public space from the beginning, but it took decades to become a car-free pedestrian area. Initially, a large part of the square was a parking lot.

Source: © Damjan Gale (in Vodopivec & Žnidaršič, 2010).

Dominant value and impact of the surroundings

Republic Square is Ljubljana's largest square and one of the city's central landmarks. For the city's inhabitants it has strong utilitarian and non-utilitarian values. Thus, it is difficult to determine its dominant value unequivocally. There is a kind of balance in this respect. On the one hand, the square is a symbolic space and a landmark of the city with a strong historical connotation. On the other hand, it is a service centre whose functions are mainly administrative, business, commercial and cultural. Since the founding of Slovenia as an independent state, the place has therefore combined the characteristics of a Central Business District

(CBD) and the centre of the country, that is to say, economic and political logic, and is viewed as a carrier of Slovenian national identity.

Republic Square is perceived primarily as a symbolic legacy of the Slovenian state-building, where existence value comes to the fore. This is because, as a CBD, it is a source of economic value "here and now." However, Slovenian society also sees its role as a carrier of deeper cultural values and national identity. Key was the fact that the independence of the Republic of Slovenia was proclaimed there on 25 June 1991. This event led to the perception of Republic Square as a "witness to the history" of Slovenia and a place where a new national identity was built. This value is reinforced by the presence of the revolution memorial and the Parliament building – the National Assembly (lower house) and the legislature's National Council (upper house). In addition, the square is seen as a place of an official character. Its space is used as a venue for many state ceremonies – parades or state ceremonies with military honours for foreign delegations (see Picture 4.39).

The historical-symbolic significance of Republic Square is confirmed by a survey conducted in 2018 (Hočevar, 2018). It indicated that for the vast majority of Ljubljana's residents, the entire complex of Republic Square is an important place for the national identification of the inhabitants, and that they experience it primarily as a square of "state" character.

The symbolic value of Republic Square also stems from its perception as a symbol of progress. In the 1950s, when the two towers were built, Republic Square (called Revolution Square at the time) was perceived as a sign of development and progress, not only architectural but also technological – something innovative in the city space (Bojc, 2014). This public perception of the square has not changed. What has changed, however, is the interpretation of this progress. The way the square has developed, its functionality, and the physical scale of the two skyscrapers still evoke positive feelings. They are associated with the transformation and development of Slovenia.

Moreover, the symbolism of this space is also built by the name of the urban composition created by the two towers. The two twelve-storey, three-sided "skyscrapers" created a symbolic portal that alludes to Ljubljana's geographical location in a mountain basin between two hills. In local circles, this layout is referred to as the "Gate of Ljubljana" or the "Double Lantern" of the modern city.

The utility value of Republic Square is created primarily by the service functions located in the two Ravnikara towers. The square is a popular shopping area, mainly due to the location of Ljubljana's largest shopping centre (Maximarket) in one of the towers. The other one houses a branch of a large bank. These two large service functions of this space are supplemented with numerous complementary activities, mainly gastronomic (e.g. cafes, bars and pizzerias). In addition, the variety of services in the buildings located in the immediate vicinity of Republic Square (including a cultural centre, a gallery, a library, schools and an orthodox church) make this space vibrant and represent one of the most important urban-architectural areas of the city.

Despite its great architectural and functional diversity, Republic Square is perceived as a harmonious and coherent space in the heart of the city. It successfully combines seemingly incompatible architecture and functions while the monumental architecture of the two towers blends into the existing urban environment. One of the guiding principles of the original design was to take into account the existing urban fabric, creating a physical and visual dialogue with the medieval and baroque heritage of the neighbourhood.

Republic Square and its immediate surroundings make up an urban and functional whole. The modernist architecture of the towers is well integrated into the surrounding urban fabric. The buildings and functions located close to the square emphasize its symbolic value. They are primarily the headquarters of the National Museum of Slovenia and the Cultural and Congress Centre (Cankarjev Dom), which hosts large and symbolic, often patriotic cultural events. This centre is the central Slovenian institution, which promotes the cultural life not only of the capital but also of the entire country.

The integration of the square with the surrounding space is also ensured by the empty spaces and bridges on the ground floor of the two towers. Not without significance for the perception of the square are the numerous green areas in the adjacent surroundings, which display the architectural and urban values of the square and reinforce its multi-functionality. Located on the western edge of Republic Square, a park with tall trees is the location of several monuments from the socialist Yugoslav era. Seemingly incompatible with the existing development, Ravnikar's towers created a coherent composition of the urban landscape and a modernist atmosphere in the city centre.

Socio-economic embeddedness and local uniqueness

In the past, Republic Square was appropriated by a surface car park, representation functions and state ceremonies. Its functionality was organized top-down, and the square was excluded from use for other purposes. However, due to a change in social consciousness (observed among CEE countries over the last two decades), there has been a shift in how the value of Republic Square is perceived. There has been an evolution in how its symbolic value is defined – from a place of representation and appropriation by government ceremonies to a place for the free expression of opinions and views. Today, Republic Square has become a space to build civil society, express one's freedom and get a sense of community. In the last two years, in particular, Republic Square has witnessed numerous public protests against the way the country is governed. For more than a hundred Fridays in a row, demonstrations by city residents have taken place here. The authorities have tried to prevent peaceful protests (supported by artistic actions) by fencing off the square and restricting access, further provoking strong public resistance. Nowadays, the symbolism of Republic Square goes beyond the construction of national identity (as it did before), and its perception as a place to express views and build civic attitudes is gaining importance.

In recent years, the community has become increasingly more aware of the value of the square and much more interested in its condition and development. This has been confirmed by grassroots reactions from city residents and protests over attempts to remove the digital clock from one of the skyscrapers. The attempt to place flagpoles between the square and the Parliament is also an example of the social revival around the square. In 2021, during the Slovenian Presidency of the European Union, a line of flagpoles of all EU Member States was erected parallel to the main facade of the Parliament, along with the flag of the city of Ljubljana. The composition of the poles represented a visual and physical dividing line between Republic Square and the Parliament building, which aroused much public controversy. The majority of the city's residents accept the square as it is now, but reject any significant change to its physical structure (Hočevar, 2018). However, there is agreement among the local community for occasional and temporary changes in the use of the square, but only for things that do not permanently alter the fundamental aspects of its appearance and its functions.

Influenced by grassroots demands, the functionality of Republic Square has changed in recent years. The modernization of the square's slab, which was carried out in 2014, and the permanent closure of the surface car park, made it possible to strengthen the integrative and recreational functions of the square. The square is now exclusively open to pedestrian traffic and hosts a variety of social, artistic and sporting events (including an ice rink in winter). It is also a popular meeting place and training ground for young amateur acrobats on skateboards and sports bikes. In this way, an open and inclusive public space emerged in the city centre that combines monumental and modernist styles. The multifaceted symbolic function of the square has been consolidated, and its utilitarian and integrative values have been strengthened.

Notes

1 At the time, the Bulgarian lev was not convertible to Western currencies, and the administrative exchange rate (close to one US dollar for one lev) was out of line with black market exchange rates. However, assuming that two leva per US dollar were paid in tourist traffic in the 1960s and 1970s, it can be assumed that the amount collected reached the rather sizable sum of about 8 million US dollars.

2 Among them: Vladislav Paskalev, Kuncho Kanev, Velichko Minekov, Valentin Starchev, Hristo Stefanov, Ioan Leviev, Dimitar Boykov, Mihail Benchev, Ivan Kirkov, Toma Varbanov, Alexander Terziev, Georgi Trifonov, Ivan Stoilov – Bunkera, Ivan B. Ivanov, Grigor Spiridonov, Dimitar Kirov, Stoimen Stoilov.

3 Stoilov made a mistake here, as Filippo Brunelleschi, an Italian architect, designer and sculptor, designed the dome of the Santa Maria del Fiore cathedral in Florence (1420–1461). It means that Stoilov's point of reference was the dome of the Pantheon.

4 Decision of the Council of Ministers No. 731/30.09.2011 on the free transfer of properties – private state property, owned by the Bulgarian Socialist Party/Buzludzha Mountain Monument Complex.

5 Exhibition: *Towards Concrete Utopia. Architecture in Yugoslavia, 1948–1980*, curators: Martino Stierli, Vladimir Kulić, The Museum of Modern Art, New York, 15 July 2018 to 13 January 2019.

References

Amiot, H. (2018). De Tito à Aalexandre : Vers la construction d'un paysage urbain postsocialiste à Skopje (République de Macédoine) ? *Belgeo*, *4*, 1–25. https://doi.org/10.4000/belgeo.21184

Architektura. (1973). Dworzec kolejowy w Katowicach [Katowice railroad station]. *Architektura*, *10*, 370–373.

Auškalnytė, V. (2012). *Sovietinio laikotarpio Vilniaus miesto visuomeninės paskirties pastatų interjerai* [Vytautas Magnus University]. https://gs.elaba.lt/object/elaba:1843690/1843690.pdf

B.A.C.U. (2019). *Urbană, Birou pentru artă şi cercetare* [Office for Art and Urban Research]. https://bacu.ro/

B.A.C.U. (2021). *Socialist modernism*. Socialist Modernism. http://socialistmodernism.com/

Barucki, T. (1987). *Wacław Kłyszewski, Jerzy Mokrzyński, Eugeniusz Wierzbicki*. Arkady.

Basista, A. (2001). *Betonowe dziedzictwo: Architektura w Polsce czasów komunizmu* [Concrete legacy: Architecture in communist Poland]. PWN.

Bell, J. D. (1986). *Bulgarian communist party from Blagoev to Zhivkov*. Hoover Institution Press.

Blatter, J. K. (2008). Case study. In L. M. Given (Ed.), *The SAGE encyclopedia of qualitative research methods* (pp. 68–71). SAGE Publications.

Bojc, S. (2014, September 24). Ljubljanski Trg republike: Velika ambicija, ki je dišala po osamosvojitv [Ljubljana's Republic Square: A great ambition that smelled of independence]. *Delo*. https://old.delo.si/novice/ljubljana/ljubljanski-trg-republike-velika-ambicija-ki-je-disala-po-osamosvojitvi.html

Borowik, A. (2019). *Nowe Katowice. Forma i ideologia polskiej architektury powojennej na przykładzie Katowic (1945–1980)* [New Katowice. Form and ideology of Polish post-war architecture on the example of Katowice (1945–1980)]. Neriton.

Borowik, A. (2020). Smutek odchodzenia architektury. Historia wyburzenia dworca kolejowego w Katowicach [The sadness of architecture passing away. The history of the demolition of the railway station in Katowice]. In M. J. Sołtysik & M. Stępa (Eds.), *Modernizm w Europie – Modernizm w Gdyni. Architektura XX wieku: Zachowanie jej autentyzmu i integralności w Gdyni i w Europie* [Modernism in Europe - Modernism in Gdynia. Architecture of the 20th century: Preservation of its authenticity and integrity in G] (pp. 171–180). Urząd Miasta Gdyni-Wydział Architektury Politechniki Gdańskiej. https://www.gdynia.pl/zabytki/module/Files/controller/Default/action/downloadFile/hash/f3a6d71ef7c98dbb183d29193397a71f

Brsakoska, J. (2021). Public space transformation in the case of 'Skopje 2014.' *Urbana*, *22*, 1–20. https://doi.org/10.47785/urbana.4.2021

Buzludzha Project Foundation. (2022). *Buzludzha Project*. https://www.buzludzha-project.com/

Černauskienė, A. (2016). Novelty of artistic forms in contemporary Lithuanian architecture. *Architecture and Urban Planning*, *11*(1), 6–13. https://doi.org/doi:10.1515/aup-2016-0001.

Černauskienė, A. (2020). Idea of in the evaluation of Lithuanian concrete architecture. *Architecture and Urban Planning*, *16*(1), 26–31. https://doi.org/doi:10.2478/aup-2020-0005

Chaubin, F. (2011). *CCCP. Cosmic communist constructions photographed.* Taschen.

Ciarkowski, B. (2018). Integralna część krajobrazu czy element obcy? Architektura modernistycznych domów wczasowych z czasów PRL [Integral part of the landscape or strange element? Architecture of modernist resort houses from the Peoples Republic of Poland's era]. In W. Kobylińska-Bunsch (Ed.), *Architektura w krajobrazie: Harmonia – Kompromis – Konflikt* [Architecture in the landscape: Harmony – Compromise – Conflict] (pp. 377–384). Instytut Historii Sztuki UW.

Cooke, C., & Reid, S. E. (2007). Modernity and realism, architectural relations in the cold war. In R. P. Blakesley & S. E. Reid (Eds.), *Russian art and the west. A century of dialogue in painting, architecture, and the decorative arts* (pp. 172–194). Northern Illinois University Press.

Deskova, A., Deskov, V., & Ivanovski, J. (2019). Challenging disregard: The case of the telecommunication center in Skopje. *Studies in History and Theory of Architecture*, 7, 205–219. https://doi.org/10.54508/sITA.7.14

Dremaitė, M. (2017). *Baltic modernism: Architecture and housing in Soviet Lithuania*. DOM Publishers.

Drėmaitė, M. (2018). Eduardas Chlomauskas: Vilnius concert and sports palace (Vilniaus Sporto Rūmai), 1965–1971. In O. Elser, P. Kurz, & P. C. Schmal (Eds.), *SOS Brutalism: A global survey* (1st ed.). Park Books. https://www.sosbrutalism.org/cms/15802395#15963855

Europa Nostra. (2013). *The 7 most endangered*. https://7mostendangered.eu/

Eysenck, H. J. (1976). Introduction. In H. J. Eysenck (Ed.), *Case studies in behaviour therapy* (pp. 1–15). Routledge.

Flyvbjerg, B. (2006). Five misunderstandings about case-study research. *Qualitative Inquiry*. https://doi.org/10.1177/1077800405284363

Franta, A. (1999). Mój ulubiony budynek. Dworzec Tygrysów [My favorite building. Tiger's Station]. *Architektura-Murator*, 7, 76–77.

Grekov, P. (1981). Za Ideyniya i Emotsionaliniya Zaryad Na Edna Slozhna Arhitektura Zadacha [About the idea and emotional charge of a complex architectural project]. *Arhitekura*, *10*, 6–22.

Grotowska, S. (2016). Czy architektura czasów PRL ma znaczenie? Analiza wydarzenia Medialnego [Does the architecture of the Polish People's Republic mean anything? An analysis of a mass media event]. *Opuscula Sociologica*, *3*(17), 33–44. http://cejsh.icm.edu.pl/cejsh/element/bwmeta1.element.desklight-91f3e24a-758d-4f34-a8b5-ce48487a8011

Gzowska, A. (2012). *Szesnaście żelbetowych kwiatów. Nowy dworzec w Katowicach* [Sixteen reinforced concrete flowers. Railway station in Katowice]. Wydawnictwo Naukowe "Śląsk".

Hatherley, O. (2012). Socialist Googie, Gothic futurism and hierarchical tunnels. In G. Piątek (Ed.), *AR/PS. The architecture of Arseniusz Romanowicz and Piotr Szymaniak* (pp. 210–216). Centrum Architektury.

Higgins, A. (2022). On a remote mountain, the 'Sistine Chapel of Socialism' awaits its fate. *New York Times*. https://www.nytimes.com/2022/05/22/world/europe/on-a-remote-mountain-the-sistine-chapel-of-socialism-awaits-its-fate.html

Hočevar, M. (2018). *Anketa o Trgu Republike* [Survey about Republic Square]. https://www.ljubljana.si/assets/Uploads/Publikacija-Anketa-o-trgu-republike.pdf

Jackiewicz, M. (2018). Nieistniejące dzielnice Wilna. Pióromont i Łosiówka. Zabłocki i mydło [Non-existent districts of Vilnius. Pióromont and Łosiówka. Zablocki and soap]. *Znad Wilii*, *3*(75), 102–110.

Janev, G. (2017). Burdensome past: Challenging the socialist heritage in Macedonia. *Studia Ethnologica Croatica*, *29*(1), 149–170.

Janković-Beguš, J. (2017). Between East and West': Socialist modernism as the official paradigm of Serbian Art Music in the Socialist Federal Republic of Yugoslavia. *International Journal of Music Studies*, *1*(1), 141–163. https://doi.org/10.33906/MUSICOLOGIST.373187

Jasiński, R., Piekarczyk, A., & Galman, I. (2010). Badania głównych elementów konstrukcji dworca PKP w Katowicach [Investigation of major elements of construction railway station in Katowice]. *Inżynieria i Budownictwo*, *3*, 129–134.

Jaśniok, M., Jaśniok, T., & Zybura, A. (2010). Badania korozyjnego zagrożenia zbrojenia kielichowej konstrukcji budynku dworca kolejowego w Katowicach [The tests of goblet construction corrosion risk of railway station building in Katowice]. *Inżynieria i Budownictwo*, *5–6*, 249–253. https://www.inzynieriaibudownictwo.pl/images/archiwum/2010/05-06-2010.pdf

Jedlecki, P. (2020, December 22). Dziesięć lat temu rozpoczęło się wyburzanie katowickiego dworca PKP [Ten years ago, the demolition of Katowice's railway station began]. *Gazeta Wyborcza*. https://katowice.wyborcza.pl/katowice/5,35063,19457808.html

Jencks, C. (1975). *Le Corbusier and the tragic view of architecture*. Penguin Books.

Jencks, C. (1977). *The language of post-modern architecture*. Academy Editions.

Jencks, C. (1980). *Late-modern architecture and other essays*. Rizzoli.

Kaleva, E. (2014). The best examples of the architectural heritage of socialism in Bulgaria. In *Socialist realism and socialist modernism. World heritage proposals from Central and Eastern Europe* (pp. 80–84). Hendrik Bäßler.

Kaleva, E., & Vasileva, A. (2018). Unity, creativity, beauty – Decline and survival of socialist memorial sites in Bulgaria. In J. Haspel, S. Brandt, L. Kondrashev, A. Kudryavtsev, & J. Ziesemer (Eds.), *A future for our recent past. Model projects of modern heritage conservation in Europe* (pp. 130–136). hendrik Bäßler.

Kaplan, F. I. (1968). *Bolshevik ideology and the ethics of Soviet labor*. Philosophical Library.

Katerina, K., Lechevska, K., Borovska, V., & Blazeva, A. (2013). *Skopje 2014 project and its effects on the perception of Macedonian identity among the citizens of Skopje*. https://www.isshs.edu.mk/wp-content/uploads/2017/05/1.-sk2014-eng.pdf

Kistyakovsky, A. Y. (1973). *Proyektirovaniye sportivnykh sooruzheniy* [Sports facilities design]. Высшая школа [Vysshaya shkola].

Konstantinov, J. (1970). Objekt Telekomunikačiskog centra PTT u Skopje [Facility of the PTT telecommunication center in Skopje]. *Čovjek i Prostor*, *4*, 12.

Koselj, N. (2018a). Edge and metaphor. The authentic modernism of Edvard Ravnikar. In A. Tostões & N. Koselj (Eds.), *Metamorphosis. The continuity of change* (pp. 36–47). Docomomo International & Docomomo Slovenia.

Koselj, N. (2018b). Edvard Ravnikar and the heart of the city. The genesis of cultural centers in Slovenia and in ex-Yugoslavia. *Docomomo Journal*, *59*(2), 55–59. https://doi.org/10.52200/59.A.B3CK6W9A

Koselj, N. (2020). The roots of Slovenian structuralism: From Plečnik to Ravnikar and beyond. Centenary of the Ljubljana school of architecture. In M. J. Sołtysik

& M. Stępa (Eds.), *Modernizm w Europie – Modernizm w Gdyni. Architektura XX wieku: Zachowanie jej autentyzmu i integralności w Gdyni i w Europie* [Modernism in Europe - Modernism in Gdynia. Architecture of the 20th century: Preservation of its authenticity and integrity in G] (pp. 65–70). Urząd Miasta Gdyni-Wydział Architektury Politechniki Gdańskiej.

Kotkin, S. (2007). Mongol Commonwealth? Exchange and governance across the post-Mongol space. *Kritika: Explorations in Russian and Eurasian History*, *8*(3), 487–531. https://doi.org/10.1353/kri.2007.0040

Kozina, I. (2019). *Ikony architektury w województwie śląskim w XX i XXI w.* [Architectural icons in the Silesian Voivodeship in the 20th and 21st centuries]. Muzeum Śląskie.

Kulić, V. (2013). Edvard Ravnikar's liquid modernism: Architectural identity in a network of shifting references. In I. Berman & E. Mitchell (Eds.), *ACSA 101: New constellations, new ecologies* (pp. 802–809). Association of Collegiate Schools of Architecture.

Kulić, V. (2017). Building the socialist Balkans: Architecture in the global networks of the cold war. *Southeastern Europe*, *41*(2), 95–111. https://doi.org/10.1163/18763332-04102001

Larsson, N. (2018, August 6). Socialist modernism: Remembering the architecture of the eastern bloc. *The Guardian*. https://www.theguardian.com/cities/2018/aug/06/socialist-modernism-remembering-the-architecture-of-the-eastern-bloc

Machat, C., & Ziesemer, J. (2017). *Heritage at risk. World report 2014–2015 on monuments and sites in danger.* Hendrik Bäßler. http://openarchive.icomos.org/id/eprint/2108/1/HR2014_2015_final.pdf

Mačiulis, A. (2002). *Lietuvos architektai* [Lithuanian architects]. Vilnius Art Academy Publishing House.

Malkowski, T. (2007a, July 7). Zburzenie dworca będzie przestępstwem [Demolition of the station will be a crime]. *Gazeta.Pl.* http://wiadomosci.gazeta.pl/wiadomosci/1,114873,4286242.html

Malkowski, T. (2007b, October 4). Katowice: Nowy dworzec jak królik z kapelusza [Katowice: New train station like a rabbit out of a hat]. *Gazeta.Pl.* http://wiadomosci.gazeta.pl/wiadomosci/1,114873,4548831.html

Malkowski, T. (2010, September 28). W Katowicach runął mur obywatelskiej obojętności [A wall of civic apathy has collapsed in Katowice]. *Gazeta Wyborcza.*

Metalkova-Markova, M. (2008). Another kind of modernism - Trends in postwar architectural ideology and practice in socialist Bulgaria 1944–1989. In T. H. M. Prudon & H. Lipstadt (Eds.), *Proceedings: VIIIth International Conference Import-Export: Postwar Modernism in a Expanding World, 1945–1975* (pp. 175–181). DOCOMOMO. https://docomomo-us.org/resource/files%2F5lv-jp7okfskf04a.pdf

Mikučianis, A. V. (1972). Sporto rūmai Vilniuje [Sports palace in Vilnius]. *Statyba Ir Architektūra*, *1*(152), 1–5.

Miłobędzki, A. (1994). *Architektura ziem Polski* [Architecture of Polish territories]. Międzynarodowe Centrum Kultury w Krakowie.

Minorski, J. (1960). Z konkursu na projekt dworca kolejowego w Katowicach [From the design competition for Katowice railway station]. *Architektura*, *4*, 137–140. http://mbc.cyfrowemazowsze.pl/dlibra/docmetadata?id=81543&from=publication

Mokrzyński, J. (1979). Katowicki dworzec kolejowy [Katowice railroad station]. *Przegląd Budowalny*, *9*, 517–518.

Molecki, A. (2014). Nowy i "stary" dworzec kolejowy Katowice Osobowa – Analiza porównawcza [New railway station of Katowice – Comparative analysis]. *Systemy Transportowe*, 7(8), 48–55. https://yadda.icm.edu.pl/baztech/element/bwmeta1.element.baztech-55c5237f-7c45-44d7-80cc-64593a06d0d3/c/Molecki.pdf

Mrduljaš, M., & Kulić, V. (2012). Between Utopia and pragmatism: Architecture and urban planning in the former Yugoslavia and the successor states. In M. Mrduljaš & V. Kulić (Eds.), *Unfinished modernisations - Between Utopia and pragmatism* (pp. 6–13). Croatian Architects' Association.

Murzyn-Kupisz, M. (2015). Values of cultural heritage in the context of socio-economics. In B. Szmygin (Ed.), *Heritage value assessment systems. The problems and the current state of research* (pp. 147–164). Lublin University of Technology-Polish National Committee of the International Council on Monuments and Sites (ICOMOS).

National Party Meeting of Architects (1949). Rezolucja Krajowej Partyjnej Narady architektów w dniu 20-21 czerwca 1949 r. w Warszawie [Resolution of the national party meeting of architects on June 20–21, 1949 in Warsaw]. *Architektura*, *6–8*, 162.

Nekrošius, L. (2020). Soviet era architecture and the meaning it holds for people in Lithuania. In D. Kopec & A. M. Bliss (Eds.), *Place meaning and attachment. Authenticity, heritage and preservation* (pp. 28–40). Routledge.

Nemeikaitė, S. (2006). Sovietmečio architektūra – Akistatoje su istorijos ženklais [Architecture of Soviet times in confrontation with history signs]. *Statyba Ir Architektūra*, *10*, 41–47.

Nettmann-Multanowska, K. (2022). *Warszawa rysuje Skopje* [Warszawa draws Skopje]. Fundacja Centrum Architektury.

Nora, P. (2009). Preface to English language edition: From Lieux de memoire to realms of memory. In P. Nora (Ed.), *Realms of memory: Rethinking the French past*. Columbia University Press.

Norwilla, J. (2022). *Russian warship, go F**k yourself! (Tale of an overdue Vilnius cultural version)*. Defending History. https://defendinghistory.com/russian-warship-go-fk-yourself/111607

Pahor, P. (2011, April 2). Trg republike spet v občinske roke [Republic Square is back in municipal hands]. *Dnevnik*. https://www.dnevnik.si/1042435218/lokalno/ljubljana/1042435218

Parasonis, J. (2007). Šiuolaikiniai pastatai: Ar statomi tikrai patikimai? [Modern buildings: Are they built really reliably?]. *Statyba*, 6, 1.

Pedio, R. (1976). Centro Di Telecomunicazioni a Skopje, Macedonia, Architetto Janko Konstantinov [Telecommunication center in Skopje, Macedonia, architect Janko Konstantinov]. *L'architettura, Cronache e Storia*, 6(254), 88–93.

Perović, M. R. (2003). *Srpska arhitektura XX veka: Od istoricizma do drugog modernizma* [Serbian architecture of the 20th century: From historicism to the second modernism]. Arhitektonski fakultet Univerziteta u Beogradu.

Petrulis, V. (2007). Manifestations of politics in Lithuanian architecture: Examples of architectural dehumanisation during the transition from a Soviet to a post-Soviet society. *Meno Istorija Ir Kritika*, *3*, 209–216. https://epubl.ktu.edu/object/elaba:6081433/6081433.pdf

Putnik, V. (2017). From socialist realism to socialist aestheticism: Three contrasting examples of state architects in Yugoslavia. In C. Preda (Ed.), *The state artist in Romania and Eastern Europe. The role of the creative unions* (pp. 347–373). Editura Universitéaţii din Bucureşti.

Ravnikar, E. (1974). Trg Revolucije [Revolution square]. *Sinteza*, *30–32*, 81–96.

Ravnikar, E. (2010). Layout of the revolution square, Ljubljana. In A. Vodopivec & R. Žnidaršič (Eds.), *Edvard Ravnikar. Architect and teacher* (pp. 157–182). Springer.

Ravnikar, V., Zorec, M., Gregorie, T., & Koselj, N. (2000). *Evidenca in valorizacija objektov slovenske modern arhitekture med leti 1945–70*. http://www.evidenca.org/evidenca_1945-70.pdf

Reklaite, J., & Leitanaite, R. (2011). *Vilnius, 1900–2012: Naujosios architektūros gidas* [Vilnius, 1900–2012: A guide to new architecture]. 'Baltu Lanka' Publishing House.

Stake, R. E. (1994). Case studies. In N. K. Denzin & Y. S. Lincoln (Eds.), *Handbook of qualitative research* (pp. 236–247). SAGE Publications.

Smolorz, M. (2006, August 11). Nos dla tabakiery [Nose for snuffbox]. *Gazeta Wyborcza. Katowice*, 12.

Snopek, K. (2014). *Bielajewo: Zabytek przyszłości* [Bielajewo: Monument of the future]. Bęc Zmiana.

Spassov, S., & Morten, R. (2022). *The Buzludzha Monument*. https://buzludzha-monument.com/

Štelbiene, A. (2019). Po betono sparnu: Žmonių santykių su Vilniaus koncertų ir sporto rūmais fenomenas [Under the wing of concrete: The phenomenon of human relationships to the Vilnius palace of concerts and sports]. *Archiforma, 3–4*, 68–77.

Stoilova, L. (2018). Metamorphoses of cultural memory and the opportunity to safeguard the modern movement heritage in Bulgaria. In A. Tostões & N. Koselj (Eds.), *Metamorphosis. The continuity of change* (pp. 122–131). Docomomo International & Docomomo Slovenia.

Szafer, T. P. (1979). *Nowa architektura polska. Diariusz lat 1971–1975* [New Polish architecture. Diary of the years 1971–1975]. Arkady.

The Allen Consulting Group. (2005). *Valuing the priceless: The value of heritage protection in Australia*. Heritage Chairs and Officials of Australia and New Zealand. https://heritagecouncil.vic.gov.au/wp-content/uploads/2021/12/hearing-submission-The-Allen-Consulting-Group-Valuing-the-Priceless-The-Value-of-Historic-Heritage-in-Australia-Research-Report-2-November-2005-3-June.pdf

Trajanovski, N. (2021). The City of Solidarity's diverse legacies: A framework for interpreting the local memory of the 1963 Skopje earthquake and the post-earthquake urban reconstruction. *Journal of Nationalism, Memory & Language Politics, 15*(1), 30–51. https://doi.org/doi:10.2478/jnmlp-2021-0007

Trilupaitytė, S. (2017). Sovietinės architektūros paveldas naujų politinių įtampų fone: Apie Vilniaus Koncertų ir sporto rūmų (nu)vertinimą [The heritage of Soviet architecture against the background of the new political tensions on the (de)valuation of the Vilnius Palace of Con]. *Acta Academiae Artium Vilnenis, 86–87*, 351–364. http://etalpykla.lituanistikadb.lt/fedora/objects/LT-LDB-0001:J.04~2017~1541692154271/datastreams/DS.002.0.01.ARTIC/content

Vasileva, A. (2019). Elitist or egalitarian? Stefka Georgieva and the peculiar face of Bulgarian "socialist" brutalism. In A. Stiller & A. Bulant-Kamenova (Eds.), *Stefka Georgieva. An architect in Bulgaria in the 1960s* (pp. 43–55). Muery Salzmann.

Vasileva, A., & Kaleva, E. (2017). Recharging socialism: Bulgarian socialist monuments in the 21st century. *Studia Ethnologica Croatica, 29*(1), 171–192. https://doi.org/10.17234/SEC.29.5

Vasileva, N. (2013). *On the instability of monument. Monuments in Bulgaria from period of the communist regime 1944–1989.* University College London. https://www.academia.edu/12412882/On_the_Instability_of_Monuments_Monuments_in_Bulgaria_from_the_Period_of_the_Communist_Regime_1944_1989

Vladova, T. (2012). Heritage and the image of forgetting: The mausoleum of Georgi Dimitrov in Sofia. In M. Rampley (Ed.), *Heritage, ideology and identity in Central and Eastern Europe. Contested pasts, contested presents* (pp. 131–153). Boydell.

Vodopivec, A. (2010). Edvard Ravnikar's architecture: Locally adjusted modernism. In A. Vodopivec & R. Žnidaršič (Eds.), *Edvard Ravnikar. Architect and teacher* (pp. 15–32). Springer.

Vodopivec, A., & Žnidaršič, R. (2010). *Edvard Ravnikar. architect and teacher* (A. Vodopivec & R. Žnidaršič (Eds.)). Springer.

Weiss, S. J. (2010). Skopje scomparira [Skopje will disappear]. *Abitare*, *7–8*, 82–95.

Wyporek, B. (2009). *Daleko od Warszawy: Architekta zapiski z trzech kontynentów* [Far from Warsaw: The architect's notes from three continents]. Bogdan Wyporek.

Yin, R. K. (2003). *Applications of case study research* (2nd ed.). SAGE Publications.

Yugoslavia: Socialism of Sorts. (1966, June 10). *Time*. https://content.time.com/time/magazine/article/0,9171,942012,00.html

Zalewski, W. (2013). Intuicja inżyniera [Engineer's intuition]. *Architektura-Murator*, *4*, 30–35.

Załuski, D., & Rzepnicka, S. (2018). Dworzec Katowice w świetle współczesnej doktryny ochrony zabytków i rozwoju przestrzennego śródmieścia Katowic [Katowice railway station in the light of contemporary doctrine of monument protection and spatial development of downtown Katowice]. In M. Kapias & D. Keller (Eds.), *Węgiel, polityka, stal, ludzie. Studia z historii kolei na Śląsku* [Coal, politics, steel, people. Studies in the history of railways in Silesia] (pp. 515–530). Muzeum w Rybniku.

Živančević, J. (2012). Socijalistički realizam u arhitekturi [Socialist realism in architecture]. In M. Šuvaković (Ed.), *Istorija umetnosti u Srbiji XX vek* [History of Art in Serbia XX century] (pp. 277–302). Orion Art.

Żmudzińska-Nowak, M. (2017). Architektura i urbanistyka [Architecture and urban planning]. In M. Żmudzińska-Nowak & I. Herok-Turska (Eds.), *Reflektory. Interdyscyplinarne spojrzenie na dziedzictwo architektury Górnego Śląska drugiej połowy XX wieku* [Spotlights. An interdisciplinary look at the architectural heritage of Upper Silesia in the second half of the 20th century] (pp. 134–209). Biblioteka Śląska.

Summary

Since value may be interpreted in so many different ways and since it has both a utilitarian and a non-utilitarian dimension, both immeasurable and measurable, where does this lead architecture, urban planning and urban studies? We have tried to show the diversity of approaches to value in architecture, emphasizing its different dimensions. We started with the most profound philosophical dimension, through social value in its many facets, to the most mercantile aspect, related to income generation and providing jobs here and now.

Our reflections have led us to a place where we claim that even if measuring the immeasurable is complicated and sometimes impossible, it is still worth attempting. However, it should be done not to monetize heritage but to get the tools to compare heritage value over time and space. In this book, we have also tried to show that the urban context is critical in capturing value – both spatially and socio-economically. We have seen a significant role in these dimensions. We also noticed in each of the cases studied that the discussion of the concrete heritage of the (still) controversial social-modern architecture is governed by slightly different rules at the national and local levels. This "zoom" is essential; generally, the local treatment of the ambiguous heritage of concrete architecture is more gracious than the national. We see that territorial proximity and embeddedness also tend to be a source of positive developmental impulses.

The examples presented in the book reveal the plurality of the local conditions and the value transformation trajectories of the architecture studied. They demonstrate the interactions between the legacy of soc-modernist architecture, community and territorial development. In our cases, architectural heritage has become a catalyst for creating new assets and territorial capital. This heritage acts as a stimulus for development. It often provides conditions to develop sophisticated economic activities (the example of artistic events in Skopje) and co-creates national identity (the example of Republic Square in Ljubljana). It becomes a social binder that builds territorially rooted relations (the example of Katowice and the railway station) or creates historical awareness as a carrier of collective memory (the example of the Palace of Sports in Vilnius).

The transformation in the countries of Central and Eastern Europe shows an attitudes evolution towards soc-modern architecture. The transformation of perception is apparent: from unwanted heritage to the discovery of its new values and meanings; from the social negation of its values to growing popularity and enthusiasm for brutalism in diverse social spheres; from scepticism and indifferent social attitudes to active involvement in its protection and the struggle to preserve its original functions and values. It increasingly seems that the architecture of late modernism no longer evokes negative connotations. After all, half a century has passed since its heyday – enough time to understand its value. The architect Zdzisław Bieniecki noticed a regularity in the assessment of the achievements of earlier generations contained in the aphorism that "the times of [our] parents are simply funny, those of [our] grandparents – charming" (Bieniecki, 1969, p. 83). The "caesura of two generations" he proposes, which separates us from what we consider a monument, is noteworthy. It allows us to free ourselves (at least partially) from the subjective judgements of those involved in creating particular objects (monuments). It allows us to acquire a proper cognitive distance. It mitigates subjective sympathies and prejudices. On the other hand, contemporary times sometimes require conservators to act at lightning speed. There is often a race between conservation services and the free market (represented by property owners and developers). The care of an object is no longer the result of striving to perpetuate what the collective memory records but a preventive measure to protect the architecture of exceptional value from destruction.

Nowadays, the cases recalled in the book are mostly sites protected by law as cultural heritage. The only exceptions are the Telecommunication Centre in Skopje and the railway station in Katowice (as of October 2022), which is a reconstruction of the original brutalist building (moderately successful, we should add). It leads to the overly optimistic conclusion that the outstanding examples of soc-modernist architecture that have survived are recognized as part of cultural heritage and, as such, are legally protected. It allows us to look optimistically to the future. The discussion on preserving the architecture of post-war modernism is becoming an increasingly broader phenomenon that goes beyond architectural history and preservationism, integrating social or ecological issues. Public awareness of concrete heritage values is growing – especially among people born in the 1980s and later and, therefore, not influenced by the communist system. The activity of organizations such as Docomomo International, Europa Nostra or more minor, local associations means that the number of "monuments of the younger generation" will increase shortly. As will their ambiguity. However, as the creators of the term themselves point out, differences of opinion – whether actual or potential – are an intrinsic part of any heritage (Tunbridge, 2019, p. 14).

In discussing unwanted or ambiguous heritage, there should also be a move away from the still arguably lingering notion of the "inferiority" of use value versus option, existence and bequest value. In the cases, we studied – most thoroughly in Warsaw and more generally in the other cities – we were always dealing with a tension between use value and non-use value (Table 4.1 in Chapter 4). In one case (Skopje), the former prevailed in our opinion, and in another (the Buzludzha Monument), the latter. Nevertheless, in the other cases, the matter was not straightforward. Not even the more sophisticated and primary data-intensive methods of capturing the value helped to solve the concerns. In the case of the Warsaw railway, as well as in Katowice, Vilnius and Ljubljana, it is not easy to decide whether the commercial approach prevails (often at the expense of eradicating the legacy of concrete soc-modernism) or a brighter future awaits the sites. The scales tilt towards preserving this kind of heritage for future generations either when:

- The use value is associated with good memories (the Palace of Culture and Sports in Vilnius).
- Representative and symbolic elements are strong (Republic Square in Ljubljana).
- Many grassroots cultural activities strongly reinforce the utilitarian function, and the value of this kind of architecture is highlighted (which succeeded in the case of most railway stations in Warsaw but failed – despite efforts – in Katowice).

At the end of the day, time, space (especially local embeddedness) and knowledge of the concrete heritage of modernism are crucial to how the value is perceived.

However, this changing attitude towards soc-modernist architecture does not limit the tensions around specific sites in specific locations. Their turbulent and nuanced histories illustrate the intertwining of historical, cultural and economic forces. The legacy of socialist modernism reveals a wide range of attitudes towards its use and non-use value. What is often valuable to professionals and the local community may be "unwanted" to the authorities, who, under intense pressure from commercial investors, are inclined to take actions that degrade the value of this architecture. Such heritage and its close surroundings are still an easy path to gain attractive land for profitable new developments that are often located in central, prestigious urban areas. These strategies are also beneficial for the sites' owners as they can eliminate their concerns about the need to protect troublesome heritage. The local community plays a different, positive role in this process. They often rediscover this architecture's value and become the impetus for conservation efforts. These grassroots and often spontaneous social movements built up in many places create a unique territorial capital, extracting valuable elements from a commonly undesired heritage.

In this context, what does the future hold for soc-modernist architecture? Will the outstanding works of late modernism, structuralism or brutalism erected in the 1960s and 1970s in the countries of Central and Eastern Europe become full-fledged monuments in the eyes of their citizens? Or will the odium of their Communist pedigree weigh so heavily on them that even in a few decades, they will be an "undesirable heritage" condemned to *damnatio memoriae*? The attempt to answer these questions, and many others, leads us to reflect on the mechanisms of heritage creation.

An inherent concept in heritage is memory. A building, or, more broadly, a place, can become a space in which a community stores its collective memories. They are often different from the original intentions of the creators. Thus, the Palace of Sports in Vilnius and Republic Square in Ljubljana have become symbols of Lithuanian and Slovenian independence, even though they form part of the modernization policy pursued by the authorities of the USSR and communist Yugoslavia, respectively. More than 30 years after the fall of communism, its architectural relics no longer arouse such strong emotions. However, it would be a mistake to conclude that "anti-communist iconoclasm" is a tune of the past. Only its character has changed. At the beginning of the systemic transformation, there was a spontaneous grassroots "iconoclasm," an enthusiastic turn towards a capitalist, "Western" reality and a rejection of everything that could be associated with the unwanted communist past (Wiśniewski, 2012). The political turn towards a populist right based on strong anti-communist resentments, which took place in the first decade of the twenty-first century, resulted in a top-down "anti-communist iconoclasm." Its manifestations are laws such as the Polish Decommunization Act (*Ustawa o Zakazie Propagowania Komunizmu Lub Innego Ustroju Totalitarnego...*, 2016) (aimed mainly at monuments) or the "Skopje 2014" programme, whose victims are brutalist buildings from the 1960s. Such approaches reject the modernist aesthetic as a carrier of foreign, "bad" values.

Protecting ambiguous architecture requires an integrated approach to preserving its value and considering the process's social, economic and spatial aspects. Such an approach points to the need for a new perspective on social-modern heritage. There is a need to shift from analyzing a single object's value to looking at it in terms of territory and the social production of heritage values. The challenge becomes to take a holistic view and apply a place-based policy approach. It implies the need to build partnerships and integrate the actions of local institutions and actors. As a result, the preservation policy for the soc-modern legacy should not only focus on protecting architectural values but also consider specific and local conditions.

References

Addae-Dapaah, K. (2012). Appraisal and cost-benefit analysis. In S. J. Smith (Ed.), *International encyclopedia of housing and home* (pp. 70–75). Elsevier. https://doi.org/10.1016/B978-0-08-047163-1.00607-X

Affelt, W. J. (2008). Dziedzictwo techniki w kontekście rozwoju zrównoważonego. In B. Szmygin (Ed.), *Współczesne problemy teorii konserwatorskiej w Polsce* (Międzynaro, pp. 7–16). http://bc.pollub.pl/Content/629/PDF/wspolczesneproblemy.pdf

Affelt, W. J. (2009). Dziedzictwo techniki, jego różnorodność i wartości. *Kurier Konserwatorski*, *5*, 5–20.

Affelt, W. J. (2012). Moc i niemoc estetyczna – Rozważania o zabytkach techniki. In E. Szmit-Naud, B. J. Rouba, & J. Arszyńska (Eds.), *Wokół zagadnień estetyki zabytku po konserwacji i restauracji* (pp. 435–452). Narodowy Instytut Dziedzictwa.

Aizpurva, L. M. (2019). The 60s of the 20th century: Modern movement public catering buildings in Latvia. *Architecture and Urban Planning*, *15*(1), 101–105. https://doi.org/10.2478/aup-2019-0014

Amable, B. (2003). *The diversity of modern capitalism*. Oxford University Press.

Amiot, H. (2018). De Tito à Alexandre : Vers la construction d'un paysage urbain postsocialiste à Skopje (République de Macédoine) ? *Belgeo*, *4*, 1–25. https://doi.org/10.4000/belgeo.21184

Angermann, K. (2017). Architektura modernistyczna w Niemczech Wschodnich: Historia ochrona. In M. J. Sołtysik & R. Hirsch (Eds.), *Architektura XX wieku i jej waloryzacja w Gdyni i w Europie* [20th century architecture and its valorisation in Gdynia and Europe] (pp. 195–200). Urząd Miasta Gdyni. https://www.gdynia.pl/zabytki/cykl-modernizm-w-europie-modernizm-w-gdyni,7219/architektura-xx-wieku-i-jej-waloryzacja-w-gdyni-i-w-europie-wersja-elektorniczna,545726

Appalardo, G., Toscano, S., & Pecorino, B. (2020). Assessing the effects of 'appeal to authority' in the evaluation of environmental goods. Evidences from an economic experiment in Mt Etna, Italy. *Aestimum*, *77*, 113–125. https://doi.org/10.13128/aestim-8365

Architektura (1973). Dworzec kolejowy w Katowicach [Katowice railroad station]. *Architektura*, *10*, 370–373.

Arnheim, R. (2016). *Dynamika Formy architektonicznej* [Dynamics of architectural form]. Officyna.

Arrhenius, T. (2013). The fragile monument: On Alois Riegl's modern cult of monuments. *Nordisk Arkitekturforskning/Nordic Journal of Architectural Research, 16*(4), 51–55. http://arkitekturforskning.net/na/article/download/296/256

Arrow, K. J. (1951). *Social choice and individual values.* Yale University Press.

Ashworth, G. J. (2013). Heritage and local development: A reluctant relationship. In *Handbook on the economics of cultural heritage* (pp. 367–385). Edward Elgar Publishing. https://econpapers.repec.org/RePEc:elg:eechap:14326_18

Auškalnytė, V. (2012). *Sovietinio laikotarpio Vilniaus miesto visuomeninės paskirties pastatų interjerai.* Vytautas Magnus University. https://gs.elaba.lt/object/elaba:1843690/1843690.pdf

Babić, D., Kaptan, M. V., & Esquerra, C. M. (2019). Heritage literacy: A model to engage citizens in heritage management. In B. Bojanić Obad Sćitaroci, M. Obad-Šćitaroci, & A. Mrđa (Eds.), Cultural urban heritage development, learning and landscape strategies. Bojanić Obad Sćitaroci, Bojana Obad-Šćitaroci, Mladen Mrđa, Ana. (pp. 1–18).

B.A.C.U. (2019). *Urbană, Birou pentru artă şi cercetare* [Office for Art and Urban Research]. https://bacu.ro/

B.A.C.U. (2021). *Socialist modernism.* http://socialistmodernism.com/

Báez, A., & Herrero, L. C. (2012). Using contingent valuation and cost-benefit analysis to design a policy for restoring cultural heritage. *Journal of Cultural Heritage, 13*, 235–245. https://doi.org/10.1016/j.culher.2010.12.005

Banham, R. (1966). *The new brutalism: Ethic or aesthetic?* Reinhold Publishing Corporation.

Barucki, T. (1987). *Wacław Kłyszewski, Jerzy Mokrzyński, Eugeniusz Wierzbicki.* Arkady.

Basista, A. (2001). *Betonowe dziedzictwo: Architektura w Polsce czasów komunizmu* [Concrete legacy: Architecture in communist Poland]. PWN.

Bateman, I., Carson, R., Day, B., Hanemann, M., Hanley, N., Hett, T., Jones-Lee, M., & Loomes, G. (2002). *Economic valuation with stated preference techniques. A manual.* Edward Elgar. https://doi.org/10.4337/9781781009727

Bell, D. (1972). The cultural contradictions of capitalism. *Journal of Aesthetic Education.* https://doi.org/10.2307/3331409

Bell, J. D. (1986). *Bulgarian communist party from Blagoev to Zhivkov.* Hoover Institution Press.

Benton-Short, L. (2006). Politics, public space, and memorials: The brawl on the Mall. *Urban Geography, 27*(4), 297–329. https://doi.org/10.2747/0272-3638.27.4.297

Białynicka-Birula, J. (2003). Wartość dzieła sztuki w kontekście teorii estetycznych i ekonomicznych. *Zeszyty Naukowe Akademii Ekonomicznej w Krakowie, 640*, 63–75.

Bieniecki, Z. (1969). Potrzeba i drogi ochrony obiektów architektury najnowszej [The necessity of and modes of modern architecture objects' protection]. *Ochrona Zabytków, 2*(22), 83–116. https://bazhum.muzhp.pl/media//files/Ochrona_Zabytkow/Ochrona_Zabytkow-r1969-t22-n2_(85)/Ochrona_Zabytkow-r1969-t22-n2_(85)-s83-116/Ochrona_Zabytkow-r1969-t22-n2_(85)-s83-116.pdf

Birdsall, C., Halauniova, A., & van de Kamp, L. (2021). Sensing urban values: Reassessing urban cultures and histories amidst redevelopment agendas. *Space and Culture, 24*(3), 348–358. https://doi.org/10.1177/12063312211000654

Blackledge, M. (2009). *Introducing property valuation.* Routledge.

Blatter, J. K. (2008). Case study. In *The SAGE encyclopedia of qualitative research methods* (pp. 68–71). SAGE Publications.

Boardman, A. E., Greenberg, D. H., Vining, A. R., & Weimer, D. L. (2018). *Cost-benefit analysis. Concepts and practice* (5th ed.). Cambridge University Press.

Boeing, G. (2019). Urban spatial order: Street network orientation, configuration, and entropy. *Applied Network Science*, *4*(1), 67. https://doi.org/10.1007/s41109-019-0189-1

Bogunia-Borowska, M. (2015). *Fundamenty dobrego społeczeństwa. Wartości.* Znak.

Boito, C., & Birignan, C. (2009). Restoration in architecture: First dialogue. *Future Anterior*, 6(1), 68–83. https://doi.org/10.1353/fta.0.0026

Bojc, S. (2014, September 24). Ljubljanski Trg republike: Velika ambicija, ki je dišala po osamosvojitv [Ljubljana's Republic Square: A great ambition that smelled of independence]. *Delo.* https://old.delo.si/novice/ljubljana/ljubljanski-trg-republike-velika-ambicija-ki-je-disala-po-osamosvojitvi.html

Bollier, D. (2014). *Think like a commoner. A short introduction to the life of the commons.* New Society Publishers.

Boltanski, L., & Thevenot, L. (2006). *On justification: Economies of worth.* Princeton University Press.

Borowik, A. (2019). *Nowe Katowice. Forma i ideologia polskiej architektury powojennej na przykładzie Katowic (1945–1980)* [New Katowice. Form and ideology of Polish post-war architecture on the example of Katowice (1945–1980)]. Neriton.

Borowik, A. (2020). Smutek odchodzenia architektury. Historia wyburzenia dworca kolejowego w Katowicach [The sadness of architecture passing away. The history of the demolition of the railway station in Katowice]. In M. J. Sołtysik & M. Stępa (Eds.), *Modernizm w Europie – Modernizm w Gdyni. Architektura XX wieku: Zachowanie jej autentyzmu i integralności w Gdyni i w Europie* [Modernism in Europe – Modernism in Gdynia. Architecture of the 20th century: Preservation of its authenticity and integrity in G] (pp. 171–180). Urząd Miasta Gdyni-Wydział Architektury Politechniki Gdańskiej. https://www.gdynia.pl/zabytki/module/Files/controller/Default/action/downloadFile/hash/f3a6d71ef7c98dbb183d29193397a71f

Bowitz, E., & Ibenholt, K. (2009). Economic impacts of cultural heritage – Research and perspectives. *Journal of Cultural Heritage*, *10*(1), 1–8. https://doi.org/10.1016/j.culher.2008.09.002

Brandi, C. (1963). *Teoria del restauro.* Edizioni di Storia e Letteratura.

Breidert, C., Hahsler, M., & Reutterer, T. (2006). A review of methods for measuring willingness-to-pay. *Innovative Marketing.* https://doi.org/10.3111/13696998.2011.644408

Brett, D. (1996). *The construction of heritage.* Cork University Press.

Brosch, T., & Sander, D. (2016). From values to valuation: An interdisciplinary approach to the study of value. In T. Brosch & D. Sander (Eds.), *Handbook of value. Perspectives from economics, neuroscience, philosophy, psychology, and sociology* (pp. 397–404). Oxford University Press.

Brown, B., Perkins, D. D., & Brown, G. (2003). Place attachment in a revitalizing neighborhood: Individual and block levels of analysis. *Journal of Environmental Psychology*, *23*(3), 259–271. https://doi.org/10.1016/S0272-4944(02)00117-2

Brsakoska, J. (2021). Public space transformation in the case of 'Skopje 2014'. *Urbana*, *22*, 1–20. https://doi.org/10.47785/urbana.4.2021

Buchanan, J. M. (1991). Opportunity cost. In J. Eatwell, M. Milgate, & P. K. Newman (Eds.), *The new Palgrave: The world of economics* (pp. 520–525). Palgrave Macmillan. https://doi.org/10.1007/978-1-349-21315-3_69

Buzludzha Project Foundation. (2022). *Buzludzha project*. https://www.buzludzha-project.com/

Camagni, R. (2008). Regional competitiveness: Towards a concept of territorial capital. In *Modelling regional scenarios for the enlarged Europe: European competiveness and global strategies* (pp. 33–47). Springer.https://doi.org/10.1007/978-3-540-74737-6_3

Camagni, R. (2012). Creativity, culture and urban milieux. In T. Baycan, L. F. Girard, & P. Nijkamp (Eds.), *Sustainable city and creativity: Promoting creative urban initiatives* (pp. 183–197). Routledge.

Camagni, R. (2019). Territorial capital and regional development: Theoretical insights and appropriate policies. In R. Capello & P. Nijkamp (Eds.), *Handbook of regional growth and development theories* (2nd ed., pp. 124–148). Edward Elgar.

Camagni, R., & Capello, R. (2013). Regional competitiveness and territorial capital: A conceptual approach and empirical evidence from the European Union. *Regional Studies*, *47*(9), 1383–1402. https://doi.org/10.1080/00343404.2012.681640

Camagni, R., Capello, R., Cerisola, S., & Panzera, E. (2020). The cultural heritage – Territorial capital nexus: Theory and empirics. *Capitale Culturale*, *11*, 33–59. https://doi.org/10.13138/2039-2362/2547

Capello, R. (2019). Interpreting and understanding territorial identity. *Regional Science Policy & Practice*, *11*(1), 141–158. https://doi.org/10.1111/rsp3.12166

Capello, R., Caragliu, A., & Nijkamp, P. (2009). *Territorial capital and regional growth: Increasing returns in cognitive knowledge use* (No. 09-059/3; Tinbergen Institute Discussion Papers). https://www.econstor.eu/bitstream/10419/86826/1/09-059.pdf

Capello, R., & Perucca, G. (2017). Cultural capital and local development nexus: Does the local environment matter? In H. Shibusawa, K. Sakurai, T. Mizunoya, & S. Uchida (Eds.), *Socioeconomic environmental policies and evaluations in regional science* (Vol. 24, pp. 103–124). Springer. https://doi.org/10.1007/978-981-10-0099-7_6

Carmona, M. (2016). *Public places urban spaces. The dimensions of urban design* (3rd ed.). Routledge.https://doi.org/10.4324/9781315158457

Cerisola, S. (2019a). A new perspective on the cultural heritage–development nexus: The role of creativity. *Journal of Cultural Economics*, *43*(1), 21–56. https://doi.org/10.1007/s10824-018-9328-2

Cerisola, S. (2019b). *Cultural heritage, creativity and economic development*. Edward Elgar.

Černauskienė, A. (2016). Novelty of artistic forms in contemporary Lithuanian architecture. *Architecture and Urban Planning*, *11*(1), 6–13. https://doi.org/10.1515/aup-2016-0001

Černauskienė, A. (2020). Idea of in the evaluation of Lithuanian concrete architecture. *Architecture and Urban Planning*, *16*(1), 26–31. https://doi.org/10.2478/aup-2020-0005

Chalana, M. (2015). Chandigarh: City and periphery. *Journal of Planning History*, *14*(1), 62–84. https://doi.org/10.1177/1538513214543904

Chalana, M., & Spragu, T. S. (2013). Beyond Le Corbusier and the modernist city: Reframing Chandigarh's 'world heritage' legacy. *Planning Perspectives*, *28*(2), 199–222. https://doi.org/10.1080/02665433.2013.737709

Charciarek, M. (2020). *Relation between the idea an matter in concrete architecture*. Wydawnictwo PK.

Chaubin, F. (2011). *CCCP. Cosmic communist constructions photographed*. Taschen.

Chauvin, E. (2015). The city of Le Havre – The story of a modernist Utopia. In M. J. Sołtysik & R. Hirsch (Eds.), *20th century architecture until the 1960s and its preservation* (pp. 131–134). Urząd Miasta Gdyni. https://www.gdynia.pl/zabytki/cykl-modernizm-w-europie-modernizm-w-gdyni,7219/nr-2-3-en-20th-century-architecture-until-the-1960s-and-its-preservation,555278

Chen, D., & Li, J. (2021). Process-led value elicitation within built heritage management: A systematic literature review between 2010 and 2020. *Journal of Architectural Conservation*, *27*(1–2), 1–16. https://doi.org/10.1080/13556207.2021.1909900

Choi, A. S., Ritchie, B. W., Papandrea, F., & Bennett, J. (2010). Economic valuation of cultural heritage sites: A choice modeling approach. *Tourism Management*. https://doi.org/10.1016/j.tourman.2009.02.014

Christaller, W. (1933). *Die Zentralen Orte in Süddeutschland. Eine ökonomisch-geographische Untersuchung über die Gesetzmässigkeit der Vorbereitung und Entwicklung der Siedlungen mit städtischen Funktionen*. Fischer.

Ciarkowski, B. (2016). Trudne dziedzictwo łodzi – Historyczna narracja w przestrzeni dawnego Litzmannstadt Ghetto. *Przegląd Kulturoznawczy*, *1*(27), 49–59. https://doi.org/10.4467/20843860PK.16.004.5044

Ciarkowski, B. (2017a). Dissonant heritage: Decoding the historical narrative of rationalist architecture in fascist Italy. *Acta Academiae Artium Vilnensis*, *86–87*, 319–328.

Ciarkowski, B. (2017b). Harmonia czy dysonans – Rozwój architektury uzdrowiskowej w Karpatach i Sudetach w latach 60. i 70. XX wieku. *MAZOWSZE Studia Regionalne*, *20*, 13–24. https://doi.org/10.21858/msr.20.01

Ciarkowski, B. (2017c). *Odcienie szarości. Architekci i polityka w PRL-u* [Shades of grey. Architects and politics in the Polish People's Republic]. Wydawnictwo Uniwersytetu Łódzkiego.

Ciarkowski, B. (2017d). Unwanted heritage and its cultural potential. Values of modernist architecture from the times of the Polish People's Republic. *MAZOWSZE Studia Regionalne*, *22*, 71–83. https://doi.org/10.21858/msr.22.05

Ciarkowski, B. (2018). Integralna część krajobrazu czy element obcy? Architektura modernistycznych domów wczasowych z czasów PRL [Integral part of the landscape or strange element? Architecture of modernist resort houses from the Peoples Republic of Poland's era]. In W. Kobylińska-Bunsch (Ed.), *Architektura w krajobrazie: Harmonia – Kompromis – Konflikt* [Architecture in the landscape: Harmony – Compromise – Conflict] (pp. 377–384). Instytut Historii Sztuki UW.

Cilliers, E. J., Timmermans, W., van den Goorbergh, F., & Slijkhuis, J. S. A. (2015). Designing public spaces through the lively planning integrative perspective. *Environment, Development and Sustainability*, *17*(6), 1367–1380. https://doi.org/10.1007/s10668-014-9610-1

Colletis, G., & Pecqueur, B. (2005). Révélation de ressources spécifiques et coordination située. *Économie et Institutions*, 6–7, 51–74. https://doi.org/10.4000/ei.900

Convention concerning the protection of the world cultural and natural heritage. (1972) (testimony of UNESCO). https://whc.unesco.org/archive/convention-en.pdf

Cooke, C., & Reid, S. E. (2007). Modernity and realism, architectural relations in the cold war. In R. P. Blakesley & S. E. Reid (Eds.), *Russian art and the west. A century of dialogue in painting, architecture, and the decorative arts* (pp. 172–194). Northern Illinois University Press.

Costa, A., Foucart, A., Arnon, I., Aparici, M., & Apesteguia, J. (2014). 'Piensa' twice: On the foreign language effect in decision making. *Cognition*, *130*(2), 236–254. https://doi.org/10.1016/j.cognition.2013.11.010

Coyle, D. (2011). *The economics of enough: How to run the economy as if the future matters*. https://doi.org/10.1177/0094306112468721f

Crowley, D. (2015). Nakierowani na przyszłość [Oriented to the future]. *Autoportret*, *3*(50), 77. https://autoportret.pl/

Czarnecki, M. (2017). Formy ekspresyjne jako przykład twórczych dążeń w architekturze powojennego modernizmu w Polsce. In M. J. Sołtysik & R. Hirsch (Eds.), *Architektura XX wieku i jej waloryzacja w Gdyni i w Europie* [20th century architecture and its valorisation in Gdynia and Europe] (pp. 209–214). Urząd Miasta Gdyni. https://www.gdynia.pl/zabytki/cykl-modernizm-w-europie-modernizm-w-gdyni,7219/architektura-xx-wieku-i-jej-waloryzacja-w-gdyni-i-w-europie-wersja-elektorniczna,545726

Czembrowski, P., Łaszkiewicz, E., & Kronenberg, J. (2016). Bioculturally valuable but not necessarily worth the price: Integrating different dimensions of value of urban green spaces. *Urban Forestry & Urban Greening*, *20*, 89–96. https://doi.org/10.1016/j.ufug.2016.07.010

Dalmas, L., Geronimi, V., Noël, J. F., & Tsang King Sang, J. (2015). Economic evaluation of urban heritage: An inclusive approach under a sustainability perspective. *Journal of Cultural Heritage*. https://doi.org/10.1016/j.culher.2015.01.009

Dardot, P., & Laval, C. (2019). *Common. On revolution in the 21st century*. Bloomsbury Academic.

Davoudi, S., Evans, N., Governa, F., & Santangelo, M. (2008). Territorial governance in the making. Approaches, methodologies, practices. *Boletín de La Asociación de Geógrafos Españoles*, *46*, 33–52.

de la Torre, M. (2002). *Assessing the values of cultural heritage: Research report*. https://www.getty.edu/conservation/publications_resources/pdf_publications/pdf/assessing.pdf

Della Spina, L. (2018). The integrated evaluation as a driving tool for cultural-heritage enhancement strategies BT – Smart and sustainable planning for cities and regions. In A. Bisello, D. Vettorato, P. Laconte, & S. Costa (Eds.), *Smart and sustainable planning for cities and regions* (pp. 589–600). Springer International Publishing.

Deskova, A., Deskov, V., & Ivanovski, J. (2019). Challenging disregard: The case of the telecommunication center in Skopje. *Studies in History and Theory of Architecture*, *7*, 205–219. https://doi.org/10.54508/sITA.7.14

Despland, M. (1969). The moral ambiguity of modernity. *Islamic Studies*, *8*(2), 167–184.

Dewey, J. (1922). *Human nature and conduct: An introduction to social psychology*. Holt.

Dewey, J. (1939). Theory of valuation. *Philosophy of Science*, 6(4), 490–491. https://books.google.pl/books?id=ZUOwAQAACAAJ

Diamond, D. B., & Tolley, G. S. (1982). The economic roles of urban amenities. In D. B. Diamond & G. S. Tolley (Eds.), *The economics of urban amenities* (pp. 3–54). Academic Press.

Domański, H. (2017). Stratyfikacja klasowa Polsce: 1982–2015. In M. Gdula & M. Sutowski (Eds.), *Klasy w Polsce. Teorie, dyskusje, badania, konteksty* (pp. 15–29). Instytut Studiów Zaawansowanych.

Dremaitė, M. (2017). *Baltic modernism: Architecture and housing in Soviet Lithuania*. DOM Publishers.

Drėmaitė, M. (2018). Eduardas Chlomauskas: Vilnius concert and sports palace (Vilniaus Sporto Rūmai), 1965–1971. In O. Elser, P. Kurz, & P. C. Schmal (Eds.), *SOS Brutalism: A global survey* (1st ed.). Park Books. https://www.sosbrutalism.org/cms/15802395#15963855

Durusoy Özmen, E., & Omay Polat, E. (2021). Assessing the values-based context of conservation for modern architectural heritage: A study on the Headquarters Building of the T.R. 17th Regional Directorate of Highways Complex, Istanbul. *Journal of Architectural Conservation*, 27(1–2), 84–103. https://doi.org/10.1080/13556207.2021.1930714

Dvořák, M. (1929). Alois Riegl. In J. Wilde & K. M. Swoboda (Eds.), *Gesammelte Aufsätze zur Kunstgeschichte* (pp. 279–299). R. Piper & Co.

Dwyer, O. J. (2002). Location, politics, and the production of civil rights memorial landscapes. *Urban Geography*. https://doi.org/10.2747/0272-3638.23.1.31

Elden, S. (2010). Land, terrain, territory. *Progress in Human Geography*, *34*(6), 789–806. https://doi.org/10.1177/0309132510362603

Erikson, R., & Goldthorpe, J. H. (1992). *The constant flux: A study of class mobility in industrial countries*. Oxford University Press.

Erikson, R., Goldthorpe, J. H., & Portocarero, L. (1979). Intergenerational class mobility in three Western European Societies: England, France and Sweden. *The British Journal of Sociology*, *30*(4), 415–441. https://doi.org/10.2307/589632

EU. (2011). *Territorial state and perspectives of the European Union*. https://ec.europa.eu/regional_policy/sources/policy/what/territorial-cohesion/territorial_state_and_perspective_2011.pdf

Europa Nostra. (2013). *The 7 most endangered*. https://7mostendangered.eu/

Eysenck, H. J. (1976). Introduction. In H. J. Eysenck (Ed.), *Case studies in behaviour therapy* (pp. 1–15). Routledge.

Faro Convention on the Value of Cultural Heritage for Society. (2005). https://www.coe.int/en/web/conventions/full-list/-/conventions/treaty/199?module=treaty-detail&treatynum=199

Fée, D., Colenutt, B., & Schäbitz, S. C. (Eds.). (2020). *Lessons from British and French new towns: Paradise lost?* Emerald Publishing Limited.https://doi.org/10.1108/9781839094309

Ferretti, V., Bottero, M., & Mondini, G. (2014). Decision making and cultural heritage: An application of the multi-attribute value theory for the reuse of historical buildings. *Journal of Cultural Heritage*, *15*, 644–655. https://doi.org/10.1016/j.culher.2013.12.007

Fields, L., Slomka, M., & Shepherd, M. (2020). *A formula for success: Reviewing the social discount rate*. https://www.oxera.com/insights/agenda/articles/a-formula-for-success-reviewing-the-social-discount-rate/

Fine, B., & Saad-Filho, A. (2018). Marxist economics. In L. Fischer, J. Hasell, J. C. Proctor, D. Uwakwe, & Z. Ward-Perkins (Eds.), *Rethinking economics: An introduction to pluralist economics* (pp. 19–32). Routledge.

Fine, S. H. (1992). *Marketing the public sector. Promoting the causes of public & nonprofit agencies*. Transaction Publishers.

Fleischer, A. (2012). A room with a view — A valuation of the Mediterranean Sea view. *Tourism Management*, *33*(3), 598–602. https://doi.org/10.1016/j.tourman.2011.06.016

Flint, A. (2018). *Modern man: The life of Le Corbusier, architect of tomorrow*. Amazon Publishing.

Florencka, K. (2018). *Warszawa/Rozpoczęto badania architektury stacji WKD Śródmieście* [Warsaw. A study on the WKD Śródmieście station architecture has been started]. Nauka w Polsce [Science in Poland]. https://naukawpolsce.pl/aktualnosci/news%2C30441%2Cwarszawa-rozpoczeto-badania-architektury-stacji-wkd-srodmiescie.html

Flyvbjerg, B. (2006). Five misunderstandings about case-study research. *Qualitative Inquiry*. https://doi.org/10.1177/1077800405284363

Forty, A. (2009). Beton i pamięć [Concrete and memory]. *Konteksty*, *1–2*, 284–285. http://www.konteksty.pl/numery/16,284-285

Forty, A. (2012). *Concrete and culture: A material history*. Reaktion Books.

Foster, S. R. (2013). Collective action and the urban commons. *Notre Dame Law Review*, *87*(1), 57–134.

Foster, S. R., & Iaione, C. (2019). Ostrom in the city: Design principles and practices for the urban commons. In H. Blake, J. Rosenbloom, & D. H. Cole (Eds.), *Routledge handbook of the study of the commons*. Routledge. https://www.routledge.com/Routledge-Handbook-of-the-Study-of-the-Commons/Hudson-Rosenbloom-Cole/p/book/9780367659608

Franta, A. (1999). Mój ulubiony budynek. Dworzec Tygrysów [My favorite building. Tiger's Station]. *Architektura-Murator*, *7*, 76–77.

Fredheim, L. H., & Khalaf, M. (2016). The significance of values: Heritage value typologies re-examined. *International Journal of Heritage Studies*, *22*(6), 466–481. https://doi.org/10.1080/13527258.2016.1171247

Frodl, W. (1963). Denkmalbegriffe, Denkmalwerte und ihre Auswirkung auf die Restaurierung. Institut für Österreichische Kunstforschung.

Frycz, J. (1975). *Restauracja i konserwacja zabytków architektury w Polsce w latach 1795–1918*. Wydawnictwo Naukowe PWN.

Gadacz, T. (2010). Wartości w czasach zamętu. In M. Madurowicz (Ed.), *Wartościowanie współczesnej przestrzeni miejskiej* (pp. 17–30). Wydział Geografii i Studiów Regionalnych Uniwersytetu Warszawskiego – Urząd Miasta Stołecznego Warszawy.

Galster, G. C. (2003). Neighbourhood dynamics and housing markets. In K. Gibb, D. Maclennan, & A. O'Sullivan (Eds.), *Housing economics and public policy. Essays in honour of Duncan Maclennan* (pp. 153–171). Blackwell Science.

Galusek, Ł. (2015). *Chciałbym, żeby socmodernizm był Neutralnym Terminem* [I wish socmodernism was a neutral term]. dzieje.pl Portal Historyczny. https://dzieje.pl/kultura-i-sztuka/lukasz-galusek-chcialbym-zeby-socmodernizm-byl-neutralnym-terminem

Garnett, R. (2002). The impact of science centers/museums on their surrounding communities: Summary report. Association of Science-Technology Centers, Questacon. https://www.ecsite.eu/sites/default/files/impact_study02.pdf

Gehl, J. (2011). *Life between buildings: Using public space* (6th ed.). Island Press.

Georgescu-Roegen, N. (1976). *Energy and economic myths*. Pergamon Press.

Ghosh, N. (2016). Modern designs: History and memory in Le Corbusier's Chandigarh. *Journal of Architecture and Urbanism*, *40*(3), 220–228. https://doi.org/10.3846/20297955.2016.1210048

Gibson, L., & Pendlebury, J. (2009). Introduction: Valuing historic environments. In J. Pendlebury & L. Gibson (Eds.), *Valuing historic environments* (1st ed., pp. 1–16). Routledge. https://doi.org/10.4324/9781315548449

Gibson, R., Tanner, C., & Wagner, A. F. (2017). In Brosch, Tobias Sander, David (Eds.), Protected values and economic decision-making. In *Handbook of value: Perspectives from economics, neuroscience, philosophy, psychology and sociology* (pp. 223–241). Oxford University Press.

Ginzarly, M., Houbart, C., & Teller, J. (2019). The historic urban landscape approach to urban management: A systematic review. *International Journal of Heritage Studies*, *25*(10), 999–1019. https://doi.org/10.1080/13527258.2018.1552615

Ginzarly, M., Pereira Roders, A., & Teller, J. (2019). Mapping historic urban landscape values through social media. *Journal of Cultural Heritage*, *36*, 1–11. https://doi.org/10.1016/j.culher.2018.10.002

Glaeser, E. L., Kolko, J., & Saiz, A. (2001). Consumer city. *Journal of Economic Geography*, *1*(1), 27–50. https://doi.org/10.1093/jeg/1.1.27

Gospodini, A. (2004). Urban morphology and place identity in European cities: Built heritage and innovative design. *Journal of Urban Design*, *9*(2), 225–248. https://doi.org/10.1080/1357480042000227834

Granovetter, M. S. (1985). Economic action and social structure: The problem of embeddedness. *American Journal of Sociology*, *91*(1), 481–510. https://doi.org/10.1086/228311

Granovetter, M. S. (2017). *Society and economy: Framework and principles*. The Belknap Press of Harvard University Press.

Grazuleviciute-Vileniske, I., Seduikyte, L., Daugelaite, A., & Rudokas, K. (2021). Links between heritage building, historic urban landscape and sustainable development: Systematic approach. *Landscape Architecture and Art*, *17*(17), 30–38. https://doi.org/10.22616/j.landarchart.2020.17.04

Grekov, P. (1981). Za Ideyniya i Emotsionaliniya Zaryad Na Edna Slozhna Arhitektura Zadacha [About the idea and emotional charge of a complex architectural project]. *Arhitekura*, *10*, 6–22.

Grillitsch, M. (2015). Institutional layers, connectedness and change: Implications for economic evolution in regions. *European Planning Studies*, *23*(10), 2099–2124.

Grotowska, S. (2016). Czy architektura czasów PRL ma znaczenie? Analiza wydarzenia Medialnego [Does the architecture of the Polish People's Republic mean anything? An analysis of a mass media event]. *Opuscula Sociologica*, *3*(17), 33–44. http://cejsh.icm.edu.pl/cejsh/element/bwmeta1.element.desklight-91f3e24a-758d-4f34-a8b5-ce48487a8011

Grüb, B., & Martin, S. (2020). Public value of cultural heritages – Towards a better understanding of citizen's valuation of Austrian museums. *Cultural Trends*, *29*(5), 337–358. https://doi.org/10.1080/09548963.2020.1822142

Grzesiuk, K. (2015). *Zakorzenienie społeczne gospodarki. Koncepcja Marka Granovettera*. Wydawnictwo Katolickiego Uniwersytetu Lubelskiego.

Guzmán, P. C., Pereira-Roders, A. R., & Colenbrander, B. J. F. (2017). Measuring links between cultural heritage management and sustainable urban development:

An overview of global monitoring tools. *Cities*, *60*, 192–201. https://doi.org/10.1016/j.cities.2016.09.005

Gzowska, A. (2012). *Szesnaście żelbetowych kwiatów. Nowy dworzec w Katowicach* [Sixteen reinforced concrete flowers. Railway station in Katowice]. Wydawnictwo Naukowe "Śląsk".

Habermas, J. (1987). *The theory of communicative action*. Beacon Press.

Hanackova, M. (2014). Team 10 and Czechoslovakia. Secondary networks. In Ł. Stanek (Ed.), *Team 10 East: Revisionist architecture in real existing modernism* (pp. 73–100). Museum of Modern Art.

Hartwick, J. M. (1977). Intergenerational equity and the investing of rents from exhaustible resources. *American Economic Review*, *67*(5), 972–974.

Harvey, D. (2001). Heritage pasts and heritage presents: Temporality, meaning and the scope of heritage studies. *International Journal of Heritage Studies*, *7*(4), 319–338. https://doi.org/10.1080/13581650120105534

Harvey, D. (2012). *Rebel cities. From the right to the city to the urban revolution*. Verso.

Hatherley, O. (2012). Socialist Googie, Gothic futurism and hierarchical tunnels. In G. Piątek (Ed.), *AR/PS. The architecture of Arseniusz Romanowicz and Piotr Szymaniak* (pp. 210–216). Centrum Architektury.

Hatherley, O. (2016a). *Landscapes of communism. A history through buildings*. Penguin.

Hatherley, O. (2016b). Renowacja czy rekonstrukcja [Renovation or reconstruction]. *Autoportret*, *2*(53). https://autoportret.pl/artykuly/renowacja-czy-rekonstrukcja/

Hatuka, T., & Forsyth, L. (2005). Urban design in the context of glocalization and nationalism: Rothschild Boulevards, Tel Aviv. *URBAN DESIGN International*, *10*(2), 69–86. https://doi.org/10.1057/palgrave.udi.9000142

Hausner, J. (2017). Value economics vs. economic value. In B. Biga, H. Izdebski, J. Hausner, M. Kudłacz, K. Obłój, W. Paprocki, P. Sztompka, & M. Zmyślony (Eds.), *Open eyes book* (pp. 23–75). Fundacja Gospodarki i Administracji Publicznej.

Hayakawa, S., Costa, A., Foucart, A., & Keysar, B. (2016). Using a foreign language changes our choices. *Trends in Cognitive Sciences*, *20*(11), 791–793. https://doi.org/10.1016/j.tics.2016.08.004

Heinle, E., & Bacher, M. (1971). *Building in visual concrete*. Technical Press.

Hess, C. (2009). Mapping the new commons. *SSRN*.

Hess, M. (2004). 'Spatial' relationships? Towards a reconceptualization of embedded ness. *Progress in Human Geography*, *28*(2), 165–186. https://doi.org/10.1191/0309132504ph479oa

Hicks, J. R. (1940). The valuation of the social income. *Economica*, *7*(26), 105–124.https://doi.org/10.2307/2548691

Higgins, A. (2022). On a remote mountain, the 'Sistine Chapel of Socialism' awaits its fate. *New York Times*. https://www.nytimes.com/2022/05/22/world/europe/on-a-remote-mountain-the-sistine-chapel-of-socialism-awaits-its-fate.html

Higgins, B. (2018). Francois Perroux. In B. Higgins & D. J. Savoie (Eds.), *Regional economic development. Essays in honour of Francois Perroux* (2nd ed., pp. 31–47). Routledge.

Higgins, E. T. (1997). Beyond pleasure and pain. *American Psychologist*, *52*, 1280–1300. https://doi.org/10.1037//0003-066x.52.12.1280

Historic England. (2008). *Conservation principles: Policies and guidance for the sustainable management of the historic environment*. English Heritage. https://historicengland.org.uk/images-books/publications/conservation-principles-sustainable-management-historic-environment

Hočevar, M. (2018). *Anketa o Trgu Republike* [Survey about Republic Square]. https://www.ljubljana.si/assets/Uploads/Publikacija-Anketa-o-trgu-republike.pdf

Hofstede, G. (1997). *Cultures and organizations: Software of the mind*. McGraw-Hill.

Hoover, E. M. (1937). *Location theory and the shoe and leather industries*. Harvard University Press. https://doi.org/10.2307/359958

Hudson, J. (2007). Conservation values, climate change and modern architecture. *Journal of Architectural Conservation*, *13*(2), 47–67. https://doi.org/10.1080/13556207.2007.10784995

Hultkrantz, L. (2021). Discounting in economic evaluation of healthcare interventions: What about the risk term? *The European Journal of Health Economics*, *22*(3), 357–363. https://doi.org/10.1007/s10198-020-01257-x

Hutter, M., & Rizzo, I. (1997). *Economic perspectives on cultural heritage*. Palgrave Macmillan. https://doi.org/10.1007/978-1-349-25824-6

Iacono, F., & Këlliçi, K. L. (2016). Exploring the public perception of communist heritage in post-communist Albania. *EX NOVO Journal of Archaeology*, *1*(1), 55–69. https://doi.org/10.32028/exnovo.v1i0.398

Iaione, C. (2012). *City as a commons*. http://dlc.dlib.indiana.edu/dlc/bitstream/handle/10535/8604/Iaione_prelversion.pdf

Ikonnikow, A. V., Fabrycki, B. B., & Szmielow, I. P. (1975). *Współczesna architektura radziecka* [Contemporary soviet architecture]. Aurora.

Ingerpuu, L. (2018). Socialist architecture as today's dissonant heritage: Administrative buildings of collective farms in Estonia. *International Journal of Heritage Studies*, *24*(9), 954–968. https://doi.org/10.1080/13527258.2018.1428664

International Charter for the Conservation and Restoration of Monuments and Sites (The Venice Charter 1964). (1965). https://www.icomos.org/charters/venice_e.pdf

Isard, W. (1960). *Methods of regional analysis: An introduction to regional science*. John Wiley & Sons.

Jackiewicz, M. (2018). Nieistniejące dzielnice Wilna. Pióromont i Łosiówka. Zabłocki i mydło [Non-existent districts of Vilnius. Pióromont and Łosiówka. Zablocki and soap]. *Znad Wilii*, *3*(75), 102–110.

Jacobs, J. (1969). *The economy of cities*. Random House.

Jahandideh-Kodehi, G., Kavoosi-Kalashami, M., & Motamed, M. K. (2021). Landscape valuation of historical tourism site in Northern Iran: A case study from Sheikh-Zahed Tomb. *GeoScape*, *15*(1), 79–89. https://doi.org/10.2478/geosc-2021-0007

Janev, G. (2017). Burdensome past: Challenging the socialist heritage in Macedonia. *Studia Ethnologica Croatica*, *29*(1), 149–170.

Janković-Beguš, J. (2017). 'Between East and West': Socialist modernism as the official paradigm of Serbian Art Music in the socialist federal Republic of Yugoslavia. *International Journal of Music Studies*, *1*(1), 141–163. https://doi.org/10.33906/MUSICOLOGIST.373187

Jasiński, R., Piekarczyk, A., & Galman, I. (2010). Badania głównych elementów konstrukcji dworca PKP w Katowicach [Investigation of major elements of construction railway station in Katowice]. *Inżynieria i Budownictwo*, *3*, 129–134.

Jaśniok, M., Jaśniok, T., & Zybura, A. (2010). Badania korozyjnego zagrożenia zbrojenia kielichowej konstrukcji budynku dworca kolejowego w Katowicach [The tests of goblet construction corrosion risk of railway station building in Katowice]. *Inżynieria i Budownictwo*, 5–6, 249–253. https://www.inzynieriai-budownictwo.pl/images/archiwum/2010/05-06-2010.pdf

Jedlecki, P. (2020, December 22). Dziesięć lat temu rozpoczęło się wyburzanie katowickiego dworca PKP [Ten years ago, the demolition of Katowice's railway station began]. *Gazeta Wyborcza*. https://katowice.wyborcza.pl/katowice/5,35063,19457808.html

Jencks, C. (1975). *Le Corbusier and the tragic view of architecture*. Penguin Books.

Jencks, C. (1977). *The language of post-modern architecture*. Academy Editions.

Jencks, C. (1980). *Late-modern architecture and other essays*. Rizzoli.

Jencks, C. (1982). *Le Corbusier. Tragizm współczesnej architektury* [Le Corbusier. The tragism of modern architecture]. Wydawnictwa Artystyczne i Filmowe.

Jevons, W. S. (1871). *The theory of political economy*. Macmillan.

Jewtuchowicz, A. (2005). *Terytorium i współczesne dylematy jego rozwoju*. Wydawnictwo Uniwersytetu Łódzkiego.

Jost, J. T., Basevich, E., Dickson, E. S., & Noorbaloochi, S. (2016). The place of values in a world of politics: Personality, motivation, and ideology. In T. Brosch & D. Sander (Eds.), *Handbook of value. Perspectives from economics, neuroscience, philosophy, psychology, and sociology* (pp. 351–374). Oxford University Press.

Kahneman, D., & Tversky, A. (2000). *Choices, values, and frames*. Cambridge University Press.

Kaldor, N. (1939). Welfare propositions of economics and interpersonal comparisons of utility. *The Economic Journal*, *49*(195), 549–552. https://doi.org/10.2307/2224835

Kaleva, E. (2014). The best examples of the architectural heritage of socialism in Bulgaria. In *Socialist realism and socialist modernism. World heritage proposals from Central and Eastern Europe* (pp. 80–84). Hendrik Bäßler.

Kaleva, E., & Vasileva, A. (2018). Unity, creativity, beauty – Decline and survival of socialist memorial sites in Bulgaria. In J. Haspel, S. Brandt, L. Kondrashev, A. Kudryavtsev, & J. Ziesemer (Eds.), *A future for our recent past. Model projects of modern heritage conservation in Europe* (pp. 130–136). Hendrik Bäßler.

Kanbur, R. (1987). Shadow pricing. In J. Eatwell, M. Milgate, & P. K. Newman (Eds.), *The new Palgrave: A dictionary of economics. Volume IV* (2nd ed., pp. 316–317). Palgrave Macmillan.

Kant, I. (1797). *Die Metaphysik der Sitten* [The metaphysics of morals]. Nicolovius.

Kaplan, F. I. (1968). *Bolshevik ideology and the ethics of Soviet labor*. Philosophical Library.

Katerina, K., Lechevska, K., Borovska, V., & Blazeva, A. (2013). *Skopje 2014 project and its effects on the perception of Macedonian identity among the citizens of Skopje*. https://www.isshs.edu.mk/wp-content/uploads/2017/05/1.-sk2014-eng.pdf

Keynes, J. M. (1936). *The general theory of employment, interest and money*. Palgrave Macmillan.

Khan, H.-U. (2009). *International style: Modernist architecture from 1925 to 1965*. Taschen.

Khan, Z., & Devanshi, S. (2021). Anne Lacaton & Jean-Philippe Vassal, the 2021 Pritzker laureates for whom demolition is an act of violence. *Stirworld.Com*. https://www.stirworld.com/see-news-anne-lacaton-jean-philippe-vassal-the-2021-pritzker-laureates-for-whom-demolition-is-an-act-of-violence

Kincaid, H. (2002). Social sciences. In P. Machamer (Ed.), *The Blackwell guide to the philosophy of science* (pp. 290–311). Blackwell Publishing.

Kistyakovsky, A. Y. (1973). *Proyektirovaniye sportivnykh sooruzheniy* [Sports facilities design]. Высшая школа [Vysshaya shkola].

Kollock, P., & Smith, M. A. (1996). Managing the virtual commons. In S. Herring (Ed.), *Computer-mediated communication: Linguistic, social, and cross-cultural perspectives* (pp. 109–128). John Benjamins.

Konstantinov, J. (1970). Objekt Telekomunikačiskog centra PTT u Skopje [Facility of the PTT telecommunication center in Skopje]. *Čovjek i Prostor*, *4*, 12.

Koselj, N. (2018a). Edge and metaphor. The authentic modernism of Edvard Ravnikar. In A. Tostões & N. Koselj (Eds.), *Metamorphosis. The continuity of change* (pp. 36–47). Docomomo International & Docomomo Slovenia.

Koselj, N. (2018b). Edvard Ravnikar and the heart of the city. The genesis of cultural centers in Slovenia and in ex-Yugoslavia. *Docomomo Journal*, *59*(2), 55–59. https://doi.org/10.52200/59.A.B3CK6W9A

Koselj, N. (2020). The roots of Slovenian structuralism: From Plečnik to Ravnikar and beyond. Centenary of the Ljubljana school of architecture. In M. J. Sołtysik & M. Stępa (Eds.), *Modernizm w Europie – Modernizm w Gdyni. Architektura XX wieku: Zachowanie jej autentyzmu i integralności w Gdyni i w Europie* [Modernism in Europe – Modernism in Gdynia. Architecture of the 20th century: Preservation of its authenticity and integrity in G] (pp. 65–70). Urząd Miasta Gdyni-Wydział Architektury Politechniki Gdańskiej.

Kotkin, S. (2007). Mongol commonwealth? Exchange and governance across the post-Mongol space. *Kritika: Explorations in Russian and Eurasian History*, *8*(3), 487–531. https://doi.org/10.1353/kri.2007.0040

Kozina, I. (2019). *Ikony architektury w województwie śląskim w XX i XXI w.* [Architectural icons in the Silesian Voivodeship in the 20th and 21st centuries]. Muzeum Śląskie.

Krawczyk, J. (2013). Dialog z tradycją w konserwatorstwie – Koncepcja zabytkoznawczej analizy wartościującej. *Acta Universitatis Nicolai Copernici. Zabytkoznawstwo i Konserwatorstwo*, *XLIV*, 507–529. https://doi.org/10.12775/AUNC_ZiK.2013.021

Królikowski, K. (2017). *Bloki*. Media Dizajn.

Kronenberg, J., & Andersson, E. (2019). Integrating social values with other value dimensions: Parallel use vs. combination vs. full integration. *Sustainability Science*, *14*(5), 1283–1295. https://doi.org/10.1007/s11625-019-00688-7

Krupowicz, J. (2005). Metody heurystyczne. In M. Cieślak (Ed.), *Prognozowanie gospodarcze. Metody i zastosowania* (4th ed., pp. 201–222). Wydawnictwo Naukowe PWN.

Krygier, K., & Sumień, T. (1973). Dzielnica mieszkaniowa Retkinia [Retkinia residential district]. *Architektura*, *5*(6), 208–211.

Kucharska-Stasiak, E. (2016a). *Ekonomiczny wymiar nieruchomości*. Wydawnictwo Naukowe PWN.

Kucharska-Stasiak, E. (2016b). Wycena nieruchomości w gospodarce globalnej. *International Business and Global Economy*, *35*(1), 429–440.

Kulić, V. (2013). Edvard Ravnikar's liquid modernism: Architectural identity in a network of shifting references. In I. Berman & E. Mitchell (Eds.), *ACSA 101: New constellations, new ecologies* (pp. 802–809). Association of Collegiate Schools of Architecture.

Kulić, V. (2017). Building the socialist Balkans: Architecture in the global networks of the cold war. *Southeastern Europe*, *41*(2), 95–111. https://doi.org/10.1163/18763332-04102001

Van Laerhoven, F., & Ostrom, E. (2007). Traditions and trends in the study of the commons. *International Journal of the Commons*, *1*(1), 3–28. https://doi.org/10.18352/ijc.76

Lamprakos, M. (2014). Riegl's 'modern cult of monuments' and the problem of value. *Change Over Time*, *4*(1), 418–435.

Lancaster, K. J. (1966). A new approach to consumer theory. *Journal of Political Economy*, *74*(2), 132–157. https://doi.org/10.1086/259131

Lange, O. (1971). *Political economy*. Pergamon Press.

Langemeyer, J., Baró, F., Roebeling, P., & Gómez-Baggethun, E. (2015). Contrasting values of cultural ecosystem services in urban areas: The case of park Montjuïc in Barcelona. *Ecosystem Services*, *12*, 178–186. https://doi.org/10.1016/j.ecoser.2014.11.016

Larsson, N. (2018, August 6). Socialist modernism: Remembering the architecture of the eastern bloc. *The Guardian*. https://www.theguardian.com/cities/2018/aug/06/socialist-modernism-remembering-the-architecture-of-the-eastern-bloc

Łaszkiewicz, E., Nowakowska, A., & Adamus, J. (2022). How valuable is architectural heritage? Evaluating a monument's perceived value with the use of spatial order concept. *SAGE Open*, *12*(4), 21582440221142720. https://doi.org/10.1177/21582440221142720

Launhardt, W. (1882). Die Bestimmung des Zweckmäßigsten Standortes einer gewerblichen Anlage. *Zeitschrift Des Vereins Deutschen Ingenieure*, *XXVI*, 105–116. https://books.google.pl/books?id=zgM-AQAAMAAJ&pg=RA1-PA106&redir_esc=y#v=onepage&q&f=false

Le Corbusier (1923). *Vers une architecture*. L'Esprit nouveau. https://en.wikipedia.org/wiki/Le_Corbusier

Leszczyński, A. (2013). *Skok w nowoczesność: Polityka wzrostu w krajach peryferyjnych 1943–1980* [Leap into modernity – Political economy of growth on the periphery, 1943–1980]. Wydawnictwo Krytyki Politycznej.

Lévesque, B. (2008). Contribution de la «nouvelle sociologie économique» à l'anlayse des territoires sous l'angle de l'économie plurielle. In G. Massicotte (Ed.), *Sciences du territoire. Perspectives québécoises* (pp. 231–258). Presses de L'Universite du Quebec.

Levine, N. (2015). *The urbanism of frank Lloyd Wright*. Princeton University Press.

Light, D. (2000). An unwanted past: Contemporary tourism and the heritage of communism in Romania. *International Journal of Heritage Studies*, *6*(2), 145–160. https://doi.org/10.1080/135272500404197

Linstone, H. A., & Turoff, M. (1975). *The Delphi method. Techniques and applications*. Addison-Wesley Publishing Company.

Lipe, W. D. (1984). Value and meaning in cultural resources. In H. Cleere (Ed.), *Approaches to the archaeological heritage* (pp. 1–11). Cambridge University Press.

Logan, W., & Reeves, K. (2009). *Places of pain and shame. Dealing with 'difficult heritage'*. Routledge.

Loos, A. (2013). *Ornament i zbrodnia: Eseje wybrane* [Ornament and crime: Selected essays]. Fundacja Centrum Architektury.

Lösch, A. (1940). *Die räumliche Ordnung der Wirtschaft. Eine Untersuchung über Standort, Wirtschaftsgebiete und internationalem Handel*. Fischer.

Louviere, J. J. (2001). Choice experiments: An overview of concepts and issues. In J. Bennett & R. Blarney (Eds.), *The choice modelling approach to environmental valuation* (pp. 13–36). Edward Elgar.

Łukasik, M. (2014). Redefinition of modernist architecture in the context of creating "the social". *SGEM 2014 International Multidisciplinary Scientific Conferences on Social Sciences and Arts*, 939–946.

Lyons, J. (1989). *Semantyka*. Państwowe Wydawnictwo Naukowe.

MacDonald, S. (2006). Undesirable heritage: Fascist material culture and historical consciousness in Nuremberg. *International Journal of Heritage Studies*, *12*(1), 9–28. https://doi.org/10.1080/13527250500384464

MacDonald, S. (2009). *Difficult heritage: Negotiating the Nazi past in Nuremberg and beyond*. Routledge.

Macel, O. (2002). Post-war modern architecture in the former Eastern Bloc. In H.-J. Henke & H. Heynen (Eds.), *Back from Utopia. The challenge of the modern movement*. 010 Publishers.

Machat, C., & Ziesemer, J. (2017). *Heritage at risk. World report 2014–2015 on monuments and sites in danger*. Hendrik Bäßler. http://openarchive.icomos.org/id/eprint/2108/1/HR2014_2015_final.pdf

Mačiulis, A. (2002). *Lietuvos architektai* [Lithuanian architects]. Vilnius Art Academy Publishing House.

Madden, K., & Schwartz, A. (2000). *How to turn A place around: A handbook for creating successful public spaces*. Project for Public Spaces.

Malkowski, T. (2007a, July 7). Zburzenie dworca będzie przestępstwem [Demolition of the station will be a crime]. *Gazeta.Pl*. http://wiadomosci.gazeta.pl/wiadomosci/1,114873,4286242.html

Malkowski, T. (2007b, October 4). Katowice: Nowy dworzec jak królik z kapelusza [Katowice: New train station like a rabbit out of a hat]. *Gazeta.Pl*. http://wiadomosci.gazeta.pl/wiadomosci/1,114873,4548831.html

Malkowski, T. (2010, September 28). W Katowicach runął mur obywatelskiej obojętności [A wall of civic apathy has collapsed in Katowice]. *Gazeta Wyborcza*.

Mankiw, N. G. (2009). *Principles of microeconomics* (5th ed.). South-Western Cengage Learning.

March, J. G., & Olsen, J. P. (1989). *Rediscovering Institutions. The organizational basics of politics*. Simon and Schuster.

Maroević, I. (1996). Croatian architecture between socialism and new tradition. *ICOMOS – Issues of the German National Committee*, *20*, 110–114. https://doi.org/10.11588/ih.1996.0.22243

Marshall, A. (2013). *Principles of economics*. https://doi.org/10.1057/9781137375261

Marx, K. (1906). *Capital. A critique of political economy*. The Modern Library.

Matera, R., & Sokołowicz, M. E. (n.d.). Does history affect regional resilience in the long term? Path-dependence lessons from Poland. In *Resilience and regional development. New roadmaps*. Edward Elgar.

Mayakovsky, V. (1972). *Poems*. https://monoskop.org/images/e/ec/Mayakovsky_Vladimir_Poems_1972.pdf

McConnell, V., & Walls, M. (2005). *The value of open space: Evidence from studies of nonmarket benefits*. Resources for the Future. https://media.rff.org/documents/RFF-REPORT-Open20Spaces.pdf

McDowell, S. (2008). Heritage, memory and identity. In B. J. Graham & P. Howard (Eds.), *The Ashgate research companion to heritage and identity* (pp. 37–53). Ashgate Publishing.

McGuirk, J. (2018). The unrepeatable architectural moment of Yugoslavia's concrete Utopia. *The New Yorker*. https://www.newyorker.com/culture/culture-desk/the-unrepeatable-architectural-moment-of-yugoslavias-concrete-utopia

Meadows, D. H., Meadows, D. L., Randers, J., & Behrens, W. W. III (1972). *The limits to growth*. Pan.

Menger, C. (1871). *Grundsätze der Volkswirtschaftslehre*. Braumüller.

Merciu, F.-C., Petrişor, A.-I., & Merciu, G.-L. (2021). Economic valuation of cultural heritage using the travel cost method: The historical centre of the municipality of Bucharest as a case study. *Heritage*, *4*(3), 2356–2376. https://doi.org/10.3390/heritage4030133

Merta-Staszczak, A. (2018). *Niechciane Dziedzictwo. Nieruchomości zabytkowe na Dolnym Śląsku w latach 1945–1989*. Wydawnictwo Naukowe SCHOLAR.

Metalkova-Markova, M. (2008). Another kind of modernism – Trends in postwar architectural ideology and practice in socialist Bulgaria 1944–1989. In T. H. M. Prudon & H. Lipstadt (Eds.), *Proceedings: VIIIth International Conference Import-Export: Postwar Modernism in a Expanding World, 1945–1975* (pp. 175–181). DOCOMOMO. https://docomomo-us.org/resource/files%2F5lv-jp7okfskf04a.pdf

Mikołajczyk, M., & Raszka, B. (2019). Multidimensional comparative analysis as a tool of spatial order evaluation: A case study from Southwestern Poland. *Polish Journal of Environmental Studies*, *28*(5), 3287–3297. https://doi.org/10.15244/pjoes/91944

Mikučianis, A. V. (1972). Sporto rūmai Vilniuje [Sports palace in Vilnius]. *Statyba Ir Architektūra*, *1*(152), 1–5.

Miłobędzki, A. (1994). *Architektura ziem Polski* [Architecture of Polish territories]. Międzynarodowe Centrum Kultury w Krakowie.

Mind Tools Content Team. (2021). *Cost-benefit analysis. Deciding, quantitatively, whether to go ahead*. Mind Tools. http://www.mindtools.com/pages/article/newTED_08.htm

Minorski, J. (1960). Z konkursu na projekt dworca kolejowego w Katowicach [From the design competition for Katowice railway station]. *Architektura*, *4*, 137–140. http://mbc.cyfrowemazowsze.pl/dlibra/docmetadata?id=81543&from=publication

Mitchell, D. (2003). *Cultural geography: A critical introduction*. Blackwell Publishing.

Mokrzyński, J. (1979). Katowicki dworzec kolejowy [Katowice railroad station]. *Przegląd Budowalny*, *9*, 517–518.

Molecki, A. (2014). Nowy i "stary" dworzec kolejowy Katowice Osobowa – Analiza porównawcza [New railway station of Katowice – Comparative analysis]. *Systemy Transportowe*, *7*(8), 48–55. https://yadda.icm.edu.pl/baztech/element/bwmeta1.element.baztech-55c5237f-7c45-44d7-80cc-64593a06d0d3/c/Molecki.pdf

Molnár, V. (2005). Cultural politics and modernist architecture: The Tulip debate in postwar Hungary. *American Sociological Review*, *70*(1), 111–135. http://www.jstor.org/stable/4145352

Mrduljaš, M., & Kulić, V. (2012). Between Utopia and pragmatism: Architecture and urban planning in the former Yugoslavia and the successor states. In M. Mrduljaš & V. Kulić (Eds.), *Unfinished modernisations – Between Utopia and pragmatism* (pp. 6–13). Croatian Architects' Association.

Murzyn, M. A. (2008). Heritage transformation in Central and Eastern Europe. In B. J. Graham & P. Howard (Eds.), *The Ashgate research companion to heritage and identity* (pp. 315–345). Ashgate Publishing.

Murzyn-Kupisz, M. (2015). Values of cultural heritage in the context of socio-economics. In B. Szmygin (Ed.), *Heritage value assessment systems. The problems and the current state of research* (pp. 147–164). Lublin University of Technology-Polish National Committee of the International Council on Monuments and Sites (ICOMOS).

Myrdal, G. (1974). *Against the stream. Critical essays on economics.* Palgrave Macmillan.

Myrdal, G. (2017). *The political element in the development of economic theory.* Routledge.

National Party Meeting of Architects (1949). Rezolucja Krajowej Partyjnej Narady Architektów w dniu 20-21 czerwca 1949 r. w warszawie [Resolution of the National Party Meeting of Architects on June 20–21, 1949 in Warsaw]. *Architektura*, *6–8*, 162.

Nawratek, K. (2005). *Ideologie w przestrzeni – Próby demistyfikacji* [Ideologies in space – Attempts at demystification]. Universitas.

Nekrošius, L. (2020). Soviet era architecture and the meaning it holds for people in Lithuania. In D. Kopec & A. M. Bliss (Eds.), *Place meaning and attachment. Authenticity, heritage and preservation* (pp. 28–40). Routledge.

Nemeikaitė, S. (2006). Sovietmečio architektūra – Akistatoje su istorijos ženklais [Architecture of soviet times in confrontation with history signs]. *Statyba Ir Architektūra*, *10*, 41–47.

Nesticò, A., Morano, P., & Sica, F. (2018). A model to support the public administration decisions for the investments selection on historic buildings. *Journal of Cultural Heritage*, *33*, 201–207. https://doi.org/10.1016/j.culher.2018.03.008

Nesticò, A., & Sica, F. (2017). The sustainability of urban renewal projects: A model for economic multi-criteria analysis. *Journal of Property Investment and Finance*, *35*(4), 397–409. https://doi.org/10.1108/JPIF-01-2017-0003

Nettmann-Multanowska, K. (2022). *Warszawa rysuje Skopje* [Warszawa draws Skopje]. Fundacja Centrum Architektury.

NID. (2013). *Społeczno-kulturowe oddziaływanie dziedzictwa kulturowego. Raport z badań społecznych.* https://ksiegarnia.nid.pl/wp-content/uploads/2022/08/Spoleczno-gospodarcze-oddzialywanie-dziedzictwa-kulturowego.Raport.pdf

Niebrzydowski, W. (2018). *Architektura Brutalistyczna a idee Nowego Brutalizmu* [Brutalist architecture and the ideas of the new brutalism]. Oficyna Wydawnicza Politechniki Białostockiej.

Nijkamp, P., & Ratajczak, W. (2015). The spatial economy: A holistic perspective. In P. Nijkamp, A. Rose, & K. Kourtit (Eds.), *Regional science matters. Studies dedicated to Walter Isard* (pp. 15–26). Springer.

Niżankowski, R., Bała, M., Dubiel, B., Hetnał, M., Kawalec, P., Łanda, K., Plisko, R., & Wilk, N. (2002). *Analiza opłacalności*. Uniwersyteckie Wydawnictwo Medyczne VESALIUS.

Nora, P. (2009). Preface to English language edition: From Lieux de memoire to realms of memory. In P. Nora (Ed.), *Realms of memory: Rethinking the French past*. Columbia University Press.

North, D. C. (1986). The new institutional economics. *Journal of Institutional and Theoretical Economics*, *142*(1), 230–237.

North, D. C. (1997). *Institutions, institutional change and economic performance*. Cambridge University Press.

Norwilla, J. (2022). *Russian warship, go F**k yourself! (Tale of an overdue Vilnius cultural version)*. Defending History. https://defendinghistory.com/russian-warship-go-fk-yourself/111607

Novikov, F. (2016). *Behind the iron curtain: Confession of a soviet architect*. DOM Publishers.

Nowacki, M. (2009). Skłonność do zapłaty a cena wstępu do atrakcji turystycznej. *Zeszyty Naukowe Uniwersytetu Szczecińskiego. Ekonomiczne Problemy Turystyki*, *568*(13), 101–114.

Nowakowska, A. (2018). Od regionu do terytorium – Reinterpretacja znaczenia przestrzeni w procesach rozwoju gospodarczego. *Gospodarka Narodowa*, *3*, 5–22.

Nowakowska, A., Guz, J., & Łaszkiewicz, E. (2020). How is the multidimensional perception of modern architectural objects associated with their surroundings? An example of Warsaw Ochota urban railway station. In Z. Gál, S. Z. Kovács, & B. Páger (Eds.), *Proceedings of the 7th CERS Conference* (pp. 323–336). European Regional Science Association. http://real.mtak.hu/116284/7/cers-kotet-2020.pdf

Nowakowska, A., & Walczak, B. (2016). Dziedzictwo przemysłowe jako kapitał terytorialny. Przykład Łodzi. *Gospodarka w Praktyce i Teorii*, *4*(45), 45–56. https://doi.org/10.18778/1429-3730.45.04

Nowicki, J. J. (1960). O kierunkach w architekturze współczesnej [On trends in contemporary architecture]. *Architektura*, *5*, 169–170.

O'Brien, D. (2010). *Measuring the value of culture: A report to the Department for Culture, Media and Sport*. https://www.gov.uk/government/publications/measuring-the-value-of-culture-a-report-to-the-department-for-culture-media-and-sport

O'Brien, D. (2012). Managing the urban commons: The relative influence of individual and social incentives on the treatment of public space. *Human Nature*, *23*(4), 467–489.

Ochkovskaya, M., & Gerasimenko, V. (2018). Buildings from the socialist past as part of a city's brand identity: The case of Warsaw. *Bulletin of Geography*, *39*(39), 113–127. https://doi.org/10.2478/bog-2018-0008

OECD. (2001). *Territorial outlook*. https://doi.org/10.1787/9789264189911-en

Orszag, P. R., Barnes, M. C., Douglas, D., & Summers, L. (2010). *Developing effective place-based policies for the FY 2012 budget*. https://obamawhitehouse.archives.gov/sites/default/files/omb/assets/memoranda_2010/m10-21.pdf

Orwell, G. (1945). *Animal farm: A fairy story*. Secker and Warburg.

O'Sullivan, A. (2007). *Urban economics*. McGraw Hill-Irwin.

Pahor, P. (2011, April 2). Trg republike spet v občinske roke [Republic square is back in municipal hands]. *Dnevnik*. https://www.dnevnik.si/1042435218/lokalno/ljubljana/1042435218

Palander, T. (1935). *Beitrdge zur Standortstheorie*. Almqvist and Wiksells.
Parasonis, J. (2007). Šiuolaikiniai pastatai: Ar statomi tikrai patikimai? [Modern buildings: Are they built really reliably?]. *Statyba*.
Parker, D. (2016). *International valuation standards. A guide to the valuation of real property assets*. John Wiley & Sons.
Pearce, D. W., & Atkinson, G. D. (1993). Capital theory and the measurement of sustainable development: An indicator of 'weak' sustainability. *Ecological Economics*, *8*(2), 103–108. https://doi.org/10.1016/0921-8009(93)90039-9
Pedio, R. (1976). Centro Di Telecomunicazioni a Skopje, Macedonia, Architetto Janko Konstantinov [Telecommunication center in Skopje, Macedonia, architect Janko Konstantinov]. *L'architettura, Cronache e Storia*, 6(254), 88–93.
Perović, M. R. (2003). *Srpska arhitektura XX veka: Od istoricizma do drugog modernizma* [Serbian architecture of the 20th century: From historicism to the second modernism]. Arhitektonski fakultet Univerziteta u Beogradu.
Perroux, F. (1950). Economic space: Theory and applications. *Quarterly Journal of Economics*, *64*(1), 89–104.
Perroux, F. (1955). Note sur la notion de pôle de croissance. *Économie Appliquée*, *8*, 307–320.
Perry, R. B. (1926). *General theory of value*. Harvard University Press.
Petrulis, V. (2007). Manifestations of politics in Lithuanian architecture: Examples of architectural dehumanisation during the transition from a soviet to a post-soviet society. *Meno Istorija Ir Kritika*, *3*, 209–216. https://epubl.ktu.edu/object/elaba:6081433/6081433.pdf
Petrulis, V. (2015). "Socialist realism": Timeline in Lithuania. In ICOMOS (Ed.), *Socialist realism and socialist modernism world heritage proposals from Central and Eastern Europe* (pp. 90–94). ICOMOS. https://doi.org/10.11588/ih.2013.4.20091
PFSRM. (2011). *Międzynarodowe standardy wyceny* (M. Trojanek, J. Konowalczuk, & T. Ramian (Eds.)). Polska Federacja Stowarzyszeni Rzeczoznawców Majątkowych.
Philokyprou, M., & Michael, A. (2021). Environmental sustainability in the conservation of vernacular architecture. The case of rural and urban traditional settlements in Cyprus. *International Journal of Architectural Heritage*, *15*(11), 1741–1763. https://doi.org/10.1080/15583058.2020.1719235
Piotrowski, P. K. (2011). *Znaczenia modernizmu. W stronę historii sztuki polskiej po 1945 roku* [Meanings of modernism. Towards a history of polish art after 1945]. Dom Wydwawniczy Rebis.
Polanyi, K. (1944). *The great transformation the political and economic origins of our time*. Beacon Press.
Popper, K. (1989). Creative self-criticism in science and in art. *Diogenes*, *37*(145), 36–45. https://doi.org/10.1177/039219218903714503
Poulios, I. (2014). *The past in the present: A living heritage approach*. Ubiquity Press. https://www.jstor.org/stable/j.ctv3s8tpq
Poulot, D. (1997). *Musée, nation, patrimoine, 1789–1815*. Gallimard.
Pratt, A. C. (2004). The cultural economy: A call for spatialized 'production of culture' perspectives. *International Journal of Cultural Studies*, *7*(1), 117–128. https://doi.org/10.1177/1367877904040609
Predöhl, A. (1925). Das Standortsproblem in der Wirtschaftstheorie. *Weltwirtschaftliches Archiv*, *21*, 294–321.

Provins, A., Pearce, D., Ozdemiroglu, E., Mourato, S., & Morse-Jones, S. (2008). Valuation of the historic environment: The scope for using economic valuation evidence in the appraisal of heritage-related projects. *Progress in Planning*, *69*(4), 131–175. https://doi.org/10.1016/j.progress.2008.01.001

Purchla, J. (2015). *Dziedzictwo a transformacja*. Międzynarodowe Centrum Kultury w Krakowie.

Putnik, V. (2017). From socialist realism to socialist aestheticism: Three contrasting examples of state architects in Yugoslavia. In C. Preda (Ed.), *The state artist in Romania and Eastern Europe. The role of the creative unions* (pp. 347–373). Editura Universitéaţii din Bucureşti.

Rabinowicz, W., & Rønnow-Rasmussen, T. (2016). Value taxonomy. In T. Brosch & D. Sander (Eds.), *Handbook of value. Perspectives from economics, neuroscience, philosophy, psychology, and sociology* (pp. 23–42). Oxford University Press.

Rampley, M. (2012). *Heritage, ideology, and identity in Central and Eastern Europe. Contested pasts, contested presents*. The Boydell Press.

Rasmussen, S. E. (1964). *Experiencing architecture* (2nd ed.). MIT Press.

Ravnikar, E. (1974). Trg revolucije [Revolution square]. *Sinteza*, *30–32*, 81–96.

Ravnikar, E. (2010). Layout of the revolution square, Ljubljana. In A. Vodopivec & R. Žnidaršič (Eds.), *Edvard Ravnikar. Architect and teacher* (pp. 157–182). Springer.

Ravnikar, V., Zorec, M., Gregoriè, T., & Koselj, N. (2000). *Evidenca in valorizacija objektov slovenske modern arhitekture med leti 1945–70*. http://www.evidenca.org/evidenca_1945-70.pdf

Ready, R. C., & Navrud, S. (2002). Why value cultural heritage? In *Valuing cultural heritage. Applying environmental valuation techniques to historic buildings, monuments and artifacts* (pp. 3–9). Edward Elgar Publishing.https://doi.org/10.4337/9781843765455.00009

Recommendation on the Historic Urban Landscape. (2011). http://portal.unesco.org/en/ev.php-URL_ID=48857&URL_DO=DO_TOPIC&URL_SECTION=201.html

Reilly, K. D. (1973). The Delphi technique: Fundamentals and applications. In H. Borko (Ed.), *Targets for research in library education* (pp. 187–199). American Library Association.

Reklaite, J., & Leitanaite, R. (2011). *Vilnius, 1900–2012: Naujosios architektūros gidas* [Vilnius, 1900–2012: A guide to new architecture]. 'Baltu Lanka' Publishing House.

Riabuszyn, A., & Szyszkina, I. (1987). *Architektura radziecka* [Soviet architecture]. Arkady.

Ricardo, D. (2001). *On the principles of political economy and taxation*. Batoche Books.

RICS. (2015). *Code of measuring practice* (6th ed.). Royal Institution of Chartered Surveyors.

RICS. (2019). *RICS valuation – Global standards. Incorporating the IVSC international valuation standards*. Royal Institution of Chartered Surveyors.

Riegl, A. (1903). *Der moderne Denkmalkultus: Sein Wesen und seine Entstehung*. Verlage von W. Braumüller.

Ripp, M., & Rodwell, D. (2016). The governance of urban heritage. *The Historic Environment: Policy & Practice*, 7, 81–108. https://doi.org/10.1080/17567505.2016.1142699

Rokeach, M. (1973). *The nature of human values*. Free Press.

Romanow, Z. (1995). *Teorie wartości i ceny w rozwoju myśli ekonomicznej*. Wydawnictwo Akademii Ekonomicznej w Poznaniu.

Romanowicz, A. (1964). Przystanki ruchu podmiejskiego w Warszawie: "Ochota", "Śródmieście", "Powiśle" (Suburban traffic stops in Warsaw: 'Ochota', 'Śródmieście', 'Powiśle']. *Architektura*, *1*, 9–11.

Różycka-Czas, R., Czesak, B., & Cegielska, K. (2019). Towards evaluation of environmental spatial order of natural valuable landscapes in suburban areas: Evidence from Poland. *Sustainability*, *11*(23). https://doi.org/10.3390/su11236555

Rudokas, K., Landauskas, M., Gražulevičiūtė-Vilneiškė, I., & Viliūnienė, O. (2019). Valuing the socio-economic benefits of built heritage: Local context and mathematical modeling. *Journal of Cultural Heritage*, *39*, 229–237. https://doi.org/10.1016/j.culher.2019.02.016

Ruijgrok, E. C. M. (2006). The three economic values of cultural heritage: A case study in the Netherlands. *Journal of Cultural Heritage*, *7*(3), 206–213. https://doi.org/10.1016/j.culher.2006.07.002

Rusu, D. (2017). *Socialist modernism map. Protecting and interpreting cultural heritage in the age of digital empowerment*. ICOMOS. https://openarchive.icomos.org/id/eprint/2034/1/24._ICOA_1441_Rusu_SM.pdf

Samuelson, P. (1955). *Economics* (3rd ed.). McGraw-Hill.

Saquet, M. A. (2016). Territory, geographical indication and territorial development. *DRd – Desenvolvimento Regional Em Debate*, *6*(1), 4–21. https://doi.org/10.24302/drd.v6i1.1106

Say, J.-B. (1880). *A treatise on political economy, or the production, distribution, and consumption of wealth*. Claxton, Remsen & Haffelfinger.

Scarrett, D. (2008). *Property valuation. The five methods* (2nd ed.). Routledge.

Schirpke, U., Timmermann, F., Tappeiner, U., & Tasser, E. (2016). Cultural ecosystem services of mountain regions: Modelling the aesthetic value. *Ecological Indicators*, *69*, 78–90. https://doi.org/10.1016/j.ecolind.2016.04.001

Schläpfer, F., Waltert, F., Segura, L., & Kienast, F. (2015). Valuation of landscape amenities: A hedonic pricing analysis of housing rents in urban, suburban and periurban Switzerland. *Landscape and Urban Planning*, *141*, 24–40. https://doi.org/10.1016/j.landurbplan.2015.04.007

Schwartz, S. H. (1992). Universals in the content and structure of values: Theoretical advances and empirical tests in 20 countries. *Advances in Experimental Social Psychology*. https://doi.org/10.1016/S0065-2601(08)60281-6.

Schwartz, S. H. (2015). Basic individual values: Sources and consequences. In T. Brosch & D. Sander (Eds.), *Handbook of value. Perspectives from economics, neuroscience, philosophy, psychology, and sociology* (pp. 63–84). Oxford University Press.

Šćitaroci, M. O. (2019). Preface: The heritage urbanism approach and method. In M. O. Šćitaroci, B. Bojanić, O. Šćitaroci, & A. Mrđa (Eds.), *Cultural urban heritage development, learning and landscape strategies* (pp. v–xiv). Springer.

Sedlaček, T. (2009). *Economics of good and evil: The quest for economic meaning from Gilgamesh to Wall Street*. Oxford University Press.

Sen, A. (1997). *On ethics and economics*. Blackwell Publishing.

Sepioł, J. (2011). Architektura i moralność [Architecture and morality]. In B. Krasnowolski (Ed.), *Doktryny i realizacje konserwatorskie w świetle doświadczeń krakowskich ostatnich 30 lat* (pp. 117–124). Wydawnictwo WAM.

Sikorska, D., Macegoniuk, S., Łaszkiewicz, E., & Sikorski, P. (2020). Energy crops in urban parks as a promising alternative to traditional lawns – Perceptions and a cost-benefit analysis. *Urban Forestry & Urban Greening*, *49*, 126579. https://doi.org/10.1016/j.ufug.2019.126579

Silverman, H. (2011). *Contested cultural heritage. Religion, nationalism, erasure, and exclusion in a global world*. Springer.

Simon, H. A. (1955). A behavioral model of rational choice. *Quarterly Journal of Economics*, *69*(1), 99–118. https://doi.org/10.2307/1884852

Sinclair, W., Huber, C., & Richardson, L. (2020). Valuing tourism to a historic World War II national memorial. *Journal of Cultural Heritage*, *45*, 334–338. https://doi.org/10.1016/j.culher.2020.04.007

Skolimowska, A. (2012). Modulor Polski. Historia osiedla Za Żelazną Bramą [Polish modulor. History of behind the iron gate housing estate]. In Ł. Gorczyca & M. Czapelski (Eds.), *Mister Warszawy. Architektura mieszkaniowa lat 60. XX wieku* [Mister of Warsaw. Residential architecture of the 1960s] (pp. 79–102). Raster.

Śleszyński, J., & Wiewiórski, R. (2011). Wycena ekonomiczna dóbr kultury na przykładzie piwnic Pałacu Saskiego w Warszawie. *Ekonomista*, *2*, 283–295.

Smith, A. (1776). *An inquiry into the nature and causes of the wealth of nations*. W. Strahan and T. Cadell.

Smith, L. (2008). *Uses of heritage*. Routledge.

Smolorz, M. (2006, August 11). Nos dla tabakiery [Nose for snuffbox]. *Gazeta Wyborcza. Katowice*, 12. https://classic.wyborcza.pl/archiwumGW/4696555/Nos-dla-tabakiery.

Snopek, K. (2014). *Bielajewo: Zabytek przyszłości* [Bielajewo: Monument of the future]. Bęc Zmiana.

Soja, E. (1971). *The political organization of space*. Commission on College Geography Resource Paper 8.

Sokołowicz, M. E. (2015). Rozwój terytorialny w świetle dorobku ekonomii instytucjonalnej. Przestrzeń - bliskość - instytucje. In *Rozwój terytorialny w świetle dorobku ekonomii instytucjonalnej. Przestrzeń – Bliskość – Instytucje*. Wydawnictwo Uniwersytetu Łódzkiego. https://doi.org/10.18778/8088-785-4

Sokołowicz, M. E. (2017). The urban commons from the perspective of urban economics. *Studia Regionalne i Lokalne*, *70*(4). https://doi.org/10.7366/1509499547002

Sokołowicz, M. E. (2018). Urban amenities – An element of public dimension of housing stock. *Acta Universitatis Lodziensis. Folia Oeconomica*, *6*(332), 125–143.

Sokołowicz, M. E. (2022). Wartościowanie niejednoznacznego dziedzictwa modernizmu w mieście na przykładzie stacji kolejowej Warszawa Ochota [Valuating the ambiguous heritage of modernism in cities based on the case of the Warsaw Ochota train station]. *Studia Regionalne i Lokalne*, *1*(87), 86–107. https://doi.org/10.7366/1509499518706

Sokołowicz, M. E., & Przygodzki, Z. (2020). The value of ambiguous architecture in cities. The concept of a valuation method of 20th century post-socialist train stations. *Cities*. https://doi.org/10.1016/j.cities.2020.102786

Spahr, R., & Sunderman, M. (1999). Valuation of property surrounding a resort community. *Journal of Real Estate Research*, *17*(2), 227–243. https://doi.org/10.1080/10835547.1999.12090974

Spash, C. L., & Asara, V. (2018). Ecological economics. From nature to society. In L. Fischer, J. Hasell, J. C. Proctor, D. Uwakwe, Z. Ward-Perkins, & C. Watson

(Eds.), *Rethinking economics: An introduction to pluralist economics* (pp. 120–132). Routledge.

Spassov, S., & Morten, R. (2022). *The Buzludzha monument.* https://buzludzha-monument.com/

Springer, F. (2011). *Źle urodzone. Reportaże o architekturze PRL-u* [Ill-born. Polish Post-war modernist architecture]. Karakter.

Sproull, N. L. (1988). *Handbook of research methods: A guide for practitioners and students in the social sciences.* Scarecrow Press.

Stake, R. E. (1994). Case studies. In N. K. Denzin & Y. S. Lincoln (Eds.), *Handbook of qualitative research* (pp. 236–247). SAGE Publications.

Stark, D. (1985). The micropolitics of the firm and the macropolitics of reforms: New forms of workplace bargaining in Hungarian enterprises. In P. B. Evans, D. Rueschemeyer, & E. Huber (Eds.), *States vs. markets in the world-system* (pp. 247–273). Sage Publications.

Stark, D. (1989). Coexisting organizational forms in Hungary's emerging mixed economy. In V. Nee & D. Stark (Eds.), *Remaking the economic institutions of socialism* (pp. 137–168). Stanford University Press.

Stark, D. (2009). *The sense of dissonance. Accounts of worth in economic life.* Princeton University Press.

Štelbiene, A. (2019). Po betono sparnu: Žmonių santykių su Vilniaus koncertų ir sporto rūmais fenomenas [Under the wing of concrete: The phenomenon of human relationships to the Vilnius Palace of concerts and sports]. *Archiforma, 3–4*, 68–77.

Stephenson, J. (2008). The cultural values model: An integrated approach to values in landscapes. *Landscape and Urban Planning, 84*(2), 127–139. https://doi.org/10.1016/j.landurbplan.2007.07.003

Stern, N. (2007). *The economics of climate change. The Stern review.* Cabinet Office – HM Treasury. https://webarchive.nationalarchives.gov.uk/ukgwa/20100407172811/https:/www.hm-treasury.gov.uk/stern_review_report.htm

Stern, P. C. (2011). Design principles for global commons: Natural resources and emerging technologies. *International Journal of the Commons, 5*(2), 213–232. https://doi.org/10.18352/ijc.305

Stierli, M. (2018). Networks and crossroads: The architecture of socialist Yugoslavia as a laboratory of globalization in the Cold War. In *Toward a concrete utopia: Architecture in Yugoslavia, 1948–1980* (pp. 10–25). Museum of Modern Art.

Stoilova, L. (2018). Metamorphoses of cultural memory and the opportunity to safeguard the modern movement heritage in Bulgaria. In A. Tostões & N. Koselj (Eds.), *Metamorphosis. The continuity of change* (pp. 122–131). Docomomo International & Docomomo Slovenia.

Subiza-Pérez, M., Korpela, K., & Pasanen, T. (2021). Still not that bad for the grey city: A field study on the restorative effects of built open urban places. *Cities, 111*, 103081. https://doi.org/10.1016/j.cities.2020.103081

Sulima, R. (2015). Pracowitość. In M. Bogunia-Borowska, (Ed.), *Fundamenty dobrego społeczeństwa. Wartości* (pp. 121–145). Znak.

Sunstein, C. R. (2019). *The cost-benefit revolution.* MIT Press. https://doi.org/10.7551/mitpress/11571.001.0001

Susser, I., & Tonnelat, S. (2013). Transformative cities: The three urban commons. *Focaal, 66*, 105–132. https://doi.org/10.3167/fcl.2013.660110

Świdrak, M. (2017). Jak młody może być zabytek? Przesłanki normatywne do stwierdzenia "dawności" zabytków nieruchomych [How young can a monument be? The normative premises of stating the "validity" of immovable monuments]. *Protection of Cultural Heritage*, *3*, 87–94. https://doi.org/10.24358/ODK_2017_03_06

Syrkus, H., & Syrkus, S. (1948). Architekt i uprzemysłowione budownictwo [Architect and industrialized construction]. *Architektura*, *8–9*, 34–35.

Szafer, T. P. (1979). *Nowa architektura polska. Diariusz lat 1971–1975* [New Polish architecture. Diary of the years 1971–1975]. Arkady.

Szczepańska, A., & Pietrzyk, K. (2019). A multidimensional analysis of spatial order in public spaces: A case study of the town Morąg, Poland. *Bulletin of Geography. Socio-Economic Series*, *44*(44), 115–129. https://doi.org/10.2478/bog-2019-0020

Szendröi, J., Arnoth, L., Finta, J., Merényi, F., & Nagy, E. (1978). *Neue Architektur in Ungarn* [New architecture in Hungary]. Callwey Verlag.

Szmelter, I. (2015). Społeczna strategia wielokryterialnego wartościowania w ochronie dziedzictwa kultury. In B. Szmygin (Ed.), *Ochrona wartości w procesie adaptacji zabytków* (pp. 265–277). Politechnika Lubelska-Polski Komitet Narodowy ICOMOS. http://bc.pollub.pl/dlibra/docmetadata?id=12729

Taher Tolou Del, M. S., Saleh Sedghpour, B., & Kamali Tabrizi, S. (2020). The semantic conservation of architectural heritage: The missing values. *Heritage Science*, *8*(1), 70. https://doi.org/10.1186/s40494-020-00416-w

TEEB. (2011). TEEB manual for cities: Ecosystem services in urban management. In *The economics of ecosystems and biodiversity*. United Nations Environment Programme-European Commission.

The Allen Consulting Group. (2005). *Valuing the priceless: The value of heritage protection in Australia*. Heritage Chairs and Officials of Australia and New Zealand https://heritagecouncil.vic.gov.au/wp-content/uploads/2021/12/hearing-submission-The-Allen-Consulting-Group-Valuing-the-Priceless-The-Value-of-Historic-Heritage-in-Australia-Research-Report-2-November-2005-3-June.pdf

The Athens Charter for the Restoration of Historic Monuments. (1931). https://www.icomos.org/en/167-the-athens-charter-for-the-restoration-of-historic-monuments

The Australia ICOMOS Charter for Places of Cultural Significance (The Burra Charter). (1999). https://australia.icomos.org/wp-content/uploads/The-Burra-Charter-2013-Adopted-31.10.2013.pdf

The Editors of Encyclopaedia Britannica. (2015). *Encyclopaedia Britannica*. https://www.britannica.com/

The Nara Document on Authenticity. (1994). https://www.icomos.org/charters/nara-e.pdf

Throsby, D. (1999). Cultural capital. *Journal of Cultural Economics*, *23*, 3–12. https://doi.org/10.1023/a:1007543313370

Throsby, D. (2001). *Economics and culture*. Cambridge University Press. https://doi.org/10.1017/CBO9781107590106

Throsby, D. (2012). Heritage economics: A conceptual framework. In G. Licciardi & R. Amirtahmasebi (Eds.), *The economics of uniqueness* (pp. 45–74). World Bank Group.

Tims, C. (2015). A rough guide to the commons: Who likes it and who doesn't. In *Build the city: Perspectives on commons and culture* (pp. 19–31). European Cultural Foundation – Krytyka Polityczna.

Torre, A. (2015). Territorial development theory. *Géographie, Économie, Société*, *17*(3), 273–288. https://doi.org/10.3166/ges.17.273-288

Torre, A. (2018). Les moteurs du développement territorial. *Revue d'economie Regionale et Urbaine*, *4*, 711–736. https://doi.org/10.3917/reru.184.0711

Torre, A., & Rallet, A. (2005). Proximity and localization. *Regional Studies*, *39*(1), 47–59. https://doi.org/10.1080/0034340052000320842

Tóth, B. I. (2015). Territorial capital: Theory, empirics and critical remarks. *European Planning Studies*, *23*(7), 1327–1344. https://doi.org/10.1080/09654313.2014.928675

Trajanovski, N. (2021). The city of Solidarity's diverse legacies: A framework for interpreting the local memory of the 1963 Skopje earthquake and the post-earthquake urban reconstruction. *Journal of Nationalism, Memory & Language Politics*, *15*(1), 30–51. https://doi.org/0.2478/jnmlp-2021-0007

Trilupaitytė, S. (2017). Sovietinės architektūros paveldas naujų politinių įtampų fone: Apie Vilniaus Koncertų ir sporto rūmų (nu)vertinimą [The heritage of soviet architecture against the background of the new political tensions on the (de)valuation of the Vilnius Palace of Con]. *Acta Academiae Artium Vilnenis*, *86–87*, 351–364. http://etalpykla.lituanistikadb.lt/fedora/objects/LT-LDB-0001:J.04~2017~1541692154271/datastreams/DS.002.0.01.ARTIC/content

Trocki, M., & Grucza, B. (2007). *Zarządzanie projektem europejskim*. Polskie Wydawnictwo Ekonomiczne.

Trzeciak, P. (1974). *Przygody architektury XX wieku* [The adventures of 20th century architecture]. Nasza Księgarnia.

Tuan, Y.-F. (1977). *Space and place. The perspective of experience*. University of Minnesota Press.

Tunbridge, J. E. (2018). *Zmiana warty. Dziedzictwo na przełomie XX i XXI wieku* [The changing of the guard: Heritage at the turn of the 21st century]. Międzynarodowe Centrum Kultury w Krakowie.

Tunbridge, J. E. (2019). The changing of the guard. A heritage perspective through time. In R. Kusek & J. Purchla (Eds.), *Heritage and society* (pp. 13–24). Międzynarodowe Centrum Kultury w Krakowie.

Tunbridge, J. E., & Ashworth, G. J. (1996). *Dissonant heritage. The management of the past as a resource in conflict*. John Wiley & Sons.

Tyler, T. R. (2007). *Psychology and the design of legal institutions*. Wolf.

UNESCO. (2013). *Managing cultural world heritage*. https://whc.unesco.org/document/125839

Urbis, A., Povilanskas, R., & Newton, A. (2019). Valuation of aesthetic ecosystem services of protected coastal dunes and forests. *Ocean & Coastal Management*, *179*, 104832. https://doi.org/10.1016/j.ocecoaman.2019.104832

Uskokovic, S. (2013). The "uncomfortable" significance of socialist heritage in postwar Croatia: The ambivalence of socialist aestheticism. In *Socialist realism and socialist modernism. World heritage proposals from Central and Eastern Europe* (pp. 85–89). ICOMOS.

Ustawa o zakazie propagowania komunizmu lub innego ustroju totalitarnego..., Dz.U. 2016 poz. 744 (2016) (testimony of Sejm Rzeczypospolitej Polskiej). https://isap.sejm.gov.pl/isap.nsf/DocDetails.xsp?id=wdu20160000744

van der Hoeven, A. (2018). Valuing urban heritage through participatory heritage websites: Citizen perceptions of historic urban landscapes. *Space and Culture*, *23*(2), 129–148. https://doi.org/10.1177/1206331218797038

Vasileva, A. (2019). Elitist or egalitarian? Stefka Georgieva and the peculiar face of Bulgarian "socialist" brutalism. In A. Stiller & A. Bulant-Kamenova (Eds.), *Stefka Georgieva. An architect in Bulgaria in the 1960s* (pp. 43–55). Muery Salzmann.

Vasileva, A., & Kaleva, E. (2017). Recharging socialism: Bulgarian socialist monuments in the 21st century. *Studia Ethnologica Croatica*, *29*(1), 171–192. https://doi.org/10.17234/SEC.29.5

Vasileva, N. (2013). *On the instability of monument. Monuments in Bulgaria from period of the communist regime 1944–1989* [University College London]. https://www.academia.edu/12412882/On_the_Instability_of_Monuments_Monuments_in_Bulgaria_from_the_Period_of_the_Communist_Regime_1944_1989

Vecco, M. (2010). A definition of cultural heritage: From the tangible to the intangible. *Journal of Cultural Heritage*, *11*(3), 321–324. https://doi.org/10.1016/j.culher.2010.01.006

Venkatachalam, L. (2004). The contingent valuation method: A review. *Environmental Impact Assessment Review*, *24*(1), 89–124. https://doi.org/10.1016/S0195-9255(03)00138-0

Vickerman, R. (2007). Cost — Benefit analysis and large-scale infrastructure projects: State of the art and challenges. *Environment and Planning B: Planning and Design*, *34*(4), 598–610. https://doi.org/10.1068/b32112

Vidler, A. (2011). Another brick in the wall. *October*, *136*, 105–132. http://www.jstor.org/stable/23014873

Vladova, T. (2012). Heritage and the image of forgetting: The mausoleum of Georgi Dimitrov in Sofia. In M. Rampley (Ed.), *Heritage, ideology and identity in Central and Eastern Europe. Contested pasts, contested presents* (pp. 131–153). Boydell.

Vodopivec, A. (2010). Edvard Ravnikar's architecture: Locally adjusted modernism. In A. Vodopivec & R. Žnidaršič (Eds.), *Edvard Ravnikar. Architect and teacher* (pp. 15–32). Springer.

Vodopivec, A., & Žnidaršič, R. (2010). *Edvard Ravnikar. Architect and teacher* (A. Vodopivec & R. Žnidaršič (Eds.)). Springer.

von Thünen, J. H. (1826). *Der isolierte Staat in Beziehung auf Landwirtschaft und Nationalekonomie*. Perthes.

Vorkinn, M., & Riese, H. (2001). Environmental concern in a local context: The significance of place attachment. *Environment and Behavior*, *33*(2), 249–263. https://doi.org/10.1177/00139160121972972

Watts, J. (2019). Concrete: The most destructive material on Earth. *The Guardian*. https://www.theguardian.com/cities/2019/feb/25/concrete-the-most-destructive-material-on-earth

Weber, A. (1909). *Über den Standort der Industrien: Teil 1: Reine Theorie des Standorts*. J. C. B. Mohr.

Wedderburn, A. D. O., Collingwood, W. G., & Ruskin, J. (2016). *Bibliotheca pastorum. Vol. I. The economist of Xenophon*. Leopold Classic Library.

Weiss, S. J. (2010). Skopje scomparira [Skopje will disappear]. *Abitare*, *7–8*, 82–95.

While, A. (2006). Modernism vs urban renaissance: Negotiating post-war heritage in English city centres. *Urban Studies*, *43*(13), 2399–2419. http://10.0.4.56/00420980601038206

Wilkin, J. (2016). *Instytucjonalne i kulturowe podstawy gospodarowania. Humanistyczna perspektywa ekonomii*. Wydawnictwo Naukowe SCHOLAR.

Williamson, K. (2002). The Delphi method. In K. Williamson (Ed.), *Research methods for students, academics and professionals. Information management and systems* (pp. 209–220). Woodhead Publishing.

Wiśniewski, M. (2012). Spóźnione ułaskawienie. Kilka uwag o nostalgii za niechcianym dziedzictwem PRL [A belated Pardon. Some remarks on the Nostalgia for the unwanted heritage of communist Poland]. *Herito*, *7*(2), 80–96. https://herito.pl/artykul/spoznione-ulaskawienie-kilka-uwag-o-nostalgii-za-niechcianym-dziedzictwem-prl/

Wojtkun, G. (2008). Wielorodzinne budownictwo mieszkaniowe w Polsce. W cieniu wielkiej płyty [Multifamily housing construction in Poland – in the shadow of the large panel]. *Przestrzeń i Forma*, *10*, 175–194. http://yadda.icm.edu.pl/baztech/element/bwmeta1.element.baztech-article-BPS1-0033-0087

Wright, W. C. C., & Eppink, F. V. (2016). Drivers of heritage value: A meta-analysis of monetary valuation studies of cultural heritage. *Ecological Economics*, *130*, 277–284. https://doi.org/10.1016/j.ecolecon.2016.08.001

Wyatt, P. (2007). *Property valuation in an economic context*. Blackwell Publishing.

Wyporek, B. (2009). *Daleko od Warszawy: Architekta zapiski z trzech kontynentów* [Far from Warsaw: The architect's notes from three continents]. Bogdan Wyporek.

Yin, R. K. (2003). *Applications of case study research* (2nd ed.). SAGE Publications.

Yugoslavia: Socialism of Sorts. (1966, June 10). *Time*. https://content.time.com/time/magazine/article/0,9171,942012,00.html

Zalewski, W. (2013). Intuicja inżyniera [Engineer's intuition]. *Architektura-Murator*, *4*, 30–35.

Załuski, D., & Rzepnicka, S. (2018). Dworzec Katowice w świetle współczesnej doktryny ochrony zabytków i rozwoju przestrzennego śródmieścia Katowic [Katowice railway station in the light of contemporary doctrine of monument protection and spatial development of downtown Katowice]. In M. Kapias & D. Keller (Eds.), *Węgiel, polityka, stal, ludzie. Studia z historii kolei na Śląsku* [Coal, politics, steel, people. Studies in the history of railways in Silesia] (pp. 515–530). Muzeum w Rybniku.

Zarecor, K. E. (2011). *Manufacturing a socialist modernity: Housing in Czechoslovakia, 1945–1960*. University of Pittsburgh Press.

Zipf, G. K. (1949). *Human behavior and the principle of last effort*. Addison-Wesley Publishing Company.

Živančević, J. (2012). Socijalistički realizam u arhitekturi [Socialist realism in architecture]. In M. Šuvaković (Ed.), *Istorija umetnosti u Srbiji XX vek* [History of Art in Serbia XX century] (pp. 277–302). Orion Art.

Żmudzińska-Nowak, M. (2017). Architektura i urbanistyka [Architecture and urban planning]. In M. Żmudzińska-Nowak & I. Herok-Turska (Eds.), *Reflektory. Interdyscyplinarne spojrzenie na dziedzictwo architektury Górnego Śląska drugiej połowy XX wieku* [Spotlights. An interdisciplinary look at the architectural heritage of Upper Silesia in the second half of the 20th century] (pp. 134–209). Biblioteka Śląska.

Index

Note: *Italicized* and **bold** page numbers refer to figures and tables. Page numbers followed by "n" refer to notes.